COURAGE
BEYOND
WORDS

The Many Lives and Languages of
Michel Thomas

*Holocaust Witness, Nazi Hunter,
Language Teacher to the Stars*

CHRISTOPHER ROBBINS

New York   Chicago   San Francisco   Lisbon   London   Madrid   Mexico City
Milan   New Delhi   San Juan   Seoul   Singapore   Sydney   Toronto

Library of Congress Cataloging-in-Publication Data

Robbins, Christopher, 1946–
    [Test of courage]
    Courage beyond words / Christopher Robbins.
        p.   cm.
    Previously published by Free Press under the title Test of courage.
    ISBN 0-07-149911-3 (alk. paper)
        1. Thomas, Michel, 1914–2005.   2. Jews—Persecutions—France.   3. France—
    History—German occupation, 1940–1945.   4. Holocaust, Jewish (1939–1945)—
    France.   5. Anti-Nazi movement—France.   6. Military government—Germany.
    I. Title.

    DS135.F9T467   2007
    940.53'18092—dc22
    [B]   2007020797

1 2 3 4 5 6 7 8 9 10 11 12 13 14 15 16 17 18 19 20   DOC/DOC   0 9 8 7

ISBN 978-0-07-149911-8
MHID   0-07-149911-3

DEDICATION

In memory of
Freida and Idessa,
and of Georgina

CHRISTOPHER ROBBINS is the author of *Assassin*, a nonfiction book on political assassination, and two nonfiction books on the Vietnam War, *Air America* and *The Ravens*. His most recent book, *The Empress of Ireland*, a memoir of his friendship with the Irish film director Brian Desmond Hurst, received wide critical acclaim. It was chosen as the Film Book of the Year by the Cork Film Festival, awarded the Saga Prize for Wit in 2005, and picked as a Book of the Year by the *The Times*, *Guardian*, *Daily Telegraph*, *Sunday Telegraph*, *Daily Express*, *Observer*, and *Sunday Times*. A new travel book, *Apples Are from Kazakhstan*, is to be published in the United States in the spring of 2008.

PROLOGUE

As a natural sceptic I would not have been inclined to believe the biography of Michel Thomas if I had not been told about him by someone whose own wartime experiences were beyond doubt. My friend spoke of a man who had endured hell in the early years of the war through internment in concentration and deportation camps in France, but who had refused to become a victim. He had escaped to fight with the Résistance, suffered further imprisonment and torture, and then fought with the US Army. Later, in the years directly after the war, he hunted Nazis and war criminals as a special agent with American Counter Intelligence, posing in one elaborate operation as a high-ranking Nazi intelligence officer. It was a life that seemed as fascinating as it was unlikely.

And then there was Michel Thomas' equally improbable post-war reputation as one of the world's great language masters with the ability to teach students in a matter of days. His celebrity clients included people as diverse as Woody Allen, Bob Dylan and Emma Thompson, yet his main interest was reforming the education system itself, and helping disadvantaged children. People spoke of miracles and magic, and his power to hypnotise, read minds and block pain. It was also said, by one of the great secret service cryptographers of the Second World War, that it was impossible to lie to him. 'You should talk to Michel,' my friend said. 'You'll find him interesting.'

Michel Thomas proved to be a quietly spoken, soberly suited gentleman, with the old-fashioned, courtly manners of another age, but even during our first encounter, when the conversation was superficial and general, I became aware that I was in the presence of a highly unusual and unique individual.

He exuded intensity and warmth and I received an impression of immense self-confidence and inner strength that was almost tangible. In time, I would come to understand that beneath the calm exterior and easy charm, a constant anger burned white hot, and that Michel was as tough as anyone I had ever met, a man of steel. But after that first meeting I left charged with an inexplicable energy and enthusiasm. True to his reputation, he had cast a spell of sorts.

We began to meet often whenever he was in London, and I sought him out in New York and Los Angeles. He seemed perpetually on the move and forever at work. We had long lunches that lasted until evening, and dinners that stretched into the early hours of the morning. I proposed chronicling his life story and Michel agreed. We came to an understanding whereby he would answer questions about all areas of his life, and I would be free to write the book in my own way, interview whomever I wished, and pursue any and every independent avenue of research. Michel would then have access to the final manuscript to correct errors of fact, and the editing process would be one of mutual consent.

The result was hundreds of hours of taped interviews that became the foundation of this book. Few men alive can have witnessed so much raw history, and Michel's memories have been kept alive by a unique form of emotional memory – consciously developed as a child – that relives rather than recalls past events. Memory of such power and immediacy can be a painful gift, and it has endowed Michel with what he describes as, 'A past that does not pass.'

But memory, however powerful, inevitably distorts and telescopes time. Events are subconsciously ordered and re-arranged, and even if the past is held on to and not allowed to pass, it is edited and coloured and becomes blurred. Michel's past is bolstered and verified by a suitcase full of personal papers that is never far from his side. In addition I unearthed a wealth of documents that fixed the principal dates and events of every period of his life. These came from a wide range of sources: French government and court records giving the dates of internment and transportation, family letters, official accreditation cards from the Résistance, ID cards from the US Army and Counter Intelligence, reports written at the time by combat and intelligence colleagues, and numerous interviews with contemporaries from the various periods of Michel's life. There were also finds in the US National Archives and Army records.

The more I learned about Michel, the more interested I became in the connection between the experiences of his life and the revolutionary system of teaching languages that has evolved from it. I interviewed university professors and academics in an attempt to understand the technique, and spoke to scores of students – ranging from ambassadors and movie stars, to businessmen, nuns and schoolchildren – to confirm the results.

On publication of the original hardback, I felt I had provided enough documentary evidence and detailed footnotes to convince anyone who had never met Michel Thomas in the truth of his story. Certainly, had I been writing fiction I would not have expected readers to indulge me by believing in a character to whom so much had happened. A single chapter from any one of the war years would have provided more than enough for an entire novel, but terrible times of upheaval bring forward extraordinary men, and they abounded in the Second World War.

Some readers remained unconvinced, as if I had described a type no longer recognised in the modern world. Human extremes of endurance, courage and spirit seemed to strain credulity, while the claim to be able to teach anyone a language easily and quickly invited particular disbelief. It was perhaps as much a failure of imagination as genuine scepticism on the part of these stubborn doubters, or simply an aversion to footnotes, for Michel's life is better supported by documentary proof than most.

One newspaper chose to publish an article that was an attack through innuendo. The Los Angeles Times assigned a reporter to write a long and hostile feature article, which adopted a mocking tone, and raised questions about specific incidents in Michel's life. Refused the right of reply, he was forced to sue for libel, fully aware that defamation cases in the United States are notoriously difficult to win because of the protections afforded the press under the First Amendment in regard to free speech. In preparation for the court case, a small army of top-notch researchers, archivists, photo and handwriting experts, professors of linguistics and journalism, were employed to examine existing documentation, and discover new evidence. This was now required to meet a legal standard of proof, withstand hostile cross-examination in a court of law, and convince a jury. The results after many months, great expense, and thousands of hours of archival research by men and women at the top of their fields were conclusive. Every question raised in the article was successfully answered without exception.

However, the California courts refused to hear the case on legal grounds, and Michel was denied the opportunity of a hearing before a jury. It was an egregious example of the First Amendment protecting the power of the press over the rights of an individual to protect his good name and reputation. A detailed account of the controversy is recorded in an Afterword to the book.

It is perhaps worth stating, as the author of a biography of a man whose identity is rooted in his Jewishness, that I am not a Jew. I mention this to explain that there is no special pleading in this account of his life, and also to underline the integrity of Michel's universal vision in that he should permit his story to be told by an Englishman brought up as a

Christian. '*I never thought about it,*' *Michel answered, when I brought this to his attention.* '*It is not an issue.*' *(Many Polish Jews with the name Robinowski, who emigrated to America, adopted the name Robbins. My own tribe is less exotic. Mud-rooted in Wessex, it took several hundred years to get from Milton Abbas to Bristol, via Weymouth. However, in the words of the Russian poet, Yevgeny Yevtuskhenko, '*In the presence of anti-Semites, I am a Jew*'.)*

For me, the experience of researching and writing this book has been both an education and a remarkable journey. To follow the life of Michel Thomas is to be handed a human route map to some of the most disturbing history of the twentieth century, and to be guided along its treacherous roads by an eyewitness with a truly original mind. '*It seems from what I know that I am the only living survivor of many of these events. I have never pushed memory away. I have nurtured, not buried it. If I am the only survivor I owe it to those who have died to remind people of the facts. I am a witness.*'

I

On a rainy night in Manhattan, more than fifty years after the end of the Second World War, Michel Thomas pulled a packet of letters from the safe in his apartment and placed them on a writing desk. It was late, and he was alone. The study was dimly lit so he switched on a lamp beside his chair, sat down and drew the letters towards him. He spread them out in a fan, a dozen dog-eared airmail envelopes faded with age. There were two sets of handwriting, both distinctly feminine versions of an old-fashioned continental copperplate, and a single envelope that had been inexpertly typed on an antiquated machine.

The letters dated from just after the outbreak of war in Europe and were among Michel's most prized possessions. He had lost count of the number of times he had taken them from their battered, black cardboard file and set them down in front of him. It was a ritual: he picked up the letters and held them, turned them over again and again, laid them back down and stared at them. He had removed the fragile airmail sheets from their envelopes and carefully unfolded and smoothed them a thousand times. But in fifty years he had never read a single word.

The fear of their impact had haunted him since the war. Now, with the century almost spent, he felt the time was right. He was an accomplished and successful man with an international reputation as a master language teacher, and the story of his life was such a potent mix of adventure and tragedy, dream and nightmare, that it had the power of myth. But until now not even the accumulated wisdom of a long and extraordinary life had enabled him to face the small packet of letters lying on the table.

At last, he felt he was ready. The letters were from his mother, aunt and uncle to a brother in New York, written at the time of their greatest peril. He picked up the solitary, typewritten envelope. It was from his uncle and Michel thought this might be the easiest to read for the man had been a businessman who wrote a businesslike letter. It had been written in Poland after he had been arrested and expelled from Breslau, a city then in Germany. He and his wife were among fifteen thousand German Jews who had been stripped of all their possessions and forced out of the country.[1] The letter had been hand-delivered to New York by a family friend who had crossed the Atlantic by liner.

Michel removed a single typed sheet of paper from the envelope. The sight of the familiar stationery bearing the letterhead WOLF GROSS – the family wholesale wine and liquor business – already stirred powerful memories.[2]

He passed quickly over the banal opening paragraphs to reach the nub at the bottom of the first page: 'Our emigration to the United States looks very bad. A letter from the American consul-general in Berlin states we will have to wait ten to fifteen years for a quota number. What shall we do? And what will happen? Our situation is well known to you. I ask you urgently to do everything possible. To address yourself energetically to the responsible immigration officials and to intervene on our behalf to send us a visa as quickly as possible. We wish you success and wait to hear from you. With all best wishes and heartfelt greetings – we hope for good news. Your brother-in-law.'

As Michel read these words something terrible and unexpected happened to him. For the first time in his life he was gripped by homicidal fury. The feelings aroused were primitive and brutal and thrust him into an extreme and alien psychological state. He had suffered internment and torture in the war, but had never experienced such corrosive hatred. Even his involvement in the arrest and interrogation of war criminals – whip-carrying SS officers and concentration camp executioners – had never triggered wrath like this. He had felt disgust and contempt for these men but now the emotions he experienced were utterly different. The act of a consul who sacrificed human lives on the altar of an American quota system ignited a rage of such violence he could have killed without pity or compunction.[3]

Michel turned over the typewritten sheet and was slammed by another almost unbearable emotional blow as he caught sight of the handwriting of his beloved aunt. She had written a single, despairing paragraph: 'Forgive me for writing so little but I'm completely down. I am so low I cannot write myself. Everything seems hopeless. What are we to do?'

The plea for help to a brother living in the haven of the United States – not yet at war – was an unadorned, final testament from the doomed.[4] All the papers needed for entry into America had long been in order, with sworn affidavits from family members guaranteeing financial support, but everything depended on obtaining an American quota number. The hopeless tone of his uncle's letter conveyed the unwritten acknowledgement that nothing could be done – and the man who wrote it would not live to discover that the quota that could have saved him was never filled.[5]

As the rage passed, Michel was left weak and nauseous. He sat motionless for hours with the letters scattered on the desk before him. Half a lifetime of preparation for this moment found him pitifully ill-equipped to cope. He was forced to admit that even after so many years the time was not yet right to read the letters.

He was a man who thought he knew himself but suddenly he was confronted by a violent stranger. He attempted to make sense of the terrible knowledge he had come upon and the alarming emotions it had uncovered. He tried to understand his murderous rage and the fact that it was directed not against the brutes that had tortured and enslaved him but at a bureaucrat who had worked in the American Embassy in Berlin. A man who had chosen to follow the rulebook, and by declining to wield his rubber stamp had condemned the people Michel loved most in the world to death.

As dawn broke outside the study window, he folded his uncle's letter and replaced the single sheet in its envelope. He pulled the other letters towards him, slipped them back into their folder, and returned them to the safe unread.

II

The memories of Michel Thomas stretch back to the crib: a huge but benign black dog the size of a bear viewed through the wooden bars of a playpen; the sensation of being pushed in a pram in the open air; the texture of a cloth pulled from the drawer of a sewing machine and its oily smell; the glittering silver shapes of the machine's metal frets used for different stitches, and their pleasing feel and cold metallic taste when placed in the mouth. His first erotic memory, vivid and thrilling, dates from the age of three. Crawling on the floor, he looked up at the towering figure of his young nanny and glimpsed under her skirt. The girl wore no underwear. Stretching heroically, the toddler reached up and touched bare flesh. 'The naked female behind! I liked it – I still see it!'

At a very early age he began consciously to recover and hold on to these memories of what he calls his 'cradlehood'. It was his first act against being overwhelmed by a hostile world.

Michel Thomas was born Moniek Kroskof, in Lodz, Poland, under the shadow of the First World War, into a prosperous Jewish family that owned a large textile manufacturing company.[1] He was the only child of the second marriage of his mother, Freida, a strong, independent woman in her late twenties who was highly unusual for her time. Arranged marriages were then the norm among well-to-do Jewish families and at the age of eighteen Freida had married a man considered to be from a suitable family. The relationship was a failure from the start, but instead of suffering within the marriage she rebelled and demanded a divorce. It was a scandalous decision for a young girl to make, but Freida insisted in the teeth of fierce family opposition.

She later met and married Samuel Kroskof, an engineer who had worked in the oilfields of Iran and Azerbaijan. The couple lived together in Lodz where the joy felt over the birth of a baby boy was tempered by fear of war. At the outbreak of hostilities, Poland became a battleground. As the German Army advanced towards

Lodz, a part of Russian Poland at that time, the local population panicked. Poland was first partitioned by Russia, Austria and Prussia in 1772, after which the country's history became an endless cycle of insurrection and reprisal. After a nationalistic uprising in 1863, Russia imposed a harsh policy of Russification within its zone, stripping the country of all autonomy and turning it into little more than a province of the empire. Russian was adopted as the official language in schools, and the use of Polish was restricted. Jewish life became particularly difficult.[2] Treatment of the Jews, many of whose families had lived in the city for hundreds of years, became vicious. There were daily executions by hanging of those accused by the Russians of sympathising with the Germans, and the fact that a quarter of a million Jews served in the Russian Army did nothing to mitigate the prejudice against them. Shops and houses were looted, synagogues defiled, and hundreds of thousands of Jews living within the Russian partition were driven from their homes. They took to the road, carrying their possessions on carts and bicycles, struggling with suitcases and bundles, their children in their arms.

Samuel and Freida remained in Lodz with their baby during this terrible time of fear and privation. The city had always been an ugly industrial place of grime, smog and noise. Its factory chimneys belched foul smoke into sooty skies and the sun found it difficult to shine through the polluted air and dingy window panes. The city at war became dismal, its few scattered trees felled for firewood and its unpaved streets churned into liquid mud by troops and horses. Most of the remainder of the already diminished population fled, including the Russian bureaucracy that had been in the city for a century. Lodz became a ghost town.

When Michel was only eight months old, the German Ninth Army surrounded the city. The ensuing battle was waged on a monumental scale, the first great carnage of modern warfare, and for weeks the two armies fought each other to the point of exhaustion until winter paralysed them. Icy winds brought temperatures to below freezing and at dawn each day both armies removed from the trenches the corpses of those frozen to death in the night.[3]

The Germans finally took the city in December, but at a high cost: German losses in the campaign were about thirty-five thousand killed and wounded; Russian losses are unknown, but conservatively estimated to be around ninety thousand in all.[4] Germany went on to take over the whole country, stripping industry of everything valuable and sending the booty back to the homeland. Copper was collected from factories, church steeples, frying pans and even door-post amulets. The thick leather transmission belts from the textile mills were sent back to Germany for soldiers' boots, and roofs were stripped of lead. The country's raw materials were also plundered, paid for with vouchers redeemable after the war, which the locals said were not worth a plug *groschen*.[5]

German sentries stood on every corner to prevent looting and riot. Food was scarce, even for the prosperous, and milk was unobtainable. There were ration cards for the terrible bread, made from a mixture of chestnuts and potato peelings and tasting of clay. Stray dogs and cats were rounded up and rendered down for their flesh, which was sent back to Germany as animal feed. Disease raged in epidemic proportions, the worst of which was typhus. Hospitals overloaded with military casualties were obliged to leave the sick to die, and corpses without shrouds were trundled to cemeteries in wheelbarrows.

As the war ground on, one terrible year after another, the desperate conditions took their toll on the health of mother and child. It also did nothing to help a failing marriage. Freida seemed unprepared, or unwilling, to give up the degree of independence that marriage demanded and broke up with Samuel. One divorce was a scandal, a second social disaster, but Freida seemed unperturbed by the opinions of others. She remained on friendly terms with her ex-husband and later took Michel to see him regularly. The child resented the visits as a duty and an imposition, and during his formative years became emotionally distant from his father.

Michel was brought up in a world of doting women. He lived together with his mother, his aunt Idessa – two years younger than his mother and a beauty – and his grandmother. With the collapse of Tsarist Russia in the revolution of 1917, and the final defeat of Germany the following year, Poland once again became a nation. The factories of the family textile business, which had floundered and closed during the war, gradually picked up production. Michel grew into something of a wild child, independent and wilful, even as a toddler. The women in his life indulged him shamelessly. 'I felt I had two mothers. I was surrounded by love. It was like air. Love was so much part of my life it was like breathing. The security of love was very strong. I am sure that is where I have drawn my strength over the years – that absolute bedrock of mother love.'

By the age of four Michel had developed an advanced case of rickets, news of which had been kept from his mother who had been taken into hospital with typhus. He was cared for by his grandmother and aunt – his second mother. By the time Freida returned home after an extended stay in hospital the child's legs were so bowed he could hardly walk. 'I still see my mother as she came into the living room and her reaction as she saw me – my horribly curved legs.'

Rickets was common at this time and often left children permanently crippled, and his mother's initial joy at seeing her son turned to anguish. 'Oh my God,' she blurted, 'he cannot walk!'

'Yes I can,' Michel cried out, delighted to see his mother at home again and eager to please her. In a display of superhuman will and effort, he dragged himself around the dining-room table. He held on to the backs of the chairs and hauled himself from one to another. 'See, I can walk!'

Freida wrote to all the experts in the field, and consulted family friends in the medical profession in a desperate search for a cure. She developed a remedy that was an early form of health cure and radical for the time. Michel was put on a diet of fresh vegetables, fruit juices and hot honey drinks with egg yolk – and less palatable doses of cod liver oil. He was soon walking again and eventually recovered to the point that he began to excel at sport.

'When I went out with my mother, her friends would always talk down to me. Idiotic baby talk in a strained voice – endless stupid questions that were meaningless. It irritated me. So I gave them strange, unexpected answers. They would become confused and embarrassed, and always they would say, "How precocious!"' It puzzled him that adults talked to children in such a manner. 'I wondered why they talked like that. I came to the conclusion that although they had all been children they had somehow forgotten their childhood.' It was an alarming insight. 'A little while later I thought, If *they* have forgotten their childhood, when I grow up *I* will forget mine. And that horrified me! It was a terrible shock. To forget everything! To forget *me* as I am now! Every day was filled with growth and change and events – and it would all be forgotten! And I would be forgotten – cease to exist, wiped from the world! I could not let that happen.'

He carefully began to develop a system to help him remember childhood. Unable to read or write, he adopted a mental process in which he forced himself to think as far back as he could and reclaim feelings and reactions. He flagged these with a child's mental markers of colour, smell, touch and taste. In this way he could recapture and fix a moment in his memory, logging the significant events of his life into his system. It was a large task for a six-year-old but he conscientiously stuck to his method until, at the age of twelve, he spent weeks painstakingly writing the history of his childhood into a lined notebook, the Memory Book – a document sadly lost to posterity. 'I owe a lot to that child. He made a vow not to forget. He influenced my development as a man and laid out the pattern of a lifetime.'[6]

It was also at the age of six that he experienced an incident so powerful and disturbing that it forever changed his life. The family lived in a spacious apartment that had a balcony filled with oleander plants overlooking a large courtyard. In one corner was a well used as an emergency water supply on the occasions when the city's mains failed. One sunny spring afternoon his mother went out on to the balcony looking down into the quadrant where the children played. Suddenly, she became rigid. A boy and his teenage sister ran to the well, leaned over its side and began calling down into it. The urgency of the children's voices echoed through the courtyard: 'Moniek, Moniek – come back up, your mother is calling. Moniek, come up!'

Freida was filled with dread that her mischievous son had fallen into the shaft. Fearing the worst, she ran down the stairs and out into the courtyard. She peered into the well and began to call for her son. There was no reply. The surface of the water was black and still with no sign of life. She became hysterical and began to wail, ripping at her garments and hair. A large crowd gathered to watch the display of grief in silence, as if at a theatre performance.

Just then Michel ran into the courtyard. The sight of his distraught and inconsolable mother shook him to his soul. He had been climbing trees in an adjoining garden to the apartment building and had not been near the well. An adult had called him down from a tree and led him back to the courtyard that had filled with people.

Michel was led through the crowd to his mother and she fell on him in relief, hugging and kissing him. The drowning had been a cruel, brutish joke hatched by a child and fed by adults. 'These men and women who were our neighbours, non-Jewish Poles, enjoyed the spectacle of the despair of a Jewish mother. No one said anything, or tried to explain it was a joke gone too far, or that they did not mean it. *Nothing!* They were enjoying it.

'This viciousness and hatefulness traumatised me. My belief system as a child was totally shaken. It changed me. Changed the child. After that I was no longer wild but clung to my mother's side. I became a mother's boy. It took a physical toll on me and I became a sleepwalker. I would pick up a pillow from my bed, put it under my arm, and try to walk out of the house. My mother actually put a bell around my neck. I suffered nightmares – terrible nightmares! Not of the incident itself, but of horrible monsters coming through the window to get me. I was scared of the dark and the things I imagined it held. I developed chronic asthma. That trauma was so deep, so strong, I quite literally could not breathe Polish air.'

His mother grew alarmed at the severity of his condition and took him from one specialist to another without success. 'I just couldn't live in Poland, I felt the atmosphere that strongly. It was such a betrayal. At the age of six I had been made aware of the difference between a Jew and a non-Jew. I wanted out – to get away from Lodz.'

In later life, Michel analysed the virulent nature of Polish anti-Semitism. 'It was worse even than Ukrainian or Russian anti-Semitism – far worse than in Germany. It was a direct result of the teaching of contempt for Jews by the Catholic Church to a largely ignorant and illiterate peasant population. These people emerged from their churches after a Sunday sermon hating the Jews whom they had been told had murdered Christ their God.'

Freida, who was a shrewd businesswoman and held an important position in the family company, travelled all over Poland and now began to take Michel along with her. Since the trauma he had become a difficult and demanding child, and his physical and psychological states were alarming. He was touchy and sensitive and resented doing what was expected of him even when it was agreeable. He grew increasingly stubborn and disobedient. 'I had my own ways and got away with it.'

As they visited the towns of Poznan and Danzig, and other areas that had been part of the German partition of Poland, Freida noticed her son's spirits lift. 'Travelling on a train I can remember looking out at the countryside and everything seemed so beautiful . . . the cows, the horses, the landscape. Still I can see it – I can feel it, I can smell it. Through my childish eyes it was a different country because I was out of the Polish-speaking region.'

On one of these journeys, just before Michel's seventh birthday when he was at his most difficult, his mother engaged him in a long and serious conversation. They walked through the streets of Poznan together and she explained the trouble he was causing, and the problems this posed for her. 'Can you imagine if you had a son, a boy like you are? How would you handle him?'

Michel pondered the question. After some thought he recommended a regime of strict rules and harsh discipline, accompanied by draconian punishment for the least infringement. He elaborated on the rules, which were ruthless in their severity, and on the punishments that were equally extreme.

'Very interesting,' his mother said. 'I have learned a lot. You have taught me how to handle you.'

'Oh no!' The child's response was immediate. 'For me it's too late!'

The system was never introduced, and Michel kept his true feelings over the incident to himself, but he felt tricked. He had been betrayed by his own mother and was deeply hurt. 'The only time I was ever hurt by my mother. I still feel it now.'

It was evident to the child as they travelled together that his mother was both well-known and respected. Michel also came to understand that his upbringing was somehow privileged and more comfortable than that of many of the children around him. Freida took great trouble to imbue him with her own philosophy, explaining that privilege and riches could be stripped from anyone at any time, and that the only true wealth was knowledge. The mind, she insisted, was something that a human being carried with him, a treasure trove that could be endlessly enriched and never taken away. 'What you are and who you are and what you know – these are the only things that count. That has to be strong. Everything else can be destroyed.' Freida was imparting a life lesson that would pay a high dividend in the future.

Michel's condition remained extreme, but his relief when outside the Polish-speaking region was so evident that Freida decided her son's health depended upon him leaving the country. Aunt Idessa had married and gone to live in Breslau, just across the border in Germany, where her husband owned a highly successful wholesale wine and spirits business, complete with its own vineyards. Some six months after the trauma it was decided that Michel should go to live with his adored aunt, something he accepted happily. 'I was not homesick, or in tears – I was happy to be going. I knew I was not being sent away but that I was going to my aunt, who seemed like a part of my mother. I did not feel I was losing my mother – I knew she would always be with me. She was in my heart.'

But travel had been forbidden to Jews under the previous Russian regime, as had college education, and passports in the new Poland were still difficult, if not impossible, to obtain. The child would have to be smuggled out of the country. A German friend from Breslau arrived one sunny afternoon in an open convertible. Michel was excited at the prospect of the journey, which he saw as a grand adventure despite the welter of rules that seemed to govern it. Advice and instructions were piled upon him. Most important of all, he was told that during the journey he was not to speak at all in the presence of other people or attract attention in any way.

His mother pretended to be happy and excited about the journey as she saw him off. But as the car sped away and he turned to wave goodbye, he saw Freida collapse to the ground. Michel squirmed in his seat and wanted to turn back, but was assured with a comforting, adult nod from the driver that everything was as it should be.[7]

It was a long journey that took all day. The driver spoke no Polish, and Michel no German, but they drove along comfortably enough in silence. The hood of the car was down and it was a sunny day. The man occasionally turned to the child beside him and smiled kindly. Somewhere near the border he pulled the car over to the side of the road and bought punnets of the first cherries of the season. He handed one to Michel, who ate the delicious fresh fruit greedily.

They crossed the border without incident. The man seemed familiar with the German frontier guards who waved them through after only a perfunctory inspection. The young charge was delivered to his aunt in the old part of the city of Breslau. He was delighted to see Idessa, who could not have been happier to have him. Michel had shed his first identity as a Polish child, and was about to enter his life as a German youth.

And suddenly he could breathe.

As a child, Michel adored Germany. The journey from Poland had been a passage from darkness into light; his arrival rebirth and liberation. True, the financial circumstances of the Weimar Republic were disastrous in the wake of the First World War (in 1914 the mark exchanged at four to the dollar; by November 1923 it was 130 million to one) but this hardly concerned a young boy who felt he had been delivered from hell. The family seemed to have everything and lived comfortably. His health improved dramatically – although he still had to be watched at night – and while he was a rather serious child for his years, he was adventurous and enjoyed life to the full. Slowly, the trauma began to fade.

His mother visited him as often as she was able. Sometimes she would travel on a business passport that strictly limited the number of days the bearer was allowed to stay out of the country. On other occasions she would take great risks to enter Germany illegally. Even if his mother arrived in the dead of night Michel could sense her in the house, and her silent presence at the end of the bed was enough to wake him. 'I would feel just a touch on my foot when I was sleeping and know it was my mother.'

The adults led him to believe that he was living in the most civilised country in the world, and his experience confirmed it. Breslau was the biggest and most important city in eastern Germany, with more than six hundred thousand inhabitants, and was a mixture of two cultures: old-world bourgeois-merchant and modern-industrial. A bishopric for a thousand years, the city had a sombre, no-nonsense burghers' beauty and stolid charm. It had once been a fortress but Napoleon had ordered the destruction of the castle keep and walls, and only the moat remained. The city had a university, theatres, several newspapers and a number of attractive parks. It also had its monumental modern structures, such as the concert hall built in 1913 boasting the biggest cupola and organ in the world. The blocks of flats close to the factories in the working-class area were a uniform gloomy grey, but the young Michel felt he was living in paradise.[8]

He had begun to learn German immediately on his arrival, fell in love with the language and made rapid progress. 'I didn't want to hear the Polish language, and didn't speak it. As quickly as I learned German, so I erased Polish. It was total rejection.' He was also taught to ski in the mountains of Silesia, and from the age of seven grew up on skis. 'A winter without skis was unthinkable. I was not always the best, but the most daring.' His aunt taught him to dance, something that became a lifelong love. He was taken to the opera and the concert hall, and classical music became important at an early age – primarily Bach, Beethoven, Mozart and Chopin. 'I couldn't imagine life without music. I wouldn't go to sleep without listening to classical music.' He was also obliged to take piano lessons, a ten-year sentence that produced little result. 'It was not handled well. I loved music but hated to practise. I resented the imposition of those daily sessions.' It was an early example of how not to teach. 'When I finally gave the piano up I played the trumpet to join the school orchestra, and because it was my own choice I loved it. I was very loud but not particularly good.'

At the age of seven Michel met a German girl his age who initiated him into the mysteries of sex. 'She was a sweet little girl and we used to play together. She wanted to play a doctor and nurse game that was new to me and we went to the basement of her building. So we had fun, naked. But we were surprised by an old man who saw us *en passant* and walked away. It was terrible for me to be discovered like that. Terrible! I felt so guilty and ashamed!' Michel was so bothered by the experience that he confessed everything to his aunt. 'Idessa sat down with me and talked very simply about growing up and sex and love. She told me there was no reason to feel shame. She said that sex should be connected to love to make it meaningful and beautiful. "But not now! Wait until you grow up." '

Other interests were encouraged, perhaps to steer the youngster away from precocious sex, and an early love of animals developed. 'I grew up identifying with all life, and this extended to animal life. I developed a love and an understanding for animals, and ended up with dogs, cats and eighteen birds.' He was given a canary named Mouki. 'A wonderful singer! We were friends, and I always left the door to his cage open. In the morning when I had breakfast I would call him and he would come and perch on the table.'

A mate was found to keep Mouki company, and other birds followed. The family apartment in Breslau had a large balcony overlooking a garden and Michel and his birds colonised it. Half of the balcony was turned into a gigantic birdcage, modelled on one seen on a visit to the zoo, complete with grass, elaborate perches and a live tree. The outside cage was connected directly to Michel's bedroom through a window. 'I developed good personal relationships with all the birds, and they would fly around my room. I called to them individually and they would perch on my finger.'

The childish interest developed into a passion, and eventually led to a life-changing insight. At the age of eleven Michel was taken on a summer holiday in the mountains. His room had a terrace, and he discovered a bird's nest with eggs under the eaves. At first the birds flew off at his approach, but slowly they grew accustomed to his presence. 'I was very curious so every day I sat at a respectable distance until they finally accepted me. I watched the chicks hatch and saw how the parents taught them. They *taught* them. In bird language. The chicks learned to react to certain sounds – there were sounds for danger, so that they would keep quiet, and others for food when they were about to be fed. This was language, communication. And I learned with the little birds and found it fascinating.

'They had to learn how to fly, and to be daring. Some of the chicks were timid, some courageous. The very timid ones had to be pushed out of the nest. I observed definite individual behaviour in each chick almost as soon as it hatched.' These observations led to the conclusion that most animal behaviour was learned, not instinctive. It was an insight that changed the way he thought – that one of the powerful innate drives in all living beings is the urge to learn.

He became absorbed in mythology and devoured books on the subject. His imagination had been captured by the Romans and Greeks at an early age; as he grew older he was inspired by the romantic heroes of German mythology. He took a handsome leather-bound volume of *Legends of the Gods: Treasures of German Mythology* from the bookshelves of his uncle's library, and read by torchlight beneath the sheets long into the night.[9] 'They were stories about values and about heroes who stood up for those values. I completely absorbed these Nordic heroes. Siegfried was a good example.' This led to a love for the music of Richard Wagner, whose operas he heard at the Breslau opera house, especially the tetralogy *Der Ring der Nibelungen*.

Later, during the war when he learned that the great Wagner was a virulent anti-Semite, a deep conflict was created. Wagner, an extreme radical and revolutionary of his day, was Adolf Hitler's ideological mentor and the composer's political writings were his favourite reading.[10] 'Even though I learned very early on to separate the personality and character of an artist from his work, I could not listen to Wagner during the war. It took me years to go back to him.'

The German educational system of Gymnasiums demanded high academic requirements in order to move from one class to another. Only those pupils who were selected had a chance of a good education – as long as they kept up and could fulfil the academic requirements year after year. Although Michel excelled in the German language, and was good at sport – especially running, swimming and skiing – he deliberately chose to be average in most subjects. This made him popular. He understood that as a non-German he would have to do better than his peers to be accepted as an equal, but did not want to be identified with *die Streber* – the swots. Instead he found that the combination of his independent nature and prowess at athletics was enough to make him accepted as a natural leader.

On one occasion at school a mischief-maker was asked to own up to a particular misdemeanour. Silence descended on the classroom and no hands were raised. The teacher threatened the entire class with punishment unless the culprit confessed. The silence deepened. At last Michel stood and owned up to the crime. He was not the guilty party, and both his classmates and the teacher knew it, but he took the punishment. The silence had irritated him. 'I could not stand cowardice. By standing up to cowards I learned by experience what worked, and the knowledge became a tool.'

His schoolmates saw him as tough and austere, while at home he was preposterously indulged. 'Somehow I led two lives. At school I was very active in sports and was physically strong, which meant the others looked up to me. Then when I took my friends home they saw me in a different light, with women fussing over me, telling me to keep warm, pressing food on me. I was completely over-mothered. My friends were surprised. My life at home didn't fit my outside image.

'I was so pampered that eventually I rebelled against it. I threw out the feather mattress and soft pillows and slept on boards. Even in the depths of winter I slept without heating. My uncle insisted on having the door of my room insulated so that the cold did not permeate the rest of the house. I remember waking one morning with thick ice on the inside of the window pane. One of my ears was frost-bitten and I had to be taken to hospital. I would go skiing in shorts and deliberately leave the windows open in the chalet and have to break the ice in the basin to wash. I took cold showers. I adopted a Spartan regime, more German than the Germans. I overdid it!'

His school friends accepted him as a German, but he did not feel like one. 'They looked to me as a leader, so I *had* to be German. Jewishness came up at school – and in sports, and on our trips – yet it never became an issue between me and my friends, and in all my relationships I never made any distinction. I was very close with my German and non-Jewish friends. But in the end I did not feel German – I was *not* German.'

His aunt and uncle were conservative Jews with liberal values, and kept a kosher household, but they were not religious and relaxed the rules when they ate out. Idessa mixed easily with all types of people, and her closest friend was Mia Von Waldenburg, a scion of the Hohenzollern family.[11] The style of the house, like that of his mother, was universal and all-embracing. 'I was taught that if you don't need help yourself then you must give help to others – a principle that left a deep impression.'

Both his mother and his aunt had brought him up to respect other religions, on the basis that they represented what was good about human beings and promoted high human values. He was taught to remove his hat in Christian churches and his shoes in mosques. But by the age of thirteen he was thoroughly sick at having to be so reverential, and rebelled. 'There were so many things I had to respect that I wondered if they all deserved it. Did anything or any person automatically deserve respect? I had to find out for myself.'

He began to question everything. All the rules, opinions and obligations that had been foisted upon him were subjected to a rigorous analysis. 'I was working out a belief system, a personal philosophy. I seem to have had a very analytical mind as a child. It was an extension, I suppose, of the system I invented when I was six.

I would pick a subject and question it, look at it, and try to go into it as deeply as I could. I had a complete system of analytical questioning set up. Questions. Questions. Questions. I particularly questioned my own Jewishness. I threw everything out – including God.

'I would examine what I was supposed to believe and why. I had my own philosophical thoughts, and after I had pursued them as far as I could only then would I consult books and compare my ideas with other philosophers – Spinoza, Kant, Schopenhauer. I could always leave it off and pick it up, as if reading a book. And I could leave my thoughts and continue the next day, or months later, and know exactly where I left off. I might pick them up again waiting for a bus or a train. I was never bored.'

He made a study of all the major religions, with particular emphasis on early Christianity, and came to the conclusion he was an agnostic. Later, he became both vexed and fascinated by the concept of infinity. 'What was beyond the beyond? My answer was that humans were limited to the finite and could never know the answer to the question. I came to accept the concept of God and the divine – that which was beyond what we could know. So I stopped being an agnostic. But I decided that how we lived and what we did with our own lives was up to us. And rejected the law of retribution as absolute evil. The idea that a human being only did good acts because he was rewarded by God, or that one's misfortunes were a punishment from God, I found contemptible. I felt we were responsible for our own acts, and that there was no divine reward or punishment, and that we had to live with the consequences of our behaviour. Especially the consequences of what we *failed* to do.'

Despite his independence and maturity at fourteen, he still could not be left alone at night because of his sleep-walking. On one occasion when his aunt and uncle went on holiday, an eighteen-year-old girl, who was a friend of the family, was asked to stay. 'The babysitter. And it happened: my first sexual experience. It was new and exciting but I did not think of it as love. She was too old, after all, and had a fiancé. I realise now she must have been very confused by it all and in great conflict. It went on for a while. I remember that after love-making I felt like rejecting her. And I didn't like that feeling and didn't understand it.'

He crept into his uncle's library, a comfortable, masculine room furnished with leather sofas and chairs, where the bookshelves went from the floor to the ceiling. His uncle used it as a *Raucherzimmer* –

smoking room – to receive his male friends, and there were decanters full of liquor and a humidor for cigars on the sideboard. Michel had been allowed to borrow the beautifully bound books on mythology, but others, which he knew were about sex, were hidden away. He now sought these out and found a volume on sexual behaviour and psychology.

Ideal Marriage, written in 1926 by a Dutch gynaecologist, Dr van de Velde, was a book that purported to confine itself strictly to the marriage bed and described itself in an introduction as 'sober, scientific and without a scintilla of eroticism'. In fact, it was advanced for its time, advocating equal sexual pleasure for both parties and stressing the need for technique. The importance of prolongation of the act for women was stressed and methods of ejaculation deferment suggested. The pros and cons of circumcision were discussed and elaborate sexual positions described – referred to as 'attitudes', as in 'Equestrian Attitude (of the Woman)'. There was even a section on oral sex, or 'genital kissing'.[12]

The teenage Michel had no idea that sex was such a rich field and now made it an area of serious study. 'I learned a lot. I read that if a relationship was just about physical satisfaction the person became an object and that this was the reason for feelings of rejection. But this did not happen when sex was combined with feelings of love, which is what my aunt had tried to explain to me at age seven. I took all this into consideration and my whole relationship changed and the act became a whole night's activity.'

Alarmed by the intensity of her fourteen-year-old lover, the girl now drew back and began to refuse to see him, eventually locking her door against him. Naturally, this only served to increase his ardour. 'I would climb up the wall to her window, which is what lovers are supposed to do, but in reality is pretty dangerous.' At one point in the turbulent affair the girl announced that her period was late. She was reduced to misery by the fear of being made pregnant by an adolescent boy. It also had a sobering effect on the young Lothario. 'My God! I sat in class surrounded by friends idly dreaming of girls. What did they know about girls? I vowed I would never do it again.' The panic passed, and the passion with it – but he found the sexual affair had cured his sleep-walking.

Between the ages of fourteen and sixteen Michel allocated the three months of the long summer holiday to solitary travel, a period he called 'Getting to Know Me'. 'Friends wanted to come, but I always went alone. I would put myself in all types of situations and evaluate how I acted and reacted in them. I would examine if I had handled myself satisfactorily. And ask myself how I felt about it. Did I get it right? Could I have done it differently? If I found something I didn't like, or a situation that scared me or that I didn't do well in, I would attempt to repeat it in order to pass my own tests.' This personal quest took him all over Europe and the North African countries of Morocco, Algeria and Tunisia, where he lived and travelled with Arab camel caravans.

Walking in the south of France on one of these journeys he decided to confront the vexing question of rats. 'I passed a small cul-de-sac and saw a heap of trash with rats running all over it. I was repelled. *Rats!* I kept going . . . and then I stopped. Why did I react that way? Just because I had been told bad things about mice and rats? I had to know for myself what my own genuine reaction was, and whether my disgust was nothing more than a conditioned reflex. So I forced myself to go back and get to know the rats. I sat on the steps beside the trash and waited for them to come out.' He settled down for the night, and after a while the brave ones – the leaders – ventured out. Slowly, their more timid companions joined them. He watched them for hours, until the rats surrounded him and moved about as if he were not there.

Although Michel had grown to love his adopted country, he became increasingly aware as a teenager of a strong identity problem. He had rejected the country of his birth and embraced Germany, but knew he was not German. 'So who was I? It became the most important thing in my life to know who I was and to establish my identity. And I found it as a Jew. As a member of a people with a four-thousand-year history. My deeper identity, my ethnic identity was as a Jew. That gave me strength.'

But the Nazis were an ever-growing political force, and to be a Jew was to run the gauntlet in an increasingly hostile world. *Jude* had become a term of abuse, a contemptuous pejorative. 'It was as good as saying "dirty Jew". German Jews at that time called themselves "German citizens of Jewish faith", and some, "Germans of Israelitic faith", or even, "Germans of Mosaic faith". This was not to avoid the strictures of Hitler, but to identify themselves as German. I was not German, and didn't want to be. So I referred to myself as *Jude* – and I said it with emphasis and pride.'

By the age of sixteen Michel began to feel that he had outstripped the school he attended and no longer felt challenged. 'I was anxious to get it over with.' He developed a plan in which he would take extensive private instruction instead of school work, enabling him to gain a year. He took the idea to the principal, who instantly rejected it.

Undeterred, he started shopping around for alternatives, an outlandish concept for a student at that time. He chose a Gymnasium attended by children of the militaristic upper-class Junkers, a school known to be rigid in its educational methods and unforgiving in its academic standards. ('It certainly had no Jews.') But the principal, although a severe disciplinarian of the old school, was sympathetic to a teenager's passion to learn. He accepted the scheme.

At the same time, Michel sought out a private tutor. He chose a highly educated intellectual in the city, Dr Karl Riesenfeld, a musicologist who wrote opera reviews and literary criticism in the highbrow publications. 'He was a walking encyclopaedia. I explained I wanted to leave school early and go on to university, and that I wanted him to teach me personally.' When pressed, Michel admitted that he had not yet spoken to his family about the idea. Not surprisingly, the professor turned him down. Michel refused to take no for an answer.

Riesenfeld tried to brush him off, saying he was busy: 'Besides, summer is coming and I will be travelling.'

'Fine,' Michel said. 'I'll come with you.'

He was passionate and persuasive, and the professor finally agreed to talk to Michel's family, and that if they consented something might be worked out.

That same evening at dinner Michel decided it was a good time to speak to his aunt and uncle about the various far-reaching arrangements he had made for his life. 'I've quit school and I'm not going back.' He explained he had left his old school and was intending to go to a more demanding establishment, finish a year early and go to university. 'I gave them my reasons and told them what I had achieved, that a Junkers Gymnasium had accepted my plan, and that this brilliant man was prepared to talk to them about private instruction. I must say they were impressed by my initiative.' He was granted his wish, and was also allowed to travel with his chosen Aristotle.

They visited the Alpine resorts of Austria, the Italian Dolomites and the cities of northern Italy. Michel studied every day, and discussed history and art, hour after hour. 'I started looking at history through different eyes than those at school. The professor was a learned man, but brought people and places to life. I began to see great historical personages not as figures detached in time who fought some war, but as real people. I started to question what they were like and what motivated them. I developed critical thinking and evaluation – not accepting what I was told and read, which was very un-German at the time. It was one of the greatest learning experiences of my life.' He had previously been weak in mathematics, a subject he had no interest in and for which he was convinced he had no ability, but the professor changed all that. 'Through challenge and love I became a reasonable mathematician. He showed me that there is nothing so complicated that it cannot be made simple, and the concept of reducing complexities later became a cornerstone of my teaching.'

The experiment with private instruction was a success, allowing him to skip a year and pass the stiff entrance tests for the Junkerschule Elisabeth Gymnasium. He excelled at his new school and once again became accepted as a leader through athletics, particularly wrestling. A teacher took the class on extended trips into the mountains and entrusted Michel with half of the group.

By this time, late 1930, the Nazis had become the largest party in the Reichstag, and Adolf Hitler's extreme nationalism and declared anti-Semitism had been widely adopted. Michel's classroom neighbour, who shared a desk with him, began to attend school in the full Nazi uniform of the SA Brownshirt movement. He covered the front of his schoolbooks with elaborate patterns of linked swastikas. Michel responded by covering his with the Star of David.

Despite the growing Nazi influence, Michel's peers continued to follow him as a leader, the only Jew in the school. There was one other boy at school who, although born a Christian, was known to be the son of converts. 'All the boys saw him as a Jew and picked on him, and whenever I saw it I stepped in to save him. I never talked to him, because I didn't like him, but I stuck up for him. Personally, I never had any trouble. I was accepted because I was not a follower. In class if anything derogatory was said about the Jews by the teachers I stood up and challenged it. I was never a Jew who was kicked around.'

It seemed to Michel that one of the major reasons for the advent of Nazism was the German educational system. It was designed to produce a highly educated elite, while neglecting the education of the proletariat who were expected to be subservient and deferential. 'The Germans as a whole – the masses – had a very low self-image. This *Minderwertigkeitsgefühl* – literally "lesser worthiness" – expressed a class inferiority that was apparent to everyone. The maid would refer to her employer as *gnädige Frau* – "merciful lady" – and so on. All those who rose to power with Hitler had lived under and accepted *Minderwertigkeitsgefühl*. These followers who had resigned themselves to lives of the "less worthy" suddenly discovered overnight that they belonged to a new Aryan race of supermen.

'And something else. The intellectual community as a whole was thoroughly prostituted and fell down on their knees before the Nazis. The failure of those with the intellectual power and moral conscience to stand up to Hitler greatly strengthened him. The masses saw the people they had always looked up to embrace Nazism. So Germany became a nation of cowards led by social misfits to believe they were a super race. And the phrase heard everywhere that dominated daily life was *"Führer, befehl, wir folgen Dir!"* – "Führer, you order and we follow you".'

In the election of 1932 the Nazis became the most powerful political party Germany had ever seen, and Hitler the most powerful leader. Although short of a parliamentary majority (the Nazis never polled more than just over a third of the vote nationally, although the party won forty-six per cent in Breslau) it was the largest party in the Reichstag with a membership of over a million, almost fourteen million electors and a private army of four hundred thousand SA Storm Troopers and SS Blackshirts – a force four times larger than the feeble national army. The Communists had polled six million votes, won a hundred seats in the Reichstag and had their own private army, the Red Front. There were pitched battles in the streets of the larger cities between Nazis and Communists, leaving many dead.

The young Michel witnessed the violence and was repelled by the unprincipled manipulation and dictatorial tendencies of both political extremes. In the struggle for power the Communists actually helped the Nazis achieve office, openly stating they would prefer to see Hitler in charge rather than lift a finger to save the republic. They also followed the Moscow-approved policy that gave priority to the elimination of the Social Democrats – not the Nazis – as the rival working-class party.[13] 'It seemed to me that only a free society didn't create conflict between Judaism and the state. So that you could not be a Jew and a fascist, or a Jew and a communist. A Jew cannot live in a police state. I always felt those Jews who were communists had a problem with identity and were trying to escape their Jewishness.'

In January 1933, Adolf Hitler was made Chancellor of Germany. Life for German Jews became increasingly difficult and dangerous as a slew of anti-Semitic laws discriminated against them. About seventy per cent of Germany's half million Jews – less than one per cent of the population – lived in cities. Primarily middle-class, they had enjoyed legal equality since the late nineteenth century and had achieved a high degree of financial success. They were thoroughly assimilated into all walks of German life – 'quoting Goethe at every meal' – and identified closely with the country to the point of vociferously expressed patriotism.[14] Although the SA Storm Troopers were brutish and violent in their actions against Jews, Hitler preferred to pursue legal measures against them, and gave speeches in which he talked of peace and the futility of war.

Jews sought a way to live within the contradictions and confusion created by the various Nazi decrees. But it took optimism bordering on self-delusion to believe life could continue normally after the Nazi-imposed boycott in April 1933, which severely limited Jewish participation in the economy. It was during this time that Michel first identified what he came later to condemn as 'the Jewish weakness'. 'There is the inability of the Jewish mind to perceive and accept the finality of evil. They will always say, whatever happens, in whatever language, "Ach, everything will be all right!" They see the darkness, the destruction – but no, everything will be all right. It is the result of four thousand years of teaching the goodness of man, that evil cannot triumph, and that good will always prevail. Things *have* to turn out well. It is different to *hope* that things will turn out all right – that is human and very important. To *believe* it is a weakness. A weakness that can become fatal.'

It seemed to his elders around him that Michel had an uncanny ability to foretell events, and they credited him with an almost supernatural gift of premonition. But there was nothing other-worldly about it. 'As a youngster I could see things coming. And when I look back on this I realise it was just a question of thinking things through. It was an intellectual process. And, of course, there was something happening in the country which to me would obviously end in total disaster, but people avoided it and didn't want to face it. There was only one way, and that way led to war. I knew it couldn't be different. I didn't minimise the danger – I realised there was no future.'

One evening three non-Jewish German friends came to Michel's house unannounced. They were visibly upset and had important news. They had learned that he was about to be arrested and charged with acts of sabotage and wanted to warn him. The offence was minor – the slashing of a police car's tyres – but Michel was in danger because of his vocal opposition to the Nazis. 'I would have been very happy and proud to have committed these acts, but it so happened that I had not done anything.' However, he had no illusions about the fate of anyone accused of such a crime in Hitler's Germany. He left in the night for France.

Michel's aunt and uncle were away when he was warned about his imminent arrest, so he left Breslau at the age of nineteen, in May 1933, without saying goodbye. He had stopped briefly to bid farewell to Dr Riesenfeld, who gave him the typescript of an anti-Nazi article he had written for publication in an émigré newspaper in Paris. Michel planned to hitch-hike to France and, standing at the side of the road clad in a pair of knickerbockers, he looked the idealised picture of German youth and was soon given a lift. The driver asked where he was going, and when told Michel was leaving the country, asked why. '*Ich bin Jude*,' Michel replied. I am a Jew.

At Kehl he passed through German customs and crossed the bridge over the Rhine to the French city of Strasbourg. But the French refused to allow him entry on his Polish passport without a visa, so he tramped back across the bridge into Germany. He was taken by the Germans to police headquarters and questioned closely, painfully aware of Dr Riesenfeld's anti-Nazi article in the pocket of his knickerbockers. After a couple of hours he was released, and considered putting his clothes into his rucksack and swimming across the Rhine, but rejected the plan as impractical. A study of the map suggested the best chance of undetected entry into France was from the Saarland, a German state occupied by France since the end of the Great War.[15] By cutting across country over mountains he thought he would be able to slip into the Saar without passing through any checkpoints, and enter France unchallenged.

As he sat by the side of the road, a column of uniformed Hitler Youth passed singing Nazi marching songs. They shot out their right hands in the Nazi salute. Michel did not respond. It was a provocation, and two youths peeled away from the rear of the column to confront him. There was a scuffle and he struck out, using his side-satchel as a weapon. The whole column turned and came after him. And on this occasion, discretion proved the better part of valour: 'I ran.'

He studied the map again and chose a place known as Drei Zinnen – Three Peaks – to cross into the Saar. It was late in the afternoon by the time he reached the point of departure. He stopped to ask directions of three farm labourers working in the fields on their vines. One crossed himself at the mention of Drei Zinnen, and as he pointed out the path told Michel that the castle ruins on top of each of the hills were haunted. No one went there at night and he advised postponing the journey until morning. Undeterred by local superstition, Michel set off as the sun began to go down.

It was a long, steep climb through thick woods to the first set of ruins and it was dark by the time he reached them. He paused at the top of the hill to take a swig of water from his canteen and saw something that made the hairs on the back of his neck stiffen. Irregular flickering lights were moving through the trees beneath the castle walls. They were unlike anything he had ever seen and inexplicable. They were simply not of this world. 'Ghostly' was the word that came to mind to describe them. He felt terror and creeping panic. 'My first reaction was to run. But that meant losing control, which was dangerous. I controlled my breathing and forced myself to keep going at a steady pace.'

He kept the fear in check as he descended the other side of the hill. There was nothing he could think of to explain the mysterious lights, which only increased his sense of dread. He began to climb the second hill, and as he reached the top he saw more ghostly white lights among the trees and ruins. Sheer willpower kept him going, and by the time he reached the top of the third hill day was breaking, although once again he saw weak, moving lights.

A hunter dressed in green, carrying a shotgun and accompanied by a dog, appeared out of the trees. Michel had never felt happier to see a fellow human being. Exhausted by his experience, he greeted the man warmly and told him of the previous night's terrors. The hunter nodded calmly, but seemed neither surprised nor alarmed at Michel's story. The ghostly lights, he explained, were an unusual local phenomenon caused by phosphorus formed in decomposing tree trunks. 'I wish I had known this before I started my journey. It was a very, very uncomfortable night.'

Michel reached the border without incident and crossed through unpatrolled green fields into the Saar, and then hitch-hiked to Paris. At this time, France was a tolerant, cosmopolitan country and a haven for thousands of refugees from Nazi Germany. 'It was almost in vogue to be a refugee then. There were numerous refugees from Germany and Jewish groups were well organised and well funded to receive them.'

By late summer the generosity of the charities and the tolerance of the authorities were stretched to the limit as an ever-increasing stream of refugees entered the country fleeing poverty and fascism. Most spoke no French, were uneducated and impoverished, and imposed an enormous strain on an economy that was already severely depressed. Unemployment stood at record levels. The immigrants, many of whom were Jewish, were resented as a threat to the job security of the ordinary Frenchman and xenophobia and anti-Semitism grew as a result. Most refugees in Paris were moved into camps.

Michel himself lived a hand-to-mouth existence, and looked up family friends who had moved to France from Lodz many years earlier. The family had a daughter called Lucienne, whom Michel had fondly known as Luba when they had played together as five-year-olds, and in the intervening years she had developed into a beautiful young woman. Michel felt himself enormously attracted to her, and began to spend all his time at her parents' house. It was the beginning of a strong physical and emotional relationship, his first true love.

The passionate affair made life more interesting but no less difficult. It was illegal for refugees to work and his family was only allowed to send the equivalent of fifteen dollars a month. And he spoke poor French. 'I had learned it in school, but what does it mean to learn in school? I couldn't read it or speak, and wasn't able to get along at all. I simply could not communicate.'

He acquired alien skills that he exploited illegally, becoming adept at painting and decorating. Hanging wallpaper was a particular speciality. In another job he hand-packed razor blades in cellophane, one after the other, possibly the most boring task he has ever performed in a long life. He also sold gaudy hand-painted ties. His old school friend, Karl Hamburg – Kai – joined him from Breslau, another Jewish refugee from Hitler.[16] They vowed to go to a French university together, which was a challenge and something of an impertinence as both spoke bad French and were penniless refugees. But they were determined to enter university by the autumn, which gave them the spring and summer to bring their language skills up to a suitable standard. 'I found ways of applying my grammatical knowledge that made my progress in the language leap ahead.' He did not know it, but he was beginning to explore techniques that would eventually merge to become his unique language system.

The friends agreed to split up and explore various cities throughout France. Afterwards they would reunite, pool their experiences and impressions, and decide where to go. When the friends met again Michel made a strong case for Bordeaux. It was an attractive, sophisticated city with a symphony orchestra and an opera, but more importantly it was on the ocean and close to the

Pyrénées. This meant the friends could enjoy the beach in the summer and ski in the mountains in winter. Karl was persuaded, and the university accepted them both in September.

Bordeaux was also full of refugees, and Michel shared a small apartment with Kai in a house used by ladies of the night, good-natured, amiable girls who bustled clients up and down the stairs at all hours. Once again he had to make money to eat and pay for lodgings. A family restaurant was pleased to make an arrangement for free food for both of them if he was able to fill the restaurant. As president of the Jewish student body he persuaded many of them to take their meals in the restaurant, and it was soon packed.

Later, he persuaded the Bordeaux council to lend him a rundown building owned by the city on the Rue Margaux for the refugee community in exchange for an undertaking to renovate it. 'We turned it into a beautiful place, equipped it with a big kitchen, and served meals in a garden courtyard in the summer.' A busy laundry service run out of the house also became a profitable concern.

To make money Michel used his Leica camera to take pictures of children at play in the city's parks. He then went to their mothers and offered them the option of buying the photos. 'And of course they loved them – I was rarely turned down.' He worked late into the night developing and printing. He also began to paint on glass, describing his style as 'assembly line'. He worked on ten paintings at a time lined up in a row and moved from one to another adding colour. 'I knocked them out.' The first fifty were framed and taken by a dealer to a large department store. Sales were slow. Michel sent student friends to stand in front of the paintings and talk about them with excitement. Sales remained slow. He sent them back with money to buy. 'So they bought the paintings and brought them to me. Sales became quite good. The store gave me a big order and the paintings I had bought went back to the store.'

Michel had applied for a place in the chemistry department at the university, and although he passed the exams he found that he was unable to afford the course. So he switched his studies to philology, philosophy, archaeology and the history of art. He was also interested in psychology, particularly the Viennese psychoanalysts Alfred Adler and Sigmund Freud. He became particularly intrigued by the work of the nineteenth-century German philosopher and classical philologist Friedrich Nietzsche.

Another profound admirer of Nietzsche, of course, was Adolf Hitler. Never could two individuals – Michel Thomas and Adolf Hitler – have interpreted a philosophy in such contradictory terms.

One man read to challenge himself intellectually, while the other sought texts to confirm his preconceptions.

Nietzsche maintained that all human behaviour is motivated by the will to power. He argued that traditional Christian values had lost their potency in the lives of people – 'God is dead' – and that these had been replaced by a slave mentality created by weak and resentful individuals, who encouraged such concepts as 'gentleness' and 'kindness' only because they served their interests. New values were needed to replace the traditional ones to help form a superman who was secure, independent and highly individualistic. The superman would have strong feelings but would always control his passion. He would be concerned with the realities of the human world rather than the heavenly promises of religion, and would affirm life with all its suffering and pain. The superman would evolve his own 'master morality', made up only of those values he deemed valid.

The student Michel saw the positive in Nietzsche, interpreting the will to power as control over self and responsible power over others. He saw the emphasis on independence and individuality as a path to individual moral responsibility. Hitler took a different view and interpreted the philosopher's ideas to suit his own totalitarian instincts and justify a master-slave society. Nietzsche seemed to support Hitler's lack of belief in either God or conscience, which the Führer dismissed as 'a Jewish invention, a blemish like circumcision'. The concept that a nation was nothing more than nature's way of providing a few important men also suited Hitler, who felt chosen for a mission by providence and therefore exempt from ordinary human moral restraint. And while Michel might subscribe to the Nietzschean phrase 'Praised be that which toughens', Hitler would have it posted in every SS barracks.[17]

Michel attended a summer philosophy course at the Sorbonne, in Paris, where a chance remark made by one of the professors made an enormous impact: Nobody knows anything about the learning process of the human mind. The statement had a profound influence on his later life.

Despite a growing undercurrent of resentment towards immigrants and Jews, the French electorate in 1936 put into power the anti-fascist Popular Front, led by Léon Blum, a socialist and Jew. But as the economy grew worse, and the government proved inept, enemies of the Third Republic complained that a Jewish premier proved that the country had fallen into the hands of the Jews, and ruin would follow. Most of all, they feared that it would lead them into war with Hitler. (In fact, the diplomatic thrust of Blum's government was to appease Hitler – with catastrophic results.)

An important influence at this time on Michel's political thinking was Michael Nelken, a young German writer who wrote under the name Michael Ken.[18] The men had met at Bordeaux University and became good friends until Nelken returned home to Germany to visit his mother and seemed to disappear. There was no word from him for almost two years, but in one of the many fateful coincidences in Michel's life the friends bumped into each other only minutes after Nelken's return to Paris.

He was a changed man. In Germany, his writing had attracted the attention and displeasure of the Nazi government and he had been arrested. He was sent to Dachau, near Munich – the Nazis' first concentration camp opened in March 1933 to incarcerate critics and enemies of the regime.[19] Nelken was released only after the intervention of Wilhelm Furtwängler, conductor of the Berlin Philharmonic Orchestra, but not before the writer had contracted a bad case of tuberculosis.[20] On his return to France doctors recommended that he live in a warm climate in the south.

Michel could see that his friend was deathly ill and offered to accompany him as companion and nurse. The men arranged to rent a house in Grasse, in Provence, but this created a crisis in Michel's relationship with Lucienne. He had suggested that she accompany him and that they live together, a scandalous arrangement for the times. Lucienne certainly thought so, and issued an ultimatum: marriage or nothing! Michel left for the south without her.

Nelken grew stronger over time, and the friends often visited a famous neighbour, H.G. Wells, for long afternoons of conversation. Nelken began writing a book on his experiences in Dachau, a place mostly unheard of by the world, and it made grim reading. The manuscript confirmed Michel's worst fears and both men were convinced that the book's publication would cause international outrage. But it was rejected across the board by French publishers as hysterical and improbable propaganda. Worse, when a condensed account was finally published in a German refugee paper, it was bitterly attacked as fantasy. Some Jewish critics even described the book as the product of a sick imagination.

The reaction depressed Nelken deeply, but Michel was unaware of the depths of his friend's despair when he went away for several weeks. He returned to receive the terrible news from Nelken's fiancée that he had committed suicide. The writer Michael Ken had survived the brutalities of Dachau and the ravages of TB but was devastated by the rejection of his own people. The dismissal of his experiences as fantasy, and his warnings as alarmist, was more than he could bear. 'You will survive the ninety-nine blows of the whip; it will be painful and very bad, but you will survive. But you will not survive the one hundredth lash. For Michael the one hundredth blow was to tell his story as a warning and not to be believed.'

It was a time of false hope, and no one wanted to believe what Michel now saw as inevitable: there would be war. He felt compelled to visit his family and travelled to Breslau to see his aunt and uncle, and then on to Lodz to see his mother and father. The German economy had improved radically under Hitler, although it did not benefit Jews for whom life had become circumscribed, dangerous and unpleasant. In Breslau his aunt and uncle lived in hope of change, but also began to speak half-heartedly of emigration, possibly to America. In Lodz, Michel found his mother oblivious to danger and so removed from reality that she expressed the hope that he might return to live in Poland.

An intimate family dinner was organised to persuade him, held in the palatial home of great-uncle Oscar (Usher) Kohn, a man of fantastic wealth who travelled in his own private train. As the owner of a large textile factory, Widzewska Manufaktura, and the builder of the town of Widzew on the outskirts of Lodz, he took a broad, general view of things.

Usher waved his cigar and delivered an avuncular lecture. 'It's nice to travel and see other countries, but it's important to have a base. You can sail out, but you must have a home port!'

Michel understood his uncle to mean that his home was with the family in Lodz, and the great manufacturing business his future. Cocooned by his immense wealth, Usher Kohn believed he could weather any political storm and return to the safety of his home port. But Michel had plans to study psychology at the University of Vienna, birthplace of psychoanalysis and city of Sigmund Freud.

'I hate Poland!' Michel exclaimed, unable to contain himself.

Uncle Usher and Freida exchanged a glance, but the young man did not stop.

'What kind of future do you have here? A manufacturer? It's just a matter of time. Maybe in a few years the Germans will be here and it will be the end of your business. Or the Russians will be here and that will be the end of your business.'[21]

Uncle Usher shrugged, drew on his cigar and changed the subject. He did not even seem angry. He was used to spirited, outspoken hotheads in the family, which is what he had been at the same age.

In many ways Oscar Kohn was the living history of Lodz, and had been largely instrumental in the city's growth from an empty village in a sandy waste to a world-renowned centre of industry. The four dozen Jews originally allowed to live in the city had been tailors from Germany and Moravia, who had fled the poverty of towns and villages razed in the Napoleonic wars. A mighty textile manufacturing empire had grown from these modest beginnings.

Uncle Usher had witnessed war, pogroms, Cossacks and revolution and had always managed to turn a profit. There had been bad times, but he had endured. Nobody who made it in Lodz did it the easy way, and he could be cynically witty about the city's inhabitants and mores. Lodz, he would tell Michel – or anyone who cared to listen – admired nothing more than wealth, and the rabbis needed to know more about promissory notes than about the Torah, more about bankruptcy than God's law. Lodz knew that with money you could buy anything, although unlike wool or cotton, justice was not a commodity the city was concerned about. Lodz was a city of sharpies, Uncle Usher said, a town without secrets that knew what was cooking in everyone's pot. 'He's moving up' was a glowing term said of a man on the make, and the city's compliments were sharp and geared to ruthless success. A man was deemed 'smart as salt in a wound', or someone who could 'turn snow into cheese', and the greatest compliment old Lodz could bestow on a citizen was to say that he had the guts of a pickpocket.

And while Uncle Usher accepted that Hitler was a threat, he did not believe the deranged lance-corporal truly represented most Germans. It was an unfortunate political phase, an aberration. Balance and moderation would eventually be restored to the most cultured and educated country in Europe. German anti-Semitism was manufactured for political reasons and not an intrinsic part of German society at all. Not like Russia, where anti-Semitism ran deep, or Poland, where the strain was the most virulent of all.

Anti-Semitism was a fact of life, a condition Jews had to endure and overcome. Even the Jewish population in Lodz struggled endlessly among themselves for supremacy. German Jews considered themselves the cream of the crop, followed by the Poles. Both groups resented and looked down on those expelled from Russia, while Lithuanians – known as Litvaks – were considered even worse, existing only on bread and herring and dismissed as 'onionheads': 'All they brought with them to Poland were their teapots and their razors with which to shave once a week.'[22]

It was in this worldly and sophisticated manner that Uncle Usher dismissed Michel's warnings as youthful exaggerations, and no doubt Freida was greatly comforted. But as Michel left the country and made his way by train to Vienna, he was full of foreboding. His return had been a bittersweet experience that left him emotionally upset and inexplicably angry. The happiness and tears of the people he loved most in the world had moved him deeply, but he worried about the danger his aunt and uncle faced in Germany, and the uncertain future of his parents in Poland. He had savoured every moment of their company, recalled every gesture and word, committing them to memory. It was the last time he saw any of them alive.[23]

III

In the middle of a busy afternoon at the Language Centre on Fifth Avenue, New York, the secretary of Michel Thomas made the rare exception of interrupting a session in progress to put through an urgent call. She sounded concerned and upset, and announced there was a woman from France on the line long distance. And it was important. Perhaps more than important.

'Who is it?' Michel demanded. The interruption broke one of his strict rules, and he was irritated. 'What does she want?'

'I don't know . . . but you must take the call.'

There was something unusual in the tone of his secretary's voice, and she was so uncharacteristically demanding that he did not argue. He excused himself and made his way along the corridor to his private office.

'Hello, Michel Thomas speaking,' he said softly into the phone.

There was no reply, and at first he thought that the caller had hung up. He was about to replace the phone in its cradle when he heard a series of strange choking noises – a terrible, heart-rending sound of somebody in unbearable emotional pain. And he did not need to hear a voice to identify the person. He felt his own pulse beat faster and a sense of dread took hold of him.

'Suzanne?'

The reply was a low moan of distress. Michel listened, helpless. There was an attempt at speech but no words came, only a pitiable sobbing.

'My God, Suzanne – calm down! *Please!* Calm down! Try to talk to me! Please talk to me!'

He tried to soothe her, but it was useless; Suzanne would attempt to talk and then break down into uncontrollable tears. Nothing could stop the outpouring of anguish from the other end of the line. Every attempt at speech was overwhelmed by outbursts of weeping.

'I'm going to put the phone down and call you back in half an hour. Okay? Give you a chance to pull yourself together. And then we can talk. Do you understand?' The sobbing continued. 'Suzanne, I'll call you in half an hour.'

The call had shaken him and disturbed powerful memories. He sat in silence for a long time and did not move. At last he spoke to his secretary over the intercom and told her to apologise and explain to the student that he was incapable of continuing that day. As he waited to call Suzanne back, he rehearsed a hundred soothing phrases, dismissing each one as empty and inadequate. The time crawled by.

It was night in France, a little after ten, when he called. The phone rang and rang but no one answered. Ten minutes later, when he called again, it was off the hook. And it remained off the hook throughout the night, although he continued to dial the number from his home before he finally fell asleep, exhausted. When he called again in the morning the operator told him that the line had been disconnected.

He made his way to the office on foot, a man in mourning. He felt he understood the meaning behind the wordless call: Suzanne was saying goodbye. He was convinced that she was dying and knew it, and had called one last time to remind him of a lifetime of love, and to say farewell. All further attempts by Michel to phone proved fruitless. Letters were returned unopened. He wondered if Suzanne might have gone to a house she owned in Austria, and attempted to track her down there, but without success. A few months later his fears were confirmed when he learned, after contacting friends in Nice, that Suzanne had died. He had lost the great love of his youth.[1]

Michel Thomas met Suzanne Adler in Vienna in 1937 after he moved there, directly after his visit to Lodz, to attend university on a post-graduate course. He was an intense twenty-three-year-old with an enormous appetite for life, and she was a lively, highly intelligent seventeen-year-old with wavy golden-brown hair. She seemed older than her years and very mature. Suzanne was a relative of Alfred Adler, an early associate and student of Sigmund Freud.

Vienna was a lively and appealing city and Michel was spellbound by it, happy to be studying psychology and philosophy in his beloved German language. He soon made friends and liked to make the rounds of the numerous cafés and concert halls. One young friend, Hans Pohl, had been an early and enthusiastic member of the Nazi Party and SS. An investigation into his background for racial purity, however, disclosed that his mother had Jewish blood. It was an awakening that transformed the young man into an outspoken critic and sworn enemy of the Austrian Nazis. Michel received one of life's lessons from Pohl: his friend's parents ran a famous restaurant in the city and he was given the secret recipe for its highly praised and powerfully alcoholic egg-nog.

At first Michel had a collection of girlfriends, but soon after meeting Suzanne he embarked upon a serious involvement. The relationship between them in the first months of student life in Vienna grew stronger by the day, although it was not physical. He was six years older and sexually experienced, while Suzanne was a virgin. 'This held me back. I had always gone out with girls older and more experienced than myself.' He was also uncertain whether he wanted to commit himself emotionally to one woman. Suzanne had already fallen in love, but he wavered.

The couple pursued as happy and carefree a life as the times allowed. They followed a student routine in the day and at night made a habit of frequenting the Congo Bar, a club with tented booths and an orchestra where they could dance until the early hours. 'I adapted very quickly to the life of the city because I found myself in a German-speaking country for the first time since I left Breslau. My experience as a student was eventful in a pleasant and exciting way. The intensity of life during the time spent in the city – the friendliness and ambience – appealed to me immensely, and time flew by. Friendships were easily made, and I felt absolutely great in Vienna.'

As in Bordeaux, he pursued a variety of part-time occupations to make money. He continued to paint pictures on glass, while a jeweller employed him to make a line of miniature gold charms featuring scenes from famous operas. 'I also helped an impressive old gentleman in his eighties with a long beard who was blind. I read correspondence and newspaper articles in various languages to him and he would dictate replies. It became a productive personal relationship in which we discussed world affairs and politics, and I learned a lot.'

To the north in Germany, Adolf Hitler dominated the nation, while Austria seemed drained of independent political will and floundered under weak, indecisive leadership. 'As time went on one suspected that something might happen – an invasion by the German Army, perhaps – to make Austria a part of Nazi Germany. But when I discussed this with prominent leaders of the Jewish community – business people and industrialists – they rejected the idea. They felt that it could not happen, and that if it did happen it would not affect them. Whatever political upheaval occurred, the Nuremberg Laws would never be applied in Austria, and certainly not in Vienna.[2] They were integrated, accepted – they were

Austrians. The Jews in Vienna felt as removed from Nazi Germany as the American Jews in the United States. *"S'wrd schoin zan git"* the Polish Jews in Lodz always said in Yiddish – "Everything will be all right". And in Vienna it was repeated in German: *"Alles wird schon gut werden".'*

Michel felt that his psychological studies provided him with an insight into the Nazi mentality. Alfred Adler stressed a sense of inferiority, rather than the sexual drive, as the motivating force in human life. He believed that an inferiority complex acquired as a child, combined with excessive compensatory defence mechanisms created to overcome it, formed the basis of psychopathological behaviour. The function of the psychoanalyst was to discover and rationalise such feelings, and to break down the neurotic will to power and dominance they engendered – ranging in means from boasting and bullying to political tyranny. It was an interesting thesis to study in pre-war Vienna, and Adolf Hitler was a classic – if extreme – textbook case.[3]

The roar of Hitler's mechanised divisions massing on the border, however, drowned out all such psychological musings. Austrian-born, Hitler had written of the dream of incorporating Austria within a Greater Germany – *Anschluss* – in the opening pages of *Mein Kampf* and it had been Nazi party policy since 1920.[4] The idea found growing support inside Austria itself, and not just among Nazi sympathisers. There were many Austrians who accepted *Anschluss* as inevitable *Realpolitik* and sincerely believed that the country, since the loss of its Slav and Hungarian possessions in 1918, had no future without union with Germany.

By early 1938, Hitler felt strong enough to chance his hand. As news spread of the German Army at the border, a massive crowd crammed into the centre of Vienna and surrounded the Chancellery. Inside, figures in swastika armbands were already saluting each other with outstretched hands. Throughout the country local Austrian Nazis seized town halls and government offices.

German troops crossed the border unopposed at daybreak on Saturday, 12 March, and were enthusiastically greeted as saviours rather than invaders. Later the same day Hitler chose to cross the frontier in person at his birthplace, Braunau am Inn, and drove through cheering villages to Linz, the town of his childhood, where he received a hero's welcome. Tears ran down his face as he was handed the text of a law stating: 'Austria is a province of the German Reich.' That night the round-up and arrest of tens of thousands of Hitler's enemies began.

An ecstatic crowd filled the Heldenplatz and the Ring and waited day and night for the Führer's triumphant entry into the capital forty-eight hours later. Vienna had been the scene of Hitler's unhappy, impoverished youth when he eked out a living as a hack artist and lived in a hostel frequented by tramps and drunks. It was the city that had rejected him – the Academy of Fine Arts had twice refused him for lack of talent – and now he was returning as a conquering hero, an Adlerian moment if ever there was one.[5]

Michel went out on the streets to witness events and found the crowd in the grip of mass hysteria. 'The Austrians received the Nazis triumphantly, Hitler was welcomed like a Roman emperor. The streets had become human rivers. I can still hear the sound of their chanting: "*Sieg Heil! Sieg Heil! Sieg Heil! Ein Volk, Ein Reich, Ein Führer . . . Wir danken unserem Führer . . . Sieg Heil! Sieg Heil! Sieg Heil!*" – Hail to victory . . . one people, one nation, one leader! Day and night it went on – and on and on. The enthusiasm was boundless.' The euphoric atmosphere and the change in the people were unnerving. 'Suddenly there was this transformation. There had been no great show of support for the Nazis before that I was aware of as a student – I considered Vienna very friendly – but now everyone wore little metal swastikas in their left lapel to show their loyalty. They were for sale on every street corner – not official party badges, just a swastika to show loyalty and express support. Foreigners had to wear the insignia of their country in their lapel, and those who didn't were exposed as anti-Nazis or Jews. Enemies.' Typically, Michel wore the Star of David in his lapel, but remained untouched.

A gigantic portrait of Hitler dominated the square in front of the opera house, and Michel heard the senior Roman Catholic prelate, Cardinal Theodor Innitzer, urge the people to support Hitler. The cardinal had greeted the Führer with the sign of the cross and gave assurances that as long as the Church retained its liberties Austrian Catholics – the majority of the country – would become 'the truest sons of the Third Reich'. The atheist Hitler shook the cardinal's hand warmly. (Nevertheless, a few months later the cardinal's palace was sacked by Nazi thugs. Awakened to the true nature of National Socialism, Innitzer spoke against the persecution of the Church – an impotent gesture of independence that was too little too late.)[6]

'The excesses were incredible. Suddenly, the Austrians were the worst – worse than the Germans. Overnight they reached the state of hatred it had taken the German nation five years to achieve. Among the most extreme were the Sudeten Germans, who had come to Austria as refugees from Czechoslovakia. Brutes let loose on the Jewish population. I saw acts of cruelty committed by Austrians against Jews on every street. Their actions even shocked German officers, and I saw them restrain people a number of times.'

It was dangerous for sceptics to be in the streets, but Michel wanted to be everywhere, and Suzanne willingly accompanied him. 'This is history,' he told her. 'These are events that we can only remember if we live them and see them, and not hide by staying at home.' One of the most painful scenes they witnessed was quiet and undramatic, but it moved them deeply. Within the shadow of the opera house, across from the giant portrait of Hitler, they came across three men gathered around a young woman, shielding her from sight. The woman had lost control and was weeping piteously. 'Her friends did not want the mob to see that she did not share in the universal joy.'

Day after day hundreds of Jewish men and women were forced on to their hands and knees to scrub the political slogans of the previous regime from pavements and walls with acid. Storm Troopers stood over them while the crowds jeered. Elderly Jews were forced to clean the lavatories and barracks of their new masters, and Michel learned that the scholarly old gentleman whom he helped had been dragged to his knees by his beard and beaten.

One of the distinguished Viennese who had previously put a brave face on events was Sigmund Freud. Although he had promised his family to leave if the Nazis ever took over, he proved reluctant when the moment came. 'This is my post and I can never leave it,' he told an English colleague. The colleague responded with the story of an officer who survived the sinking of the *Titanic* who was asked why he had abandoned the ship. 'I never left the ship, she left me,' he replied. The argument that Austria no longer existed was a compelling one, and Freud departed for England, 'the land of my early dreams'.[7]

He was one of the fortunate few who acted before the Nazis purged the police and neutralised all opposition. Austria literally ceased to exist, its ancient name – Österreich – abolished and replaced with Ostmark, until even that was dropped and the country was administered as a series of districts directly from Berlin. Instead of a fading, imperial capital, Vienna became just another city of the Reich. Hitler's revenge on the place of his youthful humiliation was complete.

Tens of thousands of Jews were jailed and their possessions confiscated, while half of the city's one hundred and eighty thousand Jewish population attempted to purchase permission to emigrate by handing over everything they owned to the Nazis. The sole agency authorised to issue exit permits was the Office for Jewish Emigration, set up by Reinhard Heydrich of the SS. It was headed, from its inception to the end of the war, by an Austrian-born Nazi from Hitler's home town of Linz, Karl Adolf Eichmann. Emigration was a lucrative business. Later, when there was no more money to be taken from the Jews, the office switched its efforts to extermination. In the weeks immediately following *Anschluss*, the concentration camp of Mauthausen was set up on the north bank of the Danube near Enns, saving the Nazis the trouble of deporting its enemies to camps in Germany.[8]

Michel had been living in Vienna under a Polish passport, the same one he had used to leave Germany and obtain residence in France. He was now summoned to the Polish Embassy where it was confiscated by the consul-general. The Polish parliament had passed a law introducing a slew of new regulations under which citizenship could be taken away from Poles living abroad. This was aimed at preventing the Nazis from pushing tens of thousands of Polish Jews legally living in Germany – and now Austria – across the border.[9] Suddenly, at a stroke, he was stateless. 'I became *vogelfrei* – fair game. It was an impossible situation for me because I also relied on my passport for my legal residence in France as well as Austria. Now I had no papers and no legal residence anywhere. And I could not travel. I had to go into hiding from that time, moving from one friend's apartment to another.'

Cut off from parents, family and friends in Poland, he was helpless. A well-placed relative in the government in Warsaw tried to use his influence, but to no effect. Michel explored every possibility but there was nothing he could do to counter the Poles' arbitrary action. Finally, through an Austrian friend, he was able to obtain a document identifying him as a stateless person. It was not much, but it was better than nothing.

The city's numerous embassies and consulates were besieged by Jews trying to emigrate. Endless lines of desperate people waited day and night to be interviewed. 'I stood in such a line at the American consulate and was told to forget it. I was treated like an undesirable. And the consulate turned people away even though the quota was never filled. Inhuman, cruel, despicable action.'

The *Anschluss* created a Jewish refugee problem of immense proportions. American president Franklin D. Roosevelt initiated an international conference in Evian, France, where thirty-two nations gathered to find a solution. In fact the conference was merely a kind of moral posturing and an act of political hypocrisy on the part of Roosevelt. Terms agreed in advance laid down that no country would be expected to receive a greater number of emigrants than was permitted under existing legislation. Immigration law in the US was notoriously restrictive at this time. No country offered sanctuary or concrete help, and the conference achieved nothing except to set up an Intergovernmental Committee for Refugees, which in the fullness of time also achieved nothing.

The conference had been opened with a strong statement by its American chairman that the time had come for governments to act, and to act promptly. *Newsweek* reported: 'Most government representatives acted promptly by slamming their doors against Jewish refugees.' The Nazi newspaper *Völkischer Beobachter* crowed in a headline: NOBODY WANTS THEM. Hitler himself, who had offered to transport the Jews anywhere on luxury liners, gleefully drove the point home. 'They complain in these democracies about the unfathomable cruelty that Germany . . . uses in trying to get rid of the Jews . . . But it does not mean that these democratic countries have now become ready to replace their hypocritical remarks with acts of help. On the contrary, they affirm with complete coolness that over there, evidently, there is no room! In short, no help, but preaching, certainly.'[10]

At this stage, the Germans still wished to remove Jews from Germany and send them elsewhere. There was even a half-baked idea considered in senior Nazi circles to resettle them on the French island of Madagascar. Michel found the world's rejection a moral outrage. 'At the beginning the Germans would allow anyone to leave who had somewhere to go; their aim was to have a *judenrein* – Jew-free – Germany. But there was not one single country – not one single country on the face of the earth that would accept Jews. They were undesirable. There was nowhere for them to go, not a desert or a jungle, not the North or South Poles. Nowhere.'

The world's apathetic response to the fate of the Jews was a surprise to the Germans, an unexpected bonus that led directly in 1942 to the policy of the Final Solution and mass murder. 'The Nazis were given the green light by the civilised world and decided to get rid of all the Jews through the chimney. The total indifference of the world was an unpardonable sin because it was more than the physical destruction of human beings, it was the spiritual destruction of human beings – the destruction of hope.

'I make a sharp distinction between physical death and the death of the mind – the death of hope. People can die as martyrs with the belief system intact. But to go to your death with hope and faith taken away, to feel rejected by the world, to have belief torn from your heart, you become nothing . . . nobody.

'There were those who despaired and found the situation hopeless. But it is not part of my character to be nihilistic or even cynical. I was not prepared to let reality overwhelm me. I wanted to find a way to fight back.'

It was a bleak time when nothing seemed to work and hope receded hour by hour. One day Suzanne met Michel in a café in a state of great excitement and announced she had found the solution to their problems. A British priest had generously offered to get pre-dated baptismal documents identifying them as Christians, and this would enable them to leave the country.

'And you can do that?' Michel asked.

'We must go right away.' Suzanne glowed with excitement and hope. 'This will save our lives.'

'How could you offer to do such a thing?' Michel said, his anger building. 'I am a Jew and I have to survive as a Jew.'

'It's just to get false papers,' Suzanne said, exasperated. 'It isn't real. Does it mean so much to you to use fake papers?'

'No, it does not mean much to use fake papers, but to deny my Jewishness and owe my life to that, how could I live with myself? I have to face myself every day and every night – how will I after this, denying who I am?'

They both became increasingly angry. Suzanne felt Michel was being stubborn and unrealistic, while he believed he had been asked to abandon the bedrock of his identity. He told Suzanne that he was shocked she did not know him better than to suggest such a course.

'It will save our lives!' she insisted.

'Save your own life, not mine.'

'How can you say no?'

'Look, you do what you have to do. It's your life. You have to live your life and I have to live mine. But if this is what you want to do, we have to separate.'

They parted angrily. 'I felt strongly for her. It was a loving relationship and I did not want to break up. But I really didn't want to see her just then.' Suzanne was the first to make overtures, which Michel resisted until he was certain she fully understood and accepted his position. He believed absolutely that any compromise made at that dangerous time would prove fatal in the struggle ahead.

They did not see each other for ten days, until one night he returned to the apartment he was staying in, turned on the light and found Suzanne curled up in his bed. She had convinced his landlady to let her in and had waited patiently for his return. Still he held back physically, although he was deeply in love. He was moved that she should offer herself to him, but felt he could give nothing in return. For Suzanne to be involved with a stateless Jewish student in Hitler's Vienna exposed her to great dangers. He explained that he intended to find a way to return to France to re-establish his residence status, and would then try to arrange for her to join him.

Suzanne became emotional and insisted that Michel take her with him. 'You cannot go without me!'

'I'm *vogelfrei* – it's too dangerous.'

'And it's safe for a Jew to remain in Austria?' Suzanne asked drily. 'If I want to share my life with you I must also share the danger!'

The courage of Suzanne brought the lovers closer together in their final months in Vienna. But Michel was reluctant to risk exposing her to the dangers of illegal flight. He told Suzanne that they could only go forward with the plan if her mother gave consent. Secretly, Michel hoped this would not be given and expected the mother to convince her daughter to take the safer course.

Suzanne was an only child, a minor, and adored, but Frau Adler was an unusual woman. 'In normal times this meeting, and the subject of this meeting, would be absolutely unthinkable,' she said flatly. 'But this is not a normal time. It is an extraordinary time demanding extraordinary measures. I know how Suzanne feels. All I can do is to give both of you my blessing.' And on a practical note, Frau Adler obtained a document from city hall bestowing legal majority on her daughter.

The obvious route to take to France at this time was through Switzerland or Italy, but Michel felt that both would be strongly guarded by German soldiers. His plan was to cross Germany and enter France across the Siegfried–Maginot Line, the supposedly impregnable network of underground frontier fortresses. 'It was so crazy and unlikely that nobody would think of it – that was my logic.'

The couple left Vienna in October 1938 and crossed into Germany without incident. They made their way to Saarbrücken, the German town near the French border where Michel had crossed illegally before. They spent the night at a friend's house and made their way the next day to the hill country, close to Voelklingen, abutting the Siegfried–Maginot Line. The plan was to observe the

German patrols and sneak across between them. They watched patiently hour after hour, looking for an opportunity to make their move, but the moment they tried to cross they were spotted and caught. They were taken to a guard post where they sat in silence, listening to the rain drumming on the roof, awaiting the arrival of the Gestapo from Saarbrücken.

The officers turned out to be young men in the long black leather overcoats that were one of the trademarks of their profession. Michel and Suzanne were pushed into the back of a car and driven for what seemed like hours along a lonely road through woods. The uncertainty of the journey was close to unbearable, and they did not pass a single car in either direction. The driver eventually turned off on to a rough track and bumped along until they reached a low, camouflaged Gestapo building hidden among large, dripping trees. They were taken inside and interrogated in a straightforward question-and-answer session that seemed to bore their captors. Papers were filled out and stamped. One of the Gestapo men then announced they were to be driven that night to Dachau, where they would be interned. They were led back to the car.

Michel and Suzanne, of course, knew all about Dachau. Michel understood that they faced a long and lonely journey across Germany and that the present moment was possibly the only hope of escape. As they approached the car he gave a signal to Suzanne to run into the woods. She broke away and made for the trees, but one of the Gestapo officers gave chase and quickly captured her. Infuriated, he dragged her back to the car. His colleague unholstered his Luger and began shouting that he was going to shoot them both where they stood.

'Why don't you?' Michel yelled, losing his temper. 'Go on – shoot! What do you want from us? You want the Jews out of the country, and that's all we're trying to do – leave the country! And you bring us back! Where should we go? We're not allowed to stay, we're not allowed to go! You want to shoot, *shoot*!'

At first the Gestapo men seemed stunned by Michel's outburst, but then they grew quiet, perhaps checked by the inescapable logic of his argument. They waved their guns and ordered the prisoners into the back of the car.

After driving for some time along a dark, empty road, they suddenly pulled over. The Gestapo officer in the passenger seat turned to face them. 'We have decided to let you escape.'

Michel was certain they were about to be shot, victims of the classic ruse: *Auf der Flucht erschossen* – shot while trying to escape.

42

'Yes, we are going to let you go,' the Gestapo officer continued, 'but you'll have to keep your eyes and ears open because when we return to HQ we will announce your escape.'

This made no sense, and Michel prepared himself. The Gestapo officer in the passenger seat got out of the car, while his companion remained behind the steering wheel. The back door was unlocked and the couple climbed out. The Gestapo officer led them to the edge of the woods where there was a path. He gestured to Michel to follow it.

'No,' Michel said firmly, expecting to be shot in the back. 'After you.'

The Gestapo officer understood and went ahead without comment, and after walking a short distance they reached a clearing. He pointed out three lights in the far distance and explained that the two closest to them were on German territory, while the furthest was in France. He told them that if they walked straight they would come to a railway line, and once they had crossed it they would lose sight of the lights. But if they remembered the position of the third light and made towards it they would be able to cross the border unchallenged. It was a lonely part of the frontier, he continued, and it was unlikely they would run into any patrols or checkpoints. But if the French picked them up they would certainly be handed back to the Germans. And then, incongruously wishing them good luck, the Gestapo officer turned and walked back along the path.

They stood for a moment, braced for shots to ring out from the black woods. But there was nothing – only the silence of the night. Michel suspected they were trapped in a cruel game and could only guess at the pay-off. On the other hand, there was a possibility that the Gestapo had decided to throw the political small fry back into the sea. They began to walk towards the lights.

They crossed a railway line and the lights disappeared exactly as described. Michel wondered if they were being sent directly into the line of fire of some frontier post as they continued to walk. They emerged on to a road. There was no checkpoint, no armed guards or border patrol, no sudden burst of gunfire from out of the dark. A knot of people were walking along unconcernedly. And they were speaking French. Grateful, and somewhat bemused to be alive, Michel and Suzanne entered France.

It was the Eve of All Saints – Hallowe'en – 1938 when Michel and Suzanne entered a French village in Lorraine, in the area of Metz. People were still out and about celebrating the festival, lights burned in the local cafés, and they attracted little attention. Michel enquired in the village if anyone operated a taxi service, explaining they had come to see friends and stayed on too late. He was directed to a house on the outskirts of town. It was in darkness and the owner was asleep, but Michel knocked loudly on the door, rousing the man from his bed. He explained they needed to be driven to Paris immediately on urgent family business. He knew it was late, and there was a long journey ahead, but he was prepared to pay. The man dressed and took the car out of the garage, and by three in the morning they were on their way.

On the long journey across France, Michel and Suzanne discussed the strange action taken by their Gestapo captors. Nothing they came up with proved a completely satisfactory explanation, but there seemed to be a number of possibilities. The men might simply have had Hallowe'en plans and the arrest was an unwelcome interruption: a tedious night-time drive across Germany with unimportant refugees was both a low priority and a thankless chore. They might even have been persuaded by Michel's argument and felt that by letting them go the Reich had to deal with two fewer Jews. And it was just possible that these young Gestapo officers retained a streak of human decency and sympathised with the plight of two young lovers caught up in forces beyond their control.

Later in the war, when Michel interrogated numerous captured SS and Gestapo men, he often wondered what he would do if his captors came under his control. He decided that he would investigate the men's subsequent war records and, despite an Allied policy of automatic arrest and imprisonment of all such officials, he would return the favour and let them go if they had no blood on their hands.

On arrival in Paris Michel and Suzanne made straight for the house of a cousin, Dianne Dudel, on Boulevard Simon Bolivar.[11] The family not only had the unexpected pleasure of their company, but Dianne's father was also obliged to pay the enormous taxi fare. In the days that followed Michel traipsed from one government office to another in order to reinstate his residence permit and establish Suzanne's legal status. And finally, safe and saved in Paris, Michel and Suzanne became lovers.

The couple had arrived in Paris at a pivotal moment in history. A seventeen-year-old Polish Jew from Germany, Herschel Grynszpan, was living illegally in the city, supporting himself by doing odd jobs. His parents lived in Hanover. In reaction to the Polish government's decrees cancelling the passports of Poles living abroad, the Germans now ordered all male Polish Jews to be forcibly deported. (Michel did not know it, but his uncle was among them.) The Polish border guards turned them back with the result that the deportees became trapped in a no-man's land. Most ended up in a concentration camp in Poland.

Grynszpan heard of the deportations in a letter from his sister. He wrote a note to an uncle in Paris: 'My heart bleeds when I think of our tragedy. I have to protest in a way that the whole world hears my protest.' He took a pistol and walked to the German Embassy and asked to see an official. He was shown to the office of the First Secretary, Ernst von Rath, took out the gun and shot the diplomat dead.

The protest was seized upon by the Nazi government to initiate a 'spontaneous' pogrom against Jews in Germany and Austria. The streets of the Reich's cities became carpeted in the broken glass from synagogues and Jewish homes and businesses. As a result, the pogrom became known as *Kristallnacht*. Hundreds of synagogues were set alight, Jewish cemeteries were destroyed, and businesses and homes belonging to Jews were vandalised. More than a hundred Jews were murdered and many more committed suicide. It was an explosion of the vilest hatred involving Germans from all levels of society. Michel's oft-repeated prophecy had become chilling reality.

Michel and Suzanne stayed for a number of weeks in Paris, but as soon as their papers were in order they moved south to Nice, on the Côte d'Azur. The lovers were inseparable in their new life together. 'If ever anybody saw one of us they knew the other was not far away. We were one mind and one body. I knew her mind and she knew mine – we read each other's thoughts.' Although they were unable to marry, because of the lack of proper documentation, Michel always introduced Suzanne as his wife.

They found an apartment together and he began to make a good living putting on shows in the various hotels, clubs and resorts along the coast. Michel sold tickets and hosted musical soirées of classical and light music for well-to-do émigrés where one of the foolproof attractions was a bowl of his ex-Nazi friend's powerful egg-nog. The evenings served as auditions for the featured artists, and he became well-known in the town. He also returned to painting. 'The trashy paintings sold, but when I put my soul into a painting it did not sell.'

One of the serious painters Michel met in Nice was the wife of the former Polish consul, Madame de Stachiewicz, 'a Polish Jew who did not display much Judaism'. She ran an elegant salon at her home and Henri Matisse was a regular visitor. He asked Suzanne to sit for him, and she agreed. 'I went regularly to pick her up from his place at Cimiez. He refused to show me the work in progress, which I respected. Then when it was finished he showed me. She was semi-nude. I was absolutely scandalised. I blew up! How dare he paint my wife like that! How dare she let herself be painted like that for everybody to see!' The couple had their first lovers' tiff.

Michel became active among the various émigré groups in the south working under a life-and-death deadline to help Jews leave Germany and Austria. He engineered a series of complicated arrangements to help Suzanne's mother and uncle escape from Vienna. The senior conductor on the *Orient Express* was an Italian and he was bribed with a considerable amount of money to help. As the express approached the Austrian–Italian border the conductor ushered the two escapees into his tiny cabin and locked the door. Customs controls were rigorous in both countries, but the conductor was never checked. The émigrés got off the train in Venice and then crossed Italy to Ventimiglia on the border with France. They were initially refused entry and had to remain in Italy for an anxious week, while Michel pulled various legal strings and paid essential bribes to obtain entry visas. Mother and uncle then joyously entered what was to prove a treacherous haven.

Meanwhile, Michel watched helplessly as Hitler took greater and greater political risks in Europe, first seizing the Sudetenland and then taking over the whole of Czechoslovakia six months later. The world protested but did nothing, a feeble response that Hitler trumped with the signing of a non-aggression pact between Germany and the Soviet Union. Then, on 1 September 1939, he invaded Poland and pushed towards the free city of Danzig, an act that even the weak governments of France and Great Britain found intolerable. Michel knew there would be war and immediately volunteered for duty in the French Army. Two days later France and Great Britain declared war on Germany.

The Wehrmacht smashed its way through Poland and gave its hated enemy no quarter. It was the world's first experience of a new and terrible kind of warfare: *Blitzkrieg* – lightning war. The biggest armoured force in the world – ten superbly trained and equipped Panzer tank divisions backed up by the co-ordinated and deadly support of modern aeroplanes – tore across the flat countryside. Whole divisions of tanks covered thirty to forty miles a day, firing their heavy guns as they moved. Squadrons of fighter planes and bombers flew ahead of them, reconnoitring and pounding the defence. The unearthly scream of Stuka dive-bombers filled the air as they dropped out of the sky on to their targets. And behind the Panzers marched an army of a million and a half men. The earth had never seen the like of this armoured juggernaut for speed and destructive power.

The outdated Polish Army was hopelessly outclassed and looked to its Allies to attack Germany through France. But no help came. The antiquated Polish Air Force was destroyed in the first forty-eight hours of the invasion, most of it on the ground. The old-world unreality of the defenders was most graphically demonstrated by a heroic but doomed skirmish. As the tanks of the German Third Army ploughed across open land at forty miles an hour, they were confronted by the Pomorska cavalry brigade. The mounted cavalrymen charged the Panzers with lances couched, pennants carrying the Polish colours fluttering bravely from their tips. The brigade was obliterated.

Michel was impatient to be sent to fight, but was told that because of his nationality he could not join the military. However, it was felt that he might be useful to French intelligence so he returned home to await a summons. He heard nothing, and was dismayed to find that there was no stomach for war. The mood everywhere was uneasy but passive. The national reaction to Hitler's invasion of Poland was summed up by the ironic phrase '*Mourir pour Danzig?*' – Why die for Danzig?

One morning on the street in Nice, a couple of months after the declaration of war, Michel bumped into a writer-friend from Vienna, Ernst Ehrenfeld. Ernst announced that he was on his way to the army recruitment office.

'I'll take you there,' Michel said. 'I've already volunteered.'

On the way to the office Ernst explained the difficult journey he had made to France. A large group of Jewish students – around fifty or so – had been drawn together in their desire to reach France and volunteer to fight. They had left cities all over Europe, travelled south and gathered on the French–Italian border at Ventimiglia. The Italians were prepared to let them out of Italy, despite the country's fascist government, but the French border police challenged them. And although the students explained they had come to volunteer to fight for France, they were refused entry.

Thoroughly demoralised, they remained in Italy where they bribed the crews of several fishing boats to smuggle them into France at night. The captain did not want to risk an illegal landing on French soil, so while the students were still some distance out to sea they were obliged to lower themselves into the water and swim for the beach at Nice. Dripping wet, cold and disillusioned, the group collected on the shore. They split up and agreed to rendezvous outside the army recruitment office the following day.

Michel accompanied his friend and found the crowd of young men gathered on the pavement. The mood among them now was buoyant. Inside it was explained that as foreigners they could not join the army, but the Foreign Legion would be more than happy to have them. Life in the Legion was austere in the extreme, and its regiments consistently faced the sharp end of combat, but they readily agreed. They were given a medical examination, signed up for the 'duration' of the war, and were told to wait.

And then the police arrived. The students were arrested for illegal entry into the country. It did not matter to the authorities that the students had joined the Legion and volunteered to fight for France, they had no entry permits stamped in their passports. 'They were marched as prisoners through the streets of Nice to the court house. I was so angry I marched with them.' The students were kept waiting again at the Palais de Justice until late afternoon, when they were herded before a judge and sentenced to three months in prison. 'They couldn't wait to fight against a common enemy. But they had to serve a prison sentence before they were allowed to fight in the Legion.'[12]

War had been declared on Germany but little effort was made by either France or Britain to wage it. Belgium and Holland had taken the soft political option of strict neutrality, a decision that would cost them dear. A strong Allied assault at this time might well have scotched Hitler's dreams of world conquest. The German High Command certainly thought so, and worried throughout the Polish campaign that such an attack to their rear would bring collapse, knowing that any assault by the French would encounter a military screen instead of a real defence.

But the Allies did not even have an offensive plan. France had specifically guaranteed Poland that in case of attack she would launch an offensive counter-attack against Germany with the bulk of her forces. Later, the French government was told by its military leaders that it was impossible to launch such an assault in less than two years, and only then with the help of British troops and American equipment. The British commitment to Poland was general and undefined. The ill-equipped Expeditionary Force of four hundred and fifty thousand men was moved across the Channel to France, while the French Army made a half-hearted, tentative probe towards Saarbrücken (where German defences were strongest).

Even the Maginot Line – the Star Wars system of the day – was only reinforced with reservists. The modernity and scale of the Maginot Line created a false and fatal sense of security among the civilian population, and masked the ossified and almost entirely defensive military thinking that permeated the French Army. While the Poles were cut to shreds, one hundred and twelve divisions of the French Army did nothing. A British general raged, 'Facing no more than twenty-six German divisions, sitting still and sheltering behind steel and concrete while a quixotically valiant ally was being exterminated!'[13]

Another war on the scale of the First World War was beyond the imagination of the nation and was deemed impossible. Mobilisation was lethargic and the French Army – the strongest in the world – sat tight, together with its powerful air force. France felt secure behind its great concrete and steel-turreted Maginot Line guarding the two major historical invasion routes. It formed an impregnable defence of 'fortified regions' twelve miles deep and stretching ninety miles inland from the Swiss border. It had been in construction since 1930, had cost in excess of five billion francs, and was the greatest system of permanent fortification built since the Great Wall of China.

The Maginot Line included one hundred kilometres of tunnels, four hundred and fifty kilometres of roads and railways, twelve million cubic metres of earthworks, one and a half million cubic metres of concrete, and one hundred and fifty thousand tons of steel. The defences consisted of hundreds of miles of anti-tank obstructions and barbed wire, behind which advance posts of reinforced barracks and pill boxes were placed. Deep anti-tank ditches came next, protecting hundreds of small subterranean case-mates that were almost invisible above ground except for the two observation cupolas surmounting them. Every three to five miles there were massive forts, masterpieces of military engineering known as 'earthscrapers' because most of their construction was below ground. These fantastic science fiction creations bristled with numerous gun stations that included machine guns, anti-tank guns, heavy mortars and giant howitzers mounted in retractable turrets. Each fort held up to fifteen hundred soldiers, transported from their subterranean concrete barracks to combat stations by electric trains. As the men lived almost entirely underground, the forts were equipped with movie theatres, gymnasiums and recreation areas –

even sun-ray treatment rooms. Apart from the vast amount of money needed to construct the Maginot Line, it was enormously costly to maintain. As a result, the remainder of the French Army remained antiquated.[14]

Jean-Paul Sartre, who was posted to the Maginot Line at the outbreak of the war, and who spent most of his time sending up balloons and watching them through binoculars, wrote: 'There will be no fighting . . . it will be a modern war, without massacres as modern painting is without subject, music without melody, physics without matter.'[15]

In France, this uneasy limbo period of war without battle became known as the *Drôle de Guerre* – the strange war; to the Germans it became *Sitzkrieg* – the sitting war; and to the British, the phoney war. In general, the population of France was greatly relieved at the lack of combat activity, but Michel was depressed to hear the oft-repeated line, 'What do we care as long as we have our steak and wine?'

Hitler used the lull to prepare for his attack on the west, although wavered when his generals counselled against it. It was a high-risk enterprise with an uncertain outcome. Allied inaction had allowed the Wehrmacht to take Poland cheaply, but France was an entirely different proposition. Hitler, however, was prepared to take the gamble.

On 10 May 1940, the mechanised juggernaut of the German war machine launched *Blitzkrieg* on the west. Eighty-three divisions – with a further forty-seven in reserve – invaded the Low Countries, spearheaded as in Poland by ten Panzer divisions made up of three thousand armoured vehicles, a thousand of which were heavy tanks. Small forces of highly trained airborne troops were dropped by parachute and landed in gliders to capture vital bridges before they could be destroyed, and the defence systems of Belgium and Holland were quickly overrun.

Three days later Panzer tanks crossed the Meuse where it meandered through the heavily wooded Ardennes, which had been pronounced 'impenetrable'. The armoured column for this thrust was made up of forty-four divisions and was over a hundred miles long, stretching back fifty miles the other side of the Rhine. It advanced so fast and easily that both Hitler and the German High Command became alarmed that they were vulnerable to a French counter-attack from the south.

As for the Maginot Line, the German Army simply bypassed it. The bulk of the Allied forces was now exposed to attack from the rear, and there was no option for the British Expeditionary Force except retreat. An army of three hundred and thirty-eight thousand men – including one hundred and twenty thousand French troops – was lifted off the beaches at Dunkirk, much of it by small craft capable of taking only a handful of soldiers. This was made possible by the brave rearguard action of the First French Army who fought until they were surrounded, having been abandoned by their commanding generals who had been ordered to evacuate to England. The retreat had been inevitable, and its execution heroic, but to Frenchmen it seemed that their British ally only showed military verve when it came to scuttling back to their island.

The British, for their part, increasingly viewed the French with contempt. Panic gripped the nation. As the Germans pushed towards Paris, and the government left for Bordeaux, it is estimated that as many as ten million of France's citizens took to the road. Entire cities became ghost towns as old men, women and children in cars, carts and wheelbarrows choked every highway and byway in the push south.

In the meantime, the French Army was left in total chaos, often falling back to find their new positions already occupied by the Germans. French soldiers surrendered in such great numbers they became the greatest problem the German Army faced in its advance. Soldiers threw away their weapons and even stripped off their uniforms. There were instances of the murder of officers who ordered their men to stand and fight, and the inhabitants of one village lynched a tank officer who attempted to defend them. One and a half million prisoners were taken and sent back to Germany.

A French colonel who had long espoused mobile armoured warfare found himself in command of a tank division that did not exist. Scraping together a few tanks, he assembled three battalions and set out to reconnoitre the military situation. 'Along the roads from the north flowed lamentable convoys of refugees. I noticed among them many soldiers without arms. At this spectacle of a lost people and a military rout, and from the reports of the scornful insolence of the Germans, I was filled with a terrible fury. It was too awful! The war was starting unbelievably badly. But we would have to continue it. If I lived I would fight on wherever I could as long as necessary until the enemy was defeated and the stain wiped out.'[16] The defiant colonel survived to become General de Gaulle, leader of the Free French.

There were a few honourable exceptions in which French troops fought tenaciously. The two thousand five hundred cadets of the

Cavalry School at Saumur, despite being vastly outnumbered and fielding only training weapons, held up the German Army and its Panzers along a twenty-six-kilometre front on the Loire for two days. When one group of cadets holding an island in the river was finally overrun by a greatly superior force, the men lay down their weapons, lit cigarettes and refused to raise their hands. A small Alpine force of three divisions held off thirty-two of Mussolini's divisions, while on the Côte d'Azur the Italian invasion was thwarted by an NCO and seven men.[17]

Despite the dangerous and difficult times, Michel's relationship with Suzanne grew ever closer. It did not cross his mind at this time that France would not somehow continue the struggle; the government could move to north Africa, the colonial divisions remained unscathed, and the navy and the air force was intact. He still expected to be called upon by French intelligence, and often discussed with Suzanne the inevitable separation and wondered how long the war might last. They turned the subject over endlessly. How long would they be apart? Would it be months or years? Would Michel be wounded . . . or killed?

One night, as they lay in bed talking about their future, Michel asked how Suzanne felt about having a relationship with another man. If they were separated for years it was a possibility and they should discuss it. She answered quickly that Michel was her one and only lover whom she adored, and it was unthinkable that she should go with anyone else. There was a pause. Suzanne then said thoughtfully that she could only possibly imagine one situation in which she would give herself to another man.

'What do you mean?' In the darkness Michel was all attention as he waited for her to continue.

'If you were ever captured and imprisoned, and your life was in danger, or if you faced execution, I would do everything in the world to save you. And if the only way to save you was to sleep with another man then, yes, I would do it.'

'How could you ever think of such a thing?' Michel asked heatedly. The idea of such a compromise appalled him. 'How could you expect me to owe my life and my freedom to such an act? I wouldn't be able to live with myself. Or with you. I would not want to owe my freedom to this. The only thing such an act would achieve would be to make things impossible between us. It would be a betrayal of trust. All you would accomplish would be to break us up. It would not save me – I would leave you and return to captivity.'

Suzanne said nothing. She had not seen him so angry since she had suggested the conversion of convenience in Vienna in order to get papers. She knew him well enough to know that he meant what he said. A strained silence came between them and neither spoke until they fell asleep. The subject was never brought up again.

Political surrender followed military collapse with unseemly haste. 'It is with a heavy heart I tell you today that it is necessary to stop the fighting,' Marshal Henri Philippe Pétain announced over the radio on 17 June. The much-loved and respected eighty-four-year-old hero of the First World War, victor of the battle of Verdun, had been brought into the French government in desperation and given full executive powers. The old soldier had the status in France of a demigod, and was considered an incarnation of France in human form, and now it was hoped he would be her saviour. 'I have made a gift of my person to France,' he said generously, and now in his thin, quavering, old woman's voice he announced that he was asking the Germans for an armistice. He also baldly articulated his future policy of collaboration – a word then untainted with the shame it came to embrace. In Germany, at the news of France's suit for armistice, Hitler literally danced for joy.

In fact, there had not even been a vote to determine whether there should be an armistice or a fight to the finish. But no public figure raised a voice to condemn the armistice, and Pétain solemnly intoned, 'At least our honour is safe.' The French Navy and Air Force were intact, and there were soldiers still in combat in the field, but Pétain had announced an end to the fighting before he knew if Germany's conditions for an armistice were acceptable. The Germans had not even had time to answer the request.

It was a precipitous and disastrous statement the marshal later tried to excuse as misunderstood, but the troops took the marshal at his word and tens of thousands gladly abandoned their weapons. The roadsides and ditches of northern France became strewn with rifles, pistols and helmets. 'The war is over!' the soldiers called to one another. 'Why get killed when the war is over?' Entire regiments sat in their barracks awaiting the arrival of the Germans. One impatient corps commander actually surrendered over the phone. Many of the population seemed more inclined to oppose their own troops than the invading army. At Vienne, the mayor threatened to loose a thousand of the town's women on a general attempting to dynamite a strategic bridge over the Rhône. Generals who continued to resist were actually reprimanded by the High Command, and one officer on the Maginot

Line who insisted 'as a matter of honour' that his soldiers fight their way out through the German lines, was shot in the back. Generals who suggested moving land, naval and air forces to continue the battle from north Africa were rebuked by Pétain himself.

For Hitler, who had fought in the First World War as a corporal and smarted under the humiliation of his country's defeat, the conquest of France was a triumph to be relished. He ensured that the actual signing of the armistice be as symbolically painful for the French as possible. The clearing in the woods at Compiègne, where the German Empire had capitulated to France and her allies on Armistice Day in 1918, was chosen, the same *wagon-lit* from that historic occasion set in place. An eyewitness wrote a description in his diary of the perfect June day, the dappled sunlight on the stately trees, and the look on Hitler's face. His eyes brimmed with revenge, burned with anger and triumph, and his expression revealed scornful inner joy and deep hatred. The moment before he entered the railcar Hitler snapped his hands on to his hips, arched his shoulders and placed his feet wide apart in an arrogant posture of absolute victory.[18]

The terms laid down by the Germans were a *diktat* – twenty-four 'hard and merciless' clauses – to be accepted without negotiation. Germany would occupy the majority of France and the entire Atlantic coast, while a Free Zone (Zone Libre) was created consisting of two-fifths of the poorest part of the country lying to the south and south-east. Hitler considered total occupation a liability and an administrative drain on German manpower. The existence of a Free Zone also dissuaded the French government from fleeing to London or north Africa to continue the war. The armistice acknowledged Pétain's government as the government of Metropolitan France, although in the Occupied Zone it was nothing but a puppet organisation. France was forced to disband and demobilise most of her armed forces, and was only allowed to retain an army of one hundred thousand men – with fewer than four thousand officers. She was allowed to keep her fleet and empire. The country was also required to bear the cost of its own occupation: from now on sixty per cent of the national income would go to the Reich.

One of the armistice's clauses directly concerned anti-Nazi refugees from Germany, described as warmongers who had betrayed their own people. As a result of this clause, the German occupation authorities issued numerous orders to the French Ministry of Interior and the secret police to track down refugees and hand them over. And in the

Free Zone, although German agents were forbidden under the terms of the armistice, in reality they were provided with false papers by Vichy and aided by the police. The million and a half French prisoners of war were abandoned 'until the conclusion of peace'.[19]

Among the majority of the populace there seemed to be no sense of national shame, merely relief that France was out of the war. People actually wept in the streets in gratitude. The government had been reduced to asking Winston Churchill if Britain would be willing to release France from her treaty obligations, while public opinion turned against her former ally. People felt that with the French Army defeated, Britain herself would soon negotiate with the Reich for terms. The commanding general of the French Army said that the British neck would be 'wrung like a chicken'. (Later, after victory in the Battle of Britain, Churchill retorted, 'Some chicken! Some neck!')

In London, de Gaulle, then largely unknown, spoke for Michel and the minority like him. 'What shame, what revolt rises in the hearts of decent Frenchmen . . . France and the French have been delivered hand and foot to the enemy . . . This armistice is dishonourable. Two thirds of our territory occupied by the enemy – and what an enemy! Our entire army demobilised, our officers and men prisoners. Our fleet, our planes, our tanks, our arms handed over intact so that the enemy may use them against our allies. The government, you yourself [Pétain] reduced to servitude. Ah! To obtain and accept such an enslavement, we did not need the Conqueror of Verdun. Anyone else would have sufficed.'

At each day's dismal news, Michel tried to fight off his depression with defiance. It was lonely work among people who openly expressed their relief that the war was over and the certainty that Britain would soon fall. Anglophobia became rampant, especially after the government failed to respond to a British ultimatum demanding that the French fleet sail to British ports. The Royal Navy sank the fleet at Mers el Kebir, in north Africa, in a twenty-five-minute action that left twelve hundred French sailors dead. The reaction in France was understandably bitter. A stranger in the south of France at this time would have thought that the British were the enemy, not the Germans. 'There are many reasons behind the official hostility towards England,' Albert Camus wrote in his notebook. 'But nothing is said of one of the worst motives . . . fury and the base desire to see the downfall of someone who dares to resist the force that has crushed you.'[20]

The French government ended up in the provincial spa town of Vichy, met in the casino and promptly dissolved itself by voting overwhelmingly to give full powers to Marshal Pétain, who assumed a new office: Head of the French State. The parliamentary democracy of the Third Republic, which had existed since 1870, was now replaced by an unregulated authoritarian regime dedicated to working hand in glove with the Nazis.

Michel knew that France could fight its way out of military, political and material ruin, but feared she would never recover from the moral ruin she was now entering. 'It is not shameful to lose a battle, but it can be very shameful not to fight. France did not fight. France collapsed like a pack of cards and darkness came. I wanted to light a candle in that darkness. It was a desperate situation but I didn't want to despair. I believed in the power of the individual to shape events. And I believed in the power of the fist – my own two bare fists if it came down to it.' Michel began to search for like-minded people, drawing strength from a line by the German poet, Schiller: I feel an army in my fist. 'I felt that if I wanted to fight there must be others who felt the same way. I had to find them.'

Michel was among the few *Résistants de la Première Heure* – Resisters of the First Hour. After the war the myth was promulgated that the French were a people united against the Nazis, a brave nation of *résistants*. Nothing could be further from the truth. While resistance did grow as time passed, the genuine Resisters of the First Hour were a minuscule number of individuals with no structure and no support, whose numbers actually diminished during the first year of Vichy rule.[21] The Socialists reverted to traditional pacifism, while the Communists executed an about-face after the Nazi–Soviet pact, and dismissed the war against Hitler as imperial fratricide whose victor, be it the City of London or the Nazis, was of no concern to workers.

The shape the new France was to take was announced by the little men of Vichy. Officially neutral, but in reality fully in compliance with Germany's will, the new government called for a return to the cult and the practice of God, Country and Family, and saw defeat as an opportunity for a national revolution which was authoritarian, traditionalist and neutral. Pétain pronounced that defeat had been born of pleasure-seeking, atheism and national slackness. He proclaimed, 'A New Order begins . . .'

The nature of Vichy's New Order with regard to refugees and Jews was revealed almost immediately. Twelve days after Pétain became head of state, a commission was set up to review citizens naturalised since 1927 and to strip 'undesirables' of their nationality. A series of laws soon followed restricting access to public service and the medical and legal professions for those born with foreign fathers.

These laws were not specifically aimed at Jews, but as half of the three hundred and fifty thousand Jews in France were foreign-born they were particularly vulnerable.

The first openly anti-Semitic legislation was the repeal of the Marchendeau Law which had previously outlawed attack in the press on any race or religion intended to arouse hatred. A blizzard of vitriolic newspaper articles denigrating Jews, freemasons and foreigners followed. The Statut des Juifs (Statute on the Jews) was passed towards the end of 1940. This defined who was Jewish in the eyes of the law, and then excluded them from top positions in public service, the officer corps and professions that influenced public opinion. This effectively excluded Jews from the press, radio, film and theatre, and even from teaching. A quota system was introduced to limit Jews in the liberal professions. Further legislation authorised prefects to intern foreign Jews in special camps, or obliged them to live under police surveillance in remote villages (résidence forcée). Algerian Jews, who had enjoyed French citizenship for seventy-five years, lost their rights overnight.

Vichy openly and enthusiastically codified xenophobia and anti-Semitism into the law as national policy, which it would continue to pursue in various forms over the next four years of its life. The persecution of the Jews was not something reluctantly adopted because of German orders imposed on a defeated enemy, or even as a result of German pressure. It was instigated and eagerly enacted independently by Vichy itself. In the first year following defeat the German occupation authorities in the north were not overly concerned with the fate of the Jews in the Free Zone, preferring to leave Vichy to its own devices. There were no German plans in 1940 to extend their racial laws, or the seizure of property, into the Free Zone. Vichy's home-grown programmes not only rivalled those of the Germans in the Occupied Zone, but in some respects went beyond them. Michel observed, 'A neutral, unoccupied country, with embassies from all over the world in the town of Vichy, was the only one in Europe that passed these laws. The deportation and death that resulted were crimes against humanity. Something that has never been officially recognised.'

The German occupation authorities and Vichy developed competing systems of anti-Semitism that led to friction between them. When three thousand Jews expelled from Alsace were dumped in the Free Zone, Vichy protested. The Germans had plans to deport as many as two hundred and seventy thousand Jews from Germany, Austria, Bohemia and Moravia, as well as from the

Occupied Zone itself, into the Free Zone. Vichy desperately wanted to prevent this, and once again protested vehemently. The objection was logistical rather than humanitarian. When fourteen hundred Jews were sent across the Demarcation Line from Bordeaux, with assurances of freedom, Vichy promptly locked them up in a camp. The government complained to the Germans of a breach of the armistice when six thousand five hundred Jews were sent in sealed cattle cars to Lyon. Two thousand were over sixty years old – the oldest was one hundred and four – and many were children. They were shunted back and forth from zone to zone as the authorities argued over their fate. Finally submitting to the conqueror's will, Vichy sent them to an internment camp at Gurs, in the Pyrénées.[22]

Life in Vichy France was precarious for an alien Jew, but Michel typically chose the time to assert his identity by changing his name on all his documents. Instead of the Polish name Moniek – shortened to Mony by Suzanne and his friends – he adopted Mosché, the Hebrew word for Moses. It was the first of many acts of provocative defiance during this period.

Vichy chose to round up foreign Jews straight away and intern them in camps. Families who had lived in France for years suddenly received *Refus de Séjour* – Residence Refusal. The authorities had created an absurd law that was impossible to obey. A family would be given forty-eight hours by the police to leave a *département*, but would need written authorisation from another to move. This was rarely given. 'So you had to leave, but you couldn't go anywhere. Most people didn't know what to do and just did what they were told. It was all so arbitrary that in the early days I was able to intervene in many cases to help people take steps to prevent them from being sent away. I was also able in some cases to help people get out of camps after they were sent away.'

Michel became known among the Jewish and foreign community as someone with influence and connections, a man who could keep you out of jail and the refugee camps. He helped families write the correct letters in French to the authorities and guided their petitions through the bureaucratic maze. And for those who were beyond legal help, he arranged for them to hook up with *passeurs* to cross the Pyrénées into Spain, or over the Alps into Switzerland. His success through the year was such that he attracted the attention of the authorities in Nice, who considered him a thorn in their side. He was arrested, together with Suzanne, in October 1940 and charged with influence peddling – the inference being that he had charged for his services.[23]

The couple were put in jail and held for four months without a hearing. They were not mistreated, merely left entirely alone. Michel was separated from Suzanne, who was imprisoned elsewhere, and heard no personal word from her and was given no news of her welfare. He was locked in solitary confinement in his cell twenty-four hours a day except for a twenty-minute exercise period when he was allowed into the yard. He walked in circles behind the prisoner from the adjoining cell, a man charged with murder. 'A murderer, but a living being – human contact.' It was the first time in his life he had been incarcerated and, despite his strong physical and psychological state, he was profoundly shaken by the experience. 'It was terrible. *Terrible.*'

The food was swill that he found inedible at first, until he became so hungry he adapted to it. 'Except for the bread, which was impossible to eat. But it was interesting, made from some quite extraordinary ersatz material. I mixed it with water and made sculptures. If you dropped these on the stone floor they didn't break. The bread really came in very useful, and I made a serviceable pipe out of it by wrapping it around a pencil to form a hollow stem, and then made a bowl.' On his arrest he had had a packet of cigarettes on him. Worried that they might be confiscated, he had emptied the tobacco from each of the cigarettes into his jacket pocket. 'I smoked my loose tobacco in that pipe, which I kept for a long time.'

There was no reading material of any kind, so to keep himself sane during the empty days and nights he elaborated upon the intellectual system he had invented as a teenager. This was something of a challenge without books, but he would pick a subject and then attempt a process of rigorous analysis. He also wrote a dissertation in his head on the relationship between art and glass, and worked on imaginary paintings and sculptures. It kept boredom at bay, and during the process an extraordinary thing happened: 'I started hearing music. Not the classical music that I already knew, but a different sort of music entirely. Passionate, beautiful music, played by a whole symphony orchestra.'

Finally, he was put on trial. Suzanne was brought into the courtroom separately, the first time he had seen her since his incarceration. 'She looked beautiful.' But prison had taken its toll and she was thin and pale. 'It had been a terrible experience for me, so imagine the effect on a young girl alone. She was so strong.'

A gifted and articulate lawyer named Pasqualini had taken up the case for the defence and dominated the court with his oratory and theatrical manner. Michel became so carried away by the proceedings that he felt more like a privileged spectator than a defendant. 'This man should never have been brought to trial,' Pasqualini boomed, jabbing an accusing finger at the prosecutor. He turned to the judge. 'You should not be sitting in judgement on him, but humble before someone whose only so-called crime is that he helped other human beings. You should be proud of this man.'

The lawyer successfully established that Michel had not taken money and that the help he had extended was entirely within the law. In an extraordinary verdict for a Vichy court, Michel and Suzanne were acquitted and released.[24] But Pasqualini warned that they were in danger under new laws of being re-arrested and sent to a camp without trial. (Within a month of the conversation they were denied permission to reside in Nice.)[25] He advised them to seek refuge in nearby Monaco, which was technically independent and outside Vichy police jurisdiction. It had also not adopted Vichy's anti-Jewish legislation.

They moved to Monte Carlo immediately, where they were given a residence permit. Michel travelled to Nice most days to continue to help desperate refugees and keep in contact with opponents of the regime. Although he kept the apartment in Nice, he considered it too dangerous to visit but felt reasonably safe in the city as long as he never stayed overnight. For safety, Suzanne remained in Monte Carlo during his numerous excursions.

In Monte Carlo he made a daily visit to the casino, where he gambled with enough success to make money to live. The foyer was lined with primitive one-armed bandits dedicated to *boule*, a nine-number variation of roulette that paid winnings of ninety francs on a ten-franc stake. 'I studied the machine and calculated that if I pulled the lever with exactly the same pressure every time I could develop a system. So I tried it out and found that by using this method I could calculate which number would come up more or less consistently. I would cover the two adjoining numbers, in case I got it wrong, and managed to win on a regular basis. I was careful not to clear out the machine and alert the casino, but over the four months I was in Monte Carlo I won a significant amount.'

Michel often put in long hours in Nice and arrived home exhausted. After one particularly gruelling and difficult day he thought he might risk staying overnight at the Nice apartment. He set the alarm clock for four a.m. and planned to be up and out of the building before dawn.

The alarm was ringing when the police hammered on the apartment door. Exhaustion had made him careless, and he had been betrayed by either the concierge or a neighbour. He was arrested, and this time there was no trial or even the semblance of a hearing. The period in solitary confinement was to prove a light apprenticeship for what now became a descent into hell.

IV

Nothing remains today of the concentration camp of Le Vernet. The camp that once stood beside the ugly brick village of the same name in the barren plain near Pamiers, in the department of Ariège, thirty miles north of the Pyrénéan Spanish border, has been erased from the landscape as it has from the national memory. There are few survivors to recall its misery, but Michel Thomas remembers.

The camp had been built on a deserted stretch of empty country beside a small railway. Even in the spring the area is a desolate wasteland of dust and rock. Michel arrived by train and was marched the half-mile from the tiny station, in formation with sixteen other 'undesirable alien Jews', towards the nondescript prison camp.[1] It rose before him, a bland fortress of despair surrounded by a tangle of barbed wire. The guards patrolling the perimeter were not soldiers but gendarmes from the Gardes Mobiles, a force with the proven reputation of being the most brutal and reactionary in the country.[2]

Michel had been sent to Le Vernet under close guard on an ordinary train in a third-class compartment. 'We were stripped and had to surrender jewellery, watches, rings and money – except for the equivalent of about fifteen dollars. I was allowed a small case with a few personal belongings, and everything else had to be left with the guards.' Nothing was ever returned. The less fortunate travelled in sealed transports made up of cattle cars. One, carrying a hundred refugees from Belgium, took a week to arrive, during which time the prisoners went unfed. To make matters worse, the word PARACHUTISTES had been daubed on the side of the wagons, provoking outbursts of hatred whenever the train stopped. One of the refugees, unable to bear the claustrophobic misery of heat and hunger any longer, went mad. The guards shot him.[3]

The camp had originally been built during the 1914–18 war to accommodate colonial troops, and was then used for military prisoners of war. Later, during the Spanish Civil War, it was used to house refugees who had fled over the mountains, mostly men who had fought with the International Brigade. A string of such camps had been constructed along the foothills of the Pyrénées, and many of the civil war prisoners were still there at the outbreak of the Second World War.

Now the camps had a new use and would be packed with troublesome refugees from the north. The network of concentration camps – the term used by French officials themselves[4] – were of various sizes and severity, but Le Vernet was universally accepted as the worst in the country. It was a punishment camp, dubbed the French Dachau.[5] The novelist Gustav Regler described it as 'a collection of ramshackle huts without beds, without light, without heating . . . An eerie cemetery where the huts stood like great coffins on the plains.' Even among the interned undesirables of Vichy, the government considered the inmates of Le Vernet the lowest of the low, a caste of untouchables. Arthur Koestler, who was imprisoned there in 1940, complained that the place was so primitive that its inhabitants were reduced to living like Stone Age men. 'In Liberal-Centigrade, Vernet was the zero-point of infamy.'[6]

Food, sanitary conditions and accommodation in the camp at this time were considerably below the level of its Nazi equivalent. In further contrast, German prisoners of war held in France had been comparatively well cared for, with adequate rations and decent sleeping quarters. It was a crushing blow to Michel's morale to know that the enemies of France had been better treated than men who had volunteered to fight on her behalf. More than a quarter of internees in Le Vernet were sick and unable to work, despite the severe punishments meted out to malingerers, and many died from lack of medical attention.

By the end of September 1940 there were thirty-one camps in the Unoccupied Zone, some, like Gurs and Argeles, with populations of as many as twenty thousand refugees – including children – and others holding only a few prisoners. There was a special camp for women, another for the sick and the old. Ten hospitals and sixteen prisons also held refugees. Seventy per cent of internees in Vichy were Jews.[7]

Responsibility for the camps lay entirely with Vichy. The inhumanity of the administration, coupled with a lack of resources, appalled American Quakers working in France, who alerted the international press. An inspector-general was appointed as a result of the adverse publicity, which even the authorities acknowledged was justified. The inspector was a man in sympathy with the aims of Vichy, and his standards were austere, but he was deeply shocked by what he saw as he went from one camp to another. His report was so critical that it moved one government minister to declare: 'The living conditions of the internees puts the honour of France on the line.'[8]

The inspector concluded that Le Vernet provided 'highly precarious living conditions'. The camp housed a fluctuating prison population of between two and three thousand men and covered a total of fifty acres. It was divided into three sections: Unit A for common criminals – a loose term used to include anyone who did not fit into the other two categories; Unit B for veterans of the International Brigade that had fought in Spain; and Unit C for Jews. High barbed-wire fences separated each section and contact was forbidden between them. The inspector described Unit C as 'the most inadequate of all . . . the Israelites enclosed in Unit C are piled up in wooden shacks in a deplorable state, dark, unclean, where the most elementary conditions of hygiene cannot be observed'.[9]

Each of the wooden huts that housed the prisoners was thirty yards long and five wide. Inside, an upper and lower shelf of wood two yards wide ran the length of either side of each hut, with a narrow gangway between. Each side was split into ten sections divided by the wooden poles supporting the roof, and every compartment slept five men – fifty to a shelf, two hundred to a hut. This meant that each prisoner was limited to twenty-one inches of space, obliging everyone to sleep on his side. It was impossible for a man to turn without disturbing his neighbour. There was one stove that was never lit as there was no fuel. Waves of influenza passed from hut to hut, section to section, in a permanent epidemic. There were frequent outbreaks of typhus and tuberculosis, and dysentery was rife. The suffocating stench of the untended sick, combined with wet, rotting straw and human excrement, made every barracks reek like a farmyard.

Each prisoner was provided with a tin can to wash in and eat from, with no utensils, and meals were eaten standing or squatting on the ground as there were no tables or chairs. The food consisted of eleven ounces of bread daily, a cup of ersatz coffee in the morning, and weak soup at midday and in the evening. The rations barely kept a man alive, let alone fit for physical labour, and condemned him to a permanent state of gnawing hunger.

Work consisted of unnecessary road repairs and the maintenance of the camp itself. Guards carrying leather whips escorted gangs of prisoners dressed in rags to and from the camp. Once the shoes a man arrived in wore out he had to make do with thin, prison-issue galoshes to cover his naked feet. The worst work of all was carried out by the *corvée de tinette*, the latrine emptiers' squad. Twelve men empted twenty, seventy-pound bins brimming with excrement twice a day. The human effluent was dumped in the river half a mile from the camp, and if the wind was in the wrong direction the sewage of Le Vernet could be smelt for miles around.

In between so-called work sessions there were four daily roll calls, lasting up to an hour each, when prisoners were obliged to stand immobile in the open air in all weathers. Guards routinely used their fists and whips on men slow to obey, while serious offences were punished with terms of solitary confinement on bread and water. 'There was constant repudiation and fighting among friends,' Regler wrote. 'Feelings were relieved by sheer baseness; it was a dysentery of the soul.'[10] Inmates developed various forms of melancholia and neurosis, while a few went stark mad, or killed themselves.

Michel himself did not suffer physical brutality at the hands of the guards, except for the abuse and humiliation of the daily routine. 'The guards did not have to be brutal. It was enough to be locked in a camp like that and slowly starved, watched over by well-fed gendarmes.' Only the possibility of emigration kept his hope alive. 'The inmates lived, not upon food, but upon rumours – upon hope. At one time a new inmate told us of a bill before the United States Congress proposing to set up some sort of camp in the Virgin Islands, where those with emigration papers could wait in safety for their quota numbers to come up. So anyone with a visa would have been immediately released. I had signed affidavits from family in the US and all the papers except for a quota number. It raised everybody's hopes.' Nothing came of it. 'Imagine the people who would have been saved!'

The heat of high summer was unbearable in the arid region, but it was nothing compared to the misery of winter. Freezing winds from the Pyrénées – those same mountains on which Michel had happily gone skiing as a student – howled through the camp. Half the prison population slept without blankets in twenty degrees of frost. 'I have a vision of one man forever standing at the barracks' unlit stove. He stood there hour after hour, hands held out towards the cold metal to receive its imaginary warmth.'

Months of undernourishment wore the prisoners down until they took on the appearance of walking skeletons.[11] Michel developed peristaltic movement which made him involuntarily regurgitate whatever little he ate. 'The food came back into my mouth. It meant I could eat again, chew the food again. It was something that remained with me for many, many years. It became natural.' Many inmates were too weak for the work details, and some simply gave up, lying motionless on their beds of straw, awaiting death.

The authorities chose to believe that these starved and weakened creatures were dangerous enemies of the state who needed constant surveillance. A ministerial document confirming Michel's internment stated that he was a man of bad reputation and dubious morality.[12] He had disobeyed the order imposed on him denying residence, and a close watch was recommended. Despite his acquittal by a Vichy court, the report chose to repeat the charge of influence peddling.

And in a way, of course, the prisoners of Le Vernet were dangerous. Many were men of courage and conscience who had been chased from country to country in an endless cycle of harassment and imprisonment. They were witnesses to cowardice and barbarity in a country that had previously considered itself, with justification, one of the most civilised and democratic in the world. Now France had chosen to break these wretched refugees from Nazism on the wheel of inhumane internment.

The strongest individuals found symbolic ways to keep their hope and spirits alive. On Yom Kippur, the day of atonement, Michel Thomas observed the holiest holiday in the Jewish calendar by fasting. 'I did not take a piece of bread or a drop of water. The act connected me in my mind to a world community of Jews who were doing the same. That connection took me out of my isolation and loneliness. It gave me the strength not to give up.'

Inmates needed spiritual strength to combat the perpetual physical strain. 'I woke one night racked by uncontrollable vomiting. I felt that my insides were coming out. I vomited without stopping, but there was nothing there. On and on, heaving a yellow fluid on to my blanket. I felt I was vomiting my guts. I shook with a high fever.' He was moved into the hut that passed for the camp hospital where he was surrounded by men dying of typhus. 'It was just a place to die. People on either side of me were carried out dead. No one cared. I don't know how long I lay there in a delirium, but eventually I recovered enough to drag myself back to the barracks. The muscles of my stomach were severely weakened, causing my belly to drop.'

Starvation was the terror of the camp and inmates inspected their bodies daily for tell-tale signs. This usually first manifested itself in swollen ankles, the swelling slowly spreading up the legs and into the torso until it reached the head. A starving man could press his finger into his cheek and the indentation would remain until it slowly filled. Once the bloating reached the face, death soon followed. 'Every morning I woke up on my thin straw pallet and inspected my ankles to see if it had started. Then one day I saw that my ankles were swollen. Finally, my own slow and creeping disintegration had started. We all learned that starvation is a long process if there is water to drink, but it is inexorable – and it had begun. At first I reacted by fighting it, raging against it. This was followed by a strange sensation, a temptation to let myself drift peacefully into the arms of death. I had to struggle for it not to overcome me.'

Throughout the months in Le Vernet Michel received mail from Suzanne. His ankles swollen, and his belly distended from starvation, he stretched out on his straw pallet and read love letters. 'In fact, because of them, I had something close to a human exchange with a young man my age who censored the mail.'

Suzanne had moved to Lyon, together with her mother, in order to be closer to the various foreign embassies that had been set up in the city of Vichy. She reported to Michel that she was tireless in her efforts to petition one country after another. This was a bureaucratic obstacle course that involved an endless round of frustrating visits, not only to embassies, but also to the relevant French government offices and ministries. Anyone with a letter promising a visa would be sent to a transit camp where a new set of problems had to be overcome. Emigrants were usually obliged to embark from neutral Lisbon, in Portugal, which meant they needed Spanish and Portuguese transit visas as well as a French exit visa. French visas were granted by the *préfecture* of a given *département*, who in turn demanded a certificate of good behaviour issued by the local police. And as all these documents were only valid for short periods of time it often happened that one crucial paper would expire before all the others were granted. The whole process then had to begin again. Moreover, the application for any document could be held up at any stage by the most lowly functionary, allowing anti-Semites and petty tyrants to wield the weapon of bureaucratic obstruction at whim. The odds were heavily loaded against Michel, a stateless Jew the authorities considered of doubtful morality and reputation.[13]

Undeterred, Suzanne followed up on every lead suggested by the refugee rumour mill, as first one embassy and then another was touted as a possibility. But it always came to nothing. Michel read between the lines of her letters and deduced fading hope and growing desperation. However, just when things seemed most dire he was handed a letter from the camp's censor. Suzanne had written in excited, almost ecstatic prose: at last a country – Venezuela – was considering issuing a visa.

Suzanne had saved his life. After eight months in a concentration camp, slowly slipping towards death, a piece of paper gave Michel renewed hope of freedom. On 12 December 1941, he trudged to the railway halt carrying a small bag that he dropped repeatedly because he was too weak to maintain a grip on the handle. He was transported by train back across France, guarded by two gendarmes, to the transit camp of Les Milles, a disused brick and tile factory six miles south-west of Aix en Provence.[14]

A high wall and a barbed-wire fence had been constructed around the dilapidated buildings, instantly converting them into a prison compound. The camp had been created as a detention camp for German and Austrian refugees suspected of being a fifth column for the Reich, an irony that cut deep into the Jews and opponents of Hitler who formed most of the inmate population. When Michel arrived the walls were still covered with the murals of the painter Max Ernst. It had since become a holding centre for those with an 'imminent chance' of emigration.[15] In comparison with the other camps the conditions were bearable. 'The people there were, after all, expected to get out and the authorities knew they would talk about it.'

Simone, a friend from the days at Bordeaux University, and her husband, Charles, visited him in the camp. 'Simone was a French girl, a lovely person, who had married a good friend of mine, Eric Meier, a Jew from Mannheim, Germany. After the collapse of France the police went to look for her husband. Simone explained he had joined up with the British and she thought he had gone over to England during the evacuation of the army from Dunkirk. So they stopped looking for him. She soon got involved with a Frenchman called Charles Lemoine, whom she married. Which was all right, because Charles Lemoine was Eric Meier.' Charles had obtained false papers and the couple made a living from a food stand at Marseille station.

Michel had left the bulk of his belongings behind at the apartment in Nice when first arrested, and Suzanne's mother had gone there and packed them. Now that they thought he was about to emigrate they brought the most important belongings to Les Milles in three large suitcases. They were immediately taken by the guards. The initial enthusiasm over the hope of emigration was soon dampened. Suzanne learned, and subsequently made clear in her correspondence through oblique references and coded asides, that although the letter from the Venezuelan Embassy was genuine, in reality it did not mean that a visa would ever be granted. But even though the letter would not provide sanctuary in Venezuela, it did present the possibility of escape.

The letter from Venezuelan officials in Vichy entitled Michel to a one-day pass, valid from three a.m. to six p.m. – enabling him to visit the consulate in Marseille to obtain a visa. He confided to an old friend he had run into at the camp, a Czech refugee named Turner, that he did not intend to return. The man grabbed his arm and squeezed it, wishing him luck. Michel left the camp at dawn, and caught an early bus for Marseille. He waited for hours at the Venezuelan consulate, only to be informed that his letter was of no official value and that a visa was impossible. He went to the American consulate and was similarly rebuffed.

The disappointments were expected, and he now reverted to his secondary plan and took a train to Lyon to join Suzanne. It was an emotional reunion, although Michel could see that Suzanne was deeply affected by his appearance. He was gaunt, his eyes were black and sunken, and his distended belly hung over the belt of his trousers. But for a few hours all that mattered was that he was alive and the lovers were together.

They discussed the visa. Suzanne was uncharacteristically vague in her account of how the embassy letter had been obtained, suggesting it was unimportant and merely a tiresome detail of the past. She was now impatient to obtain the actual visa itself, and suggested that this is what they should concentrate upon. But Michel was relentless in his questioning and became more and more dogged as Suzanne grew increasingly evasive. 'She tried not to tell me, but I wanted to know the truth. We knew each other so well, including one another's thoughts, it was impossible to lie.'

The truth exactly replicated the circumstances the young lovers had discussed in bed in Nice before Michel's internment. During the months when Michel was in Le Vernet Suzanne had despaired when efforts to save him began to seem hopeless. Camp stories of starvation, disease and death haunted her. In her perpetual round of the embassies, a young, aristocratic attaché who worked in the Cuban Embassy in Vichy had befriended her. He was sympathetic and patient and offered to help. Refugees had grown wary of Cuban visas since the liner *Saint Louis*, carrying almost a thousand Jews, had been turned away from Havana, and its occupants returned to Europe after being subsequently denied entry into the United States.[16] The Cuban diplomat said he had a friend in the Venezuelan Embassy, and he was able to ask him for a letter promising a visa, even though the country demanded proof of Roman Catholic baptism for admission. But at least it had allowed Michel to leave Le Vernet.

Michel insisted on knowing how Suzanne had obtained such a favour. She replied that she had begged the diplomat to save the life of her lover, and that he had been moved by the appeal and agreed to help.

'No,' Michel said coldly. 'You gave in! We know each other so well. We know each other's thoughts, we never lie to each other. And now I see that you are lying and know what you did.' He said firmly that they had discussed just such a possibility, and that Suzanne surely remembered what had been said. They had argued about it. He had been adamant that the course she had chosen to take would be absolutely unacceptable to him in any circumstances. Even if it were a matter of life and death. 'It is not just a question of physical survival – it's essential now to live without compromise. I know you feel terrible about this – but you *know* me! I told you that I would never be able to owe my life to such an act. I told you in Nice two years ago that all you would achieve by this would be to break up our life together. And that I would be obliged to go back to the camp. You understand me well enough to know that I have to do what I said I would.' He stood. 'I'm leaving. It's finished.'

He turned to go. Suzanne tried to hold him back, tearfully entreating him to stay. He pulled himself away and left the apartment and walked out into the streets of Lyon.

'It was a young man's decision. Of course I have had second thoughts about it over the years . . . and third thoughts and fourth thoughts. I have agonised over it. I can honestly say that jealousy was not a part of it. It was the breach of trust. I genuinely felt that any compromise in those dangerous times might be the end of all of us. And looking back I realise this has been a leitmotif in my life. I have always asked myself in every situation and over every action how I would live with it. Egotistical, perhaps, but that has always been very important. And I could not live with that – I *couldn't*! I did not want . . . did not *dare* to owe my freedom and life to such an act of love that was also betrayal.'

And so he buried his love alive. He knew that to return now to Les Milles guaranteed internment and punishment. He had originally intended to escape under a new identity, and somehow improvise a life as an outlaw, but now his own severe standards and personal code obliged him to return. He decided to travel back the following day and present himself to the camp authorities. 'The only papers I had on me was the pass, which already made me illegal. All hotels handed in guests' registration cards to the police every morning so I knew I would have to leave early. I wanted to return voluntarily, not in chains.'

He made his way to a small hotel and took a cheap room. On each floor there was a single, shared lavatory, and Michel visited it in the middle of the night. As he entered, he turned on the light and was met by the sight of a bulging wallet lying on the floor. 'I picked it up and it was packed with money. A gift from heaven! I was very low on cash and this was a lot of money. But as I looked through the wallet I found there was also an ID card.'

The *carte d'identité* was a man's most precious possession, the single legitimising document that opened the door to a normal life: ration cards, rail and bus tickets, a residence permit. Anyone in France at this time without one – especially an escapee – would find everyday life impossible. One of the reasons there were so few escape attempts from the camps was that the lack of ID was as powerful a deterrent as the bayonets of the guards at the gate.[17]

'A gift from heaven – and I could be free! I cursed the ID card because that gave the money a proprietor.' Michel took the money from the wallet and fingered it, a wad thick enough to allow him to live frugally for months. He scrutinised the ID to see how it could be adapted to carry his own photograph. And then he caught sight of himself in the mirror poring over the wallet. It was the image of a pickpocket. 'I had refused to accept freedom because of Suzanne's act, and now I was contemplating being a thief. Stealing money. I weighed leaving the wallet with the ID, and taking only the money. But how could I live with that? I would have committed an act I would consider despicable in another human being.'

The bulging wallet began to seem less a gift from the gods than a temptation designed to weaken his resolve and make him abandon his standards. He took it down to the hotel reception and asked for the owner by name. The desk clerk was reluctant to wake a guest in the middle of the night, but in the face of Michel's insistence agreed to accompany him to the room. The clerk knocked gently on the door without result, until Michel stepped forward and hammered on it to wake the sleeping man.

He appeared at the door, dishevelled and bleary-eyed, furious at being disturbed. 'What the hell do you want?'

'Have you by any chance lost your wallet?' Michel asked.

The man blinked, stupid with sleep, and then turned in panic to check the top of a chest of drawers. 'My God! It's gone! Where is it?'

Michel handed over the wallet. He explained that he had found it lying on the floor of the lavatory, and assured the man he would find both money and ID card intact. The guest scarcely thanked him, but mumbled about leaving a reward at the desk in the morning. Michel went back to bed. He left at dawn before either his fellow guest or the police could reach him, and made his way back to Les Milles.

Turner, the Czech refugee who had wished Michel luck in his escape attempt, was mystified and enraged at his return. He listened to the stories of the visa and the wallet in incredulous silence, then exploded: 'You're crazy! *Crazy!*' Principles and high ideals, Turner suggested, were fine things in peacetime but survival and freedom took precedence in war. He grew heated as he spoke. How could anyone be so *stupid?* Turner raved at Michel as he tried to defend his action, shouting that he was talking nonsense, and dangerous, suicidal nonsense at that. Michel resigned himself to being misunderstood. He realised his friend had invested so much hope in the escape attempt that he took its abandonment as a personal betrayal.

A few days later Michel was in the latrines, which comprised holes cut in rough planks placed over open trenches. Men spent as little time as possible in the latrines, but on his brief visit he spotted a ring jammed between the earth and the edge of one of the planks. It was a beauty – a thick band of gold with a large diamond at its centre. Another *cloaca*, another gift from heaven. It was as if the gods were mocking him.

The next time he ran into Turner he told him of the incredible find. The man turned white. 'My God, that's my ring!'

'Come on!'

'No, it's my ring, I promise you.'

It had been Turner's great secret, smuggled into Les Milles when he first arrived. All the wealth the refugee owned in the world was in that ring and it represented his last chance of freedom, and then he had lost it. He described his panicked, clandestine search for the missing ring when he had crawled on his hands and knees over every inch of the courtyard, and gone through the barracks with a fine-tooth comb. The loss had plunged him into a deep depression and partly accounted for his fury at Michel's inexplicable rejection of a golden opportunity.

'Describe it,' Michel said sceptically. Turner described in detail a gold band with a square-cut diamond set in the middle. Michel dug into his pocket and held the ring out to Turner in the palm of his hand. 'Here it is. Do you want it back? According to you, I should never have told you. I should keep it.'

He handed the ring to Turner, who took the ring with tears in his eyes. 'A miracle!' he exclaimed. 'The ring's my one chance.'

Michel nodded, saying nothing. 'I wanted him to understand my actions. The loss of the ring had brought him so low, almost destroyed him because he felt he had lost his last chance at freedom. It was the same with the man and the wallet. And with Suzanne there had been a betrayal of trust. And that endangered both our lives. In those days I believed trust was more important than love.' He was aware of the harshness of his decision concerning Suzanne, but was also clear about the ruthlessness and absolute evil of the enemy. To indulge any weakness, even on the side of the angels, was to court disaster. He did not regret his stand, but would be obliged to suffer for it.

On his return to Les Milles Michel had been put down for punishment. He feared a return to Le Vernet, but there was a worse fate in store for him. The administration ordered him to be transferred to a Foreign Labour Battalion at Gardanne, a punishment camp that serviced a coal mine. The mine had been closed, he was told, since the First World War, but slave labour had allowed it to re-open with minimal expense and little regard for the safety of the workers.

'I was forced to rise before sunrise at five a.m. to go down the mine. We were let down in an elevator cage for what seemed an age, then transferred to another, smaller cage and lowered further until we arrived at a depot for a small-gauge railway. We climbed on to the coal cars and had to keep our heads down for the long ride through murky, dust-filled, suffocating tunnels until we jumped off at our work zone.'

He had now entered a twilight world of half-naked men covered in sweat and coal dust, straining to push trucks loaded with coal. The hot half-light, the swirling mist of coal dust and the silent slaves presented an image of hell. At the first sight of this diabolical tableau Michel saw in his mind's eye the words of Dante's *Inferno* hanging over them in a fiery arc: *Lasciate ogni speranza, voi ch'entrate* – All hope abandon, ye who enter here!

'Once off the train I had to crawl on my hands and knees through a maze of narrow tunnels, in and out of passageways, sometimes pushing through inky water and sludge, until I reached my work station at the face, more than an hour after I had entered the mine.' He was one of a team of eight slave-workers run by three professional Polish miners who acted as guards as well as foremen. 'We slaves were so totally controlled and intimidated by this brutal system that the French never had to send any guards into the mine. The miners were not humans but brutes. No animal has the brutality of these men.'

The foreman-miners were well fed and well paid, receiving a bonus for each car filled. The slaves, of course, received nothing. The food was marginally more sustaining than at Le Vernet, but hopelessly inadequate for hard labour. 'On the first day I was given a pick without a moment's rest from the rigours of my underground journey and immediately had to begin prying coal loose from a seam. I dared not stop. I worked for a long time until my body demanded a few moments of rest. I set the handle of the pick upon the ground and bent over it for a moment, just to catch my breath.' He was instantly grabbed by one of the Poles, who snarled, 'You'd better not stop if you want to live through the day and get out of this mine!'

The hours of work seemed interminable. 'My hands were covered with blisters that brought constant sharp pains with each blow of the pick. My empty stomach ached with hunger.' By lunchtime he was exhausted. There was a momentary rest when he only drank water, having eaten his daily ration of bread at breakfast, and watched the miners wolf large, meat-filled sandwiches. The men then returned to work without a break through the afternoon and into the evening. 'Around me, every so often, a slave would be injured or killed by some accident or cave-in. Or would collapse from exertion. No one cared. Victims were simply thrown on to the coal car and hauled off like trash.'

At the end of the day, long after darkness had fallen, Michel made the long journey back to the surface. He showered in icy water and returned to the barracks. The routine never changed, six days a week. 'I never saw the sun. Every day was an eternity.'[18]

The routine ground on. Michel entered a dark, timeless psychological zone in which he could not accurately tell if he had been working at the face for weeks or months or years. The days down in the bowels of the pit merged into a perpetual cycle of hunger, exhaustion and brutality.

On Sundays, the one day of rest, the slaves lay on their thin straw mats too exhausted to move. Some received visitors and even food parcels. An occasional visitor was an old Jewish tailor from Marseille who came to mend the prisoners' rags. He was almost as poor as they were and received a pittance for his services. Michel liked to talk to him in Yiddish as he worked. One day the old man mentioned that he had originally lived in Le Havre.

'I had a girlfriend there once,' Michel said. 'I used to visit her.'

'Jewish?' the old tailor asked.

Michel nodded. 'The family were from Lodz originally, my home town. Lebowitz.'

The tailor lowered his needle and thread. He threw back his head and roared, slapping his thigh with his hand. 'I know them . . . *I know them!*'

'I don't suppose there are many Lebowitzes in Le Havre,' Michel said.

The tailor continued to slap his hand on his thigh and grew increasingly excited. 'Incredible . . . yes, *incredible!* They're here in Marseille! The daughter is married and has a baby boy.'

'Lucienne's in *Marseille?*'

The tailor nodded. 'Lucienne, yes that's her name. I'll give her a message if you like.'

Lucienne arrived at the camp the following Sunday, and from then on became a regular visitor. She was indeed married and living in Marseille, an uncertain existence even for naturalised French Jews. On every visit she chatted in a friendly manner with one of the guards at the gate. She explained to Michel that she believed the young commander who came on duty at night was a decent man, uncomfortable in his role as slave master.

Together they devised an escape plan. When Lucienne went to leave, Michel would hide in the bushes by the gate. As the commander opened the gate, and chatted to Lucienne, Michel would slip out and be met by a friend with a truck. The following Sunday they carried out the plan. He walked to the bushes and hid, while Lucienne made for the gate. The guard opened it, lit a cigarette and stood talking. Michel took his opportunity and scuttled through.

He was taken to the outskirts of Marseille where he met Lucienne's husband and child and stayed overnight. The couple risked their lives by having him in the house. Early the next morning he made his way to the station and had Lucienne buy him a ticket to Lyon, where friends from Nice had connections with the Résistance.

Control on the Marseille–Lyon train had been tightened during the four months he had spent in Gardanne. The regime was growing increasingly efficient in its repression. Despite moving from one compartment to another, and using all his survivor's wiles to avoid detention, he was eventually confronted by gendarmes who demanded his papers. He explained that they had been stolen, together with his bags, at the station in Marseille.

He was arrested, returned to Les Milles and transferred after a few days to a punishment camp in what was then known as the Basses Alpes. Les Mées was an isolated logging camp in the mountains, near Forcalquier, and its inmates were almost entirely Jewish. Security was relatively relaxed in the camp itself as roads in and out of the mountain region were tightly controlled. And once again, any escapee without papers would be unlikely to get far.

'Had I not experienced the hell of Gardanne I might have bridled at the regime, but at least this work was in the clean open air. We had to fell large trees using only axes. Then we stripped the branches and assembled the large trunks into a sort of sled that we dragged down the mountainside through a dry river bed. As hard as it was, it was a relief by comparison to work in the mine.'

Among the sixty or so inmates, Michel found a core of like-minded individuals who expressed enthusiasm to escape and join the Résistance. They were a romantic bunch much given to elaborate stratagems and extravagant pledges. 'We banded together in the joint desire to strike out against the evils of the Vichy government and its godfather, Adolf Hitler. We made plans. We saw ourselves as two strong fists, and if ever we could free ourselves from this bondage we would remain together always, strong and courageous.'

The camp came under the control of the Vichy military commander for the region. One day Michel, together with four other inmates, was sent to build a fence around the garden of the man's private residence. The commander was not present in person, but his attractive nineteen-year-old daughter, Nicole, issued instructions to the men. Michel was aware that she seemed to pay particular attention to him and found several occasions to make light conversation. In the five days it took to build the fence an unlikely friendship developed.

On his return to the camp, Nicole began to visit him on Sundays. She became a regular and took responsibility for him to go outside of the camp. 'It was the beginning of a strange relationship. She was the daughter of a Vichy commander whom I despised passionately. And I was a slave. She came every Sunday and would bring food that I shared with my friends, and then take me out of the camp for a few hours of relief. It was a little Sunday fairy tale.' They would go for walks, picnic in mountain meadows and take bicycle trips. The couple flirted, held hands and kissed in country lanes, but Michel was careful not to take the physical relationship too far. He had tender feelings for the girl but was inhibited by the peculiarity of the situation. Something held him back. 'She was attractive, happy, affectionate, and maybe in love. She was also very spoilt by her father who gave her everything she wanted. He even tolerated her visits to me, which he knew about. She never mentioned her mother, who seemed to be absent.'

One day towards the end of July 1942, Michel received another female visitor. He was told that a young woman was waiting for him at the gate with official authorisation to take him into the village. The woman introduced herself as Yvonne, and as they walked the short distance into Les Mées she explained that the authorisation was forged and that she had been sent by the Résistance in Corrèze. An inmate of the camp who had recently been released had joined the Maquis and told them about Michel. In the village, Yvonne suggested that the safest place to talk was in the *auberge*, where she had taken a room. She told Michel of the first large round-up of French Jews in Paris, and that there were plans for the deportation of all foreign Jews.[19] The Résistance was certain that this was a death sentence. 'She was very clear. She had come to get me out.'

She had been sent to warn him that mass deportations were scheduled to begin any day. The first deportation had already been made from Drancy, a large, unfinished apartment complex in the north-east of Paris which had been hastily converted into a camp. (Yvonne could not know at this time that it served as the French ante-chamber to Auschwitz.) Deportees were taken by rail, accompanied by French police, to the eastern border where they were handed over to German soldiers. It took a further three days to reach the notorious Polish concentration camp. Most of the deportees were gassed on arrival.[20]

Yvonne added that there was a place for Michel in the Résistance – he had been vouchsafed and they wanted to arrange his escape.

'When?' Michel asked.

'Now. That's why I'm here.'

Michel hesitated, then declined. He explained about the two 'fists' of inmates who had banded together in the camp and pledged fealty to one another. He suggested that the Résistance help them all escape so they could join the struggle. It was now the turn of the woman to hesitate. His proposal was both unexpected and a tall order. The woman left unsaid the Résistance's suspicion of large groups – that there was always the risk of a weak human link and the chance of betrayal. However, she promised to take the matter up with her superiors, but stressed the urgency of the situation.

'We spent the whole day in the hotel room. She was very impressive and had come to save my life. To take me with her. It was an emotionally charged atmosphere. I could not go, but we embraced – which led to passionate kisses and lovemaking.'

Yvonne accompanied Michel back to the camp and left him with a handshake at the gate. Once inside he immediately told his companions about the deportations and discussed the urgent need for escape, something that had been mulled over endlessly on many occasions. It had always been rejected previously because of the physical difficulties of leaving the closely guarded, remote mountain region. Now it was a matter of life and death. A vote was taken and a unanimous decision made to break out in two days. The plan was to escape at night before daybreak, climb into the mountains and hide during the day. They would then make their way towards Corrèze, travelling by night, and join the Résistance there.

On the night of the planned escape Michel was again called from the barracks. Nicole was at the gate at eleven o'clock, a highly unusual time for a visit, even for someone with her connections. She was nervous and charged with energy that seemed to be a mixture of fear and excitement.

'I have to talk to you,' she said.

They walked together for a short distance.

'You have to get out. I want you to come with me.'

'What do you mean?'

'I want you to leave with me right now.'

'To go where?'

'To the safest place possible for you to live.'

'Where's that?'

'Home with me. You must come to my house.'

'You mean, your father's house?'

'Yes. I have talked to him. He has agreed to let you live with us. Under my father's roof you can be sure to be protected and safe.'

Michel was genuinely bewildered. 'Why should your father protect me?'

Nicole grew passionate. Why wouldn't he protect his only daughter's true love?

'That's very nice,' Michel replied coldly, 'but I cannot accept the protection of the man who has enslaved me. I'll make my own escape, thank you. The war will not last for ever and if I survive I'll come back to see you – but under different circumstances.'

Nicole's face had grown hard during this short speech. 'Yes, perhaps,' she said, instantly cold and remote. She shrugged, a gesture that conveyed sudden rejection and dismissal. '*Le monde est petit.*' It's a small world.

Michel tried to reach out and embrace her, but she turned her back and walked away. He returned to the barracks where his group was quietly making preparations for the escape. The visit had unsettled him, but as the atmosphere among his companions was already edgy and tense, he said nothing.

At one in the morning there was a commotion at the gate. Trucks carrying Vichy troops drove into the camp, and the entire contingent of guards turned out to meet them. The door to the barracks was flung open and everyone was ordered to dress, gather their belongings and assemble outside. 'We were put in chains and herded into the trucks at gunpoint.'

As they drove down the mountain, Nicole's impetuous behaviour of the previous night became clear. 'The troops were sent by her father the commander. Nicole had known exactly what they were planning to do. She came to save me, but only under her conditions. When I rejected those conditions she decided to let me go to hell with the phrase, "it's a small world". Small chance you will live to see me again, she was saying. That betrayal was a tremendous hurt.'

Le monde est petit. On the long, uncomfortable journey south the trite phrase repeated itself over and over in Michel's mind. 'It was true that I had no strong feelings for the girl, but I was shocked at this clue to the depths to which the human heart is capable of sinking. I had turned her down – she had condemned me to death.' As the trucks bumped along the road from Aix en Provence, and once again he saw before him the forbidding brick blocks of Les Milles, he was forced to recognise the truth in Nicole's words: his world had shrunk to the dimensions of a prison yard.

That summer marked a turning point in the fate of all Jews in France. The war was not going well for the Germans, who were bogged down in Russia. The occupied countries soon felt the effects as enormous new demands were made on manpower and goods. A request for two hundred and fifty thousand French volunteer workers from the Occupied Zone had already been made, and eventually a total of seven hundred and fifty thousand would be sent to Germany. But there was a second demand. Adolf Eichmann, head of the Judenamt (Jewish Office) of the central German security service, visited Paris in person in June to pass on a Berlin directive. It was the French blueprint of the Final Solution.

From now on the Jews of France were to be deported, regardless of citizenship. The Nazis estimated that there were one hundred and sixty-five thousand living in the Occupied Zone with a further seven hundred thousand in the Unoccupied Zone – actually an exaggerated, unrealistic figure. A census was proposed, a timetable set, and Poland and other countries to the east were ordered to prepare for the deportees' arrival. Occupation officials intended that all these measures would eventually extend to the Unoccupied Zone.

The Germans did not anticipate difficulties with this order, and they were right. Although there were reservations among certain Vichy cabinet members about the fate of French Jews, little of this was conveyed to the Germans who were, in effect, given the green light. Vichy had always resented the dumping of German Jews on their soil, and had lodged a formal complaint about it to the Armistice Commission. Now Vichy actually lobbied the Germans to include foreign Jews from the Unoccupied Zone in the deportations. Deputy Gestapo chief Reinhard Heydrich said, reasonably, that it depended on the availability of trains.

The German ambassador reported back to Berlin that the French government would not object to the deportations on political grounds as long as foreign Jews were taken first. Prime Minister Laval stated that foreign Jews had always been a problem in France and that the French government was glad to have the opportunity to get rid of them. The Wehrmacht were persuaded to provide trains to allow between ten and twenty thousand deportees to be taken east in the coming months.

The number of Jews demanded by Germany from both zones jumped to forty thousand, and then one hundred thousand. Vichy was asked to deliver fifty thousand from the Unoccupied Zone and was expected to bear the cost: seven hundred marks per Jew, plus food for a fifteen-day period during deportation. In this they were overcharged: most deportees did not live longer than five days after they left France.

To facilitate the planning of the deportations from the Unoccupied Zone, a young SS officer was dispatched across the Demarcation Line on an inspection of the camps, accompanied by the head of the police for Jewish affairs. He was disappointed to find fewer Jewish internees than expected, although he was encouraged that officials were enthusiastic about the policy. Police in Nice, for instance, told him that they longed to be rid of some eight thousand Jews in the town, and other police chiefs expressed the belief that deportation would solve the refugee problem.

More and more Jews had been interned following fatal attacks on German occupation troops the previous year. The Germans had reacted to the attacks by taking French hostages with the intention of shooting them in the wake of further assassinations. They also demanded that Vichy execute six Communists in their custody in reprisal for the murder of a naval cadet. The government complied beyond the terms of the request, assuring the occupation authorities that the death sentence would be decapitation by guillotine in a public square. The logic behind this was to demonstrate that home-grown French repression was the most effective, and that police matters, and law and order, could be left in their hands. But even public beheadings were not enough to assuage German anger, and the wholesale shooting of hostages was instituted under a decree known as the *code d'hôtage*: for every German killed between fifty and a hundred Frenchmen would die. Executions became so numerous that German officials in France asked for extra beer and cigarette rations 'to calm the nerves of the executioners' and for 'persons of colour' to bury the dead.[21]

The Vichy government condemned this new Nazi brutality, but also promised to root out those responsible for 'outrages'. The state was in no doubt about the identity of the culprits. The Minister of Defence listed them as 'Foreigners (parachutists, bomb throwers, hoodlums of the Spanish Reds), Jews and Communists'. The Vichy ambassador (actually married to a Jewess) sent a telegram to Goering blaming the trouble on 'Communists incited daily by radio broadcasts of Jewish émigrés in the pay of the British government and the Bolshevik plutocrats'.[22] He added that the entire French population deplored their criminal acts. The press thundered that 'Jews, Communists and foreign agitators constitute a national danger'.[23]

The number of Jews among the hostages – a mix of Communists, anarchists and foreigners – became disproportionately high. Repression against them was expanded further when Vichy announced that all foreign Jews who had entered France since 1 June 1936, even those who had since acquired French citizenship, would either serve in labour battalions or be interned.

Since June, Jews over the age of six in the Occupied Zone had been ordered to wear a Star of David the size of the palm of a hand on the left side of an outer garment, with the word JUIF (masculine) or JUIVE (feminine) written in black. They had to apply for the stars from the local police, pay for them and even have their textile ration cards marked. However, some ten thousand foreign nationals, and a handful of upper-class society women who were Jewish and embar-rassingly married to senior officials, were excluded from the order.

Jews in the Unoccupied Zone were not obliged to wear the star. Vichy felt that a law that branded French Jews, but exempted foreigners, was contrary to the nationalistic spirit of the regime. There was also public opinion to think about. A German decree had made certain Frenchmen strangers in their own land, and this struck a chord among the population in the Occupied Zone – especially as veterans from the First World War made a point of wearing their decorations beside the Jewish star. The move seemed to question Vichy's authority as a government, so it preferred instead to adopt a more oblique approach. Instead of forcing Jews to wear the segregationist star, it required that all their personal documents – ID card, work permit, ration card – be stamped JUIF or JUIVE. In this way, the stigma need not unsettle the man in the street, but could be clearly seen and acted upon by those in authority.

The inclusion of all the Jews in France in Nazi plans for the Final Solution called for ever greater co-operation between Germany and Vichy. The German occupation authorities in Paris would have found it difficult to carry out its anti-Jewish programme without the active help of the French administration or the police; in the Unoccupied Zone, of course, it would have been impossible. And as the war in Russia continued to go badly for the Germans, manpower and resources grew ever more stretched. They came to rely increasingly on French enforcement of their anti-Semitic policies, which were growing more violent and extreme by the day.

Only Vichy could identify, segregate, arrest and imprison Jews in the Unoccupied Zone. A census of all Jews south of the Demarcation Line had been completed the previous year with the result that they had been under police surveillance ever since. Foreign Jews were subjected to periodic police inspections and round-ups that either resulted in internment or sent them into forced residence where their every move was monitored.

Faced with the necessity of producing enormous numbers of foreign Jews to fulfil its quota, Vichy placed even more obstacles in the way of emigration. Regional prefects in the Unoccupied Zone were given the order to transport all foreign Jews who had entered France after 1 January 1936 to camps in the Occupied Zone by the end of the summer, and to cancel all exit visas. Prime Minister Laval later explained to newsmen, 'It would be a violation of the armistice to allow Jews to go abroad for fear they should take up arms against the Germans.'[24] Police, soldiers and even firemen went into action in pre-dawn raids in every department of the Unoccupied Zone. The round-ups were carried out without respite over a ten-day period with the order that 'personnel act without brutality but with the greatest firmness'.[25] A report on the round-ups prepared for the president admitted that there had, in fact, been brutality, but concluded: 'they will considerably help clear the air in the Unoccupied Zone. From all quarters, for a long time, we have been receiving complaints about the illicit activities of these foreign Jews: anti-government activity, clandestine trade, black market etc.'

Deportations were duly announced, and only a shortage of trains delayed them for three months. In the meantime, the *code d'hôtage* was made even more severe on direct orders from Hitler. Not only would hostages be executed for future killings, but a further five hundred Jews and Communists would be handed over to Himmler for deportation. Reserves for this purpose were to be kept interned.

The train that took more than a hundred Jews from Drancy to Auschwitz in third-class carriages for the first deportation was the modest beginning of an ambitious programme. Eichmann ordered four thousand more Jews to follow, and they were duly sent without protest from Vichy. There were further delays because of a shortage of rolling stock. From now on deportees would be packed into freight and cattle cars, an arrangement that had the advantage of needing fewer guards.

It was against this background that Michel returned to Les Milles, now transformed into its final manifestation: a warehouse for human beings awaiting death. Locals in and around Aix en Provence nicknamed it *l'abbatoir* – the slaughterhouse. Originally an internment camp for enemy aliens, then a transit camp – as Michel had previously known it – Les Milles would now deal only in deportation. Deportees were sent first to Drancy, the camp outside Paris, and then on to Auschwitz.

And yet Michel and his group were in high spirits when they were first driven through its gates. The fraternity of the ten – the two fists – felt that the camp offered opportunities for escape, or even an uprising. Michel was once again close to his underground contacts in Marseille and hoped to enlist clandestine support. 'We entered the deportation camp like young lions transferred to a new cage, eager to sniff around every area of the enclosure, searching for a weak spot that might offer the possibility of escape.'

The men met after their initial reconnaissance to pool intelligence. The large, open yard was enclosed completely by a high wall topped with barbed wire. The camp gate, adjacent to a spur of railroad tracks connected to the main line, was heavily guarded. Any hope of escape through or over the fence, or via the gate, had to be ruled out.

Security at Les Milles had also been strengthened at the beginning of August 1942, when municipal police reorganised inmates and guards received new orders to shoot troublemakers after three shouted warnings.[26]

The men were allocated their places in the buildings that served as barracks. They were provided with a list of basic belongings that were to be packed at all times in readiness for 'relocation'. Everything else was to be left behind. 'This for any thinking person meant a trip to death. You were not allowed money, extra clothes or jewellery – it all had to be turned over to the French authorities.'

There were as many as twenty dilapidated structures in the camp, but inmates were mostly housed in two grim brick buildings, each floor of which was divided into a series of enormous rooms. The two buildings were connected on the second floor by an enclosed wooden shaft that had been sealed at both ends, denying access from one building to the other. A small shack, also locked and seemingly unused, stood between the two buildings in the main courtyard. The discouraging conclusion of the group was that security was basic but formidable: there was no visible weak link or obvious means of escape.

The men discussed the mood of the camp and reported on conversations with various inmates. These suggested a general sense of disbelief and an inability to accept the danger of the situation. The Vichy government fed the inmates' illusions by speaking of 'relocation' rather than 'deportation'. 'Too many of the victims of Les Milles grasped at this wisp of hope because it was difficult for them to accept the total collapse of human morality. Even if the Germans were capable of annihilating an entire people and culture, it was impossible to believe that the Vichy French would join forces with them so completely. As an individual, no matter how clear the evidence that massive slaughter was under way, it was impossible to accept that it was happening to *you* – that *you* had been trapped in the web, that *you* were dumped in the middle of a system that would extinguish your existence with cold efficiency. It was simply impossible to allow yourself to believe this. Disbelief was the mind's first line of defence, and this made it difficult to persuade anyone to support the Résistance. If you were still alive and still in France, why take risks?'

The group of ten prided themselves on not sharing these illusions. They knew that 'relocation' meant 'deportation', and that both were synonyms for death. They also knew from their various experiences in different slave-labour camps that Vichy would go about its task with enthusiasm and efficiency, and intended to resist their fate to the end. They reasoned that if escape proved impossible they could try to convince their fellow inmates to stage a massive riot. They might die in the struggle, but could at least attract the attention of the world. 'Death was so close on that first night in the deportation camp that we felt willing to offer ourselves as a sacrifice in order to save thousands more who were doomed to follow us on this journey to oblivion. We curled up on our hard straw mats and dreamed of heroic scenarios.'

In many ways conditions at Les Milles, even as it became ever more crowded, were better than at Le Vernet, and certainly an improvement on Gardanne. But the psychological atmosphere of defeat was overwhelming. 'The deportation camp, far more than any other in my experience, stank of death.'

The ten were unafraid to face evil and do battle, but they were woefully unprepared for an insidious phenomenon that acted upon them almost immediately. Michel called it the Siren Song. 'I found a strange and enticing sensation gradually descend on me during the first few days and nights. I did not identify it at first. I only realised that, somehow, I was not as determined as I had been earlier. I wondered if it wouldn't be simpler to surrender myself to whatever plans Vichy France had for me. Such an idea was alien to my previous resolve, yet it was nearly impossible to shake it off. Once hope is gone, and a man accepts the certainty of his fate, hopelessness becomes a malignant non-emotion that attacks the soul. Give in to hopelessness and you cave in completely. Take away hope and you take away life.'

The same pervasive mood of resignation and acceptance affected the other members of the group. Within a week, their original commitment began to dissipate. Individual members of the ten began to avoid one another and seek alternative, less demanding company. 'My friends no longer wished to speak to me because it was easier to give in. Each day I could feel they were succumbing to their fate. They avoided me. I was a bother to them. They were gone, as surely as a prisoner on death row is gone long before he reaches the electric chair. Nature seems to provide the condemned man with an escape mechanism, a natural anaesthetic that floods the conscious mind with an all-pervasive soothing feeling, an almost euphoric invitation to surrender. It whispers enticingly, "Give in! Come into my arms. Let go!" Anyone who accepts the invitation is beyond help. Regardless of his physical circumstances he is already dead emotionally. He awaits the end as a dispassionate observer of his own demise. Death becomes a welcome relief.'

It was the Siren Song – seductive, irresistible . . . fatal. In Greek mythology the Sirens were sea nymphs with the bodies of birds and the heads of women, and such sweet voices that mariners who heard their song were lured on to the rocks where the nymphs lived, and their ships destroyed. The Greek hero Ulysses was able to resist the Sirens' song by following the advice of a sorceress. He had himself bound to the mast of his ship and sealed the ears of the crew with wax. The men were ordered to ignore his most urgent pleas to be released, and only in this way could he listen to the sweet, deadly music of the Sirens and survive.

There was another story that came back to Michel at this time. As a boy he had read about the French Revolution and remembered a vignette in which a group of victims were lined up awaiting the tumbril that would carry them to the guillotine. The guards counted eight men into each wagon, until one – the odd man out – was left standing alone as the last tumbril rumbled off across the cobblestones. He looked about him in panic, and then chased after the others all the way to the guillotine. 'I did not want to be that man, running headlong to my death. I longed for allies, but was now alone. To keep my mind focused on the battle to live I forced myself to think of the condemned awaiting the guillotine, and the story of Ulysses and the Song of the Sirens. And I envied Ulysses that he could be bound to the mast and I could not. It was the greatest struggle of my life.'

There was another sound that would come to haunt Michel: the long, shrill whistle of the locomotive engines as they pulled out of the railway sidings beyond the walls of the camp.

The first transport Michel experienced pulled into the siding with its string of cattle cars. It had scarcely come to a halt when an announcement was made over the camp's loudspeaker system. Inmates were ordered to assemble in the courtyard. Michel had long contemplated this terrible moment and had formed a number of plans. In the general confusion, as people hurried to gather their belongings, he improvised a variation of a childhood stunt where he pretended to fall down the stairs. As people made their way down into the yard he slid down the long stairway, drumming his heels on the steps, until he arrived at the bottom and feigned unconsciousness. He was hauled out of the path of the stampeding crowd and then carried by guards to the camp hospital. He lay groaning on a field bed, simulating semi-conscious agony.

The selection of people for deportation went on all day, as the authorities sorted through the requests for exemption. As it became clear that few would be saved, the camp director lost the stomach for the task, declaring that he had assumed the post to help Jews emigrate from France, not to send them to German concentration camps. The police took over the job. The chief explained: 'I certainly know that the measures we have undertaken are very painful, but if you knew what I know, you would prefer to let foreign Jews leave now instead of having good Frenchmen depart soon.'[27]

From his bunk in the hospital Michel heard in the distance the dreadful shriek of the train whistle as the transport departed. 'All my friends – our two fists – went quietly on their last journey.'

He sneaked from the hospital later the same day after witnessing the treatment meted out to genuine patients. 'The camp was after a body count and didn't care what shape inmates were in. I saw suicide attempts, who had taken pills of poison, brought in unconscious and have their stomachs pumped in order to be deported. They were not permitted to die *there* – they had to be kept alive to fill a quota so they could die elsewhere.'

The camp had now lost the majority of its population, and only the Non-Deportables walked in the yard. Non-Deportables were a race apart, made up of the very few who possessed the paperwork of hope: some letter, document or passport that offered them a haven in another country. They were usually citizens of neutral, non-belligerent countries. Turkey, for instance, formally objected to the deportation of its citizens from the outset.[28] The Non-Deportables were the envy of everyone in the camp. 'The rest of us could only hope that they would survive to carry our story to the world outside.'

New inmates were brought by truck every day and the camp began to fill in readiness for the next transport. One day a beautiful young woman with black hair appeared at the gate demanding to join her husband. She was French, and at liberty, but her husband was a Jew and she wanted to share his fate. 'At first the authorities refused, but she insisted on being with her husband. So they let her in. I watched this beautiful woman and her husband as they walked hand in hand in the courtyard, waiting for the train that would deport them. That love, that devotion, that calm – it moved me very much.'

There was also the case of a Non-Deportable in the camp who was in love with a Deportable. He knew full well what would happen and also asked to be allowed to accompany his loved one on the transport. The authorities consented with cordial indifference. 'It was so difficult to grapple with the realisation that there were creatures in uniform "doing their job" who could impassively send people to their deaths, yet there were other gentle humans who chose to die for love.'

As the days went by Michel was alarmed once again to feel the allure and pull of the Siren Song. 'Now it mocked me: *So, you have delayed your fate. So? You are locked into your destiny and you cannot escape. You may as well sink into my embrace, let yourself be taken.*' The temptation to give in never left him, and he had to be forever on his guard. 'The seductiveness of its appeal tortured me and never failed to amaze.'

Only by concentrating fully on the future could he hope to believe he had one. He filled every waking moment by making impossible plans, but it was lonely work without comrades-in-arms. In his fantasies he yearned to escape and strike back, but still had no firm idea of how to avoid the next transport. When the train pulled into the siding beside the camp, the prison population was once again summoned to the yard. This time the guards had devised a more organised and thorough system and ordered everyone to gather in lines in alphabetical order. People seemed to obey like sheep. Michel deliberately stood in the wrong line.

As inmates jostled one another and attempted to comply with orders, the French guards searched the barracks thoroughly. They were not shy of using their bayonets to prod difficult-to-reach hiding places, and one or two inmates were dragged bleeding to the cattle cars. And this time the infirm in the camp hospital were not excluded, and several patients were ordered from their beds and forced on to the train, including those who had earlier taken poison or slashed their wrists in suicide attempts.

The roll was called and, one by one, men and women walked passively to their fate. Only a very few offered resistance. As one struggling man was carried on to the train by guards, he screamed in English and in French, '*Je suis un citoyen Américain!* I am an American! I am an American citizen! I demand to see my consul!' He was ignored.

'Kroskof, Michel!' a guard called. Michel willed himself not to react and to remain stock-still. 'It is surprisingly difficult to force yourself not to respond to your own identity.'

'KROSKOF, MICHEL!' the guard shouted impatiently.

As no one stepped forward the guard conferred with an officer. An examination of all the Ks in the line failed to produce Kroskof, a notation was made on a clipboard and the roll call continued. In the muddle of activity Michel moved unobtrusively to join the Non-Deportables who stood at one end of the platform glumly watching the proceedings. One man waved a handkerchief in the direction of the cattle cars, as if waving goodbye to someone going on holiday. Michel tried to look inconspicuous and indifferent to his surroundings. He watched as the tragic pair of lovers – the French woman with the long black hair and her Jewish husband – climbed aboard their respective cattle cars.

The long, hot afternoon wore on. The process seemed interminable and people began to faint in the heat. The guards themselves grew increasingly bad-tempered and prodded and kicked their victims. Despite the blazing August weather the guards sealed each boxcar as it was filled. There was nothing in the wagons but a thin layer of straw on the floors, buckets for toilets, and an inadequate water supply. As inmates locked in cars waited in the Provençal heat they begged for a breath of air and extra water. Occasionally, guards delivered packages to the cars and, in a surreal touch, the YMCA provided boxes of books. The boarding process dragged on into the night as deportees – three hundred adults, mostly all German and Austrian Jews – were ordered aboard the cattle cars.

The Non-Deportables eventually wandered back to their quarters, and Michel went with them. He picked one of the many empty spots, lay down and remained wide awake, braced for the locomotive's parting death whistle. The train remained at the platform throughout the stifling night, delayed for one bureaucratic reason or another, while its occupants sweltered and suffered inside the cattle cars.

In the early hours of the morning yet another sad human drama was played out. The guards went from boxcar to boxcar calling the name of a woman. The precious piece of paper provided a last-minute reprieve, and she was eventually found and escorted from the train. Michel learned later that a friend or relative had arrived with papers from a foreign consulate. The tragedy of the situation was that the woman was the one whom the Non-Deportable man had insisted on accompanying. Their fates had now been reversed, and it was the man who was doomed.

The train finally pulled off in the early morning. The whistle blew. *'That sound!* I felt if I did not get out soon my emotions would die, and my body would quickly follow.'

The Vichy government might have been able to delude itself that by ridding itself of foreign Jews – many of whom, they argued, came from Germany in the first place – they had not lost their moral compass. But the fate of the children of the soon-to-be-murdered was more complicated.

Whatever reasons were concocted to rationalise the deportations of the adults, the suffering of the children was impossible to disguise. At Drancy the number of orphans grew as their parents were sent to Auschwitz. The children had their names inscribed on wooden dog tags, except for the very little ones, who often didn't know their family names. Groups of a hundred lived in bare rooms, with buckets for toilets on the landings. A diet of cabbage soup gave them acute diarrhoea. Soiled underclothes were rinsed in cold water without soap. Knots of semi-naked children milling about waiting for their underwear to dry became a permanent feature of the camp. Another was the sound of their weeping.

At first, Nazi deportation plans excluded children, limiting deportees to the ages of sixteen to forty. Indeed, before the deportation of children began, the Germans had sometimes spirited orphans from the Occupied Zone across the Demarcation Line, although Vichy was not happy to have this responsibility foisted upon them. Prime Minister Laval now requested that children under sixteen from the Unoccupied Zone be deported. He believed that not splitting up families was the right thing to do – a grotesque distortion of Vichy's pious view on the sanctity of the family.

The request was passed along to Berlin, where there was a three-week delay, suggesting reluctance even on the part of the Nazis. Finally, after repeated pressure from France, Adolf Eichmann announced that Jewish children and old people could be deported. It was a concession. Previously, the orphans had caused all sorts of troublesome administrative problems, as well as political embarrassment, when their parents were sent separately to their deaths. Prime Minister Laval again made it sound like an act of compassion that in future children would be deported with their parents. Now they would be allowed to die alongside their kith and kin.

And the orphans created by earlier deportations would also be sent. These unfortunates were packed into freight cars in batches forty to sixty strong. French police accompanied their wretched cargo to the border, where they were handed over. Six thousand children were deported to Auschwitz from Drancy in 1942 alone; more than a thousand were below the age of six.[29] German involvement was minimal. 'No one and nothing could deter us from carrying out the policy of purging France of undesirable elements without nationality,' Laval declared.

Behind the scenes the deportations created diplomatic waves, and the United States remonstrated with Laval. He asked sarcastically why America didn't take the children, a point the French government had made repeatedly over the years with justification when criticised by foreign powers. This time the US State Department offered a thousand visas with the possibility of a further five thousand for Jewish children, if the French authorities would agree to grant them permission to leave.

Laval went to the Germans with the proposal. Unsurprisingly, they raised the objection that a mass emigration of children to the United States to save them from deportation would become an occasion for anti-German and anti-French propaganda. As a result Vichy made the unrealistic demand of the Americans that there should be no publicity. Negotiations bogged down. At one stage the French agreed to issue five hundred emigration visas, but added so many qualifications that they were never granted. The instincts of the men in charge supported an ingrained bureaucratic tendency to avoid taking any course that would upset administrative routine, even one that would save children's lives. The simple truth of it was that the children helped fulfil the quota requirement.[30]

Michel fought to stave off total dejection by scouring the camp once more for some hiding place where he might disappear for a few hours to avoid the next transport. He was now a fugitive within a prison camp, as the camp authorities continued to search for him. He found nothing – until he reconsidered the sealed wooden passageway that connected the two main buildings. He had initially dismissed the shaft as an impossible option after a close inspection of the doors at either end of the passage. They were not only locked, but had planks of wood nailed across them. However, the view of the structure from the courtyard gave him a new idea. Small windows were interspersed along the passageway's length, big enough for an undernourished inmate of Les Milles to slip through. The problem was twofold: to reach the windows and remain unseen.

He took a closer look at the small shack that stood beneath and slightly back from the passageway. The gabled top of its sharply sloping roof was conceivably close enough to one of the windows for an energetic and lucky jump. This was difficult enough, but there was also the problem of climbing on to the roof of the shack in the first place. Michel made his way to the second floor of the barracks and looked out of the window. It was just possible to drop on to the roof, but any attempt would be in full view of the courtyard. 'If I was seen by the guards I was lost. But what alternative did I have? I was lost anyway.'

Suddenly, an order came over the loudspeaker to assemble in the yard. Desperate to try his plan, he fought against the human tide swarming from the barracks and made his way up the stairs to the second floor. Guards were already moving people from room to room as he climbed outside the barracks window and leapt on to the roof of the shack below. He expected at any moment to hear a shout or a gunshot, and dared not glance behind him. He looked up at the window of the passageway. It now seemed much further away than he had originally estimated, an impossible distance. He jumped and stretched for the ledge, barely gripping it with his fingertips. He hauled himself up and tumbled through the window.

Inside he found a rusting conveyor belt that had once been used to transport supplies from one building to the other in the days when the camp had operated as a brickworks. Michel squeezed beneath it. Lying face down he could see through the cracks in the wooden plank flooring into the courtyard below. The sound of people being herded towards the train drifted up to him.

This time the guards conducted a thorough and systematic search of the building, checking the internal ID cards of the Non-Deportables. He heard a number of guards talking about the need to catch Michel Kroskof and discussing the possibility of the passageway as a hiding place as they looked down upon it. Moments later he heard one help the other down from the window on to the roof of the shed. Michel feared that he had been either spotted or betrayed. 'It was all over. I knew that my life was being counted in minutes. I felt caught. The chase for me was on.'

Michel had never considered himself a pious man, but now he cried out silently to his God. 'I made a vow. A solemn covenant. "If I survive . . ."' The terms of the covenant were to remain a secret between the man and his God until he was able to fulfil them, but he swore to dedicate his life to the task.

There was a sudden cry and clatter as the guard who had been hoisted on to the roof of the shack lost his footing and tumbled noisily to the ground. His companion shouted out and left the window. He heard scuffling below him and assumed other guards were helping their fallen comrade. Then there was silence. Michel waited anxiously for their return. Time passed. The guards did not come back. The accident seemed to have taken the impetus out of the search.

Later, different guards gathered in the yard, talking and smoking cigarettes. Michel presumed they had finished their day's work of loading the cattle cars with their human cargo. The men seemed intent on loitering endlessly in the one spot. He was painfully uncomfortable and longed to change position. The blood to his left arm was cut off and it became dead, while his legs were agonisingly cramped. Added to the discomfort was an ever-increasing urge to urinate. His position made it impossible to cross his legs, and he was fearful that a single drop might fall to the ground and give him away. 'I had only willpower to fight off the incredible urge to urinate that lasted for several hours until it was dark, when the guards had moved away and I dared to move.'[31]

The train was full and sealed, but as always it did not move off until late. Once again its doleful whistle took Michel to the edge of despair. Hours passed. He remained cramped in his hiding place and dared not risk leaving it in the dark for fear of breaking his neck. Once again the camp was almost empty except for the Non-Deportables. He remained under the conveyor belt throughout the night and left at first light. He climbed out of the window and dropped on to the roof of the shack with what seemed like a terrible noise. He looked around him. The yard was deserted and he seemed to have attracted no attention. He lowered himself to the ground and crept to the cover of the barracks' wall, massaging his aching muscles. 'I had escaped once again, only to remain in hopeless confinement in constant risk of deportation.'

Early one morning, as the inmates milled about aimlessly in the courtyard or passed the time in their barrack rooms, an order came over the loudspeaker. Women and children were to assemble by the gate. No transport awaited them, but the announcement was ominous. The camp's families duly gathered, accompanied by confused fathers who stood with them, and Michel loitered to one side ready to seize any opportunity during this unusual procedure that might divert the attention of the guards.

The cowed, apprehensive crowd listened as an officer made an announcement. Children were to be separated from their parents and bused to orphanages operated by Jewish philanthropists or Quakers. A low moan of anguish went up, and some of the mothers began to scream. A convoy of buses pulled into the courtyard. Men and women who had lost the will to fight for their own lives suddenly rallied and began to struggle with the guards. In the confusion Michel saw that the door to one of the buses was open and unwatched. He made his way towards it, planning to climb aboard and hide among the children. 'But I was beaten to it by another prisoner who succeeded in doing exactly what I wanted to do. The moment was quickly gone. I was bitterly disappointed by my failure to take the one opportunity of escape that had presented itself.'[32]

Parents who understood their own fate tried not to pass on the heartbreak to the little ones, even though they feared they would never see them again. Many of the tots clung to their mothers and had to be physically separated. Parents stared at their children as they were herded on to the buses, trying to fix an image to last an eternity. As they drove away an eerie silence fell over the camp.[33]

That night, Les Milles sank to a new level of misery. Parents lay on their straw mats and sobbed, adding new force to the Siren Song. 'I remember the sight of children torn from their mothers and fathers as the most emotionally painful of my life. It tears into me.'

Renewed energy came from the unexpected pleasure derived from a friendship with one of the new arrivals. In conversation it came out that the two men were not only from Lodz but had been born in the same hospital on the same day. The coincidence created an instant bond, and Michel was eager to impart the benefit of his experiences in the camp. He told his new friend about his companions from the logging camp, and how they had succumbed to the Siren Song. He explained the seductive nature and danger of the phenomenon, and told the story of the man running to the guillotine. The man listened attentively, visibly impressed by all he heard. He vowed to remain vigilant against the insidious onslaught of hopelessness.

'At last, I thought, I have found someone. My new friend was a remarkable young man – intelligent, strong, determined to resist unto death. We agreed to stick together and do everything in our power to avoid deportation. And if we were deported we vowed to escape from the train. I felt stronger now, knowing at least I had a friend and ally.'

The men were constant companions for a couple of days, until circumstances separated them little by little. A week passed. Word came from the woman in charge of the Quakers in Marseille, who was a regular visitor, that another deportation was imminent, although no date was given. Michel sought out his friend to warn him. 'He turned towards me with a vacant stare. He no longer wanted to speak to me. He was gone.'

Feeling more forlorn than ever in the knowledge that he was utterly alone, Michel forced himself once again to plan to avoid the next transport. The passageway, risky and difficult as it was to reach, and horribly uncomfortable on arrival, still seemed to be the only hiding place. But he wanted to lessen the risk of being spotted as he jumped from the barracks window to the roof of the shack, and needed to pick his time carefully. 'If only I had known exactly when the transport would arrive!

'One morning I had a strange feeling deep in my belly that this was the day.' He walked to the window and looked down at the shack. It was early, and there were few people about – the timing was perfect. ' "Okay," I said to myself, "this is the moment!" '

But then he hesitated. A voice within asked, *What if the transport is not scheduled for today?* The memory of the extreme physical discomfort of the interminable hours in hiding was very fresh. He wanted to limit his time cramped beneath the conveyor belt to the minimum, and could not bear the thought of another day and night – or even longer – in the passageway. He stood at the window debating the issue with himself. He decided against immediate action and turned away.

He headed for the stairs and was about to go down when the camp's loudspeaker system sounded. This time everyone was ordered to stay inside the building and to stand by their beds. Guards immediately sealed the exits and prepared for a systematic room-by-room inspection. 'It was a devious change in procedure and I knew I was caught. Now there was no way out. I cursed myself for not following my original premonition. The moment of flight had passed. Like everyone else I was supposed to return immediately to my assigned room and stand next to my assigned straw mat. The problem was, I did not exist.'

Since disappearing from the first transport, he was still wanted by the authorities and realised that the new tactic of locking people inside the building was aimed at trapping him and any others like him. He no longer had an assigned place anywhere where he could take up position and stand beside a straw mat. He moved quickly through the building searching for a possible haven. Guards had already taken up position at the doors at the end of each massive room as three camp officials entered calling for Michel Kroskof.

The officials walked over and Michel stepped forward as if he were the prisoner in charge. 'Michel Kroskof? No, I don't know,' he announced forcefully.

The official nodded and moved further into the next room while the guards moved from room to room calling for Kroskof.

A prisoner on the other side of the room who had seen the exchange came across. 'Who are you?' he demanded, confronting Michel. 'What the hell are you doing here? You don't belong in this room – get out immediately! I'm in charge here!'

The man was a prisoner like all the others, and would be deported along with them, but he had been put in charge of the room and took his duties seriously. The affront to his power, and the terror of reprisals, created genuine rage. '*Please* keep your voice down!' Michel said, attempting to sound deadly and accommodating in the same breath. 'Don't attract the guards' attention – just keep your voice down!'

'Don't tell me what to do. I'm responsible here and you have to go immediately.'

'You're right – but please keep calm.'

'I don't care about calm,' the man spat. 'Get out of here!'

'Okay, okay. Just give me three minutes and I'll be gone.'

The prisoner seemed somewhat pacified that his pitiful authority had been recognised. 'Okay,' he said, relenting, 'but I want you out of this room.'

Michel walked slowly away, desperately racking his brains for a plan. He contemplated leaping from the window, or crawling along an outside ledge – wild ideas with no hope of success. He saw a blanket hanging as a curtain in a corner at the far end of the room and made towards it. And when he was certain neither the guards nor the room leader was looking in his direction, he slipped behind it. The curtain created a private area containing a small table, a couple of chairs and a field bed with cardboard boxes beneath it. He crawled under the bed and concealed himself behind the boxes as best he could. Slowly, the building emptied. The rooms were cleared and the inmates were moved outside and herded into the cattle cars. The silence of the grave fell over the barracks. A train whistle blew.

Michel lay hour upon hour without moving. He drifted off into a rocky half-sleep until he heard the sound of boots making their way across the room towards him. His first thought was that someone had seen him slip behind the curtain and the room leader had betrayed him. The voices of the guards grew louder and louder and the curtain was pulled aside.

Michel could see the boots of what appeared to be three guards. They were not searching for anyone but eager to relax after a hard day's work. Two of the guards took the chairs, while the third sat heavily on the bed. The mattress pressed down, squeezing Michel to the floor. He tried to control his fear by taking short, even breaths. Wine was opened and cigarettes lit. One of the men took out a pack of cards and they began to gamble. There was laughter, and glasses were drained and refilled. 'Characteristically, the guards seemed entirely unmoved by the fate of the human beings they had just packed into cattle cars.'

The men played cards and drank for hours until two of them finally stood. They said goodnight and made their way out of the room. The third pulled off his boots, collapsed on to the bed and was snoring loudly within minutes. Michel lay below him, desperate not to fall asleep and give himself away.

The next morning he remained beneath the bed long after the guard had gone to his post. The noise of building work came from the courtyard. Finally, he ventured from his hiding place and moved carefully among the Non-Deportables. He looked out of the window. The noises that he assumed to be construction actually came from demolition: the passageway between the two buildings no longer existed. Once again luck had intervened to save him. If he had been able to reach the previous hiding place beneath the conveyor belt he would have been caught. 'How long could I continue this game of cat and mouse?'

His continued presence now threatened the Non-Deportable elite. It was declared camp policy that anyone withholding information or assisting Michel Kroskof would be severely punished, usually by the withdrawal of Non-Deportable status. A number of the Non-Deportables with whom he had become friendly over the weeks now began to avoid him. 'It placed my few remaining friends in a difficult position. I became a non-person. No one wished to see me. They turned their backs whenever I approached. No one would talk to me. Nobody would shake hands or even look at me. I felt like a leper – worse, like a ghost! I had to sleep wherever I could without attracting attention. But no one reported me. A few pointedly left scraps of food for me, but even these would not glance in my direction.'

Late one night he heard two Non-Deportables, who worked in the hospital, discuss one of the patients, who was also a Non-Deportable. A certain Sam Fischer had been granted a rare one-day pass to go into Marseille the following morning and visit a consulate.[34] Passes were valid from three a.m. and were picked up from guards at the gate. The sad truth, the men said, was that the patient was so sick he was unlikely to be able to present himself to the guards at the gate to pick up the pass, let alone go into town. 'Imagine – a sick guy in the hospital getting a pass!' one said.

Michel moved to a quiet corner. He set to work on his internal identity card with a razor, carefully scraping his name from it and trying not to destroy the paper beneath. He lettered in the name of Samuel Fischer and slipped it back into its cellophane case. The result was the product of a desperate man rather than a master forger, and even Michel had to admit it could not hope to pass anything but the most cursory inspection. But behind the cellophane it looked convincing, and he was prepared to gamble that blasé guards would treat him with the usual disdain shown all inmates.

If he made it beyond the gate he hoped he might have at least five hours before the alarm was raised. He thought it unlikely that a sick man would drag himself from his hospital bed in the early hours of the morning, and hoped to have at least until eight o'clock – and it was possible that Fisher was so ill that he might not pick up his pass at all.

At three a.m., Michel screwed up his courage and walked down the stairs to the building's exit. All doors to the building were now locked at night and prisoners needed permission to go out to the latrines. Desperate for a prop, he bummed a cigarette and inhaled deeply, trying to remain calm as he approached the guards with studied nonchalance.[35]

'Where are you going?' one challenged him lazily.

'I have a pass.'

'Okay, come on,' the guard said, and began to walk towards the gate.

Michel pulled deeply on his cigarette.

'This one's here for his pass,' the guard announced to his colleagues at the gate. He turned, and began to make his way back to the main building.

'Name?' the guard at the gate demanded.

'Fischer, Samuel.'

Michel held out his ID. One guard looked for the pass, while a second took the ID and inspected it. Michel asked questions about the time of the first bus into Marseille and where to catch it. His heart was beating so fast he thought it would show through his shirt. The guard merely seemed to check his likeness against the photo before handing the ID back with the precious pass.

'*Bonne nuit*,' Michel said, as the gate was opened and he walked out into the dark. He had an hour's brisk walk ahead of him to get to the main road, where he could catch the bus. The night air of Provence smelt good to a free man.

After walking for ten minutes or so he saw the silhouette of a woman approaching the camp.

'Sam?' The call came through the dark, tense with pleasure. 'Sam?' As she hurried towards him she realised her mistake. 'I'm sorry. I thought you were somebody else.'

'Are you looking for Sam Fischer?'

'Yes. He's my husband.'

'I'm sure he'll be at the gate soon.'

The woman moved off in the direction of the camp and Michel pushed forward. He had calculated on having several hours – a full day even – in which to escape. Now he realised he might have only minutes. Once the woman arrived at the gate and the real Sam Fischer presented himself the alarm would be sounded.

It was a dark, cloudy night as he jumped a ditch and began to run through fields, cutting across country. Scarcely fifteen minutes passed before he heard the wail of a siren and the barking of dogs.

V

As Michel moved away from Les Milles he grew disoriented in the dark, and lost his bearings as he criss-crossed farmland to throw off his pursuers. He began to fear he might actually be heading back in the direction of the camp. At first he heard motor bikes and cars, and the occasional bark of a dog, and at one point a patrol came so close that he could hear them talking.

As the night wore on the clouds began to clear and he was able to locate the North Star. But the moonlight made it more difficult for him to conceal himself, although he could now see the patrols searching for him. He was driven to exhaustion, moving fast when he thought it was safe and hiding in ditches at the sight of humans. At daybreak he lay low behind a wall, and finally emerged on to a country road at around nine in the morning.

He struck out on foot in the direction of Marseille, stopping to seek shelter with friends he knew lived at a village en route. He had originally met the couple in Nice, but when they moved to the region of Aix en Provence they came to visit him in Les Milles. They had even brought three large suitcases of his belongings from the old apartment, thoughtfully packed by Suzanne's mother. The guards stole everything. His friends were now afraid of having him in the house, but gave him food and some money and led him to a shelter in a wood to spend the night.

The next morning he went into Marseille and arrived at the home of his friend Simone, whom he had known since his university days in Bordeaux, only to discover that her husband had been arrested on suspicion of Résistance activities. It was no longer even safe to hide in the attic. He moved on and made his way to the main post office where he sent a telegram to the address given to him for the Corrèze Résistance by Yvonne, the woman who had visited him in the logging camp. He followed the instructions she had given him to arrange a meeting, coded in a seemingly innocuous message. But Michel made the clandestine message so obscure no one in the Corrèze Maquis could understand it. The telegram was passed from hand to hand until it reached Yvonne herself. She knew immediately that it had come from Michel and travelled to Marseille to make the rendezvous.

Yvonne took him to a suburb on the outskirts of town where a wealthy couple connected to the Résistance gave them rooms in a country mansion set in a large, overgrown garden. Despite her youth and flirtatious manner, Yvonne was a veteran of the Maquis and had a cool head in a crisis. Her handbag bulged not with cosmetics but with all the paraphernalia to prepare false papers: inks, stamps, gum, and a cornucopia of stolen travel passes, identity and ration cards.

'What name do you want?' she asked cheerfully.

It was to be the first of five identities Michel was to assume in the Résistance. Impressed by the risks Yvonne seemed prepared to take, he asked to keep his first name and suggested it might be convenient if he took her family name. In that way they could pose as man and wife and spend a few days together. 'She liked the idea. And we had a very tender time in each other's arms.'

It was one of the first of many brief encounters entered into during the war. 'These were intense periods, dramatic times. Life was dangerous and uncertain. No one dared think of a future, let alone a life together . . . only the present, the moment. Everything was compressed, including emotions. Men and women who met for a day or two had a time together full of feeling because they did not have the luxury of stretching the relationship out. They were immediately open. *Nothing* was casual – the opposite of the sexual revolution of the sixties. The romance, the emotion and the physical were all connected whether it was short-lived or not. It was love, not just sex. The war pushed people together, and then the war pulled people apart.'

Yvonne returned to Corrèze and Michel moved on to Lyon with his new identity. He made contact with the Résistance through a friend he had known in Nice, Sammy Lattès, who had connections with a well-known publishing family. 'From that moment on I decided that the time for fighting was at hand. I was tired of being an impotent prisoner. Neither Vichy France nor the Germans would ever again take me without a fight.'

Lyon was proud of its reputation as the capital of the Résistance. It had first experienced the German military in June 1940 when the Place Bellecour had been turned into a parking lot for Panzer tanks. Half the city's half a million population had fled so there were few people on the streets to witness the arrival of the conquerors and see the swastika replace the tricolour over the town hall. An eyewitness

observed: 'What silence! One could sense the flow of the Rhône.'[1]
Three weeks later the city was placed in the Free Zone, under the
terms of the armistice, and the Germans duly departed. They left
behind a ghoulish, racist souvenir: discovered in the cells of the
préfecture were the rotting corpses of twenty-six black Senegalese
soldiers, members of one of the few French military units to stand its
ground in defence of the town.

The residents of Lyon had no desire to see the occupiers return and
a Résistance movement began to take form. The city had a long
history of rebellion: there had been uprisings against the clergy in the
thirteenth century, the lynching of usurers in the sixteenth, and
opposition to the Jacobins in Paris during the revolution when close
to two thousand Lyonnais were guillotined in a period of four
months. And even when the Germans had been in the city liberty
remained demonstrably close, with the border of neutral Switzerland
only eighty miles away.[2]

There were three major resistance movements in the Free Zone
centred in Lyon: Combat, Liberation-Sud and Franc Tireurs
Partisans (FTP). The groups operated independently of one another
and were often in conflict as each was ideologically distinct and
pursued its own agenda. The FTP recruited from the ranks of the
French Communist Party, which was slavish to Moscow – a trend
that continued until the end of the Cold War. The Communists had
been inactive during the Nazi–Soviet non-aggression pact and
supported the Germans, and the FTP only came into existence after
Germany invaded Russia. It took a decision, without consulting
other resistance groups, to pursue a policy of assassination against
German occupation soldiers, triggering the wholesale taking and
shooting of hostages. The FTP also had a secret agenda to gain
control of the Résistance, separate it from the Free French, and
provoke a national insurrection at the time of liberation to bring the
Communists to power.[3] 'We didn't know any of this then,' Michel
says. 'Just that the Communists had been with the Nazis in the
beginning, so we didn't trust them.'

In the early days the Résistance as a whole was disorganised,
divided and largely ineffective. The Maquis in general displayed an
amateurish quality exacerbated by factional rivalries. It was said that
a member of the Maquis in Lyon could not walk a dozen yards
without running into a secret comrade-in-arms he had to pretend not
to know. At first the clandestine excesses of *résistants* became a
national joke. Some of them actually adopted dark glasses, false
beards and briefcases.

The risks of concentrating so many *résistants* in a single city were obvious. Security was abysmal. They always tended to choose the same spots in the city for secret rendezvous, such as the Port Morand, the steps of the municipal theatre, and 'under the tail of the bronze horse' at the equestrian statue of Louis XIV in the Place Bellecour. The desire to attack and hurt the enemy, while at the same time remain secretive and discreet, was a conflict impossible to overcome. Haphazard recruitment, youthful boasting, inexperience and lack of training often led to disastrous results when the arrest of a single individual inevitably implicated a chain of colleagues.[4]

The effective reorganisation of the Résistance was largely the work of Jean Moulin, a man whose bravery and exploits became one of the lasting legends of the war. Small, reserved and nondescript, he did not look much like a hero and seemed cast more in the mould of a senior bureaucrat than a secret warrior. As the youngest regional governor in France, of the Département Eure et Loire, he had been arrested by the Germans in Chartres, where only eight hundred of the population remained after the German invasion. He was tortured when he refused to sign a document stating that Senegalese troops of the French Army had committed atrocities against civilians. He was released after he tried to commit suicide by cutting his throat with a piece of broken glass. Vichy immediately relieved him of his position on the grounds of his 'attachment to the *ancien regime*'.

He spent a year in the Free Zone making contact with Résistance groups, and then made a dangerous journey under an assumed name to London, where he joined General de Gaulle and the Free French. At the beginning of 1941 he was parachuted back into France in Provence, under the codename Max, and set to work reorganising the Résistance. His first step in the grand plan was the creation of the Armée Secrète (Secret Army), designed to co-ordinate paramilitary action among the various Résistance groups in the Free Zone. Each was reluctant to accept a single, Gaullist command structure, and it took considerable skill to convince and cajole the various factions. The Communists of the FTP refused to integrate until they were forced into making an alliance when Moulin cut off military subsidies from London.

It was this new structure – the Secret Army – that Michel now joined, travelling between Lyon and Grenoble. He had arrived in Lyon in September 1942 at a time when the popular mood was slowly turning against the Vichy government and the Résistance was beginning to take more effective shape. Attitudes among the French at large were changing towards the Germans following savage reprisals against hostages and the introduction of a forced-labour law. Volunteers had failed to present themselves in sufficient numbers to go and work in Germany with the result that Vichy now drafted young Frenchmen. Service du Travail Obligatoire (STO) affected a large section of the population so that many previously uncommitted young men joined the Maquis.

The Grenoble Résistance undertook to provide Michel with a complete set of 'genuine' false papers. He was sent to see the mayor of Villard de Lans, a small town in the heart of the Vercors region of the Alps, who issued ID papers in the name of Michel Sberro, a Frenchman from a bombed-out village in Tunisia. 'After the Allies invaded north Africa we used these identities because the Nazis couldn't check them.' He was also given demobilisation papers and a *carte d'alimentation* that enabled him to receive ration coupons.

Michel's job was to recruit the disaffected to the cause. 'Vichy France made my job easier with the forced-labour decree.' Many young Frenchmen balked at the idea of going to work in Germany after the Résistance explained that they would, in effect, be fighting for the Nazis. 'I told them it was their choice: "If you go to Germany you will replace a worker who will go to fight. So go and fight for Nazi Germany or for France."' In fact, Michel was well aware that the choice was not so simple. 'It often set them against their families. Pétainistes did not want their sons to avoid the draft and put themselves outside the law. So many wavered, unable to decide. Anyone who did not go automatically became an outlaw. But I could offer these men the opportunity to join a whole army of outlaws known as the Maquis.'[5] The impassioned call to fight for the historic French principles of liberty, equality and fraternity earned Michel the nickname among his fellow *résistants* of 'Le Patriote'.

He worked with a Catholic priest in Lyon, Abbé Alexandre Glasberg, whose humanitarian work inevitably led him into underground activity. 'Lyon was one of the few cities in France where the churches opened their doors offering sanctuary,' Michel explained, 'but the Vichy authorities blocked the doors and prevented food being brought in. Then they waited for the Jews to starve or come out and be captured.' Born a Polish Jew, Glasberg was a rumpled, myopic, untidy bear of a man who wore a tentlike black cassock. He managed to obtain the release of more than fifty adults from Gurs alone, hid Jewish families and provided them with false papers. He charmed, inveigled and browbeat mayors, prefects and policemen to agree to his plans for centres and residences to receive Jews liberated from camps. Glasberg became a one-man amateur social service, and the chaos of the times meant that numerous bureaucrats bowed to the assumed authority of this eccentric and troublesome priest. Later, he became openly defiant of Vichy and finally moved into armed resistance.[6] Michel and Glasberg had much in common and instantly took to each other, speaking in Yiddish together, but never in Polish.

Michel learned that the previous August, when he had been in Les Milles, the priest had witnessed a round-up of Jews in Lyon. He had gone to an empty factory on the outskirts of the city that had been converted into a camp to visit five hundred and fifty men, women and children who were to be transported to Drancy, and eventually Auschwitz. He found families huddled together in the dark, frightened and confused, and tried to persuade the parents to hand over their children to his care so that he might save them. It was sad work, but he officially took care of eighty-four children – and a further forty unofficially – and moved them to safe houses in Lyon.

This had been a precarious undertaking. A telegram from national police HQ to the police chief of the camp arrived at the factory the evening the departure was being organised. It specifically prohibited adults expelled to the Occupied Zone from leaving their children behind. Glasberg intercepted it and hid it in his cassock, alongside a collection of letters from prisoners for delivery to family and friends. As a result, the police chief never learned of the change in orders.

The children left at dawn on two buses, while a couple over the age limit were hidden in Glasberg's official-looking black *traction avant* Citroën, the type of government car driven by the local prefect and the Gestapo. Black government cars were saluted, not checked.

Three days later the chief of police in Lyon requested troops from the city's military commander to keep order when the Jews were loaded on to trains. General Robert de Saint-Vincent replied, 'I will never lend my troops for this type of operation.' He was immediately ordered by his superiors to resign his commission. But he did not send the troops.

When the Jews were transported, it was noted that eighty-four children had been taken by priests. Cardinal Gerlier, Archbishop of Lyon, was told over the telephone by the prefect, 'Tonight, there is a train coming from Les Milles camp with Jews that we are turning over to the Germans. We will add a car so that you can put the children that you have on board. I ask you to bring these children to the station.'

'Monsieur *le Préfet*,' Gerlier said, 'their families have entrusted these children to me. You are not going to ask a father to deliver his children to the police, I hope.' The prefect was adamant, but so was the cardinal. 'You're not getting the children,' he said, and hung up.

Priests took the children and hid them in homes with Catholic families around Lyon. The cardinal wrote an anguished pastoral letter: 'The new measures of deportation taking place against the Jews are leading to such painful scenes that we have the imperative and painful duty of protesting. We are seeing a cruel dispersion of families where nothing is spared, not age, not weakness, not illness. The heart is wrenched at the thought of the treatment received by thousands of human beings, and even more at the thought of what cannot be foreseen.'

It was a chilling glimpse into the near future.

On the morning of 11 November 1942, the Germans crossed the Demarcation Line and occupied the whole country. There was no official resistance and no bloodshed. The Germans reported gratefully that the French Armistice Army had remained 'loyal' during the operation, and that the French police had been equally helpful. The general population met the occupation with apathy, while the government adopted a bureaucratic policy of maintaining correct relations with the conqueror. The Italians now occupied the Riviera and the French Alps, including Grenoble, and created a zone separated by the Rhône.

The takeover – Operation Attila – was triggered by the unexpected news that an American invasion force was disembarking in French colonies in north Africa administered by Vichy. United States president Franklin Roosevelt appealed to the French forces not to resist the Allies, but Marshal Pétain, outraged and shaken by the invasion, ordered them to fight the American and British forces to the bitter end.

Encouraged by reports of French warships defending north Africa, Hitler sent word to the French government asking whether they were now seriously willing to join the Germans in the fight against the British and the Americans. This would entail a complete break in diplomatic relations with the Allies and a declaration of war. 'If the French government makes an unambiguous declaration like this, then we would be ready to go through thick and thin with the French government.' Hitler both hoped and expected France to join the Axis cause.

However, France's military commanders no longer shared their political leaders' aims. Admiral Darlan, the supreme commander, was already in Algiers and had switched sides to join General de

Gaulle and the Free French. Hitler reacted by ordering the disarmament of Pétain's forces – in particular the hundred-thousand-man Armistice Army that had been so loyal. The French fleet in Toulon – three battleships, an aircraft carrier and more than thirty destroyers – was scuttled. France had now lost everything – her military forces and control of her colonies – and Vichy had lost its credibility.[7] Perceptions among a growing section of the population changed, and now German victory seemed less than certain. New graffiti began to appear: VIVE L'AMÉRIQUE!

In Lyon, German tanks rolled into the Place des Terreaux and once again the swastika replaced the tricolour over the entrance to the city hall. But there was no fuss as the Germans took over prisons, hospitals and military barracks. Eighty SS officers, including Klaus Barbie, arrived in the city. The Gestapo made its headquarters in the Hotel Terminus, beside the Perrache railway station, on the tip of the peninsula formed by the Rhône and Saone rivers. Forty officers remained in Lyon, while thirty were posted to surrounding towns and villages.

Barbie, as head of the Gestapo, had a large staff working under him, and inherited a network of French agents and informers from Vichy. These included prostitutes, criminals, and the barman at Le Perroquet. Informers and collaborators were everywhere. At first the Gestapo went about its business surreptitiously, and the locals were both surprised and relieved to find that life under German occupation was little worse than that under Vichy. Then, at the end of November, two young men on bicycles shot and wounded a German soldier in the Place Bellecour, setting off a series of arrests and reprisals. But still the repression seemed nothing much out of the ordinary, the lull before the storm.

On the surface nothing had changed, and Michel continued his activities with the Résistance. He was now living in Grenoble, a safer place to be because it came under the control of the Italians who now oversaw eight French *départements*. The Italian Army, Foreign Ministry, diplomatic corps and common soldiers went to extraordinary lengths to protect Jews and confound the Germans and Vichy authorities. Although officially anti-Semitic, the Italians ignored repeated demands to deport Jews living in their zone, conspiring to create frustrating bureaucratic obstructions to thwart both the Germans and Vichy, and disregarding all sorts of official anti-Jewish directives and laws. They resorted to subterfuge, feigned incompetence and outright lies.

Not only did the Italians protect French Jews, they also extended their protection to include foreign refugees. This led to direct confrontation with the Vichy administration when, in December 1942, the arch-collaborationist prefect of the Alpes-Maritimes, who was a personal friend of Marshal Pétain, ordered all foreign Jews in his *département* in the Italian zone to be sent to enforced residence in the German zone, where subsequent deportation was then inevitable. Italian Foreign Ministry officials simply cancelled the order, claiming that non-French Jews came under their care. Prime Minister Laval protested. The Italians ignored him and prevented the introduction of other anti-Jewish measures. They forbade the word 'Jew' to be stamped on ID papers and ration books, and refused to allow forced-labour camps in their zone. They went as far as to order the Vichy government to annul the arrest and internment of all Jews in the Italian zone, which meant the immediate release of a hundred people awaiting deportation and death. Italian soldiers actually showed up at the prison in Grenoble to ensure their safe passage. The Germans were enraged, but powerless to do anything.[8]

Michel, meanwhile, worked to establish a separate Jewish unit within the Secret Army that would fight under its own flag. Headquarters had given its approval to recruit for such a force and agreed to supply it, but the response from Jewish organisations was not enthusiastic. Michel was greatly disappointed to be turned down flat by the secret local Zionist organisation in Grenoble that insisted its priority was to hide Jewish families and keep them together. 'To me it made no sense. I told them of my escape and that deportation meant death. It was stupidity.' Rebuffed by the Zionists in Grenoble, Michel spent more time in Lyon where he undertook the lengthy and risky process of recruiting one individual at a time.

Even with a full set of forged documents, Michel had to exercise great care in his daily life. He took to carrying a portfolio of his own paintings, a cover that gave him the added benefit of not having to declare a fixed place of work. At any time whole streets would be cordoned off in sudden raids and anyone in them subjected to a *contrôle* – when the police checked papers. 'These were nerve-racking. Through experience I had learned not to run away from danger but to confront it and do the unexpected. If caught within a *contrôle* I would walk up to the police and ask for information, like the address of an official building. Often they would answer instead of checking my documents. At other times, I would get indignant and complain that my papers had been checked only minutes before. "Goddamn it, this is the fourth time I've been asked!" Sometimes they would wave me on, occasionally even with an apology.'

It was during this period in Lyon that he met a French girl who had her own apartment. 'It was good to have a relationship with an independent girl who was strong and successful. We became close immediately and both needed each other emotionally and physically. I was so pleased to have found her and to have found a safe place to stay with a non-Jewish girl who had strong feelings about the Résistance. Then on the night we became lovers she started crying bitterly. We were getting along very well, there had been no argument or anything, so I just couldn't understand.' At first the girl refused, or was unable, to explain her anguish. Then she blurted out that she knew Michel was a Jew.

'Circumcision had given me away. It was very rare among non-Jews in those days. And then the girl told me what it meant to her that I was Jewish and why it made her so distraught. She too was Jewish, living an unsafe life with false papers. She had been so happy to meet a Frenchman she cared for who was not Jewish. She had held out so much hope. And there we were – two people pretending not to be Jews discovering that the other was Jewish. She felt it threatened her life, and the only way to survive was to be far removed from it, and to avoid all contact with Jews. I understood. I too had been happy under the illusion she was not Jewish. She needed it and I needed it, and when we found out the truth it was over.'

The following morning he left the apartment early and never saw her again.

One cold winter's morning, Michel made his way to visit the main Lyon office of the Union Général des Israelites de France, an officially recognised Jewish welfare organisation that was a magnet for the numerous German and Austrian refugees in the city. Before the occupation the UGIF had maintained good relations with Vichy, and one of their reports written in June stated: 'We are finding understanding and even cordiality from most of the authorities. This goes for most of the civil servants and employers.'

After the arrival of the Germans the organisation openly continued to provide services for Jewish refugees, offering money, work and help in communicating with relatives incarcerated within France. It also paid for doctors and lawyers. In secret, it smuggled Jews into Switzerland and provided false papers. The organisation was an obvious target for the Gestapo, but continued to operate under an unrealistic and false sense of security. The reason there had been no extra pressure on foreign Jews since the arrival of the Gestapo was because no trains had been available for deportations since November due to military disasters on the Russian front. In Berlin, Adolf Eichmann was concerned that the French had fallen behind in terms of meeting their quota of Jews, and with the beginning of a new year he looked for improvements. Trains were promised by mid-February and the Gestapo in France was expected to fill them.[9]

Michel's destination on 9 February 1943 was the UGIF office at 9 Rue St Catharine where refugees congregated at the beginning of each week. 'In the past I had been able to supply ration cards to the committee, but on that day I was in search of recruits for a Jewish fighting unit for the Secret Army.' The office was always crowded on Mondays when money was paid out and a doctor and nurse were on hand. The refugees were made up mostly of individual German or Austrian Jews from dispersed families, people without belongings or a place to stay. The UGIF had attempted to enrol the help of rich Jewish families in the city, but reported, 'Alas! The results have been so disappointing we don't even dare quote the number of replies.'[10]

It was a miserable, grey day as Michel pushed his way through the streets carrying his portfolio of art under his arm. He battled the bitter wind and rehearsed his recruitment pitch, in which he warned of the dangers of deportation by telling stories of his experiences in Les Milles, and extolling life in the Résistance. He arrived at the building and began to climb the stairway to the office.

Halfway up the stairs he paused, overtaken by a profound sense of foreboding. 'Something told me to stop.' He looked around him but nothing seemed out of the ordinary. 'I shook off the feeling and continued on my way. But it persisted, grew stronger and stronger. I stopped again.' But there was nothing. He told himself that he was merely suffering from the inevitable paranoia that accompanied the clandestine life. It was simply a case of nerves.

On arrival at the second floor the feeling became overwhelming. 'This time I heard an inner voice, clear and frightening: *Don't go!* Of course I knew it was in my mind and tried to ignore it, but the voice kept on: *Don't go – the Gestapo is there.*' The Gestapo at this time had not become visible in the daily life of the city and Michel had never concerned himself about them before. 'Why should the Gestapo be here? Why am I standing listening to voices? Can Le Patriote go back to his headquarters and say, "Yes, I was on my way to the meeting but I heard voices so I turned back"?'

He calmed himself and continued, almost laughing out loud at the absurdity of his fears. He forced himself to walk along the corridor to the door of the office, but was unable to shake off the sense of dread. 'I approached the door cautiously, listening for anything abnormal. I asked myself what the matter was. What is it? I told myself that I wouldn't go in. That I was just going to listen, and if I heard anything strange I'd go away.'

He stood outside the door. Again, nothing. He was now thoroughly ashamed of himself. He was just plain scared, he told himself – a coward. The thought shocked him, but unable to shake off the premonition he decided on a compromise. He would push the door open a little, just a crack, and peer inside. If anything was out of the ordinary he would follow his instincts and leave.

As he turned the knob and gently eased the door open, it was yanked violently from inside. A uniformed Gestapo officer grabbed him by the scruff of the neck and pulled him forward. '*Kommen Sie'rein!*' he barked in German – come in! '*Geheime Staatspolizei!*'

A group of Gestapo officers stood in the small reception area.

'I must have made a mistake,' Michel said in French. 'I must be in the wrong place.'

'Oh no, this is the right place,' one of the agents replied in German. 'Who are you? Where are your papers?'

Michel, of course, understood every word but decided to play the role of a French artist who had dropped by to sell his paintings. The Gestapo had raided the place to arrest Austrian and German refugees and expected everyone to speak German. The officer continued to rant at him in German when the door opened and more people entered. They too were grabbed and berated by the Germans. 'I knew two of them from the cafés and my heart jumped. If one gave the slightest sign of recognition my little game was over. But they were either too stunned or too scared to acknowledge my presence.'

He was part-pulled, part-pushed into a large room that served as the main office. Cowed refugees were huddled everywhere, pressed against the walls. The Gestapo had arrived early in the morning and detained everyone who entered the office, and by the day's end there would be a hundred of them. Michel was steered towards a man in civilian clothes, the only person in the room who was seated. He was behind a table that served as a desk and Michel was ordered to stand a respectful distance in front of it. The man was Klaus Barbie, although Michel did not hear the name at this time and would not have recognised it if he had. The only obviously striking thing about him was how small he was compared to the other Gestapo officers.

111

One of them now explained to his chief that Michel had arrived on his own and did not seem to be part of any group. 'This one only seems to speak French.'

Barbie inspected Michel closely, and barked, '*Ihre Ausweispapiere!*' – identity papers! Michel knew enough about the deportation policy to know he was doomed if he was suspected of being a German-speaking foreign Jew. Barbie repeated the question. '*Wo sind Ihre Ausweispapiere?*'

Michel pretended to be bewildered and protested in French that he did not know what was going on. He insisted that he had made a mistake and had come to the wrong place, and begged somebody to translate for him. 'It's a mistake . . . a mistake! Isn't there anybody here who speaks French?'

Barbie nodded at one of the Gestapo men standing behind Michel. He heard what sounded like a gun being taken from its holster. The officer spoke calmly in German to his colleague. '*Na, ich werde den da einfach abschiessen*' – Ach, I'll just shoot him down. He leaned close and spoke to the back of Michel's head. '*Wie soll ich das tun? Einen Schuss ins Genick? Oder eine Kugel in den Kopf? Oder ins Ohr?*' – How shall I do it? Shall I shoot him through the neck? Or a bullet through the head? Or into the ear?

Michel remained deadpan. 'I could show no reaction. No reaction at all. I knew that I had to remain calm and I could not betray the slightest acknowledgement that I understood. Any reflex on my part suggesting I understood what he was saying would have meant death.'

Barbie watched the performance carefully as the game played itself out, then suddenly seemed to lose interest. He jumped up, held out his hand and snapped, '*Verdammt noch mal! Haben Sie denn keine Identitätspapiere?*' – Goddamn it, don't you have any identity papers?

Michel pretended to latch on to the word *identitätspapiere* because of its similarity to the French equivalent *pièces d'identité*. '*Ah, vous voulez mes pièces d'identité!*' he said, feigning enormous relief. '*Mais oui, bien sûr! Voilà!*' He handed over documents that identified him as the Frenchman Michel Sberro from Tunisia.

Barbie sat down, spread the documents across the table and began to question him in reasonable French. He was subjected to a lengthy and detailed interrogation, frequently interrupted as other refugees arrived and were brought into the room. 'So I told my cover story. That I was a freelance artist. That was why I was carrying my portfolio of paintings. I had met a gentleman with an address in the building who had expressed interest in buying, but evidently I made a mistake and came to the wrong office.'

Barbie listened, but looked sceptical. He opened the portfolio and inspected the contents, looking at each painting. Suddenly, he gathered up the ID papers, returned the paintings to their portfolio and handed them back. 'You can leave. *Au revoir.*'

Au revoir. Until we meet again.[11]

The incident had a profound influence not only on the way Michel thought, but on the way he acted for the rest of the war. 'It taught me to trust my instincts and premonitions. Before that I had been a strict rationalist. I learned to listen to my inner voices.'

Once outside the building, Michel went to a phone and placed a number of calls to Résistance friends and Jewish organisations. They immediately went to visit the various cafés used by the refugees to alert them of the Gestapo trap in the Rue St Catharine. 'We warned as many as we could and also set up a network of people in the area to interrupt anyone on their way to the office. Despite the danger there were people who didn't want to believe me. I had to insist.'

That winter's day in February 1943 marked the beginning of Barbie's terror operations in the city, and the brutality of his methods would earn him the title 'Butcher of Lyon'. Almost a hundred foreign Jews were arrested at the office in the Rue St Catharine, and eighty-six were transported to Auschwitz and their deaths. Later, Barbie would claim that he did not know the fate of those he sent away, but when a UGIF committee member tried repeatedly to persuade Barbie not to shoot arrested Jews, he replied, 'Shot or deported, there's no difference.' It is estimated that by the end of the war seven thousand, five hundred and ninety-one people were deported from Lyon by the Gestapo.

The Gestapo had commandeered sixty rooms on the second and third floors of the Hotel Terminus, twenty of which were for the interrogation of prisoners brought daily from Montluc prison. Barbie, then aged twenty-nine, divided his department into six specialist sections: Résistance and Communists; Sabotage; Jews; False ID; Counter-intelligence; and Intelligence. At first there were twenty-five men working under him, a number that gradually increased over time as he became responsible for an area covering fifteen thousand square miles. He was a hard-driving, efficient workaholic feared by his own men, with the absolute power of life and death over his victims. He also carried a personal grudge against the French: his father had been seriously wounded in the First World War.

In the weeks following the takeover of the city, Barbie worked to build up his connections with Frenchmen he considered sympathetic and trustworthy. Special kiosks for denunciations were introduced at which queues formed every day. Later, he said, 'Without them I could never have done my job so well . . . At the beginning it was very hard for us. We had very few contacts. Everything was new. I had to build an effective team, carefully handpicking each recruit. We were showered with denunciations of the Résistance by the French and I usually tried to find long-term collaborators from amongst the denunciators.'[12]

These French collaborators, handpicked by Barbie, came to form a private army one hundred and twenty strong dedicated to fighting terror with terror: 'Millionaire Jews, bourgeois freemasons, you who subsidise and arm the assassins, you will pay with your life.' The Gestapo expanded its torture facilities when it took over a large military school where three vast cellars were converted into cells. After initial interrogation on the ground floor, the prisoners were taken to specially equipped rooms on the fourth. Each room had one or two baths, a table with leather straps, a gas oven for heating pokers red hot, and electrical prongs. As music played in the background, men and women were stripped naked and hung from the ceiling by their wrists; children were tortured in front of their parents. The tortures imposed were a diabolical blend of ancient and modern: victims were plunged into freezing or boiling water, burned with cigarettes, had three-inch needles rammed into their rib cages, and acid injected into their bladders. They were savaged by dogs and had their backs broken with a spiked iron ball. Fingers and toes were severed with blunt knives, nipples ripped off with metal tongs, and one man had his eyes put out and was scalped. The workaholic Barbie was often present at these torture sessions. In between the ministrations of his experts he chose to work victims over with a leather cosh, pausing only to sip from a glass of beer or take a bite from a sandwich.

The escape from the encounter with this monster at Rue St Catharine saved Michel from a similar fate. His superiors in the Secret Army now considered him to be in great danger in Lyon. To slip through the fingers of Klaus Barbie once was great good luck; a second meeting would almost certainly prove fatal. Michel was issued with yet another identity and told to remain in Grenoble.

The pace of Michel's Résistance activities quickened, and he worked around the clock, happy to be fighting back. His dedication and steely resolve soon attracted the attention of local leaders who burdened him with new duties and responsibilities. He still occasionally ran the gauntlet of *contrôles* and road blocks to go into

Lyon, but most of the workload revolved around Grenoble. Although the city came under the jurisdiction of the tolerant Italians, the Gestapo employed the Milice, its home-grown French equivalent, to carry out its dirty work in the region.

The Milice was a political police force that had been created at the beginning of the year and was to give the Gestapo a run for its money in terms of violence and ruthlessness. The struggle between the Résistance and the Milice over the next eighteen months would take on the vicious nature of a civil war. The Milice was led by Joseph Darnand, a conspicuous and eager collaborator. He was the son of a railway worker and had little education but was a genuine hero of the First World War, one of only three men in 1918 to be given a citation ordaining them 'artisans of the final victory'. He had been awarded the nation's highest soldier's decoration, the *médaille militaire*, by Marshal Pétain himself, although the old man had remarked that Darnand possessed 'as much political intelligence as a kerbstone'. Despite his great personal bravery, and love of military life, the army did not consider him officer material. After the war Darnand ran a garage in Nice, nursing his bitterness about being passed over for a commission, and became a militant fascist denouncing Jews, Communists and Freemasons.

Darnand's speciality in war had been guerrilla exploits behind enemy lines, and now the poacher turned heartless gamekeeper. His view on the Résistance was straightforward: 'What is this Résistance shit? Shepherds to whom the archangel appeared?' His view of de Gaulle was similarly robust: 'He's surrounded by Jews and Freemasons and assorted deserters.'[13]

As local police, and even some German military units, lost their stomach for civilian repression, Darnand's Milice filled the gap. At last the Nazis had what they had always hoped for in France – a paramilitary political police force manned by native toughs. It numbered twenty-nine thousand men and women throughout the country, and its members were chosen for ideological fervour rather than professional competence. The fanatic and unscrupulous Darnand, together with eleven of his senior men, were granted the great honour of being allowed to take the oath of loyalty to Hitler and being admitted into the Waffen-SS.

The uniform of the Milice comprised a dark blue jacket and trousers, khaki shirt, black tie and beret. Its emblem was a white gamma, the zodiacal sign of the ram. It had a marching song that proclaimed: 'For those who brought our defeat/No punishment is harsh enough.' The oath of allegiance made it clear exactly who was responsible for France's defeat. Members swore to 'fight against democracy, against Gaullist insurrection and against Jewish leprosy'.

The moment the Germans crossed the Demarcation Line, Darnand proudly declared his intention to work with the occupiers, an action that bestowed power on the Milice out of all proportion to its membership. While other French military units were disarmed, the Milice received weapons from the Germans and *carte blanche* to pursue Jews, as well as the power to denounce those in authority who did not demonstrate their zeal for collaboration. The Milice became intensely unpopular among fellow Frenchmen of all persuasions, who accurately saw its members as thugs in the pay of the Germans.[14]

The Nazis found the work of the Milice exemplary, and commended them in particular for their single-minded pursuit of Jews. The Germans, after all, were strangers to the area and could be fooled, as Michel had demonstrated, but the *miliciens* were locals with none of the growing moral doubt or increased reluctance displayed by many of the police. And it was local knowledge that led to Michel's arrest at the end of March.[15]

He was sitting in a café in the town with a Résistance colleague when four members of the Milice entered and took them to the local HQ in Grenoble. It became clear during questioning that Michel's interrogators knew about his role in the Résistance, although he naturally denied everything. Strangely, the Milice seemed disinclined to argue. The questioning stopped and the men sat in silence, regarding him with little more than disinterested curiosity.

The door to the interrogation room opened and a young Résistance member of his group was pushed into the room. He was in bad shape and had obviously been beaten, and Michel knew at once the source of the Milice's information.

'Do you know him?' one of the officers asked Michel, pointing at the young man.

'No, I don't.'

'Is this the one?' they asked the young man, nodding towards Michel.

'No,' the *résistant* said firmly. 'You made a mistake. I don't know this man.'

The Milice went into action. The man was thrown to the floor where he was punched and kicked. Two men held him down while a third appeared with a short metal rod. He rammed it into a pressure point between the man's neck and shoulders and he screamed in pain. He began to babble, confirming Michel's identity as his Résistance cell leader. Then he lay on the floor sobbing before he was carried out.[16]

The Milice now turned their attention to Michel. His fake papers no longer served as a cover, although he continued to deny he was a member of the Résistance. He insisted that he did not know the young man, who had implicated him merely to save his own skin.

His interrogators did not bother to contest his protestations of innocence. 'We know you are scheduled to have a meeting,' one said. 'Save us time and trouble, and yourself a lot of pain, by telling us when and where.'

At first, Michel denied all knowledge of any meeting, but he had already seen what was in store for him if he continued to keep silent. 'Their information was correct. The meeting was scheduled for five o'clock that afternoon. We had a rule that if any individual was more than five minutes late for a rendezvous the others must scatter. I needed to gain time – delay the arrival of the Milice until after the deadline.' He told them he knew nothing of any meeting.

At first the Milice merely intensified their questioning, and then made a series of physical threats, culminating with a beating. 'Just tell us where the meeting is and when. Save yourself unnecessary pain.'

Michel pretended to give in and began to talk, naming the place and time. He knew that the next step would be torture, and was unsure how he would react. He reasoned that he would gain enough time to ensure that the meeting would be abandoned if he sent them on a false trail. 'There's to be a meeting at the station at five,' he said, slowly. The Milice demanded names. Michel pretended to be reluctant to give these and was encouraged to speak with the threat of another beating. He gave them half a dozen unconnected first names.

'What are their family names?'

'We don't use family names.'

'Give us a description.'

A fantasy description of every one of the half dozen was forced from him, and he gave a convincing performance. The meeting had genuinely been set for five, but far away from the station.

He was locked in a dark room where he contemplated the return of the Milice from their wild goose chase. He had sent violent and dangerous men on a false trail, and when they discovered the truth they would come for him to vent their anger. He vividly recalled the precision with which one of the *miliciens* had used the metal rod on the young *résistant*, and the man's unearthly screaming. 'All I knew for certain was that I would be tortured soon, and I wondered how I would take it. Would I be able to stand it, how would I react, would I talk, would I break down? I tried to prepare myself. We cannot evaluate or judge ourselves unless we go through certain experiences. I had learned in the Résistance that strong men who looked the embodiment of heroism, who talked big, could fall apart at the first sign of danger. While seventeen-year-old girls, little frail wisps of things, could be so very brave. There were weak-looking men who never cracked under torture, and tough guys who wept and broke in the first moments. There was no pattern, no rule.'

He was brought back to the interrogation chamber to face his persecutors once again. There was a distinct change of atmosphere. The men seemed settled into a calm, deadly anger, and their body language suggested they had resigned themselves to a late night of hard work. Their leader said they had checked Michel's papers and determined that they were false. They had gone to the place he had told them about and found no one. So they would have to start all over again. They wanted to know everything about him and his Résistance activities. And he could start by telling them his real name.

Michel repeated what he had originally told them. They waited, almost politely, for him to finish and then one of them moved towards him. 'Come on,' Michel said quietly. 'You're stronger here – show your strength! I promise not to defend myself. I am ready for you. You can do it – go ahead!'

The man stopped, momentarily uncertain of how to proceed. He looked back at his colleagues for support. There was a moment of hesitation before they moved upon him as a single being. They punched and kicked him, shouting obscenities. One pushed a thumb between his neck and collarbone and the pain was so great he thought he would pass out. He cried out and they stopped briefly to question him.

'Tell us who you are! We want your true identity now!'

He was knocked to the ground and held while his hands and feet were placed in a press. As the screws were slowly tightened they screamed at him to tell them his name. 'I knew I had to tell them something new. I could not revert to my real name – Michel Kroskof was a condemned Jewish escapee from Les Milles. So I focused all my concentration on inventing a new identity, one that I had to make them think was real and that I wanted to protect.

'Every time I stopped talking they resumed their torture. So the secret was obviously to keep talking, but the only time I was able to think and concentrate on a new story was under torture. I was concentrating so strongly on making up a believable story that I wasn't talking. So they were applying more and more torture. And then I noticed something that really alarmed me. I did not feel the pain.'

He not only felt nothing but also showed no pain, so his torturers continued to tighten the screws on the press, slowly crushing the bones in his toes and knuckles. One of the Milice was so frustrated by his victim's lack of response that he clubbed him a terrific blow on the right shoulder, instantly creating a huge lump he would carry for the rest of his life.

He heard a distant, angry voice: '*Merde*, he doesn't show any pain.'

Oh God, Michel thought, I do not show pain! I do not feel pain! He knew that if he did not react they would kill him. 'So I began to fake the pain, grimacing in agony. I kept repeating to myself over and over, like a broken record: "Show pain, show pain, show pain!"'

The need to be seen to react to the torture interfered with the intense concentration on what to say. It took him hours to make up a story plausible enough to tell them when he judged it was time to feign breakdown. Meanwhile, he was smashed in the left eye, which began to swell and close, and he saw his persecutors take out the same steel rod used on his colleague. The rod was applied to pressure points on both shoulders between the neck and the collarbone. 'But still I felt nothing. The pain never reached me, although now I acted convincingly as if it did.'

During the six hours of torture and interrogation he supplied his interrogators with his identity and activities. He told them he was a Pole by the name of Kowalski who had been in the army and put in a POW camp in Belgium at the beginning of the war. He had escaped and made it to France where he had been reduced to making a living from the black market selling food stamps. He calculated that by confessing to the lesser crime of black-marketeering, he might escape the consequences of the greater crime of being a Jew. He was very convincing, occasionally breaking into long bursts of distraught Polish. 'I could not prove it, of course, but I had constructed a completely viable false identity they could not disprove.'

Satisfied that the 'broken' man had told everything, the Milice threw him into a large, gloomy room containing a dozen prisoners. 'I was a mess. The other prisoners couldn't believe what I was like.

They looked at me in horror. They couldn't believe how I had got into such a terrible state without hearing me scream.'

The next morning he was moved to a jail in Grenoble. Conditions were predictably awful and prisoners had to tolerate bedbugs, lice and fleas, while crabs lodged in their pubic hair. He remained untreated in jail as he slowly regained his strength and health. His spirit had not been broken, but now he did feel pain, a constant hurt that racked his body from his swollen eye and damaged shoulders to his crushed fingers and toes. He tried to understand what resource he had drawn from to mask the pain of torture. 'I contemplated the untapped reserves of the human mind. The great hidden depths of the brain. I learned from it.'[17]

There was a daily turnover of prisoners. No one knew whether those who left were shot or released, and nobody much wanted to find out. A new arrival brought hope in the shape of a message for him from the Résistance: DO NOT DESPAIR – WE ARE WORKING FOR YOU!

One morning the guards came for him. He was ordered out of the cell and marched along the corridor. With every step he feared his fate might be a bullet in the back of the head in some gloomy, echoing courtyard. He was loaded into a prison van and taken to the Grenoble court house where he was formally charged with black-marketeering, being in possession of false papers and illegal entry into France. As he looked about him he felt a surge of hope as he spotted Sammy Lattès among the spectators, one of the leaders of the Grenoble Résistance. Lattès had made an arrangement with the judge, who was a secret Résistance sympathiser. Michel was sentenced to a period on parole, which meant immediate release.

The black-marketeer Kowalski was taken to the home of René Gosse, a distinguished professor at the university. Gosse, a mathematician, had been Dean of the Faculty of Science at Grenoble and, as a socialist and vocal anti-fascist throughout the 1930s, had used his position to oppose the armistice. As a result he had been relieved of his administrative post, although he was allowed to remain at the university as a professor. His efforts at sedition had been so successful that he was largely responsible for a report sent to the Prefect of the Ministry of the Interior: 'Grenoble is the centre of propaganda which is anti-government, Anglophile and Gaullist.'[18]

The Secret Army now decided that Michel would no longer be safe or effective in Grenoble, and that he should move out of town into the mountains. He was given a set of false documents for his fifth and final identity in the Résistance, the name he has chosen to live under ever since: Michel Thomas. 'The papers were provided by Sammy Lattès, whom I have always considered my godfather. Sammy was very active in the Grenoble Résistance and it was his family in Lyon who had first helped me. I consider that he saved my life and gave me the papers for my chosen identity. So I owe him my life and my name.'[19]

Michel was posted to the village of Biviers, situated on an Alpine slope nine miles outside Grenoble, and billeted on a sixty-five-year-old spinster. Mademoiselle Thérèse Mathieu had been a teacher all her life, and had retired as head of the region's teacher training college, École Normale. A tall, dignified and correct woman, her reserved exterior concealed enormous strength and courage. Thérèse Mathieu had the heart of a lion and restored Michel's faith in the nation. 'The French seem to me a people who are capable of the very heights of human achievement and nobility – and also of plunging to the depths of human behaviour. Thérèse Mathieu, and others like her, displayed the noblest, the highest calibre of human strength and dignity. That's why my own feelings about France are not torn – divided, but I hope not torn. Because I cannot betray my feelings for Thérèse Mathieu. To me, noble people like that – and there were many of them – outweigh the evil committed by hundreds of thousands. I found that type among the French which I admire and love – a deep love. They exemplified the greatness of France.'

The moment he entered the woman's home he came under the spell of her calm, powerful presence. There was nothing, her bearing suggested, that could break the spirit of Thérèse Mathieu. She reaffirmed hope, and Michel felt she carried within her the essence of eternal France. 'She was a Catholic, a principled person with a strong value system. She had a strong, healthy love of France, which I found beautiful. She had a deep influence on me. She was a symbol of courage and the highest principles of humanity. She told me: "We don't do these things for decorations or awards. We do these things because we have to."'

Thérèse Mathieu was a highly respected citizen of Biviers, an Alpinist and skier who was in love with the mountains. It aroused the suspicion of no one when this respectable spinster took one of her many solitary skiing or hiking trips in the mountains. Except now she took a secret route across the border into Switzerland and carried vital intelligence in and out of France. The local citizenry might – or might not – have been surprised to see her seated at her kitchen table instructing new members of Michel's commando unit on how to disassemble and clean a machine gun.

For Michel was now working to create and organise the Groupe Biviers, affiliated to the Grésivaudan Secret Army which had its HQ in the Belledonne mountains. He became its administrative chief responsible for paying his "tens" and "thirties" commando groups that were now formed into a rudimentary military organisation. Each man received ten francs a day and was provided with food, clothes and arms. He built a place of refuge in the woods by digging an underground complex designed to house a dozen *résistants*. He became the liaison officer between Grésivaudan, Chartreuse and the Vercors, carrying money from one to the other, riding the only motor bike in the region. He also worked for the Service de Renseignements Départmental (Security Intelligence, which later became the Deuxième Bureau). The name of Le Patriote became widely known.[20]

Mathieu's solid, bourgeois home became the HQ for Michel's Résistance activities, and although poorly armed and supplied, the commando group went increasingly on the offensive. Raids were carried out against both Vichy and German supply depots to seize food and supplies for the increasing number of *maquisards* inhabiting the woods and caves of the region.

He had not been in Biviers long when he reluctantly entered a fateful love affair that he neither encouraged nor wanted. Her name was Diane. 'I did not return the affection because I did not want to be encumbered. Whenever I came back to the house Diane came to greet me. She would leave her house and be happy to just sit and look at me. I never touched her. I didn't want to talk to her. Just for me to be there was enough. I did not want to encourage her or reciprocate in a relationship that I couldn't afford. I never gave her anything to eat or anything to drink. There was nothing for her to get from me. I didn't reject her exactly, but I tried to ignore her.' Diane was one of a pair of Irish setters belonging to a neighbour.

When Michel was away on a mission the dog remained at her home, but the moment he returned she came and sat at his feet in Thérèse Mathieu's kitchen, her large eyes swimming with love. One day Michel was confronted by the neighbour: 'Let's face it, she's your dog. I know how Diane feels – consider her yours.'

Diane moved in and became Michel's constant companion. 'When I went into the mountains I allowed her to come. She would go ahead of me like a hunting dog. Very soon people knew that if they saw Diane, I was somewhere nearby. I did not want to face it, but she was a give-away, a liability.'

Despite the treatment by the Milice, and his contempt and hatred for them, he sought victory not revenge. So when he received an order from headquarters for his group to execute the regional leader he experienced conflicting emotions. 'I organised surveillance. We knew where he lived, established his routine, learned his habits – but I was going through the motions. He was after us and would not have hesitated to have us shot in cold blood. Whenever it came to fixing a time and a place for the act I always found an excuse not to do it. Because I couldn't. I was not an assassin.'

As *chef de section* of a region of the Secret Army, Michel laid down a strict rule that all personal contacts outside of the group must be reported. Two young *résistants* belonging to the Biviers Commando came to him one day and spoke of meeting a pair of pretty girls in Grenoble who needed to be checked out. The girls seemed too keen, and Michel was suspicious.

'Invite them to a little dinner,' Michel said. 'I'll set it up.'

The girls were delighted to be asked to a Saturday night dinner among friends. They were given a phoney location and only told at the last moment of a change in rendezvous. The sudden alteration in the arrangements did not seem to arouse their suspicions and they were driven to a house in Biviers. Members of the commando unit were already at the home of Michel's adjutant, André Valat – a fearless twenty-year-old recruited by Michel – when they arrived. There were also several women belonging to the Maquis, and the group suggested nothing more than an amiable weekend gathering of friends.

One of the girls from Grenoble, whom Michel judged to be the leader of the two, sat next to him. She was an attractive creature, with an engaging personality, although he noticed that she had self-consciously arranged a silk scarf around her neck to hide some sort of disfigurement. She was also a flirt. 'We had a great time, a good dinner with quite a bit to drink. The girls went together to the toilet, and mine left her handbag on her chair.'

While they were gone, Michel went through the bag. Among the papers was a Gestapo pass, signed by Klaus Barbie, of the type issued to French nationals allowing them to avoid curfew and receive privileged treatment from the military. Michel phoned Dax, his district commander, and explained he had found an incriminating document.[21] He gave the name on the girl's pass and explained the suspicious circumstances.

The commander immediately recognised the name. 'Does she have a mark on her neck, a scar that might have been left by a bullet wound?' Michel said that she did. 'She's wanted. We have been looking for her.'

The commander explained that the girl was actually a Francophone Swiss linked to the Milice, and specialised in infiltrating Maquis groups through gullible young males. She had been responsible for a number of deaths. Michel was ordered to keep her amused while men from outside the village were sent over. There was a momentary pause on the line . . . he ought to know, the commander said, that the Résistance had sentenced the girl to death.

Michel put down the phone and rejoined the others. He sat down beside the girl and attempted to continue the flirtation, but his heart was no longer in the game. Any moment an execution squad would arrive. The atmosphere in the room had changed subtly and the girl seemed to sense that something was wrong. 'Perhaps there was something in my manner, perhaps it was a premonition, an animal awareness of impending doom. Without warning the girl fell on my shoulder in hysterics. Her companion just seemed confused and frightened. The girl was shaken by convulsions and screamed out, *"Maman, maman – on va me tuer. Je vais mourir!"* – Mother, mother – they're going to kill me! I'm going to die!'

Unnerved, Michel picked her up and carried her to a back room used for billiards. He laid her on the table and tried to calm her as the convulsions grew so extreme that she had to be held down. Within half an hour two men arrived from HQ, headed by Aimé Recquet, a good friend of Michel who had become a Résistance legend in the Grenoble area when he single-handedly blew up a German ammunition dump.

Nothing was said. Recquet looked across the dimly lit room towards the distraught girl and indicated with a subtle movement of his head that he wanted some sign from Michel to confirm the girl was the one. 'I realised that with a gesture I could wipe out a human life. A slight nod of the head and she would be shot dead. Although I had been told of her crimes, and fully accepted that she was there to destroy us, I could not pass that sentence of death.'

He walked across the room to Recquet and spoke to him quietly. 'Yes, she is the one. But I am against this execution. We have facilities in the mountains now to hold prisoners. The end of the war cannot be very far off – the Allies will be in France soon. It is only a matter of time. Let these girls go before a French court and stand trial. They'll get their just deserts.'

Recquet heard him out, saying nothing. He clapped Michel on the shoulder. 'All right, my soft-hearted friend. We'll do it that way.'

The girl and her companion were taken outside to a waiting car. 'I was relieved. The girl's screams and hysterics – the pathetic cry for her mother – had shaken me. I was pleased to discover that I still retained a trace of humanity despite all I had gone through.'

It was only much later that he realised the extent of his naïvety. After the war he always asked Aimé Recquet on their infrequent reunions about the fate of the girls. His friend shrugged, sounded vague, promised to find out . . . and changed the subject. 'In some ways I am very sophisticated, in others very naïve. It took me years to understand that they would simply have been taken that night up into the mountains. I am certain now that they were shot.'

On the night of 5 June 1944, Résistance groups all over France finally heard the longed-for coded messages from the BBC. The order went out to the Maquis groups to go on an all-out offensive, meaning the wholesale sabotage of road, rail, telephone and power installations aimed at causing widespread German troop disruption. The Biviers Commando worked night and day cutting down telephone poles and blowing up bridges. Michel was elated, a mood that reached its height when news came of the Allied D-Day landing in Normandy. He felt that a second landing in the south could only be days away.

The Résistance in the Alps played a special, symbolic role in the national consciousness, particularly after the establishment of a free mountain state in the Vercors. The message from the BBC to the Maquis of the Vercors was *Le chamois des Alpes bondit* – the Alpine chamois bounds.[22] The regional chief of staff of the Forces Françaises de l'Intérieur – founded by de Gaulle in March 1944 and intended to be the future army of liberated France – stated: 'The Vercors is the only Maquis, in the whole of France, which has been given the mission to set up its own free territory. It will receive the arms, ammunition and troops that will allow it to be the advance guard of a landing in Provence. It is not impossible that de Gaulle himself will land here to make his first proclamation to the French people.'

The Vercors plateau in the mountains south-west of Grenoble had been chosen by the leaders of the Maquis as an impregnable plateau protected on all sides by a natural mountain wall. Only eight roads led to the interior, three of which traversed mountain ridges, so that access to the plateau could only be gained through easily defended mountain passes. Viewed from below, the great half-mile-high limestone cliffs even have the appearance of a natural fortress. Twenty-eight miles long and thirteen wide, with an altitude over three thousand feet, the plateau lies hidden and protected by these cliffs. On the map it is shaped like a crude stone arrowhead defined by two rivers, and seen from the air the terrain is a patchwork of plains and valleys, with waterfalls cascading from sheer cliffs into deep gorges. Good farming land supported a scattered population of five thousand at this time, and the plateau contained one of the largest forests in western Europe, still said to contain bear. Narrow roads linked a score of villages, hamlets and Alpine farms.

This mountain fastness carried enormous emotional and psychological significance for Michel. 'Vercors was the France of the Résistance, the France that fought for freedom, the France I felt a deep love for. Despite my ambivalence because of what happened to me, Vercors brought out the love I felt for the country.'

The day after the D-Day landings, General de Gaulle's Special Projects operations centre in Algiers promised to airlift four thousand men to Vercors. Volunteers from around Grenoble, and the entire mountain region, began to pour in on foot, bicycle, bus and car. These included many regular soldiers and officers from the disbanded Armistice Army. They gathered in previously prepared mobilisation centres, were given a cursory medical check-up, and allocated a unit. Within days the armed forces on the Vercors rose from five hundred to three thousand, and by the end of the summer their number would reach five thousand.

Morale was high. Locals and *résistants* became one. The weather was also magnificent. There were clear blue skies day after day, the mountain air was crisp and clean, and the young volunteers felt free. The French tricolour was flown openly beside the Cross of Lorraine – the flag of the Résistance – and the shame of occupation and collaboration fell away.

It was all to prove a tragic illusion. Even as the men gathered, leaders of Résistance units throughout France received a message from London reversing previous orders. 'Slow down to the utmost guerrilla activity. Impossible as of this moment to provide sufficient weapons and ammunition . . . Avoid large gatherings. Organise small, isolated groups.'

The invasion in the south, confidently expected within days, was actually two months away. The messages originally broadcast activating all Maquis units were merely part of Allied diversionary tactics to keep the Germans guessing about the true location of the D-Day invasion. Now that the troops had landed in Normandy, London tried to limit the damage to the Maquis. The landing had tied up all air support so that arms drops became infrequent and haphazard. The specific order now went out to the Vercors Maquis:

'Until such time as plans for obtaining weapons and ammunitions can be realised, avoid gathering unarmed units around forces already formed.'

This was all very well for most units of the Résistance, although bitterly disappointing, but almost impossible for the Vercors Maquis, which had been encouraged to adopt a stronghold strategy. The regional Résistance commander appealed to the Free French under de Gaulle in Algiers: 'Vercors, two thousand volunteers to be armed. Initial enthusiasm undermined by failure to send promised arms. Extremely urgent. Need men, weapons, tobacco here within forty-eight hours maximum. Full-strength attack possible. Under present conditions, impossible to resist. Failure to comply will entail merciless reprisals. Would be disastrous for regional Résistance.'

An even more desperate message was sent the following day: 'For Vercors, I repeat, urgent need for Maquis-type arms for eighteen light companies, heavy weapons for six companies. Once armed, these forces will prove absolutely indispensable to Vercors. They will then be ready for offensive operations in all directions. Mobilisation has been ordered on strength of formal assurances we would receive weapons. Failure to keep promise immediately will create tragic situation.'

The concept of a mountain guerrilla redoubt, known as Operation Montagnards, had originally been mooted early in 1943. It was the brainchild of Pierre Dalloz, an architect with a passion for mountaineering who retired with his wife to live on an isolated farm in the Vercors region. Dalloz had proposed an impregnable mountain fortress in the Vercors where the passes could easily be held by a small number of men, and the plateau itself could be prepared to receive a regular army airborne force, complete with trucks and heavy artillery. Once the Allies invaded the south of France, the Résistance of Vercors could be unleashed – a bomb that would explode in the midst of an enemy already under attack and on the defensive.

The final plan for putting the Vercors plateau to military use was ambitious. It called for seven thousand, five hundred men under fifteen commands with four hundred and fifty scouts. Weaponry was to include almost a thousand machine guns, a thousand automatic rifles, six thousand pistols, five anti-tank cannon and fifteen mortars, with ammunition amounting to ten times the total weight of the weaponry. The strategy was for the Maquis to install themselves in the mountains by stealth with the object of staging hit-and-run operations against the enemy to create maximum disorder. The Résistance would push forward in every direction, and only fall back when enemy forces proved too great.

The plan was supported by Jean Moulin, president of the National Council of the Résistance, and the general in charge of the Secret Army, who personally proposed it to de Gaulle's staff in London. The Vercors Maquis knew that the plan had been accepted when the BBC broadcast the coded message 'The Montagnards must climb to the top', and believed they had been allotted a specific and important role in the strategy of the Allied invasion.

At the beginning of 1943 there were only eighty-five *résistants* in the Vercors in a single camp on a remote farm. There had been hope of invasion in the summer, but instead it brought the arrest, torture and death of Jean Moulin, and the capture of the head of the Secret Army – both operations masterminded by Barbie.[23] Another local disaster that summer was the capture of fifteen *résistants* after a failed attack on a gasoline dump. They were tortured and somebody talked, resulting in the arrest of several of the leading Vercors Maquis.

The Résistance was reorganised with separate military commands for the northern and southern sections of the plateau. Active commandos were separated from reserves and stationed in groups of various sizes in new camps. The reserves only took up arms for specific missions and then returned to their daily lives. An elaborate warning system was set up using foresters and Résistance sympathisers within the Road and Bridges Department and the gendarmerie. In one recruitment drive that was particularly daring and innovative, the Résistance liberated Senegalese prisoners working as orderlies in Lyon for German officers, and took them back to Vercors.

Supply drops from the Allies began at the end of the year when a hundred containers filled with weapons, ammunition and equipment were parachuted in. The head of the Secret Army had hoped the Vercors Maquis would refrain from unnecessary risk until Allied operations were concentrated on the western front. But it was not easy to hold back the young, who became bored and edgy in inactivity, and failed to believe France would be liberated by endless sessions of unarmed combat.

When the Special Operations Executive (SOE) – an independent British secret service set up to conduct clandestine war against the Germans in Europe – made contact with the Vercors Maquis early in 1944 they found three thousand *résistants*, five hundred of whom were already lightly armed and organised into ten-man commando groups. But there were also men trained in heavy weapons who could make an HQ company if supplied with machine guns and mortars. 'A very effective, organised army,' was the SOE verdict, 'but their supplies are not what they need; they need long-distance weapons and anti-tank weapons.'

An attack on a German military police unit attracted enemy attention to the area, and the Germans responded with severely repressive measures. A German column of thirty trucks containing three hundred troops, spearheaded by an armoured car and backed up by two thirty-seven-millimetre cannon, forced its way into the terrain, and the Maquis proved unable to stop it.

Although the Maquis operated well militarily – holding up convoys, attacking soldiers and then disappearing into the forests and mountains – there was no defence from retribution against the civilian population. Fifty men were surrounded and twenty *résistants* killed, including eight who were burned alive in a farmhouse. A presbytery which served as a command post was dynamited, while in one area five hundred Milice instigated house searches and check-ups, interrogating and torturing inhabitants. Houses were torched, there were summary executions, and young men were handed over to the Germans for deportation. The myth of Vercors' impregnability was severely shaken. Yet, despite the clear demonstration that the Germans could penetrate the stronghold at will, the Résistance refused to learn the lesson. It responded by making plans to reinforce the plateau's defences.

The SOE Résistance organiser for the area told London that the Vercors operation made no military sense at all unless there was an invasion within three weeks. He also made repeated requests for heavy weapons as it was apparent that in any direct confrontation with the Germans the Résistance needed better weapons, particularly heavy machine guns and mortars, even artillery. London replied, 'There are scarcely enough mortars for the regular army.'

In reality, the Maquis of the Vercors, and the plan for Operation Montagnards, had never been given much serious thought in London. Although it had initially been received with enthusiasm, and fed a romantic and unrealistic view of the Résistance's military capabilities, the irregular warfare experts were opposed. The concentration of large numbers of Maquis forces in a fixed place broke all the rules of guerrilla warfare, inviting attack. In London the plan had been filed and forgotten, and it never became explicit Allied policy.

There had always been conflict between the regular army officers of the Free French and the British special warfare people. The Free French wanted to see France liberated by Résistance forces, in reality an impossibility. The FFI had formulated a plan where instead of the Maquis harrying the enemy's passage across French territory, large groups would move on to the offensive, seize control of set positions and hold them. Forgotten completely was the fundamental proviso of the originator of Operation Montagnards: it could only work as a supplementary mission to an Allied invasion of the south. Vercors was a disaster waiting to happen.

In the absence of arms and food drops the Résistance was encouraged to improvise, and they set out to steal what they could from the Germans. Michel's commando group gathered on the outskirts of a village awaiting the arrival of a truck that they were going to take on a raid to seize food supplies. As the time came for the rendezvous they found themselves surrounded by German troops. Michel immediately ordered his men to disperse, which was the only course of action possible on being directly confronted by regular German troops. The commandos scattered in every direction, and Michel moved up a small road into the mountains.

The Germans pursued him along parallel roads and shot at him across the fields. Michel was wearing a hat, trench coat, horn-rimmed glasses and a beard fashioned from one of Thérèse Mathieu's hairpieces. As he turned a curve in the road, he quickly abandoned his gun and the disguise. He then walked further up the lane, turned sharp right and made directly towards a German roadblock. He was taken for a local and allowed through.

The commandos regrouped in the late afternoon, but three of their number were missing. They returned cautiously to the site of the ambush in an attempt to discover the fate of their comrades. 'The Germans did not take the Maquis prisoners but treated them as terrorists. They had executed the wounded and left them where they lay.' Two of the men were dead, but one – André Valat, Michel's adjutant – somehow survived four bullets, three of which were fired into him at point-blank range. In the skirmish he had been wounded in the chest and leg and had been unable to walk. The Germans had found him, fired two more bullets into his neck to finish him off, and left him for dead. The bullet that had hit him in the chest actually displaced his heart without touching it. The two bullets fired into the neck exited through his cheek, leaving gaping wounds. Despite a gruelling journey to the Résistance field hospital in the mountains, which offered primitive care at best, he survived. 'We had to stage a mock funeral and bury an empty coffin in the Biviers cemetery to protect his family from interrogation.'[24]

Michel returned to join the St Marie du Mont Maquis, and reported to the regional commander, Dax. He then went to sleep, exhausted. At dawn he was woken up by Maquis guards who said that a large force of Alpine SS troops was on the way. The entire Maquis of some two hundred men retreated into a mountain position which involved scaling a steep cliff to reach a plateau. 'Dax assumed the Germans would not pursue us. In this he was completely wrong. We took up military positions and put machine guns in place.'

At the top of the cliff Michel could hear German voices drifting up from below and reported to Dax that he believed the Alpine troops were going to attack *en masse*. The commander suggested taking the one road out, but Michel advised dispersing individually into the wooded mountain terrain the men knew so well. Dax agreed, and by the time the SS troops reached the plateau the Maquis had disappeared.

'I climbed further into the mountains. On the following day I experienced the most unforgettable dawn of my life. The mist hung over the boulders, and the trees were moist with morning dew. I could hear cow bells tinkling in some distant meadow. It was a pastoral idyll, so far from the war. I felt for a brief moment that I was in a different world, away from everything. The beauty of that dawn in the mountains was an incredible moment of calm and peace in the midst of war.'

The Germans now launched a strong offensive on the village of St Nizier, situated at the northern tip of the plateau at the top of a road winding up from Grenoble. The village was both the heavily defended gatehouse to Vercors and its Achilles' heel. A force of fifteen hundred regular troops attacked two hundred and fifty *maquisards* who, in spite of being armed with only light weapons, held them off. The Germans brought in reinforcements and there was hand-to-hand fighting, but the day was saved when a section of Chasseurs Alpines – French Armistice Army troops disbanded by the Germans – arrived in a bus and strengthened the defence. The enemy retreated under a rain of grenades, leaving sixty dead. The Résistance had lost ten men and their bodies were laid out in the rear of the local church. That night triumphant *résistants* were able to look down from the heights of St Nizier on to Grenoble as it slept. One wrote in his diary how peaceful the town looked.

In the early hours of the morning Allied planes from Algiers made a parachute drop. This comprised of only light weapons and ammunition, but raised morale. It remained high throughout the day when the Germans stayed in Grenoble, content to lob forty-five heavy artillery shells into the village without result. They renewed their attack at dawn when three thousand troops stormed the village following an artillery barrage, and this time they were better armed, with heavy weapons. Mortars might have saved the situation for the Maquis but there were none. The Milice, unshaven and raggedly dressed to look like *maquisards*, infiltrated the defence, calling, 'Don't shoot, comrades!' They then opened fire with automatic weapons.

The Germans stormed the defences and set the village alight. The bodies of the dead were taken from the church and thrown into the flames. Although heavy losses were inflicted on the enemy, the Résistance lost a further twenty-four men. Another message was sent to Algiers: 'We've been attacked in force. We urge you to hurry. You are putting us in a catastrophic position. We've run out of ammunition. You bear full responsibility for our Résistance.'

The Maquis had lost control of St Nizier, the gate to Vercors, but the Germans had been confronted with far heavier fighting than expected. They did not launch another offensive for more than a month. The respite was a heady, unreal time for the Maquis, who now lived under the illusion of victory and imminent liberation. The Republic of Vercors became famous throughout the country and struck a chord in the heart of every loyal Frenchman. Newspapers all over the world talked of the magnificent heroism of the tiny republic, and volunteers flocked to the plateau. A series of parachute drops helped the command rearm and resupply its forces. The Maquis of the Vercors now became a regular military force, with staff officers, a quartermaster corps, medical service, military courts and a stockade for captured collaborators and Milice. Life took on the quality it had before the war, and the tricolour flew brazenly from houses in every hamlet and village.

In the first daytime drop to the plateau, on 25 June 1944, thirty-six American Flying Fortresses dropped eight hundred containers of equipment out of a cloudless sky. Hundreds of multi-coloured chutes fell in Alpine meadows, providing enough new weapons and ammo to equip large numbers of the Vercors army. Three days later an Anglo-American mission – Eucalyptus – was dropped in, comprising two commando units of fifteen men each – one SOE and one OSS (Office of Strategic Services). This was followed by Mission

Paquebot, a team of French military construction experts – including a woman – who began to build an airfield capable of receiving heavy weapons. For the first time the *résistants* began to feel they had back-up.

A message came from de Gaulle's chief of staff in London: 'Free French fighters of the Interior at Vercors . . . On D-Day you took up arms and, offering heroic resistance to all enemy assaults, once again you flew the French flag and the emblem of Liberation over one corner of our French land . . . Your successes will spread rapidly over our entire territory.'

Despite the drops, the Résistance still needed explosives. A daring daylight raid was planned on the ammunition dump at Fort Murier, which stood on a height above Grenoble. The fortress contained more than fifty tons of explosives kept secure behind high walls and iron gates, guarded by a company of troops belonging to the Vichy Groupes Mobiles de Reserves.

On the morning of the attack nine stolen German trucks, including one that had been converted into an improvised armoured car, set off for Fort Murier carrying fifty fully armed *résistants*. The company was led by a Mercedes flying a German flag but behind came the trucks loaded with the Maquis, wearing Résistance armbands and flying their flag, the Cross of Lorraine. Close to the fortress itself a group of *résistants* cut the telephone wires that connected the fort to the military in Grenoble. A rear guard with a machine gun was left at the crossroads beneath the fort to give the alarm if anyone approached. On arrival, all except one of the trucks were driven into a side road out of view of the fort.

The commander of the assault force, which involved a mix of local commando groups and included Michel, was Aimé Recquet. 'He was one of the tough guys, one of the heroes. If it was a difficult mission I liked to be with him. If there was anything impossible that had to be done, it involved him.' Recquet's original plan assumed that the guards would automatically open the gates to allow a German military vehicle to enter, but in this he was to be disillusioned. They were stopped and told that a new rule forbade any vehicles from entering the armoury without an order signed by the commander of the Groupes Mobiles, and countersigned by a German officer of equivalent rank.

Another, improvised plan had to be adopted. Recquet knew the area around the fort intimately and sent a large group of commandos to climb the cliff behind the armoury overlooking the courtyard.

Once in position they could draw a bead on the GMR guards, who were exposed and vulnerable. Most of the other troops remained inside the brick barracks. Three commandos with sub-machine guns slid as close as possible to the wall opposite the entrance with orders to create a distraction if given the signal; another group hid in the trees opposite the main entrance.

Recquet walked alone to the gate. Challenged by the guard through a loophole, he demanded to see the commander, saying he had a message from the chief of artillery in Grenoble. The commander came out of the barracks to talk to him, but spoke through the embrasure without opening the gate.

Recquet decided to take a bold course. 'We are here for explosives for the Résistance,' he declared. 'Open up!'

There was a moment's stunned silence, and then the commander burst out laughing. 'All precautions are in place,' he said evenly. 'Don't try to come in or we'll shoot.'

'*Mon vieux*, listen to me,' Recquet continued. 'If any of *you* move *you* are all dead.' He pointed towards the hill overlooking the courtyard. 'Look!'

The commander turned to see snipers and men with machine guns positioned in the rocks, aiming their weapons directly into the courtyard. Most importantly, the commander himself was covered from every angle and would have been the first to drop. He changed his tone and became pragmatic, demanding an assurance that his men would not be taken prisoner by force if he opened the gate. Recquet agreed.

The gate was opened and the *résistants* poured through, rapidly disarming the startled GMR troops. The trucks were brought up and driven into the courtyard and backed up to the armoury, where they were loaded with explosives. A couple of hours later they were ready to move out into the mountains.

The convoy was delayed by the arrival of the head of the rear guard who reported that a large force of GMR troops had taken up position on a hairpin bend on the road and were lying in wait. Somehow, during the loading operation, the alarm had been raised, and they were now trapped. It would not be long before German troops arrived.

Recquet discussed the situation with his adjutants and came up with three options: they could risk a long and dangerous detour down into Grenoble; they could abandon the trucks and disperse on foot; or they could fight their way through the roadblock created by the GMR troops. The first option was rejected because of the treacherous state of the alternative route and the distance; five of the trucks in the convoy were *gazos* – *voitures à gazogène* – vehicles which had their petrol tanks replaced by tall gas cylinders that were only good for forty kilometres. Abandoning the trucks and their prize of explosives was rejected outright. They had not come this far to go home empty-handed. That left the third, uncomfortable option of forcing a passage with men sitting on nine vehicles loaded with dynamite.

Recquet came up with another of his bold ruses. The trucks and armoured car would make their way up the mountain and draw up in front of the Vichy roadblock. Men in the armoured car would man the machine guns, while fully armed commandos would lie in wait in the trucks out of sight. Two other groups of commandos would go further up the mountain on foot and take up positions dominating the roadblock. Meanwhile, Recquet, accompanied by Michel and another commando named Henri, moved towards the roadblock.[25]

'Just let us pass,' Recquet said. 'Nothing more. And there will be no trouble and everybody will be happy.'

The commander stepped forward. 'Certainly not!'

'Let's talk!' Recquet said. 'It's your duty as a Frenchman.'

'No. I am an officer and I have to obey my orders.'

'I am a military man as well,' Recquet said, 'and I obey General de Gaulle. Let the convoy pass – you can shoot at us afterwards.'

A junior officer began to speak in a low voice to his commander. 'Sir, perhaps we could . . .'

'No!' the commander exploded, cutting him off abruptly. 'The Germans are going to arrive from Grenoble any moment and I do not wish to be interned.'

'Yes, I'm sure the Germans are on their way,' Recquet said, adopting the tone of one reasonable man appealing to another. 'So we only have a few minutes. Let us pass.' He moved towards the commander as he spoke. 'This is nonsense. Are we going to have Frenchmen fighting against Frenchmen? Surely you could tell the Germans we had already gone through when you arrived?'

'No,' the commander repeated, unmoved. 'Absolutely not!'

During his plea, Recquet had carefully noted the position of his men out of the corner of his eye. The convoy looked harmless enough, although the armoured car had pulled to the front, and he knew the commandos would be in place higher up the mountainside. He had now moved to within inches of the officer in charge, and the men glared at each other.

Suddenly, Recquet whipped the revolver from his belt and shoved it into the man's belly. 'Put your hands up and tell your men to do the same, or we shoot!'

Four sub-machine guns appeared from the gun slots in the armoured car, and the *résistants* in the trucks stood and trained their weapons on the troops. Snipers appeared among the rocks and trees on the hill.

'You are cowards,' the commander screamed, outraged. 'You came here to negotiate. You have taken me in treachery. This is against the rules of war.'

Henri raised his hand to hit the commander, but Recquet stopped him.

'You are the cowards,' Recquet said. 'You have hidden in a ditch to make an attack on your fellow countrymen and hold us up. Even for a coward your duty was obvious.'

The sixty surrounded GMR troops were disarmed and their weapons collected. Six chose to join the Résistance, a number that disgusted Recquet. He remarked bitterly, 'The commander isn't the only coward. Out of sixty lives we respected and who were our prisoners, only six chose to follow us!' But time was pressing, and the *gazos* were spluttering.

The convoy flew the tricolour all the way back to their mountain hideout and were cheered in the villages. They did not encounter a single enemy soldier throughout the journey. The very next day Michel and his men blew up a bridge, using part of the stolen explosives. He took the time to paint and erect a sign that he left propped beside it: SOUVENIR OF MURIER.[26]

It had been a magnificent and successful operation, but there were casualties. One of the *résistants*, who acted as an observer in the rear guard, was spotted and chased by a Milice patrol. He took refuge in the home of a certain Madame Fleury, in the village of Versoud, and when the patrol hammered on her door he fled through the garden. He was later captured and handed over to the Gestapo. Madame Fleury, accused of being a Résistance sympathiser, was threatened and abused in her own home, and then badly beaten. She too was handed over to the Gestapo and deported. Recquet records: 'Nobody could make her talk. It took great physical and moral strength. Happily, she survived deportation and returned in 1945, sad and ill. She can be proud to have us say of her, "They dented their helmets with the force of the blows to her head but never loosened her teeth." A *résistant* dies but does not talk.'

On Bastille Day, three days after the raid on Murier, the Résistance held a traditional military review, including a memorial mass for those killed at St Nizier, deep in the Lente forest. On the same day

Vercors received a large supply of weaponry from forty-eight United States Air Force Flying Fortresses, filling the sky with red, white and blue parachutes. A thousand containers were retrieved full of Sten guns, ammunition and badly needed clothes – but none of the requested heavy weapons. The Germans responded within minutes of the drop with an air attack on local villages, blowing up houses and causing casualties among both *résistants* and civilians. As one member of the Maquis returned to his village from the review in the forest, he found everything in flames. The local hotel was burning furiously, but in the dining room at the rear a man was seated alone at a table, a lighted candle stuck in the neck of a bottle, defiantly consuming a baked ham.

The Germans now launched a massive attack on Vercors committing twenty thousand men. Spearheaded by the elite regiment of the 157th Alpine Division, it included two batteries of mountain guns, tank units from the 9th Panzer Division and full air support. The plan was to encircle the redoubt and seal off all escape routes, then smash through to the plateau from all points of the compass and eliminate the defenders.

At the same time, a concerted search was launched for known members of the Résistance. Michel was woken up in Biviers on the same morning by the sound of the village dogs barking furiously. He climbed out of bed and looked out of the window. German trucks full of troops were grinding their way up the mountain road. He threw on his clothes and left the house to protect Thérèse Mathieu, for the Germans killed anyone found harbouring a *résistant*. He intended to make for the mountains, but once outside he saw that a second convoy had already taken up position higher up in the village and cut the road off. 'German troops had cordoned off the entire area and there was no way out. I was surrounded, completely trapped.'

Michel began to search for a hiding place, and saw an empty house with its shutters closed. It was at this moment that Diane chose to run to his side. He ordered her to go away, but she clung to him. He began to plead. Reluctantly, the Irish setter slunk away, head hung low and feelings hurt. Michel climbed over a wall into the large fenced garden and moved quickly to a well with a wooden cover. He pulled the cover aside and saw that a metal rod ran all the way down the stone interior. He climbed into the well, pulled the cover back into place, and used the rail to lower himself until he was hanging just above the water level. He planned to submerge the moment he heard German troops approach the well.

'I hung there a long time,' Michel recalled. The Germans searched the village thoroughly. They had learned many of the Résistance's tricks during the occupation and became increasingly difficult to evade. Each patrol was assigned a certain number of houses and took their time going through cellars, checking for false floors and hidden doors. As Michel clung to the iron rod in the echoing dark, his body braced uncomfortably against the cold stone shaft, he suddenly heard scratching sounds on the cover above him. He prepared to sink into the icy well water. Then he heard the unmistakable, heartbroken whimpering of Diane.

The noise threatened to attract the attention of the Germans, so there was nothing to be done but to go back to the top and silence the dog. He had to move quickly. He hauled himself up the iron rod, slid open the cover and climbed out. Diane jumped up and began to bark with pleasure. 'Not today, *please*! Go away!' Michel hissed. 'Go!' Diane stood her ground. 'Go! Leave me!' Diane cocked her head. Once again he was forced to plead. '*Please go away . . . please!*' At last, Diane seemed to understand, and she turned and walked off.

Michel heard the crunch of soldiers' boots as a search party moved up from the lower village. It was too late to climb back down the well, because of the risk of being spotted, so he crawled on his belly towards the empty house and around to the back. A large, windowless brick tool shed with a sloping roof was attached to it, padlocked on the outside. He scaled the wall, using the house to conceal him from the search party, but once on the roof saw that he was exposed to a second patrol above him working its way down through the village.

The roof was constructed of large square tiles and he slid one aside to squeeze into the tool shed below. Holding on to the wooden frame of the roof, he pulled the tile back into position and dropped to the ground. At first he could see nothing in the dim light except for rays that filtered from under the locked door. Above, thick wire was stretched across the shed supporting a wooden plank to form a suspended storage space for hay. It offered a precarious hiding place at best, but he climbed on to a wheelbarrow, pulled himself up and buried himself under the hay.

Suspended in mid-air under hay, he felt reasonably secure. The shed was clearly locked on the outside and the wire and plank construct was more solid than it looked. And then he heard Diane barking at the side of the shed where he had climbed on to the roof.

The dog moved to the shed door and began to scratch at it and moan. 'My heart stopped beating. This was the end. I was powerless.

I could do nothing but wait for the inevitable.' He pulled out his revolver and held it against his chest. He would empty it into the enemy, saving the last bullet for himself. 'To be captured in combat meant to be tortured to death. We were branded as terrorists, and I was not going to allow myself to fall into the hands of the Germans.'

He heard one of the search parties enter the house, and the occasional shout in German as the soldiers moved from room to room. Diane suddenly stopped scratching at the door. The search party came out of the house and into the garden. There was momentary silence, and then the sound of aggressive barking as if the dog suddenly understood the source of danger and had switched her attention to the patrol. There was a shout and the noise of a soldier heaving a rock. The barking stopped. Michel lay under the hay, dreading the possibility of the dog's return, hoping the Germans might give the tool shed a miss because of the padlock.

A group of soldiers paused outside the door. One rattled the padlock. There was a pause, followed by the sound of splintering wood as the timber of the half-rotten door was kicked in. The soldier stepped inside and light flooded the shed. Michel lay still, scarcely breathing. The hay became heavy and hot and he was unbearably uncomfortable. The wait seemed endless. The soldiers looked around and walked out, apparently satisfied the shed was empty. Michel heard the patrol form up and the sound of their boots as they marched away – and Diane's barking in the distance.

He lay beneath the hay until nightfall and then dropped from his hiding place to the floor of the shed. A dark object outlined against the open door made him start. It was Diane, tail wagging happily. He slipped back to the house where the dog settled under the kitchen table, exuding the newly acquired air of a conspirator. Thérèse Mathieu told Michel that all hell had broken loose: the enemy had launched a major offensive employing thousands of troops. All Résistance groups had been put on alert. It was now too dangerous for any *résistant* to stay put, and she was going to leave the house with her rifle and climb into the mountains to join headquarters in Beldonne.[27]

The encirclement of Vercors by the Germans was completed by nightfall. The assault on the mountain fortress was launched at six the following morning in drenching rain. A heavily armed column once again climbed the road to St Nizier, while seven others scaled the escarpments and attacked defenders holding the passes. The *maquisards* fought ferociously, but were forced to fall back after twenty-four hours. The Germans sent out large reconnaissance forces probing for weak spots in Maquis positions while the *résistants* retreated. Once the enemy had identified sensitive positions they moved in to destroy them.

Despite effective ambushes inflicting heavy casualties – in one the Germans lost more than eighty men – the enemy gained a foothold on one mountain top after another. Night brought no relief as a multitude of German patrols moved through the woods. In the morning, at first light, the Germans opened up with mortars. As Alpine commandos moved on to one position, the defenders were killed one after another, and the youngest – just turned seventeen – called out, 'Tell mama that I died for France!' His commander, pipe clamped firmly between his teeth, fired his bazooka twenty-seven times. He was wounded, but continued to fight until he was encircled. Before he died he sent a radio message to his commander that his men had decided to fight to the end, signing off: 'Long live France!'

The Germans succeeded in installing mortars and cannons in mountain-top positions and were now able to fire on the Maquis below them. The military situation had been reversed. The *résistants* were fish in a barrel and the free citadel of Vercors seemed doomed. A desperate report on the enemy action was sent to Algiers: 'Demand immediate bombardment. Had promised to hold out for three weeks. Now six weeks since establishment of our organisation. Request additional men, fuel and materiel. Morale of the population excellent, but they will quickly turn against you if you do not take immediate steps, and we would have to agree with them that the leaders in Algiers and London do not understand the situation we find ourselves in and can be considered cowards and criminals. We mean what we say: cowards and criminals.'

An immediate request for commandos was made by the Free French to the Allies, but all forces were being concentrated on the projected landing in Provence. The head of the SOE for the region tried to persuade Allied command to put nearby German airstrips – where transport planes earmarked for carrying troops offered a particularly inviting target – out of action. But nothing happened. The fate of the men of Vercors was sealed. One commander remarked to a comrade: 'I have always believed that nine out of ten would never return. And yet we didn't have the right to say no.'

The only hope seemed to be the airborne troops promised by de Gaulle, and the Vercors Résistance still dared to hope that a force would be flown in, complete with heavy artillery. The construction crew had virtually completed the airstrip at Vassieux, in the centre of the plateau, which was now three thousand, three hundred feet long and four hundred and fifty feet wide, and serviceable. Three days after the Germans opened their attack there was elation as the crew spotted aircraft approaching from the south under low cloud. Word went around the strip that the Allied airborne force was here at last – and it was impressive. Altogether there were twenty planes with troop gliders in tow.

But as the gliders drew closer the awful truth struck home: they were not the long-expected Allied reinforcements at all, but German troop transports. The enemy had closely monitored the progress of the strip through aerial reconnaissance and saw a magnificent opportunity to place troops in the heart of the 'impregnable' Vercors. The gliders disgorged four hundred crack SS troops who quickly overwhelmed the Maquis defenders. The attack was a well-planned operation faultlessly executed without quarter. The Germans secured their position in the village and then fanned out on the offensive.

Résistance units were now massively outnumbered and outgunned, and hopelessly overstretched along a one-hundred-and-twenty-mile front. German reinforcements continued to be flown into Vassieux, while other troops poured through the open gate of St Nizier. Medium- and long-range artillery pounded inadequately defended set positions. By nightfall Résistance leaders understood that they would have to revert to guerrilla tactics. A decision was made to keep fighting using all possible means, and then fall back in small units. It was also decided to move the OSS commandos out of the area to the HQ of the Secret Army in the Beldonne mountains.

They reached Chartreuse, a strong Résistance area, and Michel was placed in charge of moving the OSS men across the Isère Valley and up into the Alps. The commandos were loaded into a truck and Michel led the way on a motor bike. 'I had already been able to organise lookouts all along the route within visual distance of one another. Their job was to warn us of the presence or approach of German troops. If I saw that a man was missing, or a signal was given, we would have been warned. We went like hell, and although we thought it wise to go off the road a couple of times, we had a straight run with no trouble. They were delivered to Beldonne safely.'

Back in Vercors, the SS now staged a number of brutal reprisals. They shot hostages and prisoners and massacred the inhabitants of Vassieux, mostly old men, women and children. One woman was raped by seventeen men in succession, while a German doctor held her pulse, ready to stop the soldiers when she fainted. Another was eviscerated and left to die with her intestines draped around her neck. When three children tried to save themselves by hiding behind a rock, soldiers threw hand grenades at them. All three were wounded, while one – a four-year-old boy – had his left hand torn off at the wrist. When an old lady came out of hiding to plead for him she was shot dead. Another of the children, an eight-year-old girl who had been wounded in the chest, was later carried away and hidden by her parents. They were given away by a barking dog. As the father reached into his pocket to retrieve his ID, the soldiers shot him with the cry, 'Terrorist!' They turned on the little girl and her mother. 'If you cry you'll get the same.' Sixty-four civilians died at Vassieux, and more than two hundred villagers and farmers from the region were murdered in reprisal killings.

The Résistance military hospital close to Vassieux, caring for one hundred and twenty wounded, had been evacuated during the assault. The walking wounded were left to fend for themselves. Doctors and nurses took the seats out of a number of buses, loaded the stretcher cases and headed south. News of a German column moving up from Die, a village at the southern tip of the plateau, led to them leaving the main road and heading into the mountains. They followed a rough dirt track to the grotto of La Luire, a limestone cavern sixty feet wide and twice as deep in the side of the Montagne de Beurre – Butter Mountain. The mouth of the cave was hidden by trees, and for a week the three doctors, nine nurses and chaplain cared for the twenty-six wounded, among whom were two women from Vassieux who had been wounded in the bombing, four German prisoners of war, and an American OSS lieutenant, Chester Myers, recovering from an appendix operation.

A reconnaissance plane circled the area early one morning, and in the evening fifteen German soldiers led by a Gestapo lieutenant arrived at the cave. They were visibly nervous as they entered, expecting a Résistance hide-out, and had their weapons at the ready. The wounded German POWs cried out: '*Kameraden – nicht schiessen! Dies ist ein Krankenhaus! Wir sind deutsche Soldaten! Kriegsgefangene!*' – Comrades – don't shoot! It's a hospital! We're German soldiers! Prisoners of war! The Gestapo lieutenant ripped the bandages from one of the men on the stretcher to see if his wounds were genuine. When several nurses proffered ID cards, he turned on them and said in French, 'It's useless to try and explain. Your papers are false. You're terrorists and you will be exterminated, men and women.'

The soldiers forced everyone out of the cave and took them to an abandoned farm nearby. The wounded who were able to stand were lined up against a wall and shot. The stretcher cases were executed where they lay. A letter found later on a German prisoner, who had been present, graphically described the event: 'We have exterminated all the occupants of a hospital, including doctors and nurses. There were about forty of them. We dragged them out and shot them down with our automatic pistols. That may seem atrocious, but these dogs didn't deserve anything better.'

In fact, the soldiers did not execute forty, only twenty-one, and the nurses and doctors were spared. The atrocity seems to have triggered a form of psychotic boasting. The survivors were taken to Grenoble for questioning. The eldest, a doctor in his seventies, was released. The two other doctors and the chaplain were shot. The nurses pretended they had been pressed into service with the Maquis. The eldest was asked, 'Would you nurse German soldiers?'

'Of course,' she replied. The proof of her answer was that she had been nursing four POWs when arrested.

'Then we will send you to be a nurse on the eastern front.'

The seven nurses were taken to Montluc prison in Lyon. They never reached the eastern front; instead they were transferred to Ravensbruck, a concentration camp for women fifty miles north of Berlin. Originally conceived as a model prison, complete with landscaping and designed uniforms, ninety thousand inmates died there.

More than six hundred and thirty *résistants* were killed in the battle of Vercors.[28] Scattered and divided by the enemy, some survivors made it to the Lente forest in almost inaccessible mountains. News of the defeat was sent to Algiers: 'Vercors defences pierced . . . after fifty-six hours of battle. Have ordered dispersal in small groups in order to resume the fight if that should prove possible. Everyone has performed his duty courageously in a desperate struggle, but we are saddened at being obliged to yield because of the enemy's numbers and at having been completely abandoned while the battle was in progress.'

The commander of the Secret Army in south-east France, General Henri Zeller, had managed to leave the Alps after the attack and fly to Algiers to petition de Gaulle himself. 'Thanks to their weapons – the cannon, mortars, tanks and planes – the Germans are still capable of carrying out terrible reprisals. But once they have done so, they return to huddle in their garrisons. They do not dare to send an isolated car or a liaison agent out on the road. The railroad lines are blocked. One out of every two truck convoys transporting provisions is attacked, despite armed protection. The Germans, who will never dare surrender to the "terrorists", are hoping almost as much as we are for the arrival of the Allied troops.'

De Gaulle listened attentively. He handed the colonel a blue file. 'The Allies will be landing on the coast of Provence in a few days. Here are the main features of the operations plan. Sit down at this table, study them, and give me your opinion.'

The colonel took the file and began to read. At last, the long-awaited invasion was about to happen! He was excited, but as he scanned the pages his spirits slumped. Typed before him in black and white was the expected date for the liberation of the Alpine region: *Grenoble, D-Day plus 90.*

In three months' time, he thought to himself, we'll all be long dead.

VI

The Germans continued their ruthless campaign against the Vercors Résistance for a further two weeks, destroying crops and killing cattle, burning farms and ruthlessly hunting down anyone who was suspected of being in the Maquis or of assisting it. The survivors saw the dream of liberty promised by the stand in the mountain fastness dissolve, and the rhetoric and heroics seemed to have resulted in nothing but death and defeat.

The veterans of Vercors were left with bitter feelings of resentment that in the moment of their greatest need they had been betrayed and abandoned. And yet, apart from the big set battles, the Germans had never been more vulnerable. Despite everything, the Maquis regrouped in small units and managed to go back on the offensive, attacking trucks and patrols. But now these actions were violently opposed by local inhabitants who bore the brunt of German retaliation as yet more farms were set alight.

Meanwhile, in Algiers, General Henri Zeller studied the invasion plans shown to him by de Gaulle. As commander of the Secret Army in south-eastern France, he knew the Maquis still had an essential role to play despite the price it had paid in the Alps. The calculation that the Allies would not reach Grenoble until three months after the initial landing meant that the Germans would have ample time to complete their strategy of attacking Maquis strongholds in force, one after the other, and destroying whatever pockets of resistance remained. Unless he could persuade his superiors to change their plans, and the Allies broke through quickly, thousands of Maquis fighters would be sacrificed and the fate of the mountain Résistance sealed.

De Gaulle had asked for the general's opinion of the plan, so he gave it forcefully. 'This is far too cautious. Once the coastal area has been occupied to points twelve miles inland, the Allies must be audacious and not hesitate to send out light columns, supported by armoured cars and cannon, on all the north–south roads. If the Allies advance north through the mountains, in particular the Route

Napoléon, they will be virtually unchallenged. They'll be in Grenoble in days, not months.'

De Gaulle was openly astonished at what he heard. Keenly aware of the disaster of Vercors, he had interpreted the rout to mean that the Résistance in the region had been broken. Zeller established a different reality as he described the military situation in the mountains. The Germans had powerful forces that were invincible when applied against poorly armed *résistants*, but there were large areas they no longer controlled where they were always at risk. 'Virtually the whole of the French Alps is in our hands for all practical purposes,' Zeller said. 'Once the assault troops have a firm bridgehead, it is vital that we lose no time in thrusting some armed columns north. With the support of the FFI they cannot fail to advance very fast.' And the strategy could be successful with a force of only a couple of thousand men. Once in Grenoble, the Allies would be able to strike west and cut off the enemy's retreat from the coast.

'Are you sure?' de Gaulle asked, sceptically.

'Absolutely.' The Germans would be no match for Allied armour operating in Alpine country, where it would not only have the military support of the Maquis, but would also be provided with accurate intelligence of enemy positions and movements.

'This is extremely important,' de Gaulle said, convinced. He ordered Zeller to leave immediately for Naples to explain the situation to General Alexander Patch, the American in command of the invasion force. Zeller gave an equally impressive and persuasive performance in front of the commander and his senior staff, and it was agreed to adapt the invasion plan accordingly.

On 15 August 1944, the Allies finally made their landing in southern France, in near perfect conditions. Operation Anvil-Dragoon comprised an invasion force of twelve hundred ships carrying three hundred thousand men made up of divisions from the newly constituted American Seventh Army and the French Second Army. The assault force made an amphibious landing and airdrop on the Côte d'Azur, between Hyères and Cannes. By nightfall some ninety-four thousand men and more than eleven thousand vehicles were already ashore, with fewer than two hundred Allied killed and wounded. The German coastal defence, made up of two second-line infantry divisions, was broken and over two thousand prisoners taken. The prayers of the Alpine Résistance had been answered, and as news of the landing reached the mountains, hope returned.

The French troops turned west towards Toulon and Marseille, while the American Seventh Army thrust north. Eighteen units of an armoured brigade advanced up the Route Napoléon, where nearly one hundred and thirty years earlier Bonaparte had led his men on the march to Paris after his escape from the island of Elba.

Unknown to Michel, Suzanne had begun to work in Lyon for Allied intelligence. She had continued to live a precarious existence in the city, sharing an apartment with her mother, and worked closely with a young German officer who had deserted the Wehrmacht. They were now sent south to liaise with the invasion force and supply the Americans with important intelligence regarding troop strength and positions around Lyon. Both were supplied with false papers and money, and Suzanne – a veteran of wartime uncertainty – took along her jewellery.

As they approached the Riviera, they passed unruly bands of gun-toting Frenchmen at the side of the road. These groups had sprung up all over France since the Allied invasions and were anarchic, undirected and dangerous. Most of them had nothing at all to do with the genuine Résistance but belonged to a breed dubbed, in a phrase of scorching irony, Résistants de la Dernière Minute – Resisters of the Last Minute.

The car was waved down at an improvised roadblock set up by one of these gangs and Suzanne and her colleague were ordered out and asked for their papers. The German explained that they were on an urgent mission to meet with advance units of the Allied invasion force. As he spoke, the most aggressive of the 'résistants' leaned forward, listening intently. The agent's French was not very good, and betrayed a distinct German accent. The group of volatile bandits became convinced they had found a member of the German occupation force making his escape. He was dragged roughly from the car, together with Suzanne, and the vehicle was searched. This turned up the false papers and a large amount of money and jewellery. Explanation only served to enrage the young hotheads, while Suzanne's accent with its Austrian tang further convinced them that they had caught Nazis on the run.

Sensing the danger, Suzanne attempted to calm everyone down as the gang grew increasingly excited and belligerent. The agent quoted the code names of contacts in Lyon who could prove his story, but these meant nothing to the men around him who seemed to have had no direct affiliation to any of the Résistance groups. Nobody was listening anyway. There was shoving and pushing, and one of the gang moved towards the German waving a pistol. A single shot sounded, an almost insignificant noise amid the raised, angry voices. He fell down dead.

Suzanne was manhandled back into a car, driven along the coast road to Nice and handed over to the authorities. She was put in a cell in the same jail where she had awaited trial by a Vichy court for influence peddling, except now she was accused of collaborating with the enemy.

True to General Zeller's passionate advocacy, advance US Army units were a few miles south of Grenoble in five days rather than three months. Life for the occupying enemy inside the city had become increasingly circumscribed. A force of two thousand men had been mobilised in the Isère by the Résistance and isolated the Germans by sabotaging rail and road links in and out of the city. Traffic to Chambéry was cut off completely, and only one or two convoys a day left Grenoble, escorted by armoured and repair trains. A strict curfew came into force after six in the evening, when the Germans withdrew into a cordon of armed posts that inspected every vehicle that went in and out. The only life in the streets consisted of the numerous German patrols of frightened troops. They panicked easily and recklessly opened fire on anyone and anything: doctors visiting patients, night workers, lamp-posts and stray dogs.

The Résistance groups were ordered to penetrate the city on the night of 21/22 August at the same time that the Germans began to pull out, an act they announced by blowing up their ammunition dumps. Retreating enemy convoys came under fierce attack on all routes, and there was sporadic fighting within the city itself. Michel states proudly: 'It should never be forgotten that in the end Grenoble was liberated by the Résistance.'

The population awoke the following morning to find themselves free for the first time in four years. Colonel François Huet, who had commanded the Maquis in Vercors, bicycled furiously to meet the American armoured column rumoured to be a few miles south of the town. He came upon an American tank in the village of Le Pont-de-Claix and demanded to be taken to the officer in charge. The commander of the unit, Lieutenant-Colonel Philip Johnston, greeted him warmly.

'You can push on into the city,' Huet told him through an interpreter. 'We want to see American uniforms there today!'

'But I've only got a tank squadron and an artillery battery and a company of infantry,' Johnston objected. He explained that he commanded a small advance unit and the main force was further down the road.

'*Foncez, foncez!*' Huet urged, gesturing dramatically towards Grenoble. Charge, sweep on!

Johnston did not need a translation. 'Okay,' he said, grinning.

American tanks pushed into the town and found the streets jammed with cheering locals. The taking of Grenoble turned the Germans' left flank in the Rhône valley, levering them out of all southern and eastern France. And the objective had been taken, thanks to the Résistance and the eloquence of General Zeller, not in three months but in a single week.[1]

Grenoble was liberated, but still in the war. Skirmishes between FFI forces and Vichy police units now erupted on street corners and down back alleys. More importantly, the city lay on the escape route to the north-east, and the day after liberation a retreating German column of twenty-five vehicles was reported to be advancing towards it, intending to force its way through. It was attacked by Résistance commando groups at three different points and turned back. Large concentrations of German troops were still positioned in the mountains to the east, including men from the 157th Alpine Division that had seen action on the Vercors plateau. They shelled the city with heavy 88 mm artillery in an attempt to keep the road open. American troops joined with Résistance forces to attack, and spotter planes accurately directed US artillery on to the enemy. The combined action brought about the surrender of the last Germans, who were surrounded in Grésivaudan.

Lieutenant-Colonel Johnston was standing with his French colleague, Colonel Huet, when a lieutenant from the Wehrmacht bearing a white flag was brought to him. The German officer asked to speak to Johnston alone, explaining that his orders were to surrender only to an American officer. The American draped his arm around the Frenchman's shoulders. 'My comrade and I belong to the same army of liberation,' he said. 'We will only accept your surrender together.' For the men of the Résistance, who had never surrendered, it was a powerful moment: a German officer formally conceding the defeat of a crack Wehrmacht regiment.[2]

Michel experienced his first encounter with American troops. His commando group had been active around the clock since the landing in the south and had captured a dozen German prisoners. 'They were afraid to be captured by the Résistance, for obvious reasons. They expected to be summarily executed in revenge. In fact, I had no strong feelings towards the prisoners. I saw them simply as soldiers.'

But POWs were an encumbrance, and he sought to hand them over to the American military. On a road to the north-east of Grenoble, he saw a sign indicating the field HQ of an American unit, and followed it, driving a truck flying the Cross of Lorraine, flag of the Résistance. A second truck carrying the prisoners and their commando guards brought up the rear.

America, with its ideals of individual liberty and democracy, had inspired and given hope to Michel throughout the war. The Constitution, and the human values and aspirations contained in it, was close to his heart. 'I was impressed that the US was not only fighting *against* evil, but *for* a better world.' Now, finally, after years of suffering and combat, he was to meet his first American. He prepared himself for an emotional encounter.

'We drove up to the unit and there was an officer standing there, a captain. He was not in combat fatigues, but very neat and well turned out. I stepped down from the truck and introduced myself and explained that I had come to hand over prisoners.'

The captain looked Michel up and down contemptuously, and then cast a dismissive glance in the direction of the motley collection of men who made up his force. 'Who the hell are you?' he exclaimed. It was true that at first glance the *résistants* resembled pirates more than soldiers. They were dressed in the uniform of the FFI, or a bedraggled version as close to it as they could achieve, and sported the skull and crossbones patch of Résistance commandos. 'I can't be bothered with prisoners,' the American captain added curtly. He went on to make disparaging comments about the commandos' uniforms and patches, and ignorantly questioned the validity of the Cross of Lorraine, the flag under which so many of the Maquis had died.

At first Michel remained silent, incredulous at the unexpected reception, and then his anger began to build. None of his group understood English, but the American's tone of contempt, redolent of the arrogance of officers of the German occupying army, did not need translation.

'Who the hell are *you*?' Michel yelled, his anger boiling over. 'What the hell are you doing in that American uniform? You don't belong in it!' He pointed towards the stunned POWs in the truck. 'You talk like a German – you belong with them! You should be in an SS uniform!'

He lunged at the American, grabbed his coat and began to tear it from him. The commandos watched the assault in mute confusion before a couple of GIs pulled Michel from their captain and took him to the commander. 'He was a very different man and apologised. He took the prisoners and made everything all right. But I was still furious.'

In Grenoble, the Biviers Commando was formed into a Special Police Group, and Michel was put in charge of the investigation and arrest of Milice, Vichy officials and criminal collaborators. He also served with the Deuxième Bureau (French Army intelligence).[3] It appealed to his sense of irony that the hunted had finally become the hunter. In the days following liberation, there were hundreds of arrests and Michel's unit was especially active. Those captured were taken before a judge and formally charged, but retribution was not always so measured as the population took its revenge all over the country. Members of the Milice in particular often met with rough and ready justice. They were hanged from lamp-posts, made to dig their own graves and even burned alive. 'I had nothing to do with that sort of thing and regretted it. I was not seeking revenge but intent on doing a job that I considered important. I wanted to see these people brought to justice.'

There were also swift reprisals on the day of liberation for the cruelty of the Germans in Grenoble. The populace remembered with bitterness the fate of ten young non-combatant hostages taken in the Vercors after two Germans had been killed. They were jailed for months until the SS took them from their cells, telling them they were to be set free. The hostages were driven in a truck in the early hours of the morning to the Cours Bériat and killed one by one with a shot to the neck. Their bodies were left on the pavement until noon as an example. Now, in an act of revenge, nine young French militiamen who had served beside the Germans were taken to the same place, tied to posts and shot before a jeering crowd.

Others harshly treated were the *collabos horizontales* (horizontal collaborators), the name given to French girls who had slept with German soldiers. Their heads were shaved and they were dragged through the streets, mocked and beaten. The strength of feeling against them can best be judged by a comment made by the FFI chaplain-general, a man who later became an advocate of forgiveness and reconciliation. He recorded an incident in his diary of entering a café full of German soldiers accompanied by French girls. He stared hard at one and she blushed to the roots of her hair. 'Those girls could be dipped in tar and burned in the public square and it would affect me no more than a fire in a fireplace of a neighbour's house.'[4]

Gertrude Stein, the American writer, who spent the entire war in the mountains north of Grenoble in the village of Culoz, was similarly hard-hearted to the breed. 'Today the village is excited terribly excited because they are shaving the heads of girls who kept company with the Germans during the occupation. It is called the coiffure of 1944, and naturally it is terrible because the shaving is done publicly . . . Life in the Middle Ages, it certainly is most interesting, and logical it certainly is.'[5]

One of the *horizontales* came under Michel's jurisdiction when he was asked to deliver her to the authorities. She sat meekly beside him in the jeep as she was driven to her fate. He looked across at her, a young, attractive girl apart from her crudely shaved head. 'I was tempted to let her go. And I think that any appeal or explanation on her part would have swayed me. But as I looked at her I realised she was psychologically gone. She expected punishment and was resigned totally to it. Perhaps she even welcomed it. She had no urge to escape and reminded me of those at Les Milles who had succumbed to the Siren Song, or the last man chasing the tumbril to take him to the guillotine. Had I stopped the jeep and let her go she would not have understood. She expected to be delivered, so I delivered her.'

His new role as policeman put him in constant contact with the US military and he found he got along well with Americans despite his disastrous first encounter. 'The more I met, and liked, the more I thought of how influenced we are by first impressions. They can change our lives. The captain might have turned me into an anti-American for life. I hope not, but it could have happened.'

The American Army was preparing to move on and fulfil their mission of pursuing the retreating Germans through France and into Germany itself. For the men and women of the Résistance in Grenoble, and the mountain area surrounding it, the war was finally over. But for Michel it had simply entered a new phase, and he was detached from the FFI to join the American Army as a liaison officer.

He was attached to the S-2 (Combat Intelligence) section of the 1st Battalion, 180th Infantry, of the 45th Division – known as the Thunderbirds – US Seventh Army. Although it was highly irregular for a foreign national to work in combat intelligence, the Americans were more than happy to have him. His French and English were fluent, and he spoke German like a native. From now on he would wear the uniform of the American Army, but he refused to take any pay because he felt that would make him a mercenary. 'It was all most unusual, but it was also in the midst of war. I had already established good relations with American combat intelligence. I didn't need money because everything was provided and the cigarette ration was like hard currency.'

He particularly liked the cheerful, battle-hardened 'citizen soldiers' of the Thunderbirds, and the more he learned about them and their combat record for the previous year, the more he admired them. The 45th was a National Guard infantry division, headquartered in Oklahoma City, and originally made up of non-professional 'citizen soldiers' from the states of Arizona, Colorado, New Mexico and Oklahoma. Its recruits were mostly tough young country boys who had been brought up in the hard times of the Depression. Its history was tough too, stretching back to the taming of the Wild West. Although the American Army was segregated from the time of the Civil War throughout the Second World War, the Thunderbirds included many thousands of Native American Indians from tribes such as the Cherokee, Apache, Sioux, Osage and Comanche.[6]

The fifteen thousand men of the Thunderbirds, fresh from Stateside training camps, had experienced their first taste of enemy fire as they waded ashore on the southern beaches of the island of Sicily on 10 July 1943. It was a date the green troops would come to remember as well as their birthdays. The amphibious landings on Sicily were a success, casualties were relatively light, and the Thunderbirds moved quickly across the island. The men faced their first real test when they ran head on into the newly raised Herman Goering Panzer Division, the elite of the Luftwaffe's ground troops, but after little over a month of combat the island of Sicily was taken. The performance impressed the commander of the Seventh Army, General George S. Patton: 'The 45th Division, a green outfit, went into combat with two veteran outfits, and asked no favours, made no excuses . . . I'm damned proud of every officer and man in the division.'[7]

Italy sued for an armistice on 3 September 1943, switching sides in the war, but the Germans dug in and committed themselves to defending every inch of territory. The Thunderbirds now landed at Salerno, south of Naples, in the face of well-planned and determined German resistance. The enemy finally withdrew to its defensive mountain line further north and took up winter positions. The Allies would be forced to fight their way up the Italian boot in one of the toughest struggles with the Wehrmacht on any front in the Second World War. The terrain favoured the defence, and advancing troops had to endure heavy rains which washed away bridges and turned motor pools and bivouac areas into marshes.

At the end of January 1944 an infantry battalion of the Thunderbirds landed on the beach at Anzio, and the entire division became committed to what was to prove a savage and costly campaign, one of the bloodiest battles in US military history. The plan called for an amphibious landing to the rear of the Germans' forward winter position, just thirty miles south of Rome. The attack caught the enemy by surprise, but the Allies spent too long landing men and equipment and became trapped on the beachhead. The Germans launched a furious counter-attack with the intention of liquidating the confined force. Elements of seven German divisions, with full air support from the Luftwaffe and the heaviest artillery bombardment of the Italian campaign, were brought to bear. The conflict raged over four months, involved hundreds of thousands of men, and was more akin to a First World War battle, with massive artillery bombardments and human-wave assaults. Casualties were heavy on both sides, but the tenacity of the Thunderbirds saved the beachhead.[8]

The Thunderbirds then faced months of slogging battle through Italy until they reached the south bank of the Tiber, entering Rome across a blown bridge on 5 June. A month later the division was back in the Salerno area for intensive amphibious training. And after a further two weeks they were wading ashore at St Maxime on the French Riviera. The men Michel now came across had been in combat for more than a year and displayed a battle-hardened confidence he recognised. It felt good to be among them. 'I grew to love the men of the 45th. These were combat troops from Oklahoma, a long way from home, who faced heavy fighting with great individual courage. I developed enormous respect for the capabilities and fighting spirit of the US Army.'[9]

The Americans moved north out of Grenoble. The German Army in southern France had been ordered by Berlin to conduct an orderly fighting retreat, and the military command in Lyon was ordered to hold the city until the XIth SS Panzer Division had passed through. The Wehrmacht was threatened with encirclement as the Allied armies coming from Normandy and the south moved closer to joining up. General Patton reached Orléans at the same time as the Americans reached Grenoble. Lyon found itself trapped in an ever-tightening vice.

German control of the city had been on the verge of breakdown since the liberation of Grenoble, and it now drifted towards anarchy as members of the Résistance erected barricades and mounted a sustained campaign of sniping. But the Wehrmacht held on, ruthlessly demolishing whole blocks of apartments thought to shelter snipers. German soldiers continued to patrol the streets as retreating units from infantry divisions, as well as the XIth Panzer Division, passed through unhindered.

At Gestapo headquarters, Klaus Barbie gave the order to destroy archives and begin the final 'cleansing' operation. More than twenty French collaborators complicit in Gestapo crimes were murdered in order to remove witnesses. Barbie then turned his attention to the large prison population in Montluc.

On 17 August, one hundred and nine prisoners, half of whom were Jewish, were taken to Bron airport on the outskirts of the city. They were told they were going on a work detail to fill bomb craters made by an Allied raid a few days earlier, and they were given shovels to unload a truck full of earth. A German-speaking Alsatian, who had been taken along as interpreter, tried to intercede with the adjutant on behalf of a Jewish prisoner, who had both arms in bandages.

'This man can't work,' he said.

'Tonight, he won't feel a thing,' the adjutant replied.

Later, the prisoners were pushed into unfilled craters and machine-gunned. A thin layer of earth was then spread over them.

Three days after this massacre another one hundred and ten male and female prisoners were taken from Montluc and driven to a disused fort outside the city. Among them was a priest who had hidden weapons and a radio operator in the vestry of his church. The Gestapo had cut off his ears and pulled out one of his eyes. At the fort, the prisoners' hands were tied behind their backs and they were led up a flight of stairs into a room where they were shot. According to the sworn testimony of a member of the Milice who worked in Gestapo HQ: 'The prisoners had to walk over a heap of their former comrades. Blood was pouring through the ceiling and I could distinctly hear the victims fall as they were shot. At the end, the bodies lay one and a half metres high, and the Germans sometimes had to step on to their victims to finish off those who were still moaning.'

An old woman with a wrinkled face turned to the soldier about to shoot her and said, 'I'm dying for France, but you, you bastard, you'll rot in hell.'

The dead bodies were doused in petrol and set alight. SS men lit phosphorus bricks and left the building, wiping blood and brains from their uniforms. 'While the fire was raging, we saw a victim who had somehow survived,' the Milice witness said. 'She came to a window on the south side and begged her executioners for pity. They answered her prayers with a rapid burst of gunfire. Riddled with bullets and affected by the intense heat, her face contorted into a fixed mask, like a vision of horror. The temperature was increasing and her face melted like wax until one could see her bones. At that moment she gave a nervous shudder and began to turn her decomposing head – what was left of it – from left to right, as if to condemn her executioners. In a final shudder, she pulled herself completely straight, and fell backwards.'

On 21 August, yet more prisoners were taken from Montluc to Bron airport. They too were pushed into pits and machine-gunned. A man at work in a hangar with the airport supervisor said, 'Look boss, they're shooting people.'

The supervisor went to the door of the hangar and saw a further eight men pulled from a truck by their hair and jackets. They too were pushed into a crater and shot. Later a German soldier came over to the hangar to chat.

'It's terrible what they're doing, killing them like that,' the supervisor said.

'It's nothing,' the German replied. 'It's only Jews, good to make sausage for dogs.'

The Gestapo were becoming desperate in their murder. At headquarters in Place Bellecour prisoners were shot in their cells or taken to the basement for summary execution. Eight hundred prisoners remained in Montluc. A Résistance leader, unaware of the previous massacres, sent a signed letter to the Gestapo threatening to execute all German hostages taken by the Maquis if any prisoners were harmed. The immediate response of the Germans was to select fifty Jews and shoot them.

Cardinal Gerlier, horrified by reports of the massacre at the fort, went personally to Gestapo HQ to plead for the remaining prisoners' lives. At the same time the Résistance, now aware of the murders, announced the execution of eighty German hostages. The Gestapo was informed that a further seven hundred captives would be executed unless the murder stopped.

At 9.50 on the evening of 24 August the survivors at Montluc discovered that the Germans had abandoned the prison, leaving the keys with the highest-ranking inmate. People in the streets outside the jail heard the prisoners singing an emotional rendition of 'La Marseillaise'.

Klaus Barbie was among the last Germans to leave the city, taking a train out on 30 August. He was commended by his superiors for his work while in Lyon and duly promoted. Lyon was liberated by the Americans on 3 September.[10]

The Thunderbirds rolled forward in the peculiar atmosphere created by the contrast between fierce combat and euphoric liberation. Michel immediately demonstrated his value to S-2 by establishing a network of Résistance contacts behind enemy lines able to supply vital information. 'I interrogated prisoners about the strength and location of enemy troops. I questioned suspected Nazi operatives who had been captured on issues of sabotage or espionage.' The officers in charge allowed him an increasingly free hand. And as his fellow intelligence agents wrote their reports, he was surprised to find himself frequently asked to spell words in English.

The pitiful retreat of the Germans from the region, often in trucks pulled by horses because they had no petrol, was described by Gertrude Stein, who watched motor bikes roar through her village. 'Then there came along hundreds of German soldiers, walking, it was a terribly hot dry day and in the mountains the heat is even hotter than below, and these soldiers were children none older than sixteen and some looking not more than fourteen . . . these childish faces and the worn bodies and the tired feet and the shoulders of aged men and an occasional mule carrying a gun heavier than the boys could carry and then covered wagons . . . and later we were told in them were the sick and wounded, and they were being dragged by mules . . . and about a hundred of them were on women's bicycles that they had evidently taken as they went along, it was unbelievable, the motorised army of Germany of 1940 being reduced to this, to an old-fashioned Mexican army, it seemed to be more ancient than pictures of the moving army of the American civil war . . . it was a sorry sight in every way.'

The mayor's wife remarked that the Germans probably picked young soldiers because children could set fire to homes and kill without really knowing what they were doing, while even the worst of grown men drew the line somewhere. And once the Germans left – Stein's dog, Basket, was so traumatised after a hundred soldiers moved through the house and garden that it was unable to bark for days – people awaited the Americans. A splendid rumour circulated through the village that all the officers wore ten-gallon hats, a story Stein did nothing to suppress.

The first Americans were from the Thunderbirds, and they arrived in a jeep. 'What a day of days,' Stein wrote euphorically about the liberation of her village. 'Oh happy day, that is all I can say: oh happy day . . . We talked and patted each other in the good American way, and I had to know where they came from and where they were going and where they were born . . . After at least two years of not a word with America, there they were . . . Then we went to look at their car the jeep, and I had expected it to be much smaller but it was quite big and they said did I want a ride and I said you bet I wanted a ride and we all climbed in and there I was riding in an American army car driven by an American soldier. Everybody was so excited.'[11]

The division advanced rapidly, clearing snipers out of some towns and villages, and taking others without a shot. 'The Thunderbirds surrounded a German infantry unit and delivered an ultimatum to them to surrender or be destroyed. They didn't surrender. It was insanity. So we went ahead and destroyed them.' The survivors were taken as POWs, and most proved to be untrained, while some were not truly fit enough to serve. Michel was told by prisoners that when they took their medical they were passed with the words '*Gut für die Knochenmühle!*' – good for the bone mill! He questioned the commanding officer on his motives for refusing to surrender and inviting the slaughter of his own men. 'I thought he was playing for time and waiting for reinforcements – something logical. I needed to find out, and asked him, "What were you thinking? I want to know: *what were you thinking?*"'

The officer stiffened as he answered. '*Ein deutscher Soldat hat nicht zu denken!*' – A German soldier is not supposed to think!

Michel's knowledge of the language and the country made him invaluable on reconnaissance patrols. Men volunteered to accompany him because of his confidence and demonstrable lack of fear. He began to make close friends in the S-2 unit. One, Gerhard Sachs, was a soulmate, a German Jew from Philadelphia. He had volunteered to fight despite the fact that members of his family had also been prevented from emigrating from Germany for lack of a quota number, and had subsequently disappeared.

Sachs was a respected figure who had displayed his mettle again and again in Italy. On one occasion elements of the Thunderbirds were held up by a German position dug into the side of a mountain. Sachs volunteered to go and talk to the commanding officer in German and try to convince him that both sides would suffer unacceptable casualties unless they surrendered. Someone said, 'Are you crazy? They'll shoot you soon as look at you, white flag or no white flag.' Sachs said that it was a risk he was prepared to take and disappeared up the mountain carrying a white flag. There was no sign of him for most of the rest of the day, and although no shooting was heard, his platoon began to fear he had been killed. Suddenly, they spotted Sachs coming down the mountain from the fortified position accompanied by a German officer, while behind them trooped a company of unarmed German soldiers. Afterwards his colleagues joked that he could talk anybody into anything, and there were various suggestions that he be dropped into Berlin to have a chat with Adolf and wind up the war.

As combat and conversation drew the men together, his comrade gave Michel a lucky silver dollar. It had originally been given to Sachs by his fiancée at the beginning of the war, and now he wanted his friend to have it. Michel was deeply moved by the gesture. 'It was like giving your heart.'

Sachs cheerfully told Michel, when he considered his friend overly enthusiastic about American democracy, that he had often been the butt of anti-Jewish remarks within the regiment. Prejudice ran deep, even at the front. 'I was shocked. It didn't fit with my thoughts of the United States and liberty. I was very idealistic about America. Sachs told me that outbreaks of anti-Semitism in the US were normal. This shook me up.'

As a result, Michel decided not to disclose that he was a Jew until he had won the respect of the regiment and proved himself. 'I must say I did not experience this anti-Semitism myself – not ever – but for a while the stories made me cautious. I let them think of me as "the crazy Frenchman".' It was an image he reinforced when he roared along country lanes on a captured German BMW motor bike and sidecar, with the Stars and Stripes painted on one side of the petrol tank and the French tricolour on the other. A pennant of the Cross of Lorraine flew from the handlebars.

Colonel Wilson Gibson, who was in charge of a tank battalion and became a close friend, also gave Michel a silver dollar. Gibson was from New Orleans, Louisiana, and talked long and lovingly about the city and his family. 'If we make it through this alive you've got to promise me you'll come to New Orleans.'

'Okay.'

'The first place you visit if you ever come to the States. Solemn promise?'

'Promise.'

Among the duties of S-2 was the interrogation of German prisoners, and because of Michel's fluency in the language many of the important ones were questioned by him. Most were combat troops, or their officers, but SS and Gestapo men were also caught in the net.[12] All German soldiers carried a *Soldbuch*, a military passport with a photograph that contained each man's record, including rank, unit, regimental postings, area of operation and citations. Michel was struck by the fact that almost every German soldier of whatever rank carried pornographic material of some sort. The SS officers also carried daggers and hand-crafted leather whips, custom-made to each man's individual taste.

One SS prisoner, who was a physical giant, was brought to Michel for interrogation. He demanded the *Soldbuch*, leafed through it and put it to one side. He took the man's bag and found the usual whip, dagger and pornography. He returned to the *Soldbuch* for a closer look. The officer's unit had spent time in Cracow, Poland, and tucked into the back of the *Soldbuch* was a carefully folded paper. Michel opened it, saw that it was a service citation for a military decoration, and began to read.

It was a full account of the man's activities assisting the Gestapo in Cracow and amounted to a paean of praise from his superiors. The citation extolled his dedication to duty when he had prevented a group of Jews rounded up for deportation from escaping. It was an extraordinary document in that it precisely articulated the inverted values of the Third Reich, where brutality was praised as bravery and inhumanity recognised as duty. And most disturbing of all, the man who stood before him had not thought to destroy the citation but carried it with pride.

German troops had been particularly brutal in Cracow. One scorching June day, in 1942, seven thousand Jews were rousted from their homes at dawn and marched to Harmony Square in the centre of the ghetto. They waited in the sun throughout the morning without food or water and were then moved to the railway station. A Polish Catholic chemist, with a shop in the square, witnessed the behaviour of the German troops and wrote an account of it.

'Old people, women and children pass by the pharmacy windows like ghosts. I see an old woman of around seventy years, her hair loose, walking alone . . . Her eyes have a glazed look; immobile, wide open, filled with horror, they stare straight ahead. She walks slowly, quietly, only in her dress and slippers, without even a bundle or handbag. She holds in her hands something small, something black, which she caresses fondly and keeps close to her old breasts. It is a small puppy – her most precious possession, all that she saved and would not leave behind . . .

'Old and young pass by, some dressed, some only in their underwear, hauled out of their beds and driven out. People after major operations and people with chronic diseases . . . a blind old man, well known to the inhabitants of the ghetto; he is about seventy years, wears dark goggles over his blind eyes, which he lost in the battles on the Italian front in 1915 fighting side by side with the Germans. He wears a yellow armband with three black circles on his left arm to signify blindness. His head high, he walks erect, guided by his son on one side, by his wife on the other . . .

'Immediately after him, another elderly person appears, a cripple with one leg, on crutches. The Germans close in on them. Slowly, in dance step, one of them runs toward the blind man and yells with all his power: "*Schnell!*" – Hurry! This encourages the other Germans to start a peculiar game.

'Two of the SS men approach the old man without the leg and shout the order for him to run. Another one comes from behind and with the butt of his rifle hits the crutch. The old man falls down. The German screams savagely, threatens to shoot. All this takes place right in the back of the blind man who is unable to see, but hears the beastly voices of the Germans, interspersed with cascades of their laughter. A German soldier approaches the cripple who is lying on the ground and helps him to rise.

'For a moment we think that perhaps there will be at least one human being among them unable to stand torturing people one hour before their death. Alas, there was no such person in the annals of the Cracow ghetto. No sooner were they saturated with torturing the cripple than they decided to try the same with the blind war invalid. They chased away his son and wife, tripped him, and rejoiced at his falling to the ground. This time they did not even pretend to help him and he had to rise by himself, rushed on by horrifying screaming of the SS men hovering over him. They repeated this same game several times, a truly shattering experience of cruelty. One could not tell from what they derived more pleasure, the physical pain of the fallen invalid or the despair of his wife and son standing aside watching helplessly . . . The shots are echoing all over the ghetto.'[13]

Such was the nature of events in which the SS officer who stood before Michel was involved. He slipped the *Soldbuch* with its citation into his pocket with a shaking hand. 'This was my first encounter, eyeball to eyeball, with a man who was a war criminal. A man who had committed crimes against humanity that he was proud of and for which he was honoured. My whole being was transformed. I felt I had been there in Cracow. I lost all control.'

Despite the man's size, Michel grabbed him and hit him hard in the face. He ordered him to squat and do knee bends with hands outstretched – up and down, over and over, again and again. Michel ordered him to bark, *'Ich danke meinem Führer, Sieg Heil! Sieg Heil! Sieg Heil!'* – I thank my Führer for this. The SS man eventually collapsed, but Michel was still not satisfied and took the whip he had confiscated and set about him. In the midst of the beating, three American officers walked by and one moved forward to remonstrate. He was restrained by his colleagues. 'Leave him alone,' one said. 'He knows what he's doing.'

Finally, Michel stopped. Emotionally drained, he called the Military Police to take the SS officer away. The man was trembling as if he had the shakes and the MPs gave him a blanket, thinking he was cold. 'That was the only time my rage and hatred erupted physically. When I was spent, I realised that it was a mistake to allow myself to lose control. It was the one and only time it happened, the only time I physically assaulted a prisoner. I am not proud of this. I wasn't myself. I felt I was being driven, pushed – an instrument for all those who were massacred in Cracow.'

In September 1944, in the vicinity of Aubry, one of the regiment's battalions was holding a bridge across a river when it found itself in an exposed position and threatened by counter-attack. Michel made contact with a Résistance agent in a nearby town held by the enemy and obtained vital information on their military strength. He also connected with other Résistance agents in villages in the area and received daily bulletins on enemy movements and reinforcements. When two patrols sent out to reconnoitre failed to return, he volunteered to go into the area alone.

He came across a German soldier using an abandoned house as an observation post and could have shot him but chose to make him a prisoner. Michel forced him out of the house and moved back towards the American line. At one point on the journey, the man stopped and stubbornly refused to go any further. 'I got mad and told him he would be shot if he didn't move, but he stayed firmly where he was.' It was only then that the prisoner explained they were about to enter a freshly laid minefield. They made a wide detour.

The detailed intelligence Michel provided on enemy gun emplacements allowed accurate artillery fire to be directed on to them, and the threat to the force holding the bridge was lifted. Michel's work at this time so impressed the commanding officer of the 1st battalion of the 180th that he wrote him up for a Silver Star, one of the American military's highest decorations.[14]

Michel felt secure in the army, as if he had found a family and a home. 'It was very strange for me to be in the front with the US Army. It was so different from fighting with the Résistance, where if you heard a dog bark you knew there was a stranger about and you would be up and out of your bed on alert. In the army you slept in a foxhole and were shelled, but it didn't bother me because if you heard them the danger was over. You were connected, part of an army with guards posted, and had a sense of security. I slept soundly.'

In contrast to the furtive hit-and-run tactics of the Résistance, the new experience of front-line combat revealed two things to Michel about his own nature: a disregard for personal safety and a reluctance to kill. 'A personal killing would have been very, very difficult for me. I was prepared to kill in combat, used a rifle, and certainly caused loss of life by directing artillery, but I never personally shot anybody.'

He saw the fearlessness accredited to him by fellow soldiers as nothing more than the psychological pay-off that came with continued survival. Beating the odds in combat affected people in different ways: it could either make a man overcautious or reckless. 'I felt like a gambler at the roulette table who has amassed a mountain of chips on a long winning streak. You are only cautious with the original stake and can afford to lose when you are playing with winnings. It isn't real money. That is how I felt with my life. I had a powerful wish to fight the enemy and in situations of danger I felt my life had been won. It was a part of my winnings from the camps and the Résistance.'

The Thunderbirds ran into increasingly bitter fighting as they pushed north and the Germans battled to hold up their progress. But even at the front and on the move there were moments of romance. At one French town Michel decided his men would be more effective on patrol if they had bicycles. 'So we had to organise a dozen bicycles quickly. There was this young teacher from Paris, a girl of nineteen or twenty, who arranged everything. We jumped on the bikes and went on patrol.'

They came back at nightfall and returned the bicycles. The group broke up but Michel stayed behind to talk to the pretty Parisian school teacher. They went for a long walk in the beautiful hills surrounding the town. The girl explained that she had been evacuated from Paris to the country because of the Occupation, but now the war seemed to have caught up with her. 'She was very lovely and it was a beautiful night and we found ourselves in an isolated spot. It was very romantic. It all led to intimate embraces, and as day was about to break we made love. And as we were making love I found out she was a virgin – at the same time that an American artillery position opened fire right above us in the hills. The ground moved.'

The following day Michel returned to his unit, and the teacher to her classroom. The Thunderbirds moved on in heavy rain, a condition that was to plague them for days. 'We moved with the war and I never saw her again. Later, somewhere in the front, several soldiers told me that a girl had followed the troops on a bicycle and gone from unit to unit in the rain trying to find me. That time with her remains an unforgettable experience, beautiful and painful. It made me so sad to think of her in the rain.'

As the division pushed forward, and Michel continued to reconnoitre and patrol, it was not his nerve that failed him but his sense of direction. It was a peculiar and entirely unexpected phenomenon that began to trouble him, and he had to work hard to counteract it. He would be out on patrol and lose any sense of how he arrived at the place he was in, or how to get back. The spells varied in length and severity, and at first he dismissed them as a curious form of combat fatigue, but they were alarming – and potentially life-threatening.

The division was confronted with murderous opposition in the foothills of the Vosges mountains where the terrain favoured defensive action and the Germans had dug in. There was heavy fighting around Épinal and Michel, together with an American Indian who was an excellent scout, set up an observation post in a small house. The Germans spotted them and opened up with artillery. The scout squeezed himself into a corner, hoping to protect himself, while Michel thought the house would be blown to bits. A conflict developed between them on the course of action to take next.

'We have to get out!' Michel urged.

'No! I'm staying here!'

'The shelling isn't going to stop until they've blown up the house! I'm off!'

As he moved to go a shell exploded in the garden, and the near miss served to change the scout's mind. Together, they threw themselves through the door and crawled on their bellies into a flooded ditch. As they rose to their feet and ran back towards the line, two direct hits on the house blew it to pieces.

Two days later, after non-stop fighting, a large unit of the 180th was completely surrounded. 'I didn't like it at all and there was a real fear we might be captured. I had decided that I would never allow myself to be taken alive by the Germans – I knew something about it! So I decided to do everything not to be captured and to find a way out alive. I struck out on my own and somehow made it through enemy lines, but in the tension of the moment did not bother to register any visual landmarks.'

It had been blind luck, but once reunited with American troops he was expected to lead a force back in to relieve the surrounded unit. 'They wanted me to go back the way I had come out.' Michel now found himself in an impossible position. 'I hadn't told anybody about my loss of a sense of direction. I didn't want anybody to know. It would have taken me out of the war. And now I was being asked to go back to a dangerous place in a combat zone and had no idea how to do it. What to do? If I said that I didn't know how I got out and couldn't lead them back, it would look like I was a coward and not prepared to do anything to help liberate an army unit. If I agreed and failed, it would be disaster. Possibly death. I had never found myself in such a dilemma.'

He protested that he had merely followed his nose and taken a chance, but the claim was dismissed as false modesty. Unable to refuse, he hoped to make it back in the same mysterious way that he had found his way out. Ten men followed him, including a major and two officers with radios. The plan was to call in more troops once they were in position. 'I already had quite a reputation, so they all followed me confidently, sure that I knew what I was doing. But I had no idea. I was lost. I was so happy to have got out, now it was all-important to get back in. It was a horrendous dilemma. I really don't know how I found my way back, but I did. It could have gone horribly wrong and I would have been guilty of misleading them.'

It had taken the regiment two days to crawl to the western edge of the city defended by trenches and minefields. Heavy mortar and artillery fire pinned them down, until, supported by tanks, they took the town house by house. Épinal was cleared on 24 September, and for most of the following month the Thunderbirds employed tactics using close tank and artillery support to capture and push the Germans out of one French town after another.

The division then crossed the Moselle and established a toehold among the enemy's positions in the Vosges mountains. Michel, meanwhile, put forward a plan to Allied intelligence. He felt the most effective he could now be in his personal war was as a member of the Special Forces of the French Army. His plan was to be parachuted behind enemy lines into the German Alps to organise deserters, forced labourers and opponents of the regime into resistance groups. This involved training in Besançon, so Michel organised his travel plans to take him through Lyon. He was concerned to find out how Suzanne and her mother had weathered the liberation.[15]

No one answered the bell at the apartment, so he made his way to a Latin American restaurant that had been popular during the Occupation and which he knew Suzanne had frequented. The fashionable clientele at the time included black-marketeers, police spies, German officers and Résistance agents. A young woman who ran the restaurant, who knew Suzanne well, told Michel she had been arrested in Nice on suspicion of collaboration and that her mother had gone to try to obtain her release.

Michel left for the south after a minor hiccup in Grenoble: the American Army jeep in which he had driven down was stolen. Infuriated, he made such a scene that a French general loaned him his staff car and driver. On arrival in Nice, he found Suzanne's mother through mutual friends, and she told him the whole sorry story of the arrest. He went directly to the jail where, despite his American uniform or possibly because of it, he was given the run-around. Exasperated, he insisted upon an appointment with the investigating judge handling the case, and was eventually granted one. The judge listened without expression and said that as the case was in process there was nothing he could do – the law must take its course. Justice would surely be done. He stood and offered his hand to signal that the interview was over and there was nothing more to be said.

'Who are you to tell me that?' Michel demanded angrily, rising from his chair. 'How dare you! What the hell did you do for the liberation of France? Where were you? I want to know before I allow you to talk to me like that.' Michel pulled rank he did not have and made threats he could not fulfil, and the judge began to move uneasily behind his desk. 'We're still fighting in France! I'm going to be parachuted behind German lines, and you're refusing to release a woman who worked with the Résistance from the very beginning! I'm here to investigate this case on behalf of CIC and the Deuxième Bureau. I want to know why the hell she is in jail. I want to look at the record.'

The judge quickly decided to modify his position and offered to cut through the bureaucracy and take a personal interest in the case. He explained that Suzanne had been arrested by Résistance fighters, who suspected her of working with the Germans.

'What does this prove?' Michel demanded. 'This woman works for Allied intelligence and I want to know more. Before I leave Nice I want her out, unless you can give me valid reasons to keep her in jail.'

The judge promised, after Michel's assurances, that Suzanne would be freed. Michel remained in Nice until he was certain the judge had honoured his word. Extraordinarily, both the money and the jewellery were returned to her. 'And then I left. I did not want to be present when she came out of jail. I didn't want to be in the position of receiving thanks from her.'

Michel drove on to Besançon, where he was expected to begin training with the Special Forces of the French Army. He was put through a course in radio communications, parachute jumping and commando combat. Throughout this he asked questions about preparations for his original plan, but seemed always to be put off. Finally, in a top-secret briefing, he was told there was to be an interim mission. It was dangerous, politically delicate and highly classified, and, far from having a military objective, it was connected with industrial espionage. The intention was not to damage the German war machine but to beat the Americans, British and Russians to the spoils of war. Men undertaking the mission were promised both financial reward and even property. 'I considered I was being offered a bribe to undertake something that had nothing whatever to do with the war. I was insulted.'

Disillusioned, Michel asked to be reassigned to the Thunderbirds – the Okie division fighting without financial incentive in a foreign land far from home. He rejoined them after they had moved into combat in Alsace. He was welcomed back by his tough, laconic comrades-in-arms with grins and jokes and the occasional affectionate slap on the back. It was good to be home.

The thing that every GI on the front remembers about the winter of 1944 is the cold. As the days grew shorter, troops forever on the move faced a new enemy in the weather. The only compensation was the knowledge that the Germans were similarly afflicted as they retreated. They had suffered a terrible toll in killed and wounded and were said to be thoroughly dispirited. Their defeat was certain.

The division pushed forward in knee-deep mud lashed by cold drizzle driven by raw, biting wind. Fog clung until late morning. The men cast a wistful glance in the direction of the troops on their left flank manning the eighty-five-mile Ghost Front of the Ardennes Forest, a quiet, empty area considered something of a rest camp. It was held by only three American infantry divisions and a single armoured division. And even this small force was not up to much. Two of the three infantry divisions had suffered nine thousand casualties in combat and been sent to the area to recuperate, while the third was entirely new to battle. The 9th Armoured Division was also inexperienced. The Ghost Front was a place where the artillery was fired for the sole purpose of keeping the men in practice, and patrols probed enemy lines without much danger.

As the Thunderbirds pushed deeper into Alsace they broke German resistance at Mutzig, one of the most heavily defended positions facing the Maginot Line, and set up defensive perimeters to stem an expected German counter-attack aimed at taking Strasbourg. Once they crossed the Maginot Line every town had to be fought for street by street.

Elements of the division entered Germany on 15 December. Despite the terrible weather, there was a feeling that the war was won, and morale was boosted as the Thunderbirds stepped on to the enemy's own soil. It meant another combat Christmas away from home, but no one believed the war could go on for much longer.

But all along the Ghost Front the enemy was invisibly massing in preparation for one last, great military gamble. Incredibly, almost two thousand pieces of heavy artillery, a thousand tanks and assault guns, and a quarter of a million troops moved by stealth into attack positions. Camouflage officers had been assigned to every village, strict radio silence prevailed, and truckloads of straw had been laid on the roads to deaden the sound of tanks on the move. To keep the movement of traffic to a minimum, every shell for the opening barrage was moved to the front by hand. Soldiers faced endless roll calls to prevent desertion and were issued with charcoal in order not to reveal their presence by the smoke from ordinary fires.

The objective of the German attack – code-named Autumn Mist – was to go on the offensive out of the Ardennes and smash through Blitzkrieg-style to take Antwerp. This was the major port of supply for the Allied offensive into Germany. Its loss would set the Allied attack back months, split the British and Canadian armies from the Americans, and allow both to be encircled and destroyed. The plan, masterminded by Hitler himself, was a bold gamble that caught the Allies completely by surprise.

'This battle is to decide whether we shall live or die,' Hitler declared. 'I want all my soldiers to fight hard and without pity. The battle must be fought with brutality and all resistance must be broken in a wave of terror. In this most serious hour of the Fatherland, I expect every one of my soldiers to be courageous, and again courageous. The enemy must be beaten – now or never! Thus lives our Germany!'

But the plan was a fantasy. One of the commanders of the two German armies committed to the operation articulated the military obstacles. 'All Hitler wants me to do is to cross a river, capture Brussels, and then go on and take Antwerp. And all this in the worst time of the year through the Ardennes when the snow is waist deep and there isn't room to deploy four tanks abreast let alone armoured divisions. When it doesn't get light until eight and it's dark again at four with re-formed divisions made up chiefly of kids and sick old men – and at Christmas.'

The Germans also had only a quarter of the fuel needed; forward units were expected to capture supplies from the Americans as they advanced. At dawn on 16 December, the Panzer armies attacked the weakly defended Ghost Front, which now became the worst place on earth. The eighty-five-mile line erupted into flame as mortars, rockets and heavy artillery launched the opening barrage. American soldiers on the receiving end cowered in their foxholes and wondered how they could survive such a bombardment. Thick fog and lack of communication led each unit to believe it was the victim of a heavy local attack.

When the guns stopped, giant searchlights cut through the fog like great swathes of artificial moonlight. Waves of tanks ground along the roads and infantry clad in white combat gear, looking like ghosts, moved across the snow fourteen abreast. The new Messerschmitt 262 jets, one of Hitler's promised 'miracle weapons', screamed overhead carrying thousand-pound bombs. As Field Marshal Gerd von Runstedt told the troops as he sent them into attack: 'We gamble everything!'

One American division was quickly overrun, and elements of another surrounded and cut off. Denied aerial reconnaissance because of the terrible weather, the Allied High Command failed to appreciate the magnitude of the attack, and responded to the full-scale assault as if it were a local diversion. The combat soon became a nasty, no-quarter conflict on both sides, especially after unarmed American POWs were killed in what became known as the Malmédy Massacre. As news of the massacre reached American GIs, the response from their combat commanders was immediate: Take no prisoners! The order was occasionally even put in writing: 'No SS troops or paratroopers will be taken prisoner, but will be shot on sight.'[16]

For the next eleven days the Battle of the Bulge, as Churchill dubbed it because of its appearance on the map, involved a million men. In the first days of the offensive, panic spread through the civilian population of Belgium and the Allied military were thoroughly shaken. History was repeating itself, for by relegating the Ardennes to the status of a poorly manned second front, Hitler was able to exploit the same weak point where he had attacked France four years earlier.

The campaign in the Ardennes siphoned off troops from the Seventh Army and the Thunderbirds found themselves hard-pressed on their section of the front. Four platoons were cut off for six days in one town before they were relieved. SS troops separated battalions from their regiments, one of which failed in an attempt to fight its way out. Only two men survived. At the beginning of January the division fell back to the Maginot Line and went on the defensive for the first time since Anzio.

By Boxing Day, however, the German advance had begun to slow. American armoured reinforcements blocked the enemy's Panzers and prevented them from seizing massive stockpiles of fuel. The United States 101st Airborne Division raced to Bastogne by truck, an essential road centre. Although ill-equipped to battle tanks and surrounded by the enemy, the division denied the Panzers access to the town and blocked the advance. American and British counter-attacks forced the retreat of four leading Panzer divisions, and by 16 January the front was restored.

The United States had suffered nineteen thousand fatalities and had had a further fifteen thousand men taken prisoner. The losses were heavy, but could be made good, while German losses of one hundred thousand men killed, wounded or captured were irreplaceable. They had also lost a crucial eight hundred tanks and a thousand planes. Autumn Mist had shaken the Allies, and caused a brief delay, but at the high cost to the Germans of denying men and equipment to the eastern campaign against the Red Army. The Battle of the Bulge was Hitler's last gamble, and he had lost.[17]

The Thunderbirds were taken off the line on 18 February, after eighty-six days of combat in Alsace and Germany. It fell back to the region around Épinal to rest and resupply. Stories circulated throughout the division about the wholesale massacre by the SS of unarmed American POWs at Malmédy. When the division went back into battle after a month, attitudes had hardened.

The 180th Infantry crossed the Blies river on 15 March, and the following day the Thunderbirds reached the Siegfried Line, which crumbled before its assault. Six days later the infantry crossed the Rhine. Once inside Germany, Michel was transferred to the Counter

Intelligence Corps because of his fluent German and interrogation skills. This operated on a divisional rather than a regimental level, and gave him enormous freedom of action. He became famous for running a one-man intelligence organisation within the organisation. However, it was stressed that no one outside CIC should be informed that Michel was not an American citizen, and that his reports should be signed by his senior officers.[18]

After crossing the Main river, an eight-kilometre front just south of Aschaffenburg was established. The battle for the city exemplified the type of suicidal, last-ditch defensive action the German Army was still prepared to undertake. Wounded German soldiers from five military hospitals in the region were ordered from their beds for the final battle. Aschaffenburg had a fanatical SS major as commander who organised old men, women and even children into defence squads, and ordered the hanging of those officers who suggested surrender. Their bodies were still swinging from the lamp-posts when the Thunderbirds entered the town. One young German lieutenant had a sign attached to his body: COWARDS AND TRAITORS HANG![19] As the GIs moved from street to street, fighting in the blistering heat of burning buildings, teenage girls lobbed grenades from rooftops.

In retaliation, the Allied command ordered that the garrison be annihilated and the heavily fortified city wiped from the face of the map. Artillerymen poured shells into the city and Thunderbolt pilots from the 1st Tactical Air Force rained down bombs until there was nothing left but a smoking ruin. At the end of a week of battle the German commander did what he had executed his officers for suggesting, and came out with a white flag and surrendered. It was the division's toughest fight inside Germany, in which fifteen hundred Germans were killed and another three thousand captured.[20]

'After the fighting I got into what was left of the city hall. There was all this German money in one of the offices in what was part walk-in closet, part safe. Oh God, a lot of money! Wads and wads of it. Of course, the Germans wouldn't take it and the Americans couldn't use it. It was worthless. I had the idea as a joke of wallpapering a room with it, and filled a suitcase. I called it my wallpaper money.' The GIs with him threw wads of cash into a fire to keep warm, and lit cigarettes with high-denomination notes. 'We also discovered a *cave* full of thousands of bottles of French wine and cognac. It was put under guard and requisitioned. It was not left behind.'

As the US Army moved from town to town, a system developed. Towns that were directly on the front line were evacuated, while others cleared of the enemy had a strict curfew imposed upon them. No unauthorised person could be out on the streets after dark, and it was ordered that buildings and streetlights should be blacked out.

One day, Michel was passing through a small town during curfew, driven by a tough, daring CIC agent called Pico. The sound of a piano playing provocative and strident Nazi marching songs filled the deserted streets. The jeep bounced across the cobblestones and pulled up outside the block of apartments where the music was being played.

Michel jumped out, went to the front of the building and hammered on the door. It was opened by a porter who quickly stepped aside the moment he saw an American soldier with a carbine slung across the shoulder. Michel climbed a single flight of stairs and knocked loudly on the door of the apartment where the piano continued to play. The music stopped.

After a pause, the door was opened by a tall, beautiful young woman who glared with undisguised hostility at Michel in his American uniform. 'I was passing by and heard the piano and wondered who could be playing so loudly at this hour?'

'I was playing. Is it wrong to play the piano?' The woman looked at him with a superior air of defiance and contempt.

Michel pushed past her and entered the apartment. 'You play very well, although I cannot say I admire your taste in music.' He glanced about him, and said casually, 'Your identity papers!'

The demand only served to increase the woman's contemptuous manner as she took a leather wallet from her handbag and rifled unhurriedly through it. Her languid action was designed to be a provocation, and Michel was provoked. He reached forward and took the wallet from her. 'It was a little trick I used when I asked for papers. I always took everything. Those who had nothing to hide didn't mind, but those who did hesitated – if only for a fraction of a second. Depending on those reactions I could read who they were. She had a reaction.'

He began to go through the documents. Another trick he employed if he found anything of interest was to skip over the document as if it were of no importance. He ignored a pass to Peenemünde, the V-2 rocket complex, signed by Goering, and inspected the woman's ID papers briefly. He returned all the documents to the wallet and handed it back.

'That piano music was very loud.' He walked to the window, opened it and called down to Pico to join him. 'I want a complete house search,' he said. 'Top to bottom. Everything!'

Pico looked surprised, but began the search as the woman maintained her detached and aloof manner. A thorough search turned up a quantity of engineering blueprints with an obvious military application.

'What are these?'

The woman lost a little of her composure. She insisted she was merely a student who had been given drawings by her professor, who had subsequently fled.

Michel put on a sad face. 'It is unfortunate that he is not available to verify your story. You'll have to come with us.'

They drove to the temporary CIC HQ, set up in an evacuated town nearby. The woman continued her open defiance and left no one in any doubt that she was an unrepentant Nazi. Michel remained silent as he listened to his CIC colleagues question her. The lengthy interrogation produced nothing, except to establish that the woman was not a student but a qualified engineer with a high-level clearance to pursue secret work. She refused to supply either details of her work or the name and location of associates. 'However hard the interrogators pushed, her attitude never changed. She never answered, and said nothing. Not a word.'

There were no facilities in the combat zone to keep prisoners, or the time and resources to pursue interrogations in depth, so it was decided to send her to the rear. Michel suggested he talk to her alone in a final attempt to break through the steely reserve. His colleagues shrugged sceptically and wished him luck.

The woman was taken to a barely furnished room and left alone to contemplate her fate. Michel then entered, sat down and started talking softly in a coaxing, conspiratorial tone.

'I want to talk to you alone, away from the others. I think you should understand that if you don't answer questions here you will be turned over to the Special Interrogation Centre. The people there do not accept silence for answers. They have ways to make a person talk. They use very unpleasant techniques. I'd rather not see you subjected to this.' There was no response, and she remained haughty as ever. Michel paused. 'That would not be very pleasant for you . . . a woman.' Once again the woman did not seem to react.

The 'Special Interrogation Centre' did not exist, but had a sinister ring, and he allowed the woman's imagination to invent the nature of questioning pursued in such a place. She would have known what went on in Nazi interrogation centres and would have no reason to think the Allies behaved any differently.

'I'm trying to avoid sending you there,' Michel continued. 'Why am I trying to avoid it? Because I understand you.' He paused for effect. 'Although you see me in an American uniform, inside is a German. I am German – *Ganz und gar ein Deutsche*. Entirely and altogether German.'

This was a performance Michel had developed to a fine art over the previous weeks – an appeal from one true German to another. He explained that his mother was from Hamburg and his father from Berlin, and that they had emigrated to America before the war. He offered the helping hand of a German brother, with a connection to the future, to a victim stranded and alone among the ruins of a doomed Nazi state. The war was lost, the Reich at an end, but an eternal Germany remained to be redeemed and rebuilt.

'Yes, I came here with the United States Army, but not to fight my people or conquer them. I am here to liberate them from tyranny. To liberate them from this insane destruction. What did you do, all of you? To my country! To my people! I came back here and found a destroyed nation. You *know* the war is lost. Between the Americans and the Russians the country will be squeezed into nothing. Continuing the war only adds to the death and destruction. Worse, the longer the war goes on the greater the danger of the Soviets chewing off more territory, more people. The rockets you developed will be used against you by the Communists.'

The spiel went on and on, aggressive and outraged. And over it hung the threat of the Special Interrogation Centre and its unspoken horrors. The woman continued to say nothing and seemed untouched by fear. 'I had never seen so much genuine contempt. Such arrogance and defiance. I think she would have withstood torture. I was impressed.'

Nothing seemed likely to move the woman from her implacable position. Michel began to wind down and said simply that if she did not co-operate he would be powerless to prevent her being sent away. No future American interrogator would ever understand her.

At first, there was no reaction. Michel sighed, and prepared to leave.

'Wait,' the woman said quietly. She seemed to find it difficult to speak. 'Maybe you're right in some of the things you say.'

'Let's talk,' Michel said. 'Who are you and what is your connection to Peenemünde? Why don't you tell me about it? Take your time.'

174

The words now came in a torrent that was a lament for a political dream destroyed and a country in ruins. Michel listened sympathetically and nodded understandingly as he gently guided the woman into revealing those areas of her life in which he was interested. 'She told me she was a physicist. That she had worked at Peenemünde on the V-2 and at other secret plants. She told me about new weapons, the latest missiles that were way beyond the V-2 – faster, more accurate, and more destructive. And that they were fully developed and ready for production. She gave me vague indications of the location where these weapons were under construction.' At the end of a long session they were both exhausted.

'I appreciate your co-operation,' Michel said. He told her that it would no longer be necessary to send her to the interrogation centre and that he would organise a place for her to stay the night. The army always requisitioned a number of abandoned houses in the combat zone for officers' use, and he now took the woman to one.

A peculiar and delicate atmosphere of trust had developed between them. The deserted house was well-furnished and comfortable, and as the electricity had been cut off, Michel lit a number of candles. 'To help her settle in I showed her the bedroom. She sat down on the bed, and as I was about to leave she began weeping. I sat down beside her to comfort her and she grabbed me, laying her head on my shoulder. Between sobs she confessed to a terrible sense of having betrayed her country, her friends, her associates. Only because of my sympathy and understanding, she told me, had she turned traitor.'

It was a charged moment: the two of them alone together in the bedroom of a comfortable house in flickering candlelight. The war seemed far away and momentarily unreal. The 'sympathy and understanding' had been completely false on Michel's part, but in the seductive atmosphere of the moment romance swept over him. 'I felt physical and emotional attraction. She was lovely, and nestling in my arms. It only would have taken my acquiescence and a hug to go further.'

But conscience nagged. The woman had been made vulnerable and amorous only through deceit. 'First I had undermined her self-discipline by inducing great anxiety about her future. Then I had stripped away her loyalty by presenting myself in a fake pose and turning her nationalism upside down. And certainly her strong attraction to me owed much to the relief she felt on escaping physical and mental pain from the "Special Interrogation Centre" through what she thought was my influence. For my part, while I retained reluctant respect for her initial defiance, I also knew she was truly one of the enemy. I had suffered too much from the Germans to become emotionally involved with one, beautiful and intelligent as she was. I pulled away from her and said good night.'

Back at the CIC offices the next morning, everyone was certain that Michel had slept with the enemy, although Counter Intelligence took a liberal position regarding such things. A strict non-fraternisation order, signed by Dwight D. Eisenhower, the supreme commander, barred military personnel from mixing with the German population except in a professional capacity. 'I didn't try to persuade them it never happened. I doubt if they would have understood my reactions any more than she did. I had been very tempted.'

Among the many prisoners processed by Michel at this time was an SS man concerned about the fate of his dog. The Wehrmacht used dogs in combat and the massive black and white Landseer-Newfoundland had been chosen for its size and strength, and trained against its nature to be an aggressive attack animal. The SS man had grown fond of his ferocious charge and was genuinely disturbed that it might be put down. He held the dog tightly on a short leash and choke chain as it snarled menacingly at anyone who came close.

'Beautiful dog,' Michel said approvingly.

As he approached, the animal rose to its feet, pulling against its leash. It seemed to roar like a lion rather than bark, and its fangs were bared behind the quivering lips of its enormous head. Without thinking, Michel moved his clenched fist towards the dog's open mouth.

'Nein!' he commanded. Confused, the Landseer growled uncertainly but obeyed.

'I'll take him,' Michel said, and the SS man handed him the leash.

The dog's name was Barry, and he proved to be a handful. Although enormous and very strong – books recommend that owners of the breed harness the animal to a small cart as part of the dog's exercise routine – the Landseer is gentle and friendly by nature. 'He had been trained to be mean. To go on the attack in battle. He barked and snarled at everyone and had been rewarded for this behaviour. I began to teach him differently. I don't train animals, I teach them. It took a while, but he slowly began to respond. He accepted me almost immediately, but he was ferocious with other people. I had a German police dog before – Rando, who got killed on the road – and knew the commands and how they were trained.

Barry began to accept the people who worked with me and was actually very friendly. But he did not allow people he didn't know anywhere near him. He proved an effective interrogation aid.'[21]

The Thunderbirds now joined the attack on Nuremberg, the Bavarian city that had hosted the massive, operatic Nazi party rallies in the 1930s. Once a beautiful walled medieval town, it was now reduced to ruins by Allied artillery bombardment and air raids. Three regiments attacking abreast moved into the city and five thousand prisoners were taken on the first day. It was a strange battle with no discernible front line, just shifting urban chaos with Americans in one street and Germans in another, slugging it out.

An American agent from the OSS (Office of Strategic Services), who had lived and worked within the city and radioed intelligence reports to the advancing troops, now found himself trapped. Michel volunteered to get him out. He changed into civilian clothes and was driven by jeep as far into the city as possible. He then slipped into the section occupied by the Germans. 'The chaotic conditions created by the battle actually made it less difficult than it sounds and I located the OSS agent fairly easily. I moved through the streets as a German civilian, and there was no fighting where I was. I had been given the address and a city plan. I then led the OSS man back to the American lines and made a rendezvous with the jeep.'

Driving back through the section of the city captured by the Americans, they were shot at from a building by German snipers. Bullets ripped into the pavement and ricocheted off walls. The driver pulled into cover while Michel took his carbine and ran towards the building, snapping off a few rounds as he went. 'In retrospect my action seems foolhardy, but I was still operating on the winner's luck of a gambler on a hot streak.'

On the ground floor, sheltering behind a window, he spotted four young men. They were attached to one of the home defence units created late in the war and had a girl with them. At the sight of Michel they ran up the stairs to the first floor, leaving the girl behind. Michel caught her and pursued the men, climbing the stairs with the girl in front of him as a human shield. The men had tried to enter the apartments on the first floor, but found all the doors bolted against them. Michel shouted in German that anyone who provided shelter would have their apartments destroyed by the American Army. Trapped at the end of the corridor, the young men threw down their weapons and surrendered.

The soldiers were handcuffed and driven in a truck to HQ. The girl sat in the back of the jeep beside Michel. She told him that she was a singer who had tagged along with her friends and been prepared to fight. At the end of their journey Michel told her that she was free to go. But she was reluctant to leave and said she wanted to be with him. That night, in a flagrant violation of the non-fraternisation order, Michel went to bed with her. 'I didn't try to seduce her – she offered herself. I suppose, looking back on it, she had become psychologically dependent on her captor. I remember it mostly because it meant nothing. It was purely physical for both of us. I felt neither intellectual nor emotional conflict about a one-night stand with this particular enemy. I can hardly recall what she looked like – in contrast to the piano-playing rocket engineer, who remains forever etched in my memory.'

After four days' fighting the city was taken. Men from the Thunderbirds raised the Stars and Stripes in Luitpold Stadium, where Adolf Hitler had once been worshipped by hundreds of thousands of the party faithful.

Amid the triumph Michel received terrible news: Gerhard Sachs, his friend and soulmate from Philadelphia, had been killed in combat. 'This brave man, this hero, who had fought all through Italy and France and Germany, killed so close to the end of the war. In Nuremberg. It was a bitter blow.'

On the road between Nuremberg and Munich stood the town of Dachau and its concentration camp. Small in comparison to the others, the camp was thought to house in excess of thirty thousand people. Rumours about conditions in the various camps and the pitiful state of the survivors had been circulating through the army since the middle of the month. There had been stories about the nature of these places for some time, but battle-weary troops were cynical and wondered if they were not further examples of wartime propaganda. The Soviet Army had overrun and liberated camps in Poland – including Auschwitz – at the end of January, but little information came from that quarter and not much of it was believed.

Then, on 11 April, the 3rd Armored Division reached Nordhausen, on the south of the Harz Mountains, and finally there were American soldiers who were eyewitnesses to the horror. Nearby were the vast caverns carved out of the mountains that housed the underground complex where the giant V-2 rockets were built, and beside them stood Camp Dora, which had once held tens of thousands of slave labourers who serviced the gigantic factory.

As the GIs approached the camp, they were confronted with walking skeletons, stumbling ghostlike along the roads. They were everywhere, shuffling along barely alive in their striped prison garb, or lying sprawled by the side of the road too weak to move. It was often impossible even to tell the sex of the survivors, who seemed to belong to a different species.

The troops then entered the camp itself. There were twenty-three thousand survivors and three thousand unburied bodies rotting inside the buildings. Thirty thousand others had already been exterminated. 'It was a fabric of moans and whimpers of delirium and outright madness,' one soldier said. 'Here and there a single shape tottered about, walking slowly, like a man dreaming.'[22] The surviving slave labourers were found in a condition 'almost unrecognisable as human. All were little more than skeletons. The dead lay beside the sick and dying in the same beds; filth and human excrement covered the floors. No attempt had been made to alleviate the disease and gangrene that had spread unchecked among the prisoners.'[23]

At one town on the way south, the Thunderbirds moved forward unexpectedly first thing in the morning, and Michel was forced to leave his things in the deserted house where he had spent the night. He returned late in the afternoon to pick them up and surprised a gang of half a dozen scraggly youths in their late teens going through his belongings. Thinking they were German looters, he unholstered his gun and yelled at them. The youths froze and dropped everything they held on to the floor as he bore down on them brandishing the automatic. Their fear was pitiful, and Michel heard one cry out in anguish, '*Oy Gottenew!*'

The despairing voice shook him to his soul. The terrified boy was saying 'Oh dear God' in Yiddish. The young men were not looters but recently liberated inmates from a camp. It was Michel's first encounter with survivors of the German concentration camps. He holstered his pistol and tried to make amends. 'Until then I forgot to cry. And still I did not cry, but tears came to my eyes. Tears of shame. It tore me, and still does. An immense hurt – an emotional stab in the eyes. That in my first encounter with Jewish survivors I had threatened and frightened them. It shames me to have shouted at them. To have waved a pistol at them. It shames me still.'

On 15 April Edward R. Murrow, the famous CBS war correspondent, broadcast a report about Buchenwald, a camp just outside Weimar. He described the barracks. 'When I entered, men crowded around, tried to lift me to their shoulders. They were too weak. Many of them could not get out of bed. I was told that this building had once stabled eighty horses. There were twelve hundred men in it, five to a bunk. The stink was beyond all description.' As he walked out into the fresh air of the courtyard, a man fell dead. He visited the part of the camp where the children were kept, some only six years old and all tattooed with a number. 'The children,' an old man said. 'Enemies of the state.' In the hospital two hundred people had died the previous day and a doctor reeled off the causes of death: 'Tuberculosis, starvation, fatigue, and there are many who have no desire to live.' In a garage Murrow found approximately five hundred bodies stacked neatly like cordwood. Five different men, who had experience of other camps, told him that they were all worse than Buchenwald. The broadcast was deeply disturbing and shocking at the time to those who heard it. There was no way of knowing that the horrors described were only the tip of the iceberg of what would become known as the Holocaust.[24]

The mission to liberate Dachau was assigned to the 3rd Battalion, 157th Infantry Regiment of the Thunderbirds, and Michel drove down independently in his capacity as a Divisional CIC agent, and steeled himself against the horrors to come. On 29 April 1945, a cold Sunday, two columns of infantry, riding on tanks and armoured bull-dozers, moved through the eerily silent town towards the camp itself.[25] As the infantry grew close to the camp they became aware of a sickening stench. One column of troops came across thirty-nine railroad cars in a siding filled with thousands of rotting human corpses. GIs began to throw up. Some broke down and wept, others entered a frozen zone of deep shock, while some exploded into vengeful combat rage. 'Let's kill every one of these bastards,' GIs started yelling. 'Don't take any SS alive!'[26]

An SS man wearing Red Cross patches tried to make a break for it and was shot down. Four others, who came out of hiding with their hands in the air, were herded into one of the railcars by an enraged lieutenant, who emptied his pistol into them. The troops were shot at as they entered the main gate of the camp and took cover. They moved forward when they saw a white flag, but SS guards opened fire again. When a second flag appeared, the troops advanced cautiously.

The smell of corrupted bodies was overpowering. 'When we entered the camp the first thing visible was the source of the odour: a small mountain of decaying bodies. Nearby stood another mountain of discarded clothes and shoes. Thousands of men, women and children stood at the wire, gaunt and unwashed, and tried to express their joy over liberation. GIs just stood on the other side of the wire staring at them in shock. Even though I had fought the Nazis for more than five years and had seen them at what I thought was their worst, Dachau stunned me. It was gut-wrenching. It is one thing to know, another to experience.'

The first concern of the military was to find the SS troops who resisted the advance. Many had changed out of their uniforms into civilian clothes in an attempt to escape in the confusion, although inmates were quick to point them out. 'The GIs shot a number of them on the spot. Technically, as they were out of uniform, these summary executions could probably be justified by the rules of war. Actually, the treachery of the fake surrender signal that led to casualties, plus outrage over camp conditions, provoked the retribution. Even in retrospect the action does not strike me as harsh, and I can't say I was upset.'

SS prisoners were herded into a coal yard, lined up and told to keep their hands above their heads. When they saw a GI load a belt of ammo into a machine gun they panicked and bolted. The machine gun opened fire and seventeen were killed. An officer rushed to the machine-gunner and grabbed him by the collar, pulled out his .45 and fired it into the air to attract attention. The machine-gunner began to shake and weep. Another sixteen SS men rousted from a guard tower were also shot down. It was becoming difficult to control the men as hardened combat troops exploded under the strain.[27]

Michel took photographs: of the dead bodies of paunchy SS soldiers in their civilian clothes; of the heap of naked corpses discarded like so much rubbish; of the mountain of old clothes awaiting its grim sorting; of the half-burned bodies in the ovens of the crematorium; of the *Brausebad* (showers) that was really a gas chamber; of a coloured mural of the SS riding pigs; and of a notice painted on the wall: REINLICHKEIT IST GÖTTLICHKEIT – Cleanliness is Godliness – Don't Forget to Wash your Hands.

The world has viewed similar images many times since the war, and they have never lost the power to sicken and shock, but on the day of liberation none of those present had seen such things. It was a vision of twentieth-century inhumanity on such a scale that the senses were overwhelmed. Michel took pictures simply because he thought no description in words could ever convey the scale and systematic nature of the horror. And also because he feared the outside world would refuse to believe it. His friend, Michael Nelken, had committed suicide when his pre-war account of Dachau had not been believed. And in those days conditions had been nothing like this.

Altogether there were thirty-three thousand survivors in Dachau, two thousand, five hundred and thirty-nine of whom were Jews. Nine thousand captives had died in the previous three months, a further fourteen thousand over the winter. Even after the liberation, thousands more died, too far gone from starvation or sickness to be helped. As Michel walked through the camp he examined the railcars full of emaciated bodies, the last death transport of the war from Buchenwald. The German guards had locked the men, women and children inside the freight cars without food or water, and they slowly starved. When the despair of some of the survivors became too loud, or efforts were made to break out, the guards shot randomly into the cars. One survivor, who was found under a pile of the dead, stood on his matchstick legs and wept as he later told a female journalist, 'Everyone is dead. No one is left. Everyone is dead. I cannot help myself. Here I am and I am finished and cannot help myself. Everyone is dead.'[28]

Another journalist who witnessed the corpses in the train described them as piled up like branches of cut-down trees, and those at the crematorium looking like a heap of crooked logs ready for some infernal fire.[29] The American Army forced Dachau civilians from the town to bury the dead, a task that continued for days. Michel went into the town to find the mayor and local officials and had them brought to the camp with their wives. All of them claimed to have been entirely ignorant of what had happened within its walls. 'Not know?' Michel shouted, turning on them in contempt. 'Mention the name Dachau to the Hottentots and they know!'

Among the prisoners Michel interrogated Emil Mahl, the man in charge of the crematorium and the camp's hangman, who referred to himself as Kapo.[30] Mahl's account of life in Dachau, related without remorse or any sense of guilt, drew a picture of a world that even Michel could scarcely imagine, despite his own experiences in camps. The banality of the lengthy confession, with its quotidian detail, described a routine of casual barbarity. After many hours of interrogation Michel handed Mahl a block of rough paper and a pencil, and told him to write down his confession. The hangman covered six pages on both sides in a neat, even script. 'Executions and hangings took place in the crematorium at least two days a week, usually on Tuesdays and Thursday . . .'[31]

Mahl was originally a common criminal who had been sent to Dachau in October 1940, where he served a year and a half of his sentence. In the inverted value system of the camp world, common criminals enjoyed preferential treatment and privileges. After a period of illness he tried for months to be given a job that provided extra and better food, and was assigned to work with a squad in Munich to remove debris after Allied bombing raids. Later, he was successful in landing a more prestigious job in the camp crematorium, obtained through the influence and special recommendation of two men working there who were about to be released and drafted into the German Army.

At first Mahl found the work and food rations satisfactory because he 'only' had to cremate corpses. However, the arrival of a new camp commander brought extra responsibilities. 'It changed, and I had to help carry out each execution.' He became the right-hand man to SS Sergeant Theo Bongartz, who soon entrusted him to become an executioner in his own right. The SS sergeant executed inmates by shooting them. Although Mahl was a willing volunteer, he was not allowed a weapon because he was an inmate, so he became a specialist in hanging. Both men were paid a bonus after every execution: a pint of schnapps, five cigarettes and a sausage. There would often be a drinking party following the executions, hosted by the sergeant and regularly attended by the camp adjutant and doctor. 'Sometimes it was a real drinking orgy, where the camp adjutant Otto played a big role . . . he threw over the table and smashed dishes and glasses.'

In addition to his duties at the crematorium, Mahl was assigned one day a week as hangman to the Gestapo in Munich. This work involved driving with SS men to any town near Munich where an execution was to take place. He hanged the victims in the presence of Dr Lobkuchner, chief of Gestapo in Munich, who never failed to show up with a couple of his officers to witness the spectacle. 'After it was done, I always had to sit down in the corner of an inn to eat my meal while they were drinking with the mayor, the town doctor or local party leaders.' A week rarely passed in which the Gestapo did not call on Mahl's specialist talents.

Later, the Gestapo took over one of the rooms of the crematorium for the interrogation of prisoners brought from Munich. Mahl was often called to give assistance, usually in the form of liberal administration of the lash. 'At each interrogation they were beating the prisoners with rawhide whips,' Mahl wrote. He added without irony that he found this 'deplorable', although he dutifully carried out his orders. 'At the last interrogation by the Munich Gestapo there were about six or eight prisoners . . . I had to hang them with the help of Sergeant Bongartz.'

Hanging by this time had become such a routine that Mahl was sometimes honestly unable to remember the exact number he had been called upon to execute. Six or eight – the death of two men a session, more or less, no longer left an impression. Michel had asked during the initial interrogation how many people Mahl thought he had executed during his years as hangman. 'It took him quite a while to reach an approximate figure, which he arrived at only by counting the average during the weeks, months and years of his activity.'

The written confession conveys the sense of pride that Mahl took in his work. He recalled an incident where an inmate was taken to the crematorium for hanging at a time when both he and the sergeant happened to be away. As the hanging had to be done immediately, two workers in the crematorium – described as 'non-specialists' – carried it out. Mahl wrote, as if affronted by such amateurism, 'I learned later the men suffered very much.'

One incident in Mahl's account was a glimpse of the fate that might have been Michel's own. The hangman described the arrival of a large rail transport – which later became known as the Phantom Train – of two thousand prisoners from southern France in July or August of 1944. The transport had originally left Toulouse – after the D-Day landing and the liberation of Paris – and been shunted across France from one city to another for a total of five weeks. 'Five hundred of them were already dead because they had not received any water . . . It was evident to me that they were intentionally deprived of water in order to be exterminated . . . It was gruesome when this transport arrived, because the corpses were lying in one car for three or four weeks already. The smell of it carried for miles . . . In cremating these five hundred corpses, we had to burn for six days, day and night.'

Eugen Seybold, one of the men who worked in the crematorium under Mahl, added his own details to the account. He remembered the sealed train and seven cattle cars stacked with bodies. He estimated they had been dead for weeks as most were dark blue, and some were black and already decomposed beyond recognition. Twelve Russian officers, prisoners in Dachau, were ordered to unload the cars. They went about their work in gas masks. 'We who worked in the crematorium were obliged to undress these corpses,' Seybold said. 'Four men worked for two days on this grisly job and then the cremation started. There was a stack of bodies five feet high filling the hall and antechamber to the crematorium.' An additional forty to fifty corpses of inmates who had died from starvation or typhus were brought to the crematorium every day, and as Mahl had already reported, the men of the detail worked in shifts, day and night for a week. It was assembly-line cremation.

August 1944 had been a hard month for the work detail at Dachau. Seybold wrote that ninety Russian officers were taken to the courtyard of the crematorium, where Mahl ordered them to strip. 'Sergeant Bongartz stood in front of the door with his pistol in hand. While the victims were preparing to die, these men (the adjutant, Bongartz and Mahl) were chatting, laughing and smoking – as if they were out to have fun.'

The first group of Russians was then marched to the place of execution, a freshly dug ditch crossed by wooden planks. The men were ordered to kneel, which they did, except for a general who refused to die on his knees and remained standing. Shots were fired from four pistols and bodies tumbled into the ditch. The general was shot twice through the neck and fell, but did not die. The remainder of the Russians were taken to the place of execution in groups of ten and gunned down. Mahl 'noticed that there were thirty to forty still living a little. We reported it to Sergeant Bongartz and to the doctor, whereupon they shot some of them again so that they should be dead. However, many of them lying underneath died after three or four hours.'

The crematorium detail was ordered to take the bodies away five at a time. 'We had to load them on the hand cart and take them to the crematorium,' Seybold wrote. 'We unload. Seven men are still alive. They are groaning. We are called again, and have to hurry, hurry – always on to the next load. Sweat breaks out on me. My arms and feet get cramped from always pulling, loading and unloading. I am trembling in all my body.'

When one of the Russian officers who had been shot but not killed stood up in the crematorium, Mahl yelled at him in a rage, 'Damn dog! Lie down. Otherwise, I'll knock you down.' Seybold wrote of the three Russian officers who were still alive: 'When we brought the first men into the crematorium, one of them raised himself from the floor and stared at me. The brain came out of his forehead, then he collapsed. He still lived for four hours.' Seybold asked if he could give the men the *coup de grâce*. Mahl snapped, 'These dogs will perish by themselves.'

Mahl's account, horrible as it is, adopts the bland, matter-of-fact tone of a man forced to perform unspeakable acts to survive. But the testimony of the four inmates who worked under him, all interviewed separately by Michel, drew a different picture. Their written statements describe Kapo as 'the all powerful in the crematorium, loyal servant and handyman of the Gestapo . . . mean to the inmates who worked under him . . . Even his superior, SS Sergeant Bongartz, came under his influence. Whatever Mahl said and suggested was considered an order . . . In his delusion of grandeur, he threatened that he would hang all of us inmates who worked with him . . . This mass murderer is cruel, nauseating and a coward . . . in brief, sadistic, beastly and bloodthirsty . . . he is the inventor and constructor of the gallows in the crematorium. That was his creation – and that's also where he should end.' None of the men forced to work with Mahl had a single redeeming thing to say on his behalf. Their accounts depict a low creature who never displayed a glimmer of humanity or a moment's compassion.[32]

Michel collated the various confessions and written testimony, attached the photographs, and sent them – and the person of Emil Mahl – over to the army war crime prosecutors. Appropriately, the trials were held in Dachau. Mahl was sentenced to death, although Michel had not heard the last of him.

A different level of human depravity, intellectually superior but morally more corrupt, was displayed by doctors at the camp who had used inmates in medical experiments. In order to find out how long an aviator could go without oxygen, the strongest and healthiest of the inmates were locked in pressure chambers which then had the oxygen pumped out. The process was filmed. It took a man a hard fifteen minutes to die, and after eight hundred deaths the doctors concluded that no one could survive above thirty-six thousand feet without oxygen. In another experiment inmates were stood in vats of sea water up to their necks. It took six hundred deaths to deduce that the human body can exist for two and a half hours in water eight degrees below zero.

Eleven thousand Dachau prisoners were inoculated with tertiary malaria, and while the fever killed off the weak, no immunisation was found. SS surgeons performed castration operations on Jews and gypsies, and sterilised foreigners accused of having sexual relations with German women. One thousand Catholic priests from Poland had streptococcus germs injected in their upper legs between muscle and bone, causing large abscesses and fever. There were thirty-one deaths after months of ceaseless pain when experimental operations performed on advanced cases failed.[33]

As Michel interrogated survivors, and moved about the hellish world of Dachau, surrounded by corpses and ghosts, a terrible dread enveloped him. Nothing short of a series of miracles had kept him alive in the camps, and he knew that for his family to survive they would need to have been similarly blessed.

The Thunderbirds moved on to take Munich, described by Eisenhower as 'the cradle of the beast', which fell with surprisingly little resistance. But furious combat would have come as a relief to Michel after the horrors of the camp. He now worked around the clock in a state of such profound psychological shock that he felt no emotion whatsoever.

Among the blizzard of intelligence reports that overwhelmed CIC at this time was one of an SS convoy of covered trucks that was thought to have come from Berlin, heading south from Munich. Michel's best agent, Fritz Spanheimer, reported that it was disguised as non-military but had SS troops with it, and that it had stopped just outside the city at a large paper mill.[34] 'I originally suspected it contained gold or treasure of some sort and took a jeep and drove to the paper mill. When I got there I saw mountains – I mean *mountains* – of documents. The SS just dumped everything, ordered it to be shredded, and fled.' Michel walked around and saw there were official government documents of every sort, and while there was no actual treasure, Michel had stumbled upon pure gold.

One of the mountains was made up of stacks of wooden filing cabinets. Michel pulled out a file to see what it contained and found original Nazi Party member profiles, complete with photos. 'I immediately understood how important these were, and their significance. Although at the time I had no idea of the scope of the find.' In fact there proved to be forty tons of them, or almost eleven million cards accounting for ninety-five per cent of the entire Nazi Party membership. The order to pulp them had been made because a fire of such magnitude would have attracted attention.[35]

He clambered over the mountain of paper, sifting and sorting through what he thought might be important, and spent hours putting together an impressive collection of document samples. He arranged for troops to guard the paper mill day and night. 'I took the samples to the military government and told them I had it under guard. It was now their job to proceed as it did not come under my jurisdiction. They said they would take care of it, but they didn't.'

The officer did not seem to attach much importance to the find and never bothered to visit the site. 'Although I tried to insist, nothing happened.' Time passed, and Michel became increasingly frustrated and annoyed. 'Then I did something that I would never usually do. I leaked its existence to the press. It was picked up, and only then did the military government take action.' The documents were moved under guard to the Army Document Centre in Munich.

The Nazi Party membership records became the jewel in the crown of what was to become known as the Berlin Document Centre, the American Army's collection of German official papers, later taken over by the State Department. These included six hundred thousand files on officers and enlisted men and women of SS units; racial purity files on two hundred and fifty thousand SS officers; the records of three hundred thousand Storm Troopers; files on party members' disciplinary infractions; loyalty files on teachers, doctors, policemen, musicians and entertainers; citizenship records of ethnic Germans whose ancestors had settled in countries conquered by Hitler; and records of Jews and other Germans stripped of their citizenship. Over the next six months twenty-four freight trains averaging more than twenty-five cars each moved documents to Berlin, including one thousand four hundred tons of documents from more than a dozen Reich ministries, and four hundred and fifty tons of Wehrmacht casualty files. They were housed in underground warehouses once used by the SS to tap telephones. The party membership records were of the highest importance for the future de-Nazification programme and the search for war criminals now launched by the Allies.[36]

The Second World War officially ended in the west at midnight on 8 May 1945. The cities of Germany were in ruins, the country's infrastructure destroyed, and at first peace brought nothing but chaos and confusion. Bridges and roads had been blown up and there was no water, electricity or phone service. Millions lived amid the rubble in cellars and makeshift shelters, while millions more on the move drifted through a soul-destroying landscape of devastation. These new armies of the displaced filled roads already clogged with every sort of military vehicle. Demobilised soldiers, homeless Germans, refugees, liberated slave labourers and camp survivors were all trying to get home.

With the surrender of Germany, the Thunderbirds took on the role of occupying army and struggled to process the vast number of captured soldiers. By the end of May the total number of captured prisoners held by the 45th Division alone approached one hundred and twenty-five thousand. Despite the non-fraternisation and de-Nazification policy, necessity demanded that German officers serve as liaison personnel to the Allies. The non-fraternisation laws applied to all Germans, including anti-Nazis, who at first were offered no role in terms of replacing the previous evil system.

In war-ravaged Munich, the doughboys of the 45th Division celebrated and looked forward to going home after two long and bloody years of combat. Following VE Day, and the reorganisation of American forces, the Thunderbirds were transferred from the Seventh Army to General George Patton's Third Army, and on 12 June 1945 they moved to a new camp beside the *Autobahn* on the outskirts of Munich.[37]

But for Michel, in Counter Intelligence, defeat brought an extra workload as the search for war criminals began. He did not talk about his fears concerning the fate of his own family. Emotionally, he entered a state of blank anxiety. The liberation of Dachau, and subsequent reports from other camps, had dealt a stunning psychological blow to his spirit.

On top of his other duties, Michel took a jeep and made his way through the chaos to visit the liberated camps. He questioned survivors in German and Yiddish. 'I gathered people up to talk because many of them came from Auschwitz where I knew my family had been. Wherever they came from I wanted to find out about my family. All the time, every day, I searched for news.'

The most disturbing moments of these visits came from the reactions of the children. 'The first time I went to a liberated camp the children ran from me and hid. Because of the uniform. They could not distinguish between a German and an American uniform. That hurt me very much, to see little children running away from me in horror. That was very painful. Non-Jewish children told me how they were put to work searching discarded clothing for hidden valuables. The older boys told stories of carefully lining up bodies, head to toe, in neat rows – when some of the corpses would be family members. It was all said in a matter-of-fact way, not expressed with horror at all. It had become natural. I listened, and was transported to some alien, nightmare world.'

The children who survived the camps were like no other children in the world. In Buchenwald an American officer, who was also a rabbi, pulled a living eight-year-old boy from a pile of corpses. Shattered by the horror of it, the adult burst into tears. He quickly tried to compose himself in order to protect the child, so he thought, and began to laugh.

'How old are you?' he asked the child in Yiddish.

'Older than you.'

'How can you say that?' the rabbi said, thinking the experience had deranged the child.

'You cry and laugh like a little boy, but I haven't laughed for years and I don't cry any more. So tell me, who is older?'[38]

In his capacity as a CIC agent, Michel was able to receive the lists of survivors compiled by the army. These were usually scarcely decipherable carbon copies of badly typed originals, often incorrectly spelt, made up of thousands and thousands of names that were neither in alphabetical nor any other order. But the crude lists were registers of the living and offered hope. 'I spent whole nights going over these lists . . . names, names, names. These were lists of life and death. To find a name meant to find a life. Not to find it . . . I lived in the suspense of not knowing whether any of my family was alive.'

The strain took a terrible emotional toll as deep down he suspected his family was dead. 'I did not hope to find their names, I *had* to find their names. When I did not find them I could not, and did not, accept what happened. For me to accept the destruction of the lives of my parents and aunt and uncle was unthinkable. I would never admit it until I had absolute proof. I could not acknowledge that they had been slaughtered.'

Night after night, week after week, he went through every name on every list. The psychological tension and emotional pain were insupportable, and he became physically unwell. He began to cough and throw up blood, and suffered such extreme rectal bleeding that he feared for his life. 'I thought I was very sick, maybe I was dying. I feared the worst.'

He confided in no one and continued with his duties. 'I didn't want to go to hospital and be taken away from my work.' He made enquiries and learned that there was a distinguished professor of medicine in Basle, Switzerland, who specialised in his condition. He packed a small suitcase, changed into civilian clothes and drove in his commandeered BMW to Basle. He checked into the professor's clinic and went through several days of tests and examinations. The professor then received him in his office and began writing prescriptions.

'What is it?' Michel asked bluntly. 'What do I have?'

The doctor answered that in his opinion Michel had gone through a deep emotional crisis and had suffered a trauma of enormous impact.

'Are you saying it's psychosomatic?'

The doctor looked at his patient in surprise, as the term was not much used then. He hesitated before he answered. 'Yes. I'm certain it is.'

'Thank you. You can tear up the prescriptions. I don't need any medication. Now I understand the cause, I can handle it.'

He left Basle relieved of an enormous burden of anxiety and drove back to Munich. 'I felt I would survive and find the strength to carry on. I could not allow myself to succumb to despair.'

On the surface he continued to show nothing of either his physical or spiritual pain, and went about his work with dogged professionalism, earning himself the reputation throughout the unit of a workaholic. All around him he heard expressed the crude desire for revenge, a course he rejected utterly. 'There was talk of putting poison in the SS prisoners' food. I found this deplorable, despicable.'

In contrast, Michel decided to throw a party just a few weeks after the end of the war. On his own initiative, and without the army's knowledge – and with the usual flagrant disregard for the strict non-fraternisation laws in force – he organised an elegant musical gala for a large, invited gathering of senior American personnel and prominent Germans. 'We had the best possible singers and musicians for a great programme of classical music planned around the world-famous opera singer of the time, Hans Hotter. I employed local artists to draw handmade invitations and sent them out with the programme to high-ranking officers of the US Army, senior figures in the military government, and important Allied intelligence people. I screened and investigated important local Germans who were known to be either anti-Nazi or non-Nazi. And we had a party.'

The location was the palatial residence of an anti-Nazi surgeon, Professor Kreckc, just outside Munich. The gala was held on a beautiful summer's evening and lanterns were hung in the trees of the large garden. 'People didn't know I had sent invitations to Germans, obviously. I organised it so they showed up after the Americans were already seated.' Even so, there were disapproving murmurs when the American brass saw the seats in the rear fill with elegantly dressed Germans. 'It was a shocker.' Michel quickly strode on to the stage and addressed the audience, first in English and then in German.

'The war is over. And with the end of hostilities we should also end hatred of the enemy because now there is no enemy. To keep on hating is self-destructive, so we have to reach out to each other. We now have two duties: to eradicate the evils of Nazism for ever, and to work together to create a new democratic Germany. Tonight I want us all to celebrate not only the end of the war but the beginning of co-operation. That is why I have invited a selection of Germans who are willing to work with us. We have to communicate. And one universal language that reaches all of us and which we all understand is the language of music. It speaks to our emotions and our hearts.'

He sat down, and the music began. Today, it is difficult to imagine how contrary this simple speech was to the spirit of the times. Six years of the most brutal war the world had ever seen, in which fifty-five million people had been killed, had filled vast reservoirs of hatred. Germany was in ruins. Michel's lone voice suggesting reconciliation was not easily understood by either side in the immediate aftermath of such carnage.

More peculiar still, if the audience could only know it, was the background of the man making the plea for a united, collaborative future with a former enemy. He had suffered so much because of the war, continued to suffer, and would always suffer, and yet sought a new beginning rather than a harsh accounting.

As the musicians played beneath the stars in the summer garden hung with lanterns, the audience fell under the music's spell and was transported from the reality of war and death. Instead of being court-martialled, Michel was later congratulated by senior officers who might have nurtured notions other than reconciliation. 'After the classical music we had laid on a large buffet with a band that played light, popular music with dancing.' That night the non-fraternisation laws went by the board and, only days after the end of the fighting, Americans and Germans danced – although still not with each other.

Today, so many years after the war, Michel's action still seems incomprehensible to him. 'I look at that young man, who was myself, and wonder: How did he do it? Why did he do it? I don't have a clear answer. Sometimes looking back I find it difficult to understand myself. At the time I was literally bleeding inside. I suppose I did not want my anger and quest for justice reduced to bitterness and lust for revenge. I refused to become one of the brutes. I wanted and needed reconciliation.'

It was one of the most significant decisions of his life, taken automatically and almost without thought. He had chosen life over death, the blessing not the curse.

VII

In the months following the defeat of Nazi Germany, five SS officers were blindfolded and driven in two separate cars into the countryside outside of Ulm, on the road to Stuttgart. It was a cold, wet night and each man felt the fear rise in him as the cars passed through an elaborate arrangement of roadblocks and security checks. The men were members of a post-war underground network representing some four thousand SS officers and men, and SD intelligence agents dedicated to the resurrection of the Nazi state. They were on their way to meet the unknown commander of a much larger and powerful umbrella group, the Grossorganisation.

The cars turned off the road on to an unpaved track and came to a halt deep among dripping woods. The blindfolded men heard a final exchange of passwords and the rattle of weapons. The roar of heavy vehicles sounded in the background as they were led along a muddy path, made slippery by trodden autumn leaves, to a building in an isolated clearing. They waited shivering in the cold rain to be summoned into the HQ of the Grossorganisation. Numerous people seemed to come and go, until at last, long after midnight, the SS men were led into the building through deep puddles of icy water.

Even inside, the blindfolds remained. The men were forbidden to speak and were kept waiting in an unheated corridor. Despite the late hour, the HQ remained furiously active as people brushed past in response to snapped commands. Doors opened and closed, heels clicked and aides scurried.

After what seemed an age, the SS men were marched down a long corridor and through a doorway. The blindfolds were removed. The sight that confronted them made every moment of the long, cold wait worthwhile. They found themselves in the vast hall of a hunting lodge where a log fire blazed. Mounted on the walls were the heads of wild boar and stag, with the portraits of leading Nazi figures hung between them, and in pride of place was a large painting of Adolf Hitler himself.

All around was an impressive display of weaponry: pistols, flame throwers, machine guns, assorted grenades, and ammunition of every calibre. Sabotage kits – the pride of the SS intelligence units – were stacked in one corner. There was also a small mountain of coffee and cigarettes – both almost impossible to obtain in post-war Germany – and an open safe filled with bundles of paper money. The lodge was clearly the heart of a powerful organisation, an unapologetic and defiant throwback to the heady days of the Third Reich. The audacity of the display was balm to bruised Nazi souls. For defeated men suffering the added humiliation of foreign occupation, the very existence of the Grossorganisation's HQ was psychologically uplifting.

Seated behind a large desk that bore a bronze bust of Hitler was an impressive man, framed between two swastika-shaped candlesticks, immaculately dressed in civilian clothes except for a military-style brown shirt. He had the manner of a high-ranking party functionary familiar with power and unquestioning obedience. Hard and unsmiling, his unblinking stare was a challenge rather than a welcome, and there was about him the unmistakable, indelible stamp of the Gestapo fanatic.

The SS men were announced with full rank and drew themselves up and flung out their arms in salute. 'Heil Hitler!' The man behind the desk returned the salute limply, in the style of Hitler himself. He made a curt gesture with his head for them to sit. A long silence followed in which he studied a dossier carefully, suddenly raising his head to glare at the leader of the SS men.

They knew this intimidating figure to be Dr Frundsberg, commander of the Grossorganisation. He immediately delivered a quiet but forceful rebuke over the existence of any unit with military potential operating outside the Grossorganisation's umbrella. No local underground splinter group, he declared with authority, could be allowed to function in any capacity as a separate entity. It must either disband or be absorbed into the Grossorganisation. The master plan was to have everything centralised under one command. Anything else was treason, and traitors would be dealt with as such.

As Dr Frundsberg spoke, there were constant interruptions as deferential messengers came and went with urgent communiqués. A field telephone rang frequently and he cut himself off in mid-sentence to answer. It was clear the doctor was a man who continued to exercise great authority, and the SS officers were made brutally aware of their own marginal importance. Visibly shaken, the SS men's leader tried to justify himself. He explained that he had been a major in the Sicherheitsdienst (SD) – the security service of the SS – with the cover name Lümmel, and was now commander of Group

9-11-23 Resistance Group West. Its charter was sabotage, espionage, resistance, and the eventual overthrow of the Allied military government. The group comprised former members of the SS and SD and carried out their activities using fake ID cards, forged residence and work permits, and phoney army discharge papers.

The leader's adjutant had been an SS *Unterscharführer* and had escaped from a French prisoner-of-war camp. The other two men present at the lodge, who happened to be twin brothers, had escaped from an Allied camp for SS prisoners. One served as head of intelligence, while the other was the head of the organisation for Rheinland-Westfalen, and the centre of operations was in Fulda.

Dr Frundsberg nodded without comment and made notes on a pad before him. Encouraged, the leader boasted of close connections to the group that had undertaken the bombing of the De-Nazification Court in Stuttgart. This had the opposite effect to the one desired, and Frundsberg rose to his feet, infuriated. He raged that such acts were rank stupidity that achieved nothing except to attract attention to the underground. The result was to put American intelligence on full alert. It was precisely because of such foolish and irresponsible freelance operations that it was vital to incorporate all groups opposed to the occupation under the Grossorganisation. Amateur and uncoordinated assaults put the entire mission at risk, and only the Grossorganisation was authorised to launch such attacks.

Dr Frundsberg then challenged the men to provide proof and details of their recruitment. They described a travelling variety show that went by the name of Black Panther and moved from town to town making contact with SS men through word of mouth. Heralded in advance by posters proclaiming THE BLACK PANTHER IS COMING, potential recruits were signed up backstage under the noses of the Allied occupation forces.

The men explained that they had been unaware of the existence of the Grossorganisation but declared they were loyal to the Nazi cause to the point of death. Dr Frundsberg seemed unimpressed and demanded more information on their organisation and its activities. Visibly intimidated, the leader of the SS men gave a full account and expressed willingness to turn over control of the group under certain conditions. Listing his qualifications as an intelligence officer, which were impressive, he laid out the intricate system he had devised for his own organisation. He asked for logistical and intelligence support, and requested that he be made head of intelligence of the Grossorganisation.

Dr Frundsberg hesitated, and seemed to give the proposal serious thought. In his reply he pointed out weaknesses in the group's intelligence apparatus, while outlining the workings of the highly developed intelligence structure of the Grossorganisation. He intimated that the leader had much to learn. The circumstances of defeat and occupation required different techniques and expertise to those used in time of open war.

After listening closely to Dr Frundsberg, the leader pulled himself up in his chair and said he had made an important decision. He agreed to place the group under the new command, and to co-operate with the commander to the utmost of his ability. He asked in a crisp, military tone: *'Und was befehlen Sie uns jetzt zu tun?'* – What do you order us to do now?

Dr Frundsberg hesitated once again, and his concentration seemed to wander momentarily. But his bullying, autocratic manner returned almost immediately as he rattled off a list of clipped commands. First of all, he demanded that all activities of the SS underground cease instantly. Secondly, only orders issued directly from him were to be carried out. Thirdly, the leader was to instruct all the groups under him to prepare for an inspection. As the orders were given the SS man wrote them down, adding his own rider: failure to obey this order is punishable by death.

Dr Frundsberg rose abruptly and marched from the room without another word. His departure announced the end of the meeting. Once again the men allowed themselves to be blindfolded and led back to the cars that had brought them. The return journey repeated the rituals enacted on the trip out, with the same random stops and exchange of passwords.

The curtness of the commands, the peremptory treatment and the severity of Dr Frundsberg at the lodge did not disturb the SS men. Indeed, the opposite was true. The harsh encounter had bolstered their confidence. To men who had spent their adult lives in an authoritarian hierarchy that demanded blind obedience, the experience had been almost religious in nature. It was a taste of old times. Somewhere, at least, the Nazi flame continued to burn bright. The men had been given a focus for their uncoordinated activities and the motivation necessary to refresh their floundering morale. And, most important of all, they had discovered an impressive leader of the old school whose confidence and authority remained unshaken. They had found a strong man to take them forward, the head of an organisation with the will and means to continue the fight.

When they were arrested months later, the SS officers refused at first to believe the outrageous prosecution claims that Dr Frundsberg was neither a Nazi nor even a German, but a United States Counter Intelligence officer named Michel Thomas.[1]

Immediately after the war Germany and Austria were split into four zones to be militarily occupied and administered by each of the Allies: America, the Soviet Union, Great Britain and France. As the armies of the various countries moved into position in their allotted territories, and the zones became reality rather than lines on a map, there was an enormous migration of people from one zone to another. Seven million ethnic Germans fled Poland, Czechoslovakia and the Russian zone to escape the Soviets. The intelligence fall-out was overwhelming.

The post-war mission of US Counter Intelligence was to protect the American zone – which included southern and eastern Germany to the Czech and Austrian borders – against espionage, sabotage and subversion. This embraced the automatic arrest policy of the Nazis, the capture and interrogation of war criminals, and the apprehension and debriefing of important German scientists and intelligence agents. It was a tall order to fulfil in the ruins of post-war Germany, and the matter was complicated by competing US government agencies that pursued contradictory policies. In addition, intrigue and deceit among supposed Allies capped the universal administrative chaos.

The Allies could not even agree on the form the new Germany should take. The Americans wanted to reduce Germany to a broken agricultural state without a real economy, while the Europeans foresaw the disastrous financial burden this would impose on the entire continent. The British, virtually bankrupted by the war, found it difficult from the outset to find the money to subsidise their zone – eighty million pounds in the first year. In order to be able to divert wheat to Germany, the new Labour government introduced bread rationing, something that had not even been in force in the war. The Soviet Union, meanwhile, was working to turn the zone it controlled – East Germany – into a totalitarian prison state.

The occupation authorities were theoretically committed to eradicating Nazism root and branch from the country, which meant cleansing schools, universities, city halls and newspapers of party members. In reality the policy was a recipe for chaos. It condemned tens of thousands of people to internment without hearings and at first denied party members any employment except manual labour. The de-Nazification policy created an unworkable world with rules described by the officials involved as 'systematic and meticulous imbecility' enacted by officers who were 'politically ignorant and morally indifferent'.[2]

The American Department of War estimated that it needed a minimum of ten thousand permanent American personnel to have any hope of success with de-Nazification. By the end of 1945 there was a staff of only two hundred designated to the task, and a third of those were German nationals. The policy to root out Nazis failed utterly, and by the autumn of 1946, out of a total of almost forty-two thousand cases compiled by de-Nazification tribunals, only one hundred and sixteen Germans were considered major offenders.[3]

In many towns the records had been destroyed, and ardent Nazis simply moved back into power. The Allies themselves knowingly appointed Nazi Party members, or sympathisers, as the mayors of Hamburg, Wuppertal, Bremen, Hanover, Kiel and many other smaller towns. Agencies of the US government, including the army, State Department, and later the newly formed CIA and air force, all created clandestine programmes to allow known Nazis who were deemed useful into the United States. Hard-headed realists, who were able to accept that a country that had been Nazi since 1933 could scarcely be expected to operate without employing numerous party members, still drew a line when it came to war criminals. But it was crossed repeatedly, and a form of *Realpolitik* was adopted by the Allies that was nakedly amoral.

Surrounded by chaos and unaware of the dark political forces playing themselves out elsewhere, Michel plunged into post-war intelligence work in Munich, eager to hunt down Nazis. 'I was in a sea full of fish to be caught.'

The CIC Munich office was established in a German government building on Ludwigstrasse, and one of the larger rooms on the ground floor was used as a reception area for arrested suspects. As the men were interrogated and processed, they were predictably vociferous in their denials of any involvement with either the Gestapo in particular or the Nazi Party in general. Michel employed a Gestapo officer with long service as his right-hand man to help discover the truth. 'He had originally been an official with the Kriminalpolizei and was then transferred to the Gestapo. He was not a bad guy and insisted that he had always worked inside the office and never gone out on raids or been involved in torture. I believed him. I thought he would be more useful to me than inside an internment camp, so instead of processing him, which was my official duty, I offered him a job.'

The man was given an office next to Michel's and put to work typing profiles on Gestapo officials to be arrested, and provided lists of likely aliases and possible addresses. He was allowed to go home to his wife and family at night. 'I felt he earned his freedom.' And every morning he would be placed in the reception area posing as another prisoner, where he would mingle and chat to fellow suspects until it was his time to be interrogated. 'And then he would come in to me and tell me who was there. It worked very well. It gave me a weapon which was taken as uncanny insight and prescience by the men who sat before me lying for their lives.'[4]

Counter Intelligence at this time was receiving a welter of reports on post-war undercover organisations dedicated to preserving Nazi ideals. One, the Organisation der Ehemaligen SS-Angehörigen – known by its initials, ODESSA – was created with the mission of re-establishing conditions favourable for the rebirth of Nazi power. In reality it was little more than a well-funded bureau that helped party members and war criminals obtain false identities and escape the country. However, in this it was highly successful. ODESSA smuggled hundreds of millions of dollars out of Germany, via Switzerland, primarily to Argentina. It arranged for the escape of thousands of wanted Nazis to the Middle East and South America, especially Argentina. A CIC team, led by Michel, raided the organisation's HQ in Munich only weeks after the end of the war. The office yielded five members, who were arrested, and all the paraphernalia for forging documents. Michel kept a printer's counterfeit die-stamp of the papal seal as a souvenir.[5]

Another well-publicised group was the Werewolves, which supposedly had access to stockpiled weapons hidden in the Tyrol enabling Nazi guerrilla fighters to wage war against the occupation armies. 'The Werewolves were the brainchildren of Propaganda Minister Joseph Goebbels. Maybe that's why in practice the outfit proved to be a lot of media bark with no bite.'[6] There was also a group that attracted considerable CIC interest at the time called Red Lilac, but eventually proved to be little more than a band of freebooters set on personal enrichment. 'Although these cabals never managed to mount a serious threat on their own, they numbered thousands of men with access to weapons and funds, trained in sabotage, espionage and assassination. These men were drifting back into society taking innocuous jobs as car mechanics and cooks. If they could have been welded into a cohesive, well-directed force they could have frustrated attempts to reconstitute the liberated countries as democracies.'

The more experience Michel accumulated with captured German officers, and later with high-ranking Nazi officials, the more contempt he developed for them. 'Most exhibited in their attitude something subservient and despicable. They revealed a leadership made up of low people and rejects. Practically all of them were easily cowed during interrogation, ready and willing to give away their friends. Most volunteered to betray colleagues. There were few who showed any rectitude. What was lacking completely was any sense of dignity. This was hardly surprising. If they didn't recognise human dignity in others, why should they have it themselves? There wasn't a trace of it.'

The willing betrayals and automatic denials of party membership became routine. One exception stood out. Michel interrogated an SS officer who not only refused to give information but also proudly stated that he remained an enthusiastic Nazi. Automatically, Michel offered the man his hand. 'It was a relief after all the evasions and lies to meet a single man who said he was a Nazi. Someone who was prepared to take the consequences for his beliefs. So I reached out and shook that Nazi's hand.'

In the midst of the war, retribution for Nazi crimes had been declared by Winston Churchill to be among the major purposes of the war, but the complexities of peace introduced a harsh *Realpolitik*. 'Revenge is, of all satisfaction, the most costly and long drawn out; retributive persecution is of all policies the most pernicious,' Churchill declared after the war, modifying his earlier position. 'Our policy . . . should henceforth be to draw the sponge across the crimes and horrors of the past, hard as that may be, and look for the sake of our salvation towards the future. There can be no revival of Europe without the active and loyal aid of all the German tribes.'[7]

There was no war crimes policy at first in either Washington or London, and when one finally emerged the necessary machinery was not in place to implement it. In the US, the War Department assumed responsibility for punishing war crimes and pressed the Intelligence Division to carry out the task. This fell to the CIC, the only section empowered to arrest war criminals, and at first the job did not seem too onerous as at the time of the D-Day landing there were only sixty-eight names on the wanted list.[8] However, public outrage generated by the murder of unarmed American POWs during the Battle of the Bulge – the Malmédy Massacre – led directly to a commitment to an international war crimes trial. Malmédy was the greatest crime committed against Americans during the entire war.

The list of wanted men mushroomed. The Central Registry of War Criminals and Security Suspects – which went by its acronym CROWCASS – became the world's biggest list of possible war criminals with eight million cross-indexed names. Created by General Dwight Eisenhower, Supreme Allied Commander, its aim was to foster international co-operation in finding and prosecuting war criminals. The registry was broken down into three lists: (1) wanted men; (2) prisoners already in custody; (3) the names of all internees and the camps they were held in. Scotland Yard and FBI experts joined forces with the French in Paris, on Rue Mathurias, where an army of three hundred clerks was put to work punching information into an IBM card-index machine. Forms had been sent out to all internment camps to be returned with every internee's photo and fingerprints. The cards flooded back at the rate of forty thousand a day, overwhelming a workforce that was only able to process a fraction of that number.

People on the lists had also changed identities, while fingerprinting proved an exercise in futility as there were no prints on record for the wanted men. On top of this, the Russians were not part of CROWCASS – which excluded thirty-five per cent of all POWs – while camps under British jurisdiction were not even returning their forms. The British officer who headed CROWCASS was eventually forced to admit the list was worthless. In the general chaos, numerous war criminals slipped through the net and were not even questioned, let alone punished.

Before the war had ended a large number of Displaced Persons seeking repatriation who needed CIC approval, particularly French and Polish speakers, were sent to Michel to be processed. It was dull, form-filling work for the most part and something he delegated as much as possible, but a Belgian, who claimed to have been released from a labour camp and wanted to be repatriated, aroused Michel's curiosity. Everything about him seemed to be in order, except there was something about the accent that seemed off-key to a highly tuned ear. It was nothing obvious or defined, and might even have been a regional variation unknown to Michel, but it made him suspicious. 'I remembered, for example, that the Belgians say "*septante* and *octante*" whereas the French say "*soixante-dix* and *quatre-vingt"* and he seemed unaware of this. It was something that insignificant.

'The DP supplied me with his basic biography: name, date of birth, home town, trade. All seemed in order except the accent continued to bother me. The man was tall and rail-thin with big ears on a narrow face. He told me he was thirty-eight years old, although he looked much younger, which struck me as odd. Most slave labourers quickly appeared older than their chronological age because of the brutal working conditions in the labour camps. He was ragged and dirty enough, and cursed the guards, camp commander and even Hitler with appropriate vigour, but all that could be a piece of theatre to fool me. I studied his hands – they showed none of the inevitable cuts and bruises and calluses of manual labour.'

Michel chatted casually in French and reminisced about his travels in Belgium before the war. The DP spoke of his brief career as a soldier in 1940 when the German Army swept through the country. 'The talk meandered for hours – innocuous questions and bland answers.'

Finally, Michel appeared to be satisfied and the DP moved in his seat, preparing to leave.

'One moment, please,' Michel said.

He told him that he knew he was not Belgian, because of inconsistencies in his conversation, and that he believed everything the man said to be a lie. He glared at the 'Belgian' and began to fire questions in an aggressive, unfriendly tone, picking away at discrepancies in statements the man had made about his career. The DP seemed to have an answer for everything, but Michel continued to chip away at him for the rest of the night. 'I did not expect him to give himself away easily. He had been too well coached to fall for simple cat-and-mouse games. But marathon question-and-answer sessions were quite effective.'

As the night wore on the man began to make small mistakes. Michel ignored these without comment and let them pile up. Then he painstakingly went back over his line of questioning until the DP grew flustered and confused. He was also exhausted, while Michel displayed the stamina to suggest he could go on for ever. 'The longer I grilled him the more he realised I was not going to buy the story. He was visibly sagging before my eyes.'

Michel sat at a table and began to write. Dawn broke, and a grey light filtered into the bleak office. The DP sat slumped in his chair, so worn down and tired that he resembled a different being to the tall, confident man who had swapped nostalgic small talk about pre-war Belgium eighteen hours earlier.

Michel looked up from his writing and fixed him with a hard stare. 'There's only one way you can save yourself. You must tell me everything and then work with me to save Germany.'

Once again, Michel resorted to the histrionic display of the outraged patriot. 'Like my piano-playing rocketeer, I knew he burned with nationalist fervour. I counted on that quality as the real hook into him.' He began to speak in German, which the man affected to have difficulty understanding. Michel trotted out his phoney family antecedents, claiming to be a genuine German patriot who had witnessed the destruction of his beloved country. 'You are a disgrace to the Fatherland. I am a German to the tips of my toes but you've damn near wiped out an entire generation of the finest young blood in Europe, and now to make matters worse you're engaged in some scheme to make it possible for a few higher-ups to live off the loot they've grabbed.' The harangue continued for an hour until the man was hallucinating from exhaustion. This was exactly the state Michel wanted him in. 'Look around you,' he said as he finished his speech, gesturing at the ruined town outside the window. 'See the glory you've brought Germany.'

The man stared at the floor and said nothing. Michel sighed, and returned to his work. The only sound in the room was that of his pen moving across paper.

At last, a low, sombre voice broke the silence: *'Ich bin Georg Lermer.'*

'Go on,' Michel said, continuing to write. 'I'm listening.'

Lermer began a long, rambling story he hoped would save his life. He was diffident at first, but gathered momentum as he was artfully prodded and steered by Michel towards a full confession. 'He was not the stupid sort who savaged prisoners in concentration camps. Undoubtedly he was responsible for more than his share of misery, but he could still reason. Like so many in the Nazi hierarchy, ideology appealed to him in direct proportion to the power it brought and the amount of personal ambition it fulfilled. I listened with fascination.'

Lermer confessed to being a German officer who had served with the RSHA (Nazi intelligence) in various occupied countries in western Europe. As he spoke, he gave the true reason for trying to get to Belgium and outlined in a flat, exhausted monotone the Regenbogen (Rainbow) plan. The brainchild of the immensely powerful Martin Bormann, head of the Nazi Party Chancellery and Hitler's private secretary, Rainbow was the secret strategy for post-war Nazis outside Germany. In anticipation of defeat, Bormann had made contingency plans in 1944 to develop an international strategy to wage underground war aimed at undermining democracies with the ultimate objective of bringing the Nazis back to power. He foresaw and encouraged unlikely tactical alliances with anyone opposed to democracy. 'The plan was to unite Communists, fascists, religious extremists and even common criminals. It may sound far-fetched now, but there was no shortage of volunteers.'[9]

Lermer, a fluent French speaker, had been given a false identity as a DP from Belgium who had been in a labour camp for years. His top-secret mission was to find his way back to Belgium, create a normal life with a job and family, and dedicate himself to Rainbow, in charge of Belgium, France and Luxembourg.

Michel's pen flew across the pad of paper on his desk, recording every detail. 'Once his tongue was loosened he kept adding information. He offered me the names of people we desperately hunted for prosecution. He revealed aliases, new identities, the hideouts of several dozen fugitives. Rainbow envisioned much more than hit-and-run killings or sabotage. Skilled operators would foment strikes, mastermind hijackings of strategic goods, counterfeit currencies to disrupt economies, start small wars and generally stir the political pot. Significantly, Rainbow operatives were never to associate directly with overt neo-Nazi groups. International agents would incite ethnic religious and racial hatred, pitting Jew against Arab, Moslem against Christian, Protestant against Catholic, white against black.' And the enterprise was carefully planned, compartmentalised for security, and well funded through Switzerland.

'Rainbow is just one more ignoble delusion,' Michel scoffed with a confidence he did not feel. 'It is not enough to destroy Germany, now you want to export the terror. Once again Germans will pay the price. Look at yourself and think how the rest of the world regards you. If the survivors of slave-labour camps could get their hands on you; if we were to turn you over to the French whose relatives were murdered as hostages; if we were to ship you to Poland or the Soviet Union, you would wish we had simply blown your brains out here.'

He described a bleak fate for members of the RSHA and emphasised Lermer's personal responsibility not only for his own activities but those of the entire Nazi government. Conscience and personal responsibility might have been suspended as long as the Third Reich existed, Michel said, but thinking Germans should now be looking inward, counting the costs and asking themselves what they had lost. 'I spoke of the need to become aware of the enormous personal and national guilt and did not allow my prisoner to evade any slivers of conscience he might have left.'

Lermer was offered a deal.

'If you want to stop it, we can talk about it.'

'How can I stop it? I am your prisoner.'

'First, I want a complete breakdown of Operation Rainbow worldwide. I want a list of those who were associated with you in western Europe. I want the names of collaborators and sympathisers. I want their probable whereabouts and their codenames. Instead of trying to make Rainbow succeed, you will help smash it.'

Lermer grabbed at the lifeline thrown to him.

'I wanted more than a spur-of-the-moment decision made after I had battered his mind with a marathon inquisition. His co-operation was his commitment. And he offered to bring in an associate who was also to be sent to Belgium.'[10]

Michel took Lermer with him to Munich and worked on a report outlining the nature of Rainbow. He attached a list of Nazis gleaned from his prisoner, and their cover names and possible whereabouts. He suggested using Lermer and his associate as part of a CIC task force to trap and arrest those involved by sending out agents posing as Rainbow couriers.

The report was sent through to the main HQ in Frankfurt and Michel was summoned by the colonel in charge of CIC to discuss putting his plan into action. The colonel was sceptical about various suggestions in the report, and seriously concerned about one in particular. There was a recommendation that both men should be given their freedom and be allowed to create the nucleus of a project designed to unmask their associates.

'How do we know this whole Rainbow thing isn't a fantasy of two down-at-heel Nazis trying to get their freedom?' the colonel wanted to know.

Although the colonel accepted the report's evaluation of the danger of Rainbow, he balked at the idea of giving the men their freedom and employing them as double agents. Michel was suggesting, in effect, the time-honoured strategy of setting a thief to catch a thief. 'The rule book called for suspects to be arrested, and then to sweat whatever intelligence you could out of them, and move against others who might be implicated. This was the routine, *respectable* approach. No one could criticise these tactics even if they brought meagre results. The other route was a risk.'

Michel argued forcefully that very little would be accomplished if each name associated with Rainbow was investigated individually. It would take too much time, and as word spread after a couple of arrests, the conspirators would go to ground. On the other hand if their prize was kept in play it might be possible to acquire precise information on hundreds, even thousands, of targets.

'How can we possibly trust these two?' the colonel objected. 'The minute we give them their freedom and they see an opportunity, they'll take off. Not only will we lose them but they'll wise up everyone else.'

'That's easy,' Michel said, comfortably. 'They both have wives and children. I know where they live. I'll let Lermer and his friend know that I know where they live.'

The colonel looked as if he were about to have a coronary. 'You may be unaware, but in the United States it is not customary to take hostages, or to punish or threaten the families of criminals,' he said in a voice of suppressed thunder. *'We don't do that sort of thing.'*

'You know that and I know that,' Michel said with a shrug. 'But our friends from the RSHA only understand the way Nazis operate. We don't have to tell them what we will do or won't do. Simply by mentioning their wives and children they'll draw their own conclusions. I don't have to threaten them – their imaginations will do the work. Because for them blackmail and murder are the laws of life.'

The colonel gave Michel a long, hard look. He then announced that CIC would act upon the report's recommendations. The plan was adopted and a task force set up, although Michel did not participate because of his workload in Munich. Lermer and his associate were incorporated into a small unit that worked to pull in people on the list.

Michel was later contacted by CIC HQ in Frankfurt and told that the mission was completed and that Lermer should now be arrested. He refused to carry out the order. A week later he received a letter from Lermer, who was interned in a camp. 'He did not complain about having been arrested or being put in a camp. He only complained that there was so much more work to be done. There was nothing I could do. I argued strongly for the task force to be re-formed, but was rebuffed. I don't know if they located and reclaimed the funds reported to be stashed in Switzerland. Or if the authorities truly understood what Rainbow meant. I heard nothing more.'

However, Rainbow gave Michel the idea for his boldest plan. He would beat the underground at its own game by creating a pseudo organisation masquerading as the main movement conceived by Himmler. The idea was to bring his fictitious organisation to the attention of the genuine underground groups in the hope they might be tempted to join forces with the more powerful organisation. The seed for Dr Frundsberg and the Grossorganisation had been sown.

The identity photograph taken by the Vichy authorities at the concentration camp of Le Vernet in the foothills of the Pyrénées in France. Imprisoned in solitary confinement in Nice, two slave labour camps, and a deportation centre, Michel did not come across a German soldier or Gestapo officer for two years.

Michel's mother, Freida –
strong, independent and
adored by her son.

Michel in Breslau, Germany,
standing between his 'two'
mothers, Freida and Edessa.

Michel in Vienna as a student, where he became an eyewitness to the violence of the Anschluss, after the invasion by Germany.

A post-war gendarme surveys prisoners in a French concentration camp. The photograph was banned by French governments because of the incriminating képi.

Prisoners arrive at a French concentration camp in the Vichy free zone.

The Vercors in the Alps, the mountain fortress that carried enormous psychological and symbolic significance for the Résistance.

Résistance fighters in the mountainous terrain around Grenoble.

Mademoiselle Thérèse Mathieiu, a member of the Maquis who became for Michel, 'a symbol of courage and of the highest principles of humanity.' She carried within her the eternal essence of France and restored Michel's faith in the country.

Young members of the Maquis are given a demonstration in the use of arms dropped by parachute – in this case Sten guns, revolvers and pistols.

Michel in the commando outfit of the Grésivaudan Maquis.

An official French government document issued after the war verifying Michel's wartime service with the Résistance and French military.

Citizens of Grenoble welcome liberating US troops.

Collabos Horizontales, French women who went with German troops
during the occupation, are led barefoot through the streets, carrying their
shoes. Their heads are shaved, their clothes partially torn off, and swastikas have
been painted on their foreheads.

An old lady regards the ruins of her home as the Thunderbirds of the US Army (45th Division) push through Germany.

One of the giant Tiger tanks used by the SS Panzer divisions in the Battle of the Bulge.

Troops from Kampfgruppe Peiper, part of the 1st SS Panzer Division, in a *Schimmwagen* (amphibious Volkswagen) on the road to Malmédy where US prisoners of war were murdered later the same day.

The killing field where eighty-four unarmed troops were murdered in the Malmédy Massacre, the greatest war crime commited against Americans in the war.

Gustav Knittel, a much sought after war criminal for his role in the murder of American POWs in the Malmédy Massacre.

Thunderbirds line up SS officers at Dachau. Battle-hardened GIs snapped under the strain of liberating the camp and shot down more than thirty SS men.

Michel was posted to Ulm in his work as a special agent for US Army CIC. The centre of the city had been destroyed by Allied bombing and shelling and only a single tree and the spire of the cathedral remained standing.

Michel at work in his office at Ulm as a special agent of the US Army Counter Intelligence.

The notorious Nazi and RSHA officer, Dr Frundsberg – aka Michel Thomas – in party spirit with American military policemen.

One of the many documents issued to Michel after the war identifying him as a special agent of the US Army's Counter Intelligence Corps.

Away from the rigours of Counter Intelligence work, Michel enjoyed skiing in the mountains.

Michel at the CIC Villa Kauderer in Ulm, with his BMW convertible and SS-trained attack dog, Barry.

The children of Izieu. Orphaned after their parents were arrested and deported, the children sought refuge in a shabby manor in a remote mountain village. In the last weeks of the war Klaus Barbie had them arrested and deported to their deaths.

Michel and Ted Kraus, head of Counter Intelligence in Ulm, in the mountains.

Michel collaborating with the enemy.

Klaus Barbie, the Butcher of Lyon, manacled and surrounded by police, as he is taken to the Lyon courthouse for trial.

Michel standing in front of the photos of many of the celebrities he has taught languages in his office in New York. They include Bob Dylan, Peter Sellers, Barbra Streisand, Raquel Welch, Woody Allen, Warren Beatty, François Truffaut, Alfred Hitchcock, Princess Grace, Emma Thompson, the Duchess of York among others.

Students from the City and Islington Sixth Form Centre, North London, with Michel. A BBC documentary film recorded their progress when they were taught French in five days.

Based in New York, Michel continues to fly all over the world to teach languages.

But a more pressing priority than catching Nazis, or even war criminals, was now imposed on CIC. A free-for-all had broken out among the Allies over the seizure of German technology and the recruitment of top scientists and engineers, particularly those involved in weapons' technology. The Allies now engaged in a ruthless drive to obtain the knowledge of German scientists and engineers, who were greatly superior in many areas of rocketry, aviation and weaponry. Thousands of Allied officers were allocated to the task, a much greater number than were charged with hunting down war criminals. Eisenhower felt that German scientists were 'the only reparations we are likely to get'.

The declared aim of Project Paperclip, as the mission was codenamed, was to locate nine thousand of Germany's top scientists, engineers and military technicians and put them under American and British control. Special American units known as T-Forces – because of a red 'T' emblazoned on their helmets – had been put in the field before the end of the war. A mobile HQ, comprising two hundred and thirty men, co-ordinated the activity of three thousand trained specialists who followed in the wake of advancing Allied armies. The T-Forces had extraordinary powers and could commandeer transport at will, including trains, and had the authority to call on military units for support.

The scientific bounty to be had from Germany was a treasure beyond price, and the welter of reports that came across Michel's desk indicated there was no limit to the loot. Significant finds were reported every day and were there for the taking under the terms of unconditional surrender. Forty-five miles south of Munich, for instance, there was a sophisticated wind-tunnel complex for testing aircraft that was far in advance of anything possessed by the Allies. At Mühldorf, east of Munich, there were repair shops above and below ground that employed ten thousand men, day and night. Heinkel blueprints were found hidden in a tunnel in the area, and a previously unknown underground Messerschmitt factory was discovered.

Michel spent time looking for a rocket production plant in Bavaria and was detached on a temporary basis from the 45th Division to the Third Army CIC so he could continue his work uninterrupted. Time was of the essence, for it was well-known that the Russians were illegally active in the American zone. The rocket blueprints were found in the basement of a building south of Munich and a truck and an agent from CIC HQ in Frankfurt were sent to collect them. 'As we went to load them we found a senior member of the French

Mission in the zone. It was a scandal – a high French official spying in the US zone and preparing to steal.' The Frenchman was declared *persona non grata* by the Americans and rapidly removed.

The sheer volume of technical intelligence, plus the mass of valuable equipment, created a competitive feeding frenzy among Allied intelligence agencies. On paper there was an inter-Allied agreement over the control of all German scientific institutions. Allied scientists and intelligence officers were supposed to collaborate in their efforts to collect and analyse the work of Germany's wartime scientists, much of whose resources were buried in safes and bunkers beneath the rubble and ruins of its destroyed cities. At first western experts freely made their findings available to the Soviets, but soon discovered their mistake when the Russians failed to reciprocate. The Russian zone was closed tight and all scientific material, and at least two thousand of the scientists themselves, were sent directly to Moscow.

The Soviets virtually kidnapped these scientists, giving them a choice between signing lucrative five-year contracts or a document stating, 'The undersigned herewith declares his unwillingness to assist in the reconstruction of the Soviet Union.'[11] Under Stalin, this amounted to a death warrant. The French, for their part, offered important scientists good jobs and citizenship, and displayed scant interest in probing murky political pasts. Army trucks picked up forty BMW engineers just after the end of the war and drove them secretly into the French zone, and eighty more followed over the next six months.

At first, the Americans and the British were more squeamish, but soon overcame their reservations in various covert operations. The American Advanced Communications Section ran a daily train – the 'Toot Sweet Express' – to take plundered equipment, drawings and technical records to a Paris depot for transportation to the United States. The British transported entire factories to England, and the French did the same to France. The Russians transported the Bosch fuel injection factory, among others, from Berlin to the Soviet Union, along with the engineers to run it. Germany was being stripped.

The rocket base of Nordhausen, together with its adjoining slave-labour camp, had been liberated by the Americans but was situated in what was to become the Russian zone. As the deadline for the Americans to withdraw westwards on 1 June neared, troops arrested four hundred V-2 rocket scientists in the vicinity. The underground tunnels of the complex contained a wealth of rocketry – a magician's cave, American scientists called it – and four hundred tons of equipment consisting of thousands of rocket parts were moved by train and truck to Antwerp for shipment to the States. The authorities were more interested in the scientists than the SS men, besides which the T-Forces had neither the resources nor the authority to pursue them. Out of a force of three thousand SS men who ran Nordhausen and Camp Dora, only thirty-nine were eventually prosecuted for war crimes.

The scientist in charge of Nordhausen, General Walter Dornberger – described as a 'menace to security' – was secretly taken to the United States and employed by the air force in a classified rocket programme.[12] Dr Arthur Rudolf, accused of committing atrocities at Nordhausen's Camp Dora, and of being 'one hundred per cent Nazi', was recruited to play a major role in the American missile programme, and was later granted US citizenship. Wernher von Braun, mastermind of the entire V-2 rocket programme, also travelled to the United States and eventually became an honoured citizen. These Nazi scientists would be instrumental in putting an American on the moon.

American officers with lists of names visited rocket bases throughout the region and told scientists to accept immediate evacuation or remain in the Soviet zone at their peril. The Seventh Army removed twenty-three aircraft engineers and two hundred university professors across the Demarcation Line, and in one instance a train carrying a thousand scientists and their families crossed into the American zone only hours before the arrival of Russian troops.

Some five thousand German scientists and engineers were forcibly uprooted, often without wives or children, and while the cream went on to new lives in America – and some in Britain – many were later abandoned with no prospect of employment. Some of the older men attempted suicide in despair. The scientists compared their fate to that of their colleagues in the French, and even the Russian, zone who received privileged treatment. Two hundred and fifty scientists moved by American Army intelligence units to Austria were left destitute.

Recruiting officers from Paperclip selected those scientists who were to be offered contracts and passage to the United States. (A host of secret projects with silly names came into being at this time: Pajamas sought German personnel for forecasting European political trends; Apple Pie recruited key figures in Nazi intelligence who were expert on industrial and economic matters, and so on.)[13] In order to compete with the French and the Russians, senior US military officers wanted German scientists to have the status of their peers in the USA, with good pay and the freedom to travel. But extending such largesse to the enemy, especially in the wake of outrage over the revelation of slave-labour and extermination camps, was not popular with the general public. Secrecy was essential if Paperclip was to avoid being smothered at birth.

The State Department, which automatically denied entry to war criminals and undesirables, was misled when Army intelligence shipped the first forty rocket scientists to America. The scientists were under arrest, so technically did not require visas, and the State Department believed that once the men had been interrogated by experts they would return to Germany within a period of four to six weeks. Many not only remained for years, but also became American citizens after their Nazi pasts had been suitably doctored by their intelligence sponsors. Later on, Paperclip was used as cover for scores of German intelligence agents who would never have passed the State Department's criteria for entry into the country.[14]

The 66th CIC, headquartered in Frankfurt, was in charge of a dozen regions throughout the American zone, each with its own headquarters and field offices. In August, Michel returned to his original unit, which had moved to Ulm, a small city between Munich and Stuttgart. The 970/35th CIC, Region I, comprised half a dozen agents in Ulm, with another four in a branch office in Heidenheim. The local HQ was in Göppingen, and the regional command in Stuttgart. Ernest T. 'Swifty' Gearheart Jr, whom Michel had served with since his transfer to CIC in France, was still in charge, and Ted Kraus, a Catholic with a German background, arrived in September as second-in-command. 'I felt very sorry for the Germans,' Kraus said. 'They lived in terrible conditions. I had empathy for them as I had a fondness for things German. There were obviously many people who had no control over their lives.'

The city of Ulm was a place of total desolation and the only things left standing in its centre were a single tree and the steeple of its seven-hundred-year-old cathedral. But despite the post-war chaos, life for the CIC agents was rather comfortable. They were billeted in a complex that included an eight-bedroom house, the Villa Kauderer, in a beautiful undamaged suburb on a hill overlooking the Danube. A German caretaker looked after the grounds, half a dozen displaced Polish girls cleaned the house, and meals were cooked by a chef who had previously worked in a top Munich restaurant.[15] 'We had to scrounge our own food,' Ted Kraus remembered. 'We would send someone to the army supply depot and he would come back with whatever provisions he could get. It's amazing what a gifted person can do, even with army rations. The excellent chef concocted delectable items.'

One of the first things Michel did in Ulm was to locate all existing documents dealing with the town's civil administration and have them brought to the villa. He then employed three German secretaries to sort through them and put aside anything to do with the Nazi Party. A policy of automatic arrest and internment was in place and applied to members of the Allgemeine and Waffen-SS, Gestapo, Wehrmacht intelligence officers, high party officials and assorted small fry in local government.

'A lot of the time was spent in meetings with the mayor or police chief of the towns we were in,' Ted Kraus said. 'And other administrative heads. A rather mundane occupation most of the time. And we would send these reports up the line.' It was clear to Kraus from the beginning that Michel had a more ambitious agenda and that he displayed superior skills as an interrogator. Although he was technically Michel's superior officer, and would later be put in charge of the Ulm office when 'Swifty' Gearheart left for the US, Kraus had the sense to leave his 'subordinate' to his own devices.

It amused Kraus that, although they all wore uniforms without rank or insignia, people referred to Michel as 'Captain Mike'. 'His presence suggested he was an important person. He had a lot of autonomy simply because he knew more about Germany than anyone else in the unit. Plus a forceful personality. Someone like that just takes charge. He went his own way and had his own informants I didn't know about. I didn't always know what he was doing, and must admit that I had very little control over him.' It took a while for the men to get to know and trust one another. 'Here was this individual who didn't say very much and was hard to draw into conversation,' Kraus remembered. 'I found out slowly that his entire family had disappeared, and that he had been tortured and imprisoned in France. Mike had a lot of crosses to bear while we were in Germany together.' Gradually, the men became close and developed a strong friendship that was to last all their lives.

'Because of his languages, culture, knowledge and German background, he would conduct most of the interrogations. He certainly got my attention by his techniques. He was a real pro and knew how to draw a person out. He seemed to know instinctively whether a person was trying to put one over on us or was lying and being deceitful. He would frame his questions in a particular way to catch the person offguard. He was *extremely* skilful. He knew the right questions and had a theatrical touch that got things out of people most interrogators would never have got close to. Most of the time he was very quiet and carried out the interrogations in a low voice, but he got what he wanted. But there were many instances, when he felt people were distorting the truth, that his anger came out. He could get *very* angry. He could be very intimidating – *very* intimidating – because it was in such contrast to his normally cool, mild demeanour. Yes, he could get very angry, but he never got physical. Never. Not ever.' Leo Marks, an acknowledged cryptographer of genius who ran the British Special Operations Executive that worked with the French Résistance, added: 'It is almost technically impossible to lie to Michel Thomas. He may not detect what the truth is, but he will know when he is not being given it.'[16]

Michel soon set up his own trademark 'organisation within an organisation' in Ulm, recruiting and paying his own informants. 'The occupation authorities reinstituted the Reichsmark as the official currency soon after the end of hostilities. My "wallpaper money" came in useful.' He still had a suitcase full of high-denomination bills liberated from Aschaffenburg and believed he could use it to more effect than the government. Even so, the Reichsmark had little value, and cigarettes were the true hard currency of the time.

Around two hundred scientists who moved from the Russian zone had settled in Heidenheim, which came under the jurisdiction of Ulm CIC. Michel went regularly to the town to carry out interrogations for Paperclip, aimed at categorising scientists in terms of quality and importance, and investigate their personal histories for any evidence of Nazi Party activity or war crimes. 'This meant that even people with Nazi pasts might be useful, if they were important enough, and should be sent up the line. But I understood very clearly from written instructions that immigration was out of the question. I thought these people would go to the United States for two months at the most for expert debriefings. They lied to us, and it was a betrayal.' He did not discover the truth for many years.

One of Michel's most important informants in Ulm was Hans Joohs, a German who had been a leader in the Hitler Youth. Aged nineteen when war broke out, Joohs was drafted into the First Alpine Division early in 1941 and sent to the Russian front, headed for the Caucasus. He was wounded in a Russian tank attack in the Ukraine, lost an arm and was sent back to hospital in Germany. He was discharged from the army in 1943 and attended university in Munich. At the end of the war Joohs made his way to his home city of Neu-

Ulm, across the Danube from Ulm. 'I moved with my bicycle and it took a day because the German Army was blocking the road. It was a mess. An unbelievable mess. I found the two cities destroyed and had to recognise that everything we had was gone. My folks' house, all the homes of my relatives, everything. It was very tough to see that.'

Joohs, who spoke reasonable English, was desperate for work and found his way to Michel's office. The German authorities had told him he was only eligible for manual labour, because of his background, and with only one arm he was doomed to starvation. Michel listened to Joohs's story and felt that he was sincere in his repudiation of Nazism, a process that had begun on the day he was wounded. 'I believed every word he said.'[17]

Michel found Joohs a job at the refugee camp in Ulm situated in a large army barracks, the Kienlesberg Kaserne. Built of brick at the end of the nineteenth century, the huge complex had survived the bombing and now housed thousands of refugees in primitive conditions. Trains arrived from the east every day – from Poland, Czechoslovakia, Romania, Hungary and even Russia – bringing back desperate Germans and others who had either fled or been expelled from those countries, every one of whom had to be screened.[18] Joohs worked as an interpreter, liaising between the camp administration and the military authorities.

'Due to the fact that I was one of the very few who spoke English, and perhaps because my nationalistic past was apparently not as hopeless as many others, I began to work with CIC,' Joohs said. He knew Michel only as 'Mike'. 'I never knew his last name or his real name. My first impression was that he was a clean-cut American officer. I had no idea he was not American. He did not speak very much and seemed very introvert. He did not ask many questions at first, but they were precise and to the point. I wouldn't say he was friendly, which I understood as I learned more about the crimes of my country, but he was a well-mannered gentleman.'

The camp had a rapid turnover. Ordinary soldiers remained about two weeks and then returned home, while those who came from the east stayed longer until they were assigned to villages where local farmers were compelled to give the refugees shelter. 'I gave Mike information about the new arrivals who came into the camp, where they came from, how long they stayed and what sort of people they were,' Joohs said. There would be periodic raids on the barracks when people were arrested. 'I would be informed twelve hours beforehand and my responsibility would be to show the MPs where the suspects were sheltered. I remember one raid when twenty-five males were arrested and later tried before a military court.'

One day two French counter-intelligence officers from the Securité Militaire came to see Michel at his office in Ulm with an interesting story. A survivor from Ebensee concentration camp, in Austria, had been shot by the SS and left for dead but had ended up in hospital in the French zone. His condition deteriorated, and when he knew he was on the point of death he asked to see someone in authority to pass on important information.

More than thirty thousand slave labourers at the camp in Ebensee had quarried stone from tunnels that went deep into the mountains. As the American Army had neared at the end of the war, the SS ordered all the prisoners into one of the tunnels. The plan was to block the entrance and detonate explosives packed inside to bury them alive. But for the first time since the prisoners' arrest, the proximity of the American Army allowed them to believe they might survive the war. They refused to move. The SS guards were uncertain how to respond to the mass rebellion. Many of the guards had already been replaced with ethnic Germans who were less dedicated and reliable in their fanaticism, and the slaughter of tens of thousands of people so close to the end of the war was impractical and unwise.[19]

The survivor in the hospital told the French intelligence officers that just before the very end of the war an SS detachment had driven into the compound and ordered a group of Jewish prisoners to carry a number of large chests into one of the three main tunnels. Each of these split into a labyrinth of smaller, subsidiary tunnels, and the prisoners carried the containers to the end of one. The chests, loaded with gold and jewellery looted from the inmates of various camps, were stacked on top of one another. The prisoners were then ordered to seal the tunnel entrance with rocks. When they had completed their work an SS guard raised his pistol and shot them. The man who survived had been left for dead but was taken to hospital, where he helped the French agents draw a map of the whereabouts of the chests in the tunnel. And then he died.

'The intelligence officers called me in Ulm and wanted to talk to me because Ebensee had ended up in the American zone and they couldn't do anything about it. And they said they were prepared to lead us to the loot. In exchange they wanted a reward which seemed to me very little. They had an idea for a business and wanted two American trucks in exchange for all those chests, and only after everything had been retrieved. There were thousands of trucks available after the war.'

Michel wrote a report recommending positive action. CIC officers arrived from regional HQ in Göppingen and, together with Ted Kraus and the Frenchmen, they all made a trip to Ebensee. The camp was now full of Jewish DPs and Michel discovered something that enraged him. Immediately after liberation the Americans had converted Ebensee into an internment camp for captured SS men. The new prisoners objected to conditions, citing the Geneva Convention, and virtually ransacked the camp in a violent rebellion. The authorities responded by moving them out of Ebensee and placing them in a camp with better conditions. Their place was taken by survivors from the death camps. 'It was not good enough for the SS, but it was good enough for the Jewish survivors.'

Accompanied by the Frenchmen, Michel and the Counter Intelligence officers from HQ went into the tunnels. Everything fitted the dying man's description, although it was understood that the French agents would not reveal the exact location until the authorities agreed to the deal. Michel had also added his own recommendation that the gold and jewellery looted from the camps should be handed over to Jewish charity organisations and not be appropriated by the army or government.

'The visit convinced all of us of the truth of the French agents' story. We got the answer from HQ in Frankfurt a couple of days later. It was negative. No deal was to be made with the Frenchmen. No reason was given. And that was that. Perhaps the authorities felt it was not worth bothering to go to all that trouble just to give the proceeds away. I never found out what happened to it, whether the French got the loot or the Germans. Or whether it was just left in the tunnel. It created an anger within me that has never gone away.'

Throughout this time the whole of the American Army and CIC in Germany had been searching for SS Major Gustav Knittel, one of the officers from Kampfgruppe Peiper, of the 1st Panzer Division, wanted for the murder of unarmed American POWs and Belgian civilians during the Battle of the Bulge – the Malmédy Massacre. A war crimes tribunal would charge officers and men of SS Kampfgruppe Peiper with the murder of a total of three hundred and fifty American POWs over ten days at twelve different locations along their line of march. One hundred and twenty-eight Belgian civilians were also shot down in cold blood.[20]

The original SHAEF – Supreme Headquarters Allied Expeditionary Force – file on the Malmédy Massacre contained only a bare
statement of the facts and the names of forty-two members of
Kampfgruppe Peiper. The investigation had been put into the hands
of a young major from the Quartermaster Corps who did not speak
German and who had no investigative experience. He wandered
from camp to camp, accompanied by an interpreter, with his list of
wanted men, only to be told, 'Hell, we don't know who we've got
here.'

But a thousand men from Kampfgruppe Peiper were eventually
tracked down, including its commander, Joachim Peiper himself.
Newly arrived American interrogators dutifully warned the prisoners
against saying anything that might be incriminating, so the SS men
said nothing. And the fact that they had been imprisoned together
allowed them ample time to construct and compare alibis. Finally, a
total of five hundred suspects – almost as many men as actually
survived from the original group – were moved to a new building at
Schwäbisch Hall prison, where they could be isolated and properly
interrogated. However, Gustav Knittel had not been captured and
was not among them.[21]

Out of the total force of five thousand, eight hundred men who
had started the attack in the Battle of the Bulge with Kampfgruppe
Peiper, including Knittel's fifteen-hundred-man Schnell (Fast)
Group, five thousand lost their lives. Knittel was known to be among
the survivors who had managed to return to Germany, but all
attempts to find him had failed. 'Everybody was looking for Knittel,
including the British. In September Frankfurt called me because of
my track record in finding and arresting war criminals. Nobody knew
where he was – he seemed to have disappeared into thin air.'

The mass killing had begun, not actually at the town of Malmédy
that gave the massacre its name, but a few miles south at a crossroads
known as Baugnetz. The Americans called it Five Points, as five roads
converged there. It was a dreary spot with only a few houses, a farm
and a single café, named after its Belgian owner, Madame Adèle
Bodarwé. At lunchtime on 17 December 1944 an American convoy
of thirty-three jeeps and trucks drove south from Malmédy and
made its way up the hill to the crossroads. The column comprised
one hundred and forty men of the lightly armed Battery B of the
285th Field Artillery Observation Battalion, known in American
military parlance as a 'sound and flash' unit with the mission to
locate enemy artillery positions.

The convoy had been on the move through cold, grey sleet since early morning. A corporal in one of the trucks became obsessed by a premonition, which he confided to his best friend in the unit. 'I'll not be going home. Something terrible is going to happen to most of us today, but you'll be going back. Tell the folks back home I love them.'

As the convoy had passed through Malmédy it found the narrow streets full of military vehicles, most of which were moving in the opposite direction. Civilians ran beside the trucks, pointing south and shouting, '*Boches! Boches!*' The commander was stopped by a colonel in the Combat Engineers, who warned of a German breakthrough, and advised him to consider another route. But the commander, worried that he might lose his position in the march column, decided to press on.

When the convoy reached the Baugnetz crossroads one of the jeeps pulled over and stopped at the Café Bodarwé. Three soldiers went in to check that the column was taking the right road and enquired as to the whereabouts of any German troops in the vicinity. Madame Bodarwé, whose son had been forced into service in the German Army, gave directions but said she knew nothing about any soldiers. A pro-German farmer from across the road, Henri Le Joly, said nothing.

The soldiers went outside and climbed back into their jeep. The lead vehicle of the convoy was scarcely five hundred yards beyond the crossroads when the battalion was fired upon. The convoy had been spotted by an advance unit of Kampfgruppe Peiper, a beefed-up battle group comprising six thousand men, many of them in their teens. It was part of the 1st Panzer Division, which traced its origins to Hitler's first bodyguard known as Leibstandarte Adolf Hitler – Hitler's Own. Numbering twenty-two thousand men altogether, it was considered one of the more powerful divisions in the German Army and had a reputation for daring and ruthlessness. Motivated to the point of fanaticism, it had served on the Russian front, where brutality on both sides was routine.

The first round from a German tank fell just in front of the American convoy's lead vehicle, and the jeep swerved and stopped. The Americans had run into two German tanks at the very point of the battle group, which immediately fired half a dozen shells each. One of the Observation Battalion's ambulances and the kitchen truck received direct hits and burst into flame. Other German tanks and SPW armoured personnel carriers joined the point vehicles and began firing as they raced to reach the convoy.

Fire from tanks, mortars and machine guns raked the column. Trucks exploded or drove off the road and GIs jumped from the vehicles and dived into the icy water of the roadside ditches. A few men returned desultory and ineffective fire from their M-1s and carbines, but the virtually defenceless Observation Battalion was hopelessly outgunned and had inadvertently crossed the path of one of the elite outfits of the German Army. Kampfgruppe Peiper was formidable and comprised more than a hundred tanks, five flak tanks and a light flak battalion, self-propelled tank destroyers, artillery, and SS Panzergrenadiers. In addition, Major Gustav Knittel's Schnell Group, made up of fifteen hundred men in tanks and half-tracks, was also part of the attack force, operating as a reconnaissance battalion.

Lieutenant-Colonel Joachim Peiper, commander of the Kampfgruppe, arrived at the Baugnetz crossroads in a captured American jeep, attracted by the sound of gunfire. Peiper, the 'Siegfried of the Waffen-SS' and one-time adjutant to Heinrich Himmler, was a natural soldier who had spent ten years with the division and stood high in Hitler's personal favour. He now reprimanded his men for needlessly expending valuable ammunition on a target that could have been captured. 'Those beautiful trucks which we need so badly, all shot up.' He ordered his troops to cease firing, and American soldiers crawled out of the ditches and emerged from behind burning trucks with their hands in the air. They were gathered into small groups and SS soldiers removed rings, watches and cigarettes. They also stripped the Americans of their gloves, which the Germans particularly prized. One SS soldier went down the line of prisoners putting a pistol against each man's forehead, saying they would all be shot in retribution for American bombing. The American commander objected that his men were prisoners of war and demanded that they be treated honourably. The German returned the pistol to its holster.

Peiper now left the scene of battle, together with the majority of his tanks and half-tracks, while about one hundred and thirty American prisoners were herded into a field next to the café. These included several GIs who had been captured after the farmer, Le Joly, had betrayed their hiding place to the Germans. The men were joined by a captured American colonel who drove up in his own jeep accompanied by two teenage SS soldiers.

The prisoners stood in the mud with their hands in the air. The farmer, still watching from the café, was surprised at the men's apparent lack of concern as they chatted easily to one another. They seemed relieved to have survived the initial strafing and now waited without apparent foreboding for trucks to arrive to take them to the rear.

A tank manoeuvred into the road alongside the field and attempted to lower its gun to cover the prisoners. It was unable to do so, and was replaced by two SPW half-track armoured personnel carriers that pulled into the field and stopped. An SS soldier in the rear of one stood, took his pistol from its holster and pointed it towards the huddled prisoners. He fired, and a GI fell backwards, knocking down several other prisoners in the tightly packed group like so many skittles. The men began to shout and scream, and those in the front row fought to get to the back.

'Stand fast!' an American officer commanded, alarmed that panic might provoke more shooting. The GIs fell silent.

A second pistol shot rang out, killing a medical officer. An order was then shouted: '*Alle kaputt machen!*' – Kill them all! Two machine guns mounted on the SPW armoured personnel carriers opened up, and panic broke out as bullets ripped into the prisoners. Some turned and ran across the field while others were cut down where they stood. The machine guns methodically raked the bodies from one end to the other, and the men cried out in fear and pain as the living tried to burrow beneath the dead for protection.

The automatic fire stopped. The brief silence was punctuated by occasional rifle and pistol shots as SS soldiers moved across the field and inspected the bodies for survivors. The low groans of the wounded sounded like the lowing of cattle.[22] The Germans called out to anyone surviving to make a sign so they could receive medical attention. Those unwise enough to do so were shot. The soldiers kicked those bodies showing signs of life in the head or groin for a reaction, and if anyone moved he was shot. One German soldier perversely allowed a medic to help a wounded comrade, and then shot them both.

Once the Germans had left, the field survivors began to call out to one another, and frozen GIs crawled out from under the bodies of their comrades. Some ran into the woods, but twelve went into the Café Bodarwé. They were seen by German troops, who moved on the café, set it alight and then shot down the unarmed men as they ran out.

Over the next two hours, as more troops from the Panzers passed the scene, some of the men fired into the pile of bodies for sport. One tank, delayed through a breakdown, arrived at the crossroads in the late afternoon and spotted the abandoned trucks and the field full of corpses. The commander, an SS sergeant, detected movement. He climbed down from the tank and went into the field, where he hauled an unwounded GI to his feet by his collar. The American was ordered to take off his watch, jacket and combat boots. As the prisoner stooped to remove his boots the SS man shot him in the back of the neck with his 9 mm Belgian automatic, and twice more in the chest as he fell. The tank gunner then pumped a burst of machine-gun fire into the bodies in the field.

Soldiers from a tank crew threatened to kill the farmer, Le Joly, even though he had delivered the hidden Americans to them. They eventually let him go after abject pro-German protestations. Adèle Bodarwé disappeared, and her body was never found. But despite all the shooting, the massacre proved to be an inefficient business. Miraculously, forty-six Americans survived the field of death. Five nights after the massacre, the bodies of their eighty-four dead comrades-in-arms were temporarily buried in a fall of deep snow.[23]

Kampfgruppe Peiper moved on to attack nearby Stavelot, where the Americans had stashed millions of gallons of fuel. Peiper summoned Knittel to his command post and ordered him to use the Schnell Group to take the town.

As he left the meeting, Knittel remarked: '*Die haben eine ganze Menge auf der Kreuzung umgelegt*' – They've killed a good few at the crossroads.

'The crossroads?'

Knittel reminded Peiper about Baugnetz, south of Malmédy, where the road turned towards Ligneuville. 'There's a lot of *Amis* [Americans] dead there.'

It was the first Peiper had heard of the killings, but he had more pressing matters on his mind, and returned to the plan of attack on Stavelot. Knittel was given three heavy Tiger tanks to strengthen his force and immediately moved his men into position. He established his tactical HQ in the cellar of the Ferme Antoine, to the west of the town near the Amblève river, and split his men into two units for the assault. The larger group was sent along the main road, while a smaller force moved north through back roads and hamlets standing on high ground. The Germans were shelled remorselessly by the Americans throughout the battle: three thousand shells were fired in such rapid succession that the artillerymen had to throw cold water over the barrels of their guns.

The attack heralded the beginning of a new slaughter by the SS men, this time random shooting of civilians, all of whom had been declared by Peiper to be 'terrorists' in reaction to resistance activity in the area. The Germans had been shot at from buildings and the SS were to take a terrible revenge. The killing was haphazard, almost casual. An SPW armoured half-track first passed through Stavelot as a machine-gunner fired into the kitchen of a house, killing a fourteen-year-old boy; a farmer was shot in his barn; a woman was killed as she lay in her bed. Locals were rounded up in small groups of two or three, taken into houses and shot. The houses were then set alight as the soldiers moved on.

In one particularly brutal killing in Stavelot, twenty men were packed into an eight-by-twelve-foot shed. A machine gun was set up outside and two belts of ammunition fired into the writhing mass of panicked humans. SS soldiers then entered, firing pistols into the heaped bodies, before they threw down straw and set the shed alight. Somehow, eight people survived the conflagration.[24] In another incident, a group of twenty-six locals sheltering in a cellar were flushed out when soldiers threw a grenade down the stairs. Unhurt, a woman called out in German that they were all civilians, and they were ordered to come up into the open. A dozen SS men – mostly in their teens, as at Baugnetz – lined up the terrified group of women, children and old men, who ranged in age from four to sixty-eight. One soldier with a rifle and another with a pistol walked down the line and methodically shot them one by one. Only three people from the cellar were spared: the woman who spoke German and her two children. Another twenty civilians were murdered at a nearby hamlet with a population of just one hundred.

Altogether, one hundred and thirty-eight unarmed Belgian civilians were killed in this way by men under Knittel's command during the battle of Stavelot. And while there is no evidence that he was present at any of these killings, or personally ordered them, the large number suggests that his troops were encouraged to behave in this manner and that their actions were condoned.

As the battle raged, the Germans' position became increasingly untenable, but Knittel held on. On the afternoon of 21 December, he left the cellar of his command post at the Ferme Antoine to investigate a report that a number of recently destroyed American tanks might be part of an advance force of forty-five armoured vehicles. Knittel was on foot and unarmed as he walked to the Amblève Bridge, passing several destroyed enemy tanks on his way. A single Tiger tank secured the road and eight German soldiers provided the only infantry cover. The commander of the giant Tiger reported that more American tanks were out of sight around the curve in the road, guarded by three Shermans hidden in the mouth of a railroad tunnel.

Knittel walked over to inspect a nearby anti-tank gun emplacement on the river bank and was alarmed to find it abandoned with the guns unmanned. He walked quickly to a deserted house standing close by and demanded an explanation from the anti-tank gun commander. The commander had bad news. An SPW had been destroyed and its crew killed, while Knittel's second-in-command had been killed in a separate incident. In a sworn statement given later, Knittel reported that he was enraged that the Americans had been allowed to break through. The death of the second-in-command, a brave man who was a favourite, particularly upset him.

'What have we thrown against them?' he asked the commander.

'I've taken the men away from the *Paks* [anti-tank guns] and ordered them to reconnoitre,' the commander replied. 'I couldn't make the drivers of the vehicle column go forward.'

Knittel fully understood the gravity of the situation. He was faced with a strong concentration of enemy tanks both in front and behind his positions, and his only possible retreat was through a wooded area difficult to reconnoitre. And there were no reserves left. Nothing. He was facing catastrophe.

As he discussed things with his commander, a badly wounded German soldier limped out of the woods.

'What's happening up there?' Knittel shouted.

'All quiet,' the soldier replied. 'Everybody seems to have taken off.'

He had scarcely finished replying when eight American GIs emerged from the woods.

'Goddamn it, those are *Amis*,' Knittel shouted. He ran with the anti-tank commander and took cover behind the wall of the abandoned house. The wounded soldier limped back into the woods.

As the Americans came closer it became apparent that they were prisoners covered by the rifles of two German soldiers following close behind.

'What are we going to do with them?' Knittel asked the commander. 'If we've got to take off we can't take them along with us through the woods.'

Knittel remembered the words of the Panzer Army's leader, Sepp Dietrich, at the opening of the campaign, reported to him by the general's adjutant: 'No foreign soldier will stand on German territory at the beginning of the New Year. Everything that helps you advance is permitted. The Führer covers you. Think of the Fatherland, which suffers under the enemy bombing terror, and be ruthless towards the civilian population. When military necessity demands it Allied prisoners of war should be shot.'[25] The solution to the American prisoners was obvious. Knittel also admitted later that he was emotionally upset by the news of the recent deaths of his men and wanted revenge.

As the soldiers came close, Knittel called out to the guards: 'From which division are they?'

'We don't know,' one replied. 'We don't speak English.'

Knittel waited until the American soldiers reached the house, then ordered their guard, *'Mach' sie fertig!'* – Finish them off!

The Americans were led in a line behind the house while Knittel and the anti-tank commander remained in the front. Five minutes later there were pistol shots. The two guards returned showing each other gold rings and watches taken from the prisoners.

'You swine!' Knittel shouted at them. 'That's not going to bring you any luck!'[26]

On Christmas Eve, Knittel was forced to accept that the situation was impossible. He gave the order to retreat. This meant snaking through heavily wooded country covered in fourteen inches of snow and infested with American paratroopers. It also involved crossing a number of rivers where the bridges had been destroyed. Exhausted by days of combat without sleep, and fuelled only by hard biscuits and occasional shots of cognac, the soldiers struggled through the woods. A sergeant and five SS men were left behind to cover the retreat and destroy the last two operational tanks of the Kampfgruppe, a pair of seventy-two-ton Royal Tigers abandoned outside the Ferme Antoine. Then, before first light on Christmas morning, they too stole away.

Knittel's men reached the icy, fast-flowing Salm river in full flood, and swam across. After covering twenty-five hellish miles and losing thirty men on the way, the survivors of Kampfgruppe Peiper – some seven hundred and seventy men in all – struggled into the German-held sanctuary at Wanne on Christmas Day.

They enjoyed only a brief respite before the remnants of the division were reorganised and sent back into battle at Bastogne on 30 December. Knittel was wounded the following day and taken out of the battle. The division fought on for another two weeks before retreating yet again to an area west of Cologne.

The Battle of the Bulge was over, and the Germans had suffered a rout. Leibstandarte Adolf Hitler was reorganised yet again, and Kampfgruppe Peiper along with it. Back on German soil it was reinforced almost to its original strength, drawing troops from every source available, and sent to Hungary where it took part in an operation designed to break through the Russian front to the Danube. Hitler's Own received another dreadful mauling, fighting in a sea of mud, and suffered appalling casualties. Unable to sustain its position the division fell back, against Hitler's express but impossible command. Infuriated, the Führer ordered that his elite bodyguard, which had fought fanatically for him in the toughest campaigns throughout the war, be stripped of its armband.

The war was lost, and on 8 May the order came for Leibstandarte Adolf Hitler to destroy its vehicles and armour. The men retreated rapidly westwards on foot, desperate to be captured by Americans rather than fall into the hands of vengeful Russians. Some men threw down their weapons, burned their uniforms and escaped into the mountains. The majority, however, crossed the Demarcation Line and were surprised to be casually waved through by American troops.

Once across, many tried to make it to their homes, but most were later arrested and put into camps, alongside three hundred thousand other prisoners. Some of the SS men, in a final irony, were among those housed in Ebensee. The senior officers were moved to the US Forces' main interrogation centre at Camp King in Oberürsel, near Frankfurt – which had been the Luftwaffe's primary interrogation centre. But Knittel had not served with the division in Hungary because of battle injuries sustained at Bastogne – the last of seven occasions on which he was wounded – and had disappeared.

Gustav Knittel had married a French woman when in Paris and they had had a baby boy together whom he had never seen. His wife had then moved from France to Germany to live in the family home in Ulm. Although she had not seen her husband since before the Ardennes offensive, and he had not returned to Ulm, Michel put her under surveillance. 'I had to set up a system to find out any possible contact he might make with family or friends. I had my people pose as insurance agents and officials to approach the family without their knowledge.'

Among the agents activated to find Knittel was a beautiful, highly intelligent twenty-eight-year-old woman named Anna Konrad.[27] 'We created the legend for her that she was actually the wife of a high-ranking SS officer who had been arrested by the Allies and charged with war crimes.' She posed as a fellow victim of Allied oppression, befriended Knittel's wife and was soon accepted by the family.

Anna became a regular at the Knittel household. She confided her terror of the American Military Police and CIC agents, who constantly questioned her, and asked to be introduced to contacts who might help her obtain a new identity through ODESSA. The occasional visit became a regular event, and Anna spent long evenings with Knittel's wife, a high-spirited if not very bright young woman in her late twenties. She became distraught at any mention of her husband's disappearance, and demonstrated genuine devotion to him that was beyond doubt. Her worst fear, she confided, was that he might be dead. But months of contact and constant surveillance revealed nothing more than the fact that Knittel's wife was as ignorant of her husband's whereabouts as CIC.

Knittel's family and friends had been subjected to constant questioning for months before Michel took over the hunt. 'I put a stop to the practice in the hope that the family would believe the heat was off, and pass this on to Knittel so he might think it safe for a visit. It seemed reasonable to believe he would surface – turn up somewhere, however briefly – to see his wife and child. I expected him to do so at Christmas, if only for a moment.' Michel was so confident of this that he even cancelled a skiing trip he had planned to take over the holidays, but Christmas came and went and Knittel did not appear. 'I went to midnight mass with Ted and found the service beautiful and moving.' Michel now became convinced that he would show up over the New Year, and once more cancelled long-overdue leave. Again, there was no sign of the fugitive. Michel began to wonder whether the SS man might be dead after all.

And then Anna reported a breakthrough. On one of her visits to the Knittel household the wife appeared to be reborn and could not contain her joy and excitement as she passed on her wonderful news: her husband was alive! He had sent word that she was to be ready at a moment's notice to meet him at a secret rendezvous. As she spoke, the depression that had dogged her lifted, and the light returned to her eyes.

A German agent now took over – one of Michel's trusted informants who had been in the police – and arranged discreet, round-the-clock surveillance of the family house. A tense period of expectation followed, but as time passed and Knittel still did not appear it seemed that they had been fed a false lead. 'Then, on the fifth of January, late at night, I got a report that his wife had left the house. She was followed to a remote area of the town where she disappeared in the dark. There were only three isolated houses in the vicinity and it was reasonable to presume she had gone into one of them, but we could not be certain.' Further action posed a dilemma: to move on the houses but fail to capture Knittel would alert both man and wife. 'I was following a hunch. I had no evidence that either Knittel or his wife were in any of the houses. It was a risk. I fought with myself whether to act or not, and followed my gut reaction and decided to strike.'

Michel and Ted Kraus called in a group of forty American troops and drove to the spot where Knittel's wife had last been seen. The soldiers were told nothing about their mission, and Michel facetiously said to one that there had been a report of somebody stealing a pram. They were divided into four groups: one secured a perimeter around all the properties, while each of the other three was assigned a house. The troops were ordered to hold everyone they found and search each building from top to bottom.

'I led a squad into one house and we quickly assembled everyone in the living room with guards over them. Frau Knittel was there, but not her husband.' Michel climbed the stairs to the first floor, kicking open bedroom doors, searching under beds and inside wardrobes. He climbed a ladder into the attic. In the gloom beneath the eaves he made out a crouched man, very much the worse for wear, hiding in a corner. Michel ordered him to stand and clasp his hands behind his head. The man was unarmed and his papers identified him as Hans Jagomast, an agricultural labourer. Demobilisation documents stated that he had formerly been a corporal in the Wehrmacht. His head was shaved, his cheeks were bloated and he looked nothing at all like SS Major Gustav Knittel. 'It looked like he had been through hard times,' Ted Kraus said. 'He hadn't shaved in a couple of weeks and was quite surprised that he had finally been caught. He admitted nothing and denied ever having been in the SS.'[28] The man said he had panicked when American soldiers had entered the house and that was the reason he had tried to hide.

Michel went carefully through his wallet and found a photograph of a woman, on the back of which was an inscription: FÜR GUSTEL, ALLES LIEBE – to Gustel, with love. Michel recognised the woman as Frau Knittel; Gustel was a form of endearment for Gustav. 'So, Gustel,' Michel said, 'you changed your name to Hans Jagomast. But it's Gustav, isn't it – Gustav Knittel?'

Knittel said nothing.

'You've done a good job to make yourself unrecognisable,' Michel continued. 'Take off your shirt and raise your arms!'

The standard SS tattoo denoting blood group was found under the left arm. Knittel sullenly admitted his real identity and said that the house they were at, number nineteen Blaicher Haag, belonged to his aunt's husband, Alfred Schiebel.[29]

As Knittel was brought out of the house under arrest, the commander of the American troops lounged against a wall, smoking a cigarette. He asked nonchalantly, 'So now can you tell us who this joker is we're freezing our arses off for in the middle of the night?'

Kraus told him they had picked up somebody important – Knittel, the SS officer suspected of murdering unarmed American prisoners at Malmédy. The American soldier's easy manner evaporated, and for a moment he looked stunned. He turned his head towards the wall and began to sob. Later, he explained that his best friend had been one of those shot at the crossroads.

There was a fear that the prisoner's life might be in danger once word spread among the GIs that he was wanted in connection with the Malmédy Massacre. Feelings ran very high against Knittel among the American troops, so Michel arranged to put him in a secure cell guarded by men he could trust.

'How could you hope to stay free?' Michel asked. 'Everyone is looking for you after this terrible crime.'

The surrender of Germany had devastated him, Knittel said, and he felt the end of the world had come. At first he had no wish to carry on but, ironically, the will to live came from the sight of Jewish survivors. Unaware that Michel was a Jew, Knittel said, 'At the end of the war I was shocked to see a Jew in the street still alive. I thought that these accursed people would have been finally wiped out for ever. How was it possible that any were still alive and free? When I saw that the Jews had managed to avoid extinction, that gave me hope. I said to myself, "If those dumb *Jews* can survive, I can survive. I'm at least as smart as any damn Jew."'

Michel said nothing.

Once in jail, Knittel seemed to take pleasure in reasserting himself as an SS major. He spoke repeatedly of his amazement at having been caught. He had been so careful, changing his identity and appearance, working quietly on a farm with no outside contact with anyone. 'It was the only time I ever came out of my hiding place,' he said. 'For a few hours at midnight. You know, I was absolutely sure I would never be caught. Never! NEVER!' Curiosity about how he had been trapped began to obsess him. 'How is it possible you caught me? Tell me!' Michel allowed the obsession to grow, aware that doubt and curiosity would gnaw at the prisoner and lead him in time to suspect his own wife.

Michel returned to the jail frequently to interrogate his prisoner, subjecting the SS major to lengthy questioning sessions. Knittel was a classic SS officer, commended by the commanding general of

Leibstandarte, Sepp Dietrich, as one of his best officers. He was well-educated, came from a middle-class background, and had joined the Nazi Party and an SS Political Alert Unit at the age of eighteen. As an officer cadet he had earned high marks for ideology and was commissioned at the age of twenty-three on 9 November 1938, the anniversary of Hitler's abortive putsch of 1923. He was wounded in combat in France and Russia, where he was awarded the Knight's Cross for cool and skilful leadership under fire.[30]

'I had him for weeks. He complained early on that he had been made to work all night to clean his cell with a toothbrush. I was enraged. I called the head of the prison and insisted that no prisoners should be touched or abused in any way.'

The questioning took the form of long conversations. 'We talked about the objectives of the Ardennes offensive, and he spoke with pride about the rapid advance made by Kampfgruppe Peiper. I remarked that he must have taken a number of American prisoners in such a breakthrough.'

Knittel said that prisoners were a problem as the division was not equipped to handle them.

'You mean you shot your prisoners?' Michel asked.

'No, I did not. I ordered them to be shot.'

Although Knittel readily confessed to giving the command to shoot unarmed American prisoners, he insisted that he was following orders issued at the beginning of the offensive. 'However, he admitted he agreed with them because the army could not afford to waste time and bother with sending prisoners to the rear.' Knittel explained dispassionately about the inability to cope with the large number of prisoners which he ascribed to American cowardice. Their deaths had been a necessity of war. 'He talked quite calmly about how they were killed. He was able to talk about it without any remorse or apparent feeling. He was candid and cool, as if mass murder was understandable to those familiar with the rigours of combat.'

But Knittel's voice changed as he spoke of his outrage when his men looted personal belongings from the dead: 'After the shooting some of my men stripped the corpses of their watches and rings. Their behaviour was a serious breach of conduct. I ordered the business stopped at once and made it clear none of the bodies was to be touched.'

As he spoke about the looting, he grew increasingly agitated. 'It was a complete switch from the dispassionate account of the killings. It was such a change that it threw me. I was confused. He practically screamed about calling his men back and preventing the looting. This enraged him, made him furious.' The contrast between the detached report of the cold-blooded murder of prisoners, and the fury over the aftermath, seemed to make no sense. At first, Michel assumed it was some arcane part of the SS military code of honour.

'Tell me, major,' he asked, 'you had just calmly ordered your men to kill unarmed soldiers, but became angry when they tried to loot the bodies. What made you so upset?'

Knittel's eyes narrowed and the answer was snarled between clenched teeth. 'Because looting the dead brings bad luck!'

Throughout the lengthy and numerous interrogations Michel never once showed any personal animosity towards his prisoner. 'Towards the end of the questioning, after he had confessed to murder, he begged me to tell him how we got on to him. He had become truly obsessed by this, as I had foreseen. He could not understand how it was that he had ventured out for such a short time and been caught. I said nothing but just watched him. He was going through terrible mental torture. I knew what was playing on his mind, and I was so tempted to look at him innocently and say, "Your wife – she's French, isn't she?" Not as an answer, but as a question. He would have been destroyed emotionally. I felt it would have sent him into such mental torture that it would have killed him. And why shouldn't he be destroyed? This murderer. This war criminal. I had no regard for Knittel's feelings. I let him beg and plead, and the more he did so the more I was tempted. It was easy to hate him. I was so tempted to sour his relationship with his wife – it would have cut deep to let him think the woman he loved had betrayed him. But I couldn't do it, and I didn't.'

Michel approached the interrogation of Gustav Knittel's wife with the same inner revulsion he felt for her SS husband. 'It was extremely difficult for me. I had considered myself French for so many years. I knew how we in the Résistance felt about French women who associated with the hated German occupiers, and here was one who had married an SS officer! Before Knittel's arrest, his wife had been questioned by the CIC agents and been given a full account of the atrocities her husband was accused of, yet she chose to stay in Germany and wait for him. I could not understand. How could a French woman betray her own country and people?'

At their first encounter Michel expressed this contempt for a French woman who could marry an SS officer. 'How could you? As a French woman! The invaders of your country – the occupiers. The brutes! *How could you?*'

The woman looked at Michel calmly and replied in a soft but firm voice, *'L'amour ne connait pas de frontière'* – Love knows no borders.

Michel could not help but be moved, and was secretly envious of such a love. It reminded him with a sharp pang of the selfless love Suzanne had displayed. 'The straightforward answer disarmed me, despite my strong feelings. It came out of her soul. She did not seek either to excuse her husband or justify him. That demonstration of devotion and loyalty, the strength of her love – ill-deserved, but true – made me see things differently. I had been so caught up in the passions of the war and my work after it that I had forgotten there were emotions stronger than hatred of an evil enemy, stronger even than a person's best interests. This woman's unconditional love for an evil man affected me strangely. I had gone to her with great anger, but left deeply moved.'

Knittel fully expected and accepted that he would be executed within a short time and asked Michel to grant him a last request. The major had married his wife in a civil SS ceremony and now wanted a religious wedding as he did not want his son to be considered illegitimate. 'I asked his wife if she wanted this and she said that she did. They were Catholics, so she chose a priest and I arranged for a wedding service to be held in prison.'

Gustav Knittel duly appeared before an American military tribunal at Dachau in May 1946, charged with murder. Along with twenty-three other officers and forty-nine non-commissioned officers or enlisted men from Kampfgruppe Peiper, the prosecution charged that the accused 'did wilfully, deliberately and wrongfully permit, encourage, aid, abet and participate in the killing, shooting, ill treatment, abuse and torture of members of the Armed Forces of the United States of America, and of unarmed civilians'. All the SS men were found guilty as charged and sentence was passed in July. Gustav Knittel was among twenty-three defendants to receive life imprisonment. His commander, Joachim Peiper, was sentenced to death, along with forty-two other SS officers and men. The remainder received lengthy prison terms.

Knittel was transferred to Landsberg Fortress, the same jail in which Adolf Hitler was imprisoned after his abortive putsch in Munich in 1923. It was the same prison that held Emil Mahl, hangman of Dachau, and Michel's involvement with both men was far from over.

CIC had developed a schizoid nature after the war. On the one hand its record for the capture of war criminals remained unrivalled, and the evidence gathered and investigative files accumulated – not least the Berlin Document Centre, initially funded by the US Army – resulted in thousands of successful prosecutions in many countries. But at the same time another, top-secret section of CIC was recruiting war criminals to work as intelligence officers, in the same manner that Project Paperclip employed Nazi scientists.

Top-secret operations that enlisted German intelligence officers with experience in covert operations gave known war criminals of dubious value a new lease of life. SS officer Otto von Bolschwing, one-time senior aide to Adolf Eichmann, volunteered his services to CIC and was used for interrogation and recruitment of other former Nazi intelligence officers. Among Bolschwing's previous career achievements was the planning and oversight of a pogrom in Bucharest. He was later picked up by the CIA and employed as a contract agent. SS officer Robert Verbelen was a contract agent in Vienna for CIC, despite a known background that included the torture of two captured American pilots. The US Army Chemical Corps hired Dr Kurt Blome, a leader in Nazi biological research. This involved experiments on humans and caused unimaginable suffering. Senior Nazi Foreign Office official Gustav Hilger was flown in secret to the US on a military transport. These men were the first of many, and typical of a breed that enjoyed protection by the American intelligence community in various programmes that continued until 1973.[31]

The most important Nazi intelligence agent to be recruited by the US was General Reinhard Gehlen, Hitler's senior expert on Russia. During the war, Gehlen's organisation had been responsible for tens of thousands of deaths when it employed ruthless methods of interrogation and torture against Russian POWs. (It is estimated that approximately four million Soviet POWs were deliberately starved to death.) As a favourite of Hitler, Gehlen enjoyed great success and meteoric promotion, but his reputation relied greatly on the smoke and mirrors of his profession. His reports were carefully crafted to be so equivocal that they often allowed him to take credit whatever the outcome.[32]

In March 1945, two months before the end of the war, Gehlen had taken out a solid-gold life insurance policy. He secretly microfilmed everything the German Army's military intelligence service had in the files on the USSR. The films were packed in fifty-two watertight steel drums and buried in three hiding places in the Bavarian Alps. Gehlen stayed with the most important of these in a chalet located at a place called Misery Meadow, and waited to be captured by

American forces. When he surrendered, together with his top aides, he bartered the priceless hoard in exchange for his life and future. 'Here are the secrets of the Kremlin,' Gehlen had boasted as he revealed the sealed steel containers containing the world's most valuable espionage files. 'If you use them properly, Stalin is doomed.'[33]

He also offered the Americans another valuable intelligence asset in the form of an espionage network already in place behind the Iron Curtain. In addition, he produced a list of agents from the OSS (Office of Strategic Services) who, he claimed, were members of the US Communist Party.[34] Dressed in an American lieutenant-general's uniform, Gehlen was flown to Washington DC together with three of his top men, in August 1945. He returned to Germany with the blessing and money of the intelligence community, and set up the Gehlen Organisation.[35]

Its early staff of fifty officers, many of whom were enlisted with false names and papers to protect them from prosecution, established themselves at Pullach, near Munich. They were a sinister crew of known war criminals. Among them were men like Willi Krichbaum, one-time Gestapo leader in south-eastern France; Fritz Schmidt, Gestapo chief in Kiel; and Hans Sommer, who had torched seven Paris synagogues in 1941. Two SS officers, Emil Augsburg and Franz Six, ran the émigré section of the organisation. Augsburg was one of the Nazi regime's leading experts on Eastern Europe, who had also led a murder squad in Russia. Apart from working for the Gehlen Organisation, Augsburg was simultaneously employed by CIC, French intelligence, a private network of ex-SS officers, and possibly British intelligence. Dr Six, as he liked to be known – his doctorates were in Nazi law and political science – had been dean of Berlin University where he ran an SS think-tank concerned with strategic intelligence on the USSR. He, too, was a wanted war criminal who had led a mobile killing squad on the eastern front.

However, despite Gehlen's protection and CIC sponsorship, another arm of CIC went ahead and prosecuted Six. He was charged with war crimes, including murder, and was sentenced to twenty years in prison by a military tribunal in 1948. But he served only four years before being granted clemency by the US High Commissioner in Germany. The clemency board specifically approved the former SS man for a position in the Gehlen Organisation, and he returned to work a few weeks after his release.[36]

Under Hitler, Gehlen had reorganised his operation so that intelligence collection was greatly improved, and he placed great value on research and analysis. He impressed high-ranking US Army officers with his forecasts of Soviet policy in post-war Europe, most of which history has since proved incorrect. His value to America was exaggerated by a scarcely credible intelligence gap with regard to the Soviet Union. The US intelligence files on Russia were virtually empty, and did not even include the most elementary information on roads and bridges, the location of major weapons factories, or even road maps and city plans. As a result the US Air Force was obliged to plan for nuclear war using dated material in the Library of Congress.[37]

Gehlen might have helped fill empty files, but his intelligence and analysis was not only tainted by Nazi ideology, it was also self-serving and self-promoting. Created and shaped by the US Army's CIC, the Gehlen Organisation was later kept in business by $200 million of CIA funding, and eventually employed four thousand people full-time. The CIA took the organisation's reports as gospel truth, and sometimes merely retyped them on their own stationery before handing them to the American president in the morning intelligence summary.[38] When West Germany regained its sovereignty, in 1949, Gehlen was appointed head of the Federal Intelligence Service, a post he held until his retirement in 1968.

The disintegration of Germany continued apace through 1946 until in the severe winter of that year, with food and fuel shortages, many Germans faced slow starvation. A third of all babies born at this time did not survive their first year. The emphasis had switched at CIC from the hunt for unrepentant Nazis and war criminals to keeping tags on the German Communist Party and those sympathetic to the USSR. The Cold War had begun and, as time passed, some in the west feared a hot war with the Soviet Union was inevitable – even imminent.

The Soviets had the foundation of an espionage establishment in place in the west in the form of the Rote Kapelle – Red Orchestra – that had operated inside Germany throughout the war. Within days of the war's end, the Russian security services, in the form of the NKVD (forerunner to the KGB) and GRU (military intelligence), were recruiting informers and establishing new spy rings. As in the west, many important ex-Nazis with skill and expertise in intelligence rose to prominence in the Russian zone when it became East Germany.

For Michel, intelligence work involving the Soviets proved to be frustrating, like trying to put together a jigsaw in which half the pieces were either missing or from another puzzle altogether. Operations seemed to have no beginning and no end, and it took subterfuge and cunning to follow them for even a part of the course. Investigations would begin, then trail off or be taken over, until it seemed that universal muddle had become official policy.

One example of this involved a Russian NKVD officer who appeared out of the rubble in Munich. He had managed to convince CIC that he could put his hands on a valuable cache of Russian documents purloined from French intelligence. CIC employed him, and he dropped into the Ulm office on his way to the French zone and seemed anxious, not to say boastful, to tell his fellow agents his story.

The man introduced himself as Pupescu, originally from Romania, where he had worked as a NKVD agent before going over to the French. He had worked for Foreign Legion intelligence in Kehl but had grown disgusted by French recruitment of SS men, or so he said, and had made off with valuable documents he intended to hand over to the Americans. His escape, as he told the story, even involved a shoot-out with French intelligence officers.

'A dramatic tale. It convinced CIC in Munich, who considered him a valuable asset, but I didn't believe it. To his immense surprise, instead of helping him on his way, I had him arrested and jailed incommunicado. The Russians were pouring their agents into the western intelligence agencies at this time, which was why I never trusted any so-called turncoats who claimed to have changed allegiance.

'I began to interrogate him. He talked a lot and I got him to write stuff down. But it still didn't fit.' Pupescu said he had gone from the NKVD to Romanian intelligence during the war, after convincing them that he had turned against Communism because of what he had seen. He expressed a passion to work against the system. 'This was not good enough on its own, so he came up with lists of dozens of genuine Communists. He led the authorities to a meeting where there were people with leaflets and incriminating material. They were arrested and he was a hero. But it didn't mean anything to the Russians to sacrifice hundreds of their own people to get one man into western intelligence.'

Michel suspected that Pupescu was a double agent, copying reports and passing them to the Russian zone. He was also convinced that the valuable 'cache' of documents had been doctored and would turn out to be falsified and misleading versions of the originals. After a while, CIC in Munich became concerned about their man and made enquiries. It came as a shock to find out that he had been jailed by another CIC office only a few miles down the road. Lobbying began for Pupescu's immediate release.

Pupescu remained in jail as Michel procrastinated, clinging to his devalued cover story, until Michel received an irate call from a Seventh Army general. 'It was very unusual to receive a call like that. These sorts of things usually went strictly through channels. He wanted to know the whereabouts of the man and ordered that he be freed immediately.'

Although very much opposed to the man's release, Michel now had no option but to follow orders, although he felt these were open to imaginative interpretation. 'At that time, Pupescu was going through a period of deep depression. He expressed again and again in his writings the certainty that he would be executed as a spy.'

Michel adopted a lugubrious manner and offered the prisoner cold comfort. 'We don't want to execute you. In fact I have the order for your release. But you know you won't live long without American protection – the Soviets will kill you as a traitor. You have outlived your usefulness to both sides.' He elaborated on the theme that release meant certain death, and Pupescu nodded glumly, unaware that he had an American general as a sponsor and that CIC in Munich was anxious to re-employ him. 'There's an option,' Michel continued. 'I can release you and put you up some place in secret where you'll be safe. Instead of being shot by the Soviets as a traitor, you can work for me.'

Pupescu's eyes filled with tears of gratitude.

Michel visited Hans Joohs in the barracks and told him to prepare isolated quarters. 'I said I was bringing somebody who was to be kept separate and to receive special treatment. He was not to eat with the other refugees but have food taken to his rooms. I told Hans that the man was technically free but needed to be under day-and-night sur-veillance and be restrained if he tried to leave. But that he should feel free and think he was free.'

Michel returned to Ulm jail, ordered the release of Pupescu, and drove him to the barracks. 'He couldn't believe it – I had saved his life!' Michel had changed into civilian clothes before collecting the prisoner in order not to draw attention to himself at the barracks. He took Pupescu to his new quarters and told him that if he gave a complete and honest account of his life in NKVD he would be protected. 'After that I always went to the barracks in civilian clothes and we would work. We talked for hours. And then I asked him to write everything down. It practically became a book. I thought of it as "Anatomy of a Soviet Spy". It was a very interesting, alarming and damning document. And I was following orders!'[39]

When the Soviet spy had written everything down, Michel sent the manuscript to CIC HQ in Frankfurt. 'There was an explosion up there! They immediately called regional HQ demanding that the man be handed over. And they got in touch with me to ask where he was.' Michel explained patiently that Pupescu had been released on the express orders of a general. Pupescu had then written his account, albeit under Michel's supervision, as a free agent on his own accord.

Military police arrived at the barracks and arrested Pupescu on suspicion of being a Soviet agent. 'I have no idea why the general ordered his release in the first place. That had nothing to do with CIC in Munich. And I don't know what happened to him afterwards.' Pupescu became another loose piece of an unfinished jigsaw.

A dinner invitation arrived at the Villa Kauderer from the general in charge of the military forces in the French zone. Michel and Ted Kraus drove together to Biberach where they were lavishly entertained with good wine and excellent food. At first, the general made the dinner seem little more than an opportunity for allies and colleagues to get to know one another, but at the end of the meal he took Michel aside for an intensely personal conversation. 'The dinner was not just a nice social gesture. He wanted to talk to me about a young woman he cared very much about.'

The woman in question, Tanya, was a *femme fatale* of great beauty, fluent in French, German, Russian and English, who Michel had under investigation on suspicion of spying for the Russians. 'I had met her and questioned her. She was something. Very lovely and seductive. Very dangerous.' Born in Monte Carlo of Russian parents, Tanya had worked at the German Embassy in Moscow during the German–Soviet pact where she met her husband, who went on to become a high official in the Gestapo. At the end of the war they were both arrested in Constance, in southern Germany, and her husband was subsequently executed by the French. 'Somehow she got out with the help of this French general. Later the relationship became known in France, where he had a wife and children, and created a scandal. As a result the authorities refused her a resident's permit in the French zone, but the general didn't want to give her up.'

The general enjoyed an agreement with a young American officer working for the military government in Ulm to allow Tanya to live in the American zone. Passes were provided by the officer so she could

regularly visit her lover. 'My enquiries interfered with this arrangement because she could not be granted a resident's permit while she
was under investigation. And I didn't want her in the American zone
because of the questions raised by her background. The French
general wanted me to drop the investigation.'

The request was made from one ladies' man to another, but
Michel refused. 'My investigations suggested that she might be a spy
for the Russians and I indicated I had very strong reasons to
continue.' There was also a complication unknown to the French
general: the obliging young American officer in Ulm had also become
romantically involved with Tanya. 'The American officer was very
much in love with her, and that bothered me a lot. Because he was
so very sincere in his feelings, despite her involvement with the
French general. Nothing seemed to matter to him. He didn't care
that she might be a Russian spy.'

Besotted, the officer also tried to block the investigation in a
clumsy manoeuvre that only served to intensify Michel's enquiries.
In frustration, the French general and the American officer arranged
for their shared mistress to slip away to Paris. One of the Ulm CIC
agents was about to be transferred to the city, and Michel briefed
him about the case. 'I gave him the address and asked him to watch
her because I suspected that she was working for the Soviets. I
warned him about her and her ways.'

In due course the agent reported back that he had contacted the
woman and everything was under control. 'He had certainly
contacted her, but things were *not* under control. I found out much
later that he had fallen in love with her. As I said, she was something.
I suspect she may have ended up in the States.'

One of the SS officers on Michel's wanted list lived in the British
zone, and plans were laid to lure him into a trap. Rudolf
Schelkmann, who had been a major in the SD (SS intelligence), was
in the habit of visiting a tavern in the American zone and the original
plan was to have him arrested there. New information had been
received, however, that suggested the major was actively involved in
an SS underground organisation.

Just at the moment when the man was about to be picked up,
Michel decided to hold off. The arrest of one man in the organisation
was insignificant when set against the possibility of infiltrating the
whole movement. 'I could well remember being aware of the danger
of German infiltration when I had been active in the Secret Army.
Infiltration usually meant doom to a whole underground network.

Now it was my turn to infiltrate, and Dr Frundsberg and the Grossorganisation were born.'

A number of trusted German agents were picked to pose as SS officers and designated to areas where underground activity was suspected. They had no contact with anyone in CIC except an assigned 'shadow' agent who liaised with Michel.

The agent who first made contact with the underground was Hans Meyer.[40] He became a regular at the bar of an inn suspected to be an underground meeting place. At the bar, over a period of weeks, he slowly revealed himself to be an unreconstructed Nazi of the old school. In this he had to be careful. He could not openly proclaim his allegiance, but by dropping occasional nationalistic remarks after a few drinks, and voicing nostalgic indiscretions on the past glories of Adolf Hitler, he established solid fascist credentials. He soon attracted the company of like-minded drinking companions.

His new friends took Meyer into their confidence and told him about a group they knew with which he might be in sympathy. Perhaps he would like to join? Meyer pretended to be less than enthusiastic. Join them? Who were they? he asked in a belittling manner. It was out of the question. Meyer bought a round of drinks, and quietly confided that he already belonged to the central underground network set up by Himmler in the last months of the war. The organisation was well-funded, fully equipped and getting ready to take direct action. After more drinks he boasted that he was the liaison officer serving the area.

His companions fell silent and studied one another. This sort of talk was dangerous, and they knew it. Then one of the men nodded to the others and Meyer was invited to join them in a quiet corner of the inn. Away from the bar, they confided that they were former SS officers who were also members of a significant underground group hampered only by its lack of supplies and weaponry. They had not known that a central body with authority from Himmler existed and wanted to arrange a meeting between their leaders.

Again, Meyer was sceptical. His outfit was extremely powerful and headed by a formidable man who had been a senior figure in RSHA – Nazi intelligence. Any contact would have to be handled with great secrecy and at the highest level. He suggested the men make a formal request for an interview on behalf of their group leader, which he could pass on. They agreed, and a meeting was arranged with the local underground's commander – who turned out to be none other than Rudolf Schelkmann.

Schelkmann told Meyer that he had always suspected a larger group with a master plan existed, and he wanted to be involved. He explained that his continued residence in the British zone put him at risk as he was sought by the authorities. He desperately wanted to move with his wife and child to the American zone, and needed to take his closest associate, SS Unterstürmführer Gerhard Laufer, with him. He wondered if Meyer's organisation could help. In the meantime, he was eager to meet with its leader under secure conditions.

Over the following weeks Meyer acted out an elaborate charade of sending and receiving coded messages. He told Schelkmann that in order for his leader to consider the request, a detailed organisational plan of the entire local movement would have to be submitted. Schelkmann was reluctant, but agreed to consider offering certain information and a general plan to the leader in person, if certain criteria were satisfied.

A meeting was agreed upon in principle, with the time and place to be set. In the meantime, acting on instructions, Schelkmann brought his staff to the inn, together with their wives or girlfriends. From there they were taken to a safe house in the small town of Dellmensingen, near Ulm. They were fed well, provided with money and even cigarettes, and were asked to remain at the house until the leader, who was said to be on an inspection tour, was available to summon them to a meeting.

'The SS officers had been taken to the house for psychological reasons. The idea was to brainwash them during the waiting period, deflate them, and create such an aura about the leader, Dr Frundsberg, that when they finally met him, he would be in a position of unchallenged strength and power. Away from their own environment, and isolated, they were entirely dependent on the Grossorganisation. They were also exposed to the seeming efficiency and wealth of the greater and more powerful outfit, and were made to realise they were but a small cog in a much greater machine.'

Every room of the safe house had been bugged, and Michel was able to monitor private conversations, uncover romantic intrigues and draw profiles of the strengths and weaknesses of each individual. The indeterminate waiting period also played on the nerves of the men and put them at a psychological disadvantage.

Another effective device employed to undermine the confidence of the SS officers was the suggestion that their forged credentials put them at grave risk. In reality, the fake documents were masterful, but the doubt had been sown. Hans Meyer drove the SS men one by one to the city hall in Ulm and arranged for new papers to be issued. Schelkmann was provided with identity and army discharge papers in the name of Rolf Heimborg – born in Karlsbad on 1 February 1920 – and Laufer became Gernot Reinemann – born in Breslau on 20 January 1921. The provision of legal, official documents worked in two ways: the men were deeply impressed by the influence of the Grossorganisation, which had contacts even within government offices, and the new papers allowed CIC to keep tabs on every individual in the group.

When Michel judged that his various psychological games had done their work, he arranged for the men to be taken to the meeting. Without advance warning, motor bikes pulled up in front of the safe house in Dellmensingen late on a wet and windy night. Schelkmann and four of his men were told they were finally being taken to a secret rendezvous to meet Dr Frundsberg, RSHA commander of the Grossorganisation.

The night had been chosen for its bad weather. The cold rain soaked the men on the back of the motor bikes, lowered their morale and made them less observant. The bikes pulled up beside two cars on a deserted road, one of which had the bonnet open and appeared to have broken down. The password 'Gustav' was given; the reply 'Adolf' received. The SS officers were split into two groups and ordered to be blindfolded. They objected at first, but were told that they must comply for security reasons as they were not yet members of the organisation. Once inducted, the blindfolds would no longer be needed. They consented to the procedure, were transferred to the cars and driven into the night.

'Counter-intelligence is partly a branch of show business. The scenario called for imagination, and throughout the trip my team had to make it seem that they were not just a handful of men but a giant military organisation. I employed about thirty people in the charade and their performance was geared to stimulate the SS officers' imagination through the auditory senses, heightened as a result of being blindfolded. I calculated correctly that these men were so disciplined they would not dream of removing their blindfolds without being ordered to do so. The cars were driven in circles so that a small group of agents was able to double and triple their roles. All along the route the cars were stopped and passwords exchanged. The five roadblocks were in fact just one encountered again and again. What sounded like the movement of trucks and equipment increased further the illusion of size and strength.'

The *coup de théâtre* was the lodge itself, and the formidable figure of the commander of the Grossorganisation, the renowned and much anticipated Dr Frundsberg. 'Before my men brought the shivering audience in from the cold and wet, they led them in circles through puddles of deep water just for the sport of it, thoroughly wetting their feet. Ted Kraus was hidden in an adjoining room to tape-record the conversation. We had installed agents to record everything. As in any well-staged drama, our actors had memorised their lines and rehearsed their movements before we raised the curtain for our momentous opening night.'

Once inside the lodge and before the commander, Schelkmann attempted to establish his importance by mentioning various SS acquaintances who had been members of RSHA. 'The names did not catch me by surprise. I was thoroughly familiar with the files of these men and could discuss them with considerable authority.'

Schelkmann's adjutant, Gerhard Laufer, from Bad Pyrmont – codename Herzog – had been an SS Unterscharführer and had escaped from a French prisoner-of-war camp. The other two men present at the lodge, twin brothers Siegfried and Johann Weber, had escaped from an SS camp. Siegfried's role in the group was head of intelligence, while Johann was the head of the organisation for Rheinland-Westfalen. The centre of operations was in Fulda.

There were a couple of difficult moments for Michel at the lodge. He was unprepared when Schelkmann requested that he be made head of intelligence of the Grossorganisation. 'I had not anticipated this. I could hardly grant the man's request without bringing him into the organisation, which was obviously impossible. I pointed out the weakness in his operation, which in reality I was forced to admire, and sketched an overall picture of the workings of my own highly advanced but non-existent system. He was speechless with admiration.'

The most dangerous time came when Schelkmann handed Michel the power with the words, 'What do you order us to do now?' It was a critical psychological moment, and as Michel hesitated he feared his mask had momentarily slipped and that he had stepped out of character. 'Oddly, I was not prepared. I had trained myself mentally for everything up to this point. Now, suddenly, for a split second, I was thrown.' If the flicker of doubt showed, it was not picked up by Schelkmann, who sat eagerly awaiting the new commander's orders. 'There were no more discussions, no more questions. Schelkmann expected nothing but orders. And orders were given.'[41]

Michel and Kraus now sent a report and the recording of the meeting to CIC HQ, which was ready to make immediate arrests. But Michel argued forcefully to hold off until he had made the inspection tour of the various SS units and pulled more people into the net. And in the back of his mind another elaborate concept was formulating: he would employ the SS intelligence officers to work unwittingly for CIC.

He needed to give his new employees something to do while they awaited their formal amalgamation into the Grossorganisation. It had been established that the bomb planted in the de-Nazification court in Stuttgart had been stolen from one of the US ammunition dumps, and Ulm CIC had been given the assignment of surveying the security of all dumps in the area. He decided to turn the job over to the SS organisation as a test of their prowess. Michel, as Dr Frundsberg, explained to his now devoted followers that the survey was important so that they would later be able to penetrate the dumps. A deadline was set.

The SS intelligence operation proved to be more than efficient. At the time of the designated deadline Michel was provided with a detailed report, including accurate maps and a complete inventory of munitions at the various dumps. And as an added bonus, a live American bomb from the US dump at Amstetten was delivered to the lodge and placed on Dr Frundsberg's desk. It was Michel's turn to be impressed, and he complimented the men fulsomely on their work. He forwarded the report to CIC HQ, adding only that the entire survey had been conducted by the SS. HQ was thoroughly unnerved. Without giving his superior officers time to gather themselves, he outlined his daring new plan.

'My mind had been whirling ever since the SS had completed their assignment. Would it not be possible for these men to be used in far more important jobs? There were many Nazi organisations actively working against the Allies. Why not use the advanced skills of SS intelligence to track down war criminals and other wanted persons? They could obviously operate far more effectively than US intelligence for they were beyond suspicion, the real thing.'

He was given grudging permission to go forward with this plan, but took it on himself to release intelligence to Schelkmann gained during his own investigative work. Believing this to be privileged intelligence gleaned from Dr Frundsberg, the SS men went to work.

Things progressed alarmingly well for a number of weeks until there was a hitch. Michel was called at three in the morning by CIC in Fulda and told that five SS Officers had been arrested by the Military Police and were being held in jail. One of them, by the name of Hans Meyer, had insisted the police call CIC. The men had been picked up at a railway station where they had gone to meet a number of Nazi group leaders. These failed to show up, but one of the SS officers recognised three old comrades as they got off the train. He approached them and struck up a conversation in which he dropped broad hints about the nature of the work he was involved in, and wondered if they might be interested. One of the SS men had undergone a change of heart since the end of the war and quietly went to the Military Police on duty at the station. Meyer and his men were promptly arrested.

Michel knew that if he secured their immediate release it would arouse suspicion, so he made contact with Meyer through his 'shadow' and outlined a plan in which the agent would initiate an escape with the help of CIC in Fulda. When they were transferred from the local jail to a detention camp their truck was held up by armed men outside the town and the prisoners were freed and bundled into waiting cars. If there had been any vestige of doubt concerning the extent of Dr Frundsberg's power in the minds of the SS men, it was now eradicated completely. The commander's reach seemed to know no limits.

Michel also took advantage of the situation to cut his new conscripts further down to size. Dr Frundsberg refused to receive Schelkmann, but raged at him over the phone. He berated him for taking risks and making foolish mistakes, accusing him of endangering the security of the entire organisation. Schelkmann was now entirely submissive, and was issued with a new set of orders to incorporate the small neo-Nazi groups he had listed into the Grossorganisation.

Ted Kraus returned to the United States at the end of the year before the final act of the drama was played out. 'Towards the end of that year we lost most of our veteran CIC agents, who were irreplaceable,' Kraus said. 'They had been an erudite group of people with many skills – lawyers, educators, administrators. They were being demobilised, having put in their time, and were ready to go home. Some of them were replaced by very second-rate people in my opinion, including untrained personnel who did not even speak German. The whole operation began to go downhill.' Kraus himself was replaced by an officer whose only concern seemed to be horseback riding. He freely admitted knowing nothing about intelligence work and showed no interest in learning about it. He rarely showed up at the Villa Kauderer during the day and left Michel alone to do as he wished.

And within weeks a new regional commander was also appointed to CIC HQ in Stuttgart, and his way of doing things was to prove diametrically opposed to the unorthodox nature of Michel's methods. The new man was a career soldier, who had been posted to Germany after the end of the war, and was determined to do things by the book. On the commander's first inspection tour of his realm, he dropped into the Ulm office unannounced. The new officer in charge was out riding, as usual, and Michel was also absent. One of the agents present attempted to put the new commander in the picture: Mike pretty much ran the operation, and everybody else stayed out of his hair or lent a helping hand as needed.

'Mike?'

'Captain Mike. Michel Thomas.'

The commander said nothing, but returned to Stuttgart determined to impose military structure and discipline upon an operation that seemed to be on the verge of becoming a rogue outfit. The more he learned about 'Captain Mike' – that he ran elaborate, unsupervised sting operations, used Nazis and SS men in intelligence work, sometimes operated in conflict with other CIC offices, had a web of his own informants and *was not even American* – the more the commander became convinced of the need for oversight and control. He assigned a 'specialist' from CIC HQ to monitor activities involving the Grossorganisation. Although the new agent spoke fluent German, he lacked imagination and had a wooden quality that made him singularly ill-equipped for a role that demanded lightning reflexes and a talent for improvisation.

'I was less than receptive to having a newcomer enter the picture at this critical time. I was frightened that the arrival of a new man would endanger the whole operation, particularly someone whose declared approach to intelligence techniques and operational methods was in direct conflict with my own. Moreover, the job called for an actor who could carry his role convincingly, and I felt the new agent fell far short in this department.'

The 'specialist', backed by the regional commander, insisted that he accompany Michel to the next meeting of the Grossorganisation, posing as Dr Frundsberg's deputy. 'I could not indulge him. If the "specialist" was so determined to serve in this capacity, he would have to do it without me. I became very upset. Up to that point, CIC knew exactly who I was and what I was doing. They may not have known the details, but they were happy with the results. And suddenly here's a man intent on running intelligence operations by the regulation book in the chaotic, complicated world of that time. I could not carry on.'

Michel promptly resigned from CIC and was out of the office within days.

The Grossorganisation came to an anti-climactic and disappointing conclusion. The new agent sent to oversee the operation unwisely took up the challenge to go ahead on his own. Abandoning the Teutonic set of the hunting lodge and its Nazi paraphernalia, he arranged a meeting with the SS men at a beer hall, and even allowed wives and girlfriends to be present. 'This immediately broke the psychological pattern of making the men journey blindfolded to Frundsberg's HQ. The ritual of the trip, the sense of awe at being summoned by the commander, and the physical impact of the Nazi hunting lodge were all gone.'

At the meeting, the SS Commando leaders submitted a ten-point terror programme for immediate action. High on the list was the bombing of the Bavarian Diet, planned to be executed within ten days. This unnerved the new agent and his performance wavered badly. Inexplicably, Dr Frundsberg's right-hand man seemed indecisive and unsure of himself. Instead of expressing enthusiasm and resolve over the ambitious attack, he appeared on the edge of panic.

The SS men sensed something was wrong and suspected foul play. Fearing for the safety of Dr Frundberg, they demanded to be taken to him. Tempers flared, and the agent was accused of betraying the commander. Schelkmann angrily demanded proof of the man's affiliation to the Grossorganisation. The CIC officer lost the little composure he had left and pulled a gun. There was pandemonium as other undercover CIC agents present in the beer hall were given no alternative but to move on the group. After a brief struggle, the unarmed SS men were arrested. 'There was nothing left to do but for CIC to roll up those SS organisations already known through the deception, and pick up whatever SS men they could.' Only a fraction of the potential haul of Nazis active in the underground was caught.

The High Military Court of Würtenberg-Baden, in Göppingen, sentenced Schelkmann to fifteen years in prison; Laufer, his deputy, received eight years. Four other associates were given lesser sentences. (Michel later investigated Schelkmann's fate: he served twelve years in prison, moved to Dortmund on his release, changed his name and ran successfully for political office.) Passing sentence, the judge declared: 'The primary object of the occupying powers in Germany is to keep Nazism down. The schemes of the SS underground might easily have had disastrous consequences for the occupying forces as well as for Germany. Every Nazi movement has to be mercilessly crushed and the occupation army is going to stay in Germany until this is done.'

Fine words, but they expressed the objectives of a policy that in reality had already been abandoned. Michel had suppressed his own desire for revenge at the end of the war and had sought a moral reckoning. He had believed that the Allied military authorities of occupation genuinely intended to work to prevent Nazis from entering new government positions, and that war criminals would be prosecuted. In this he was to be bitterly disappointed, as Nazi Party members returned to positions of power throughout the country. German scientists who had held senior SS rank and employed slave labour had their records rewritten and sanitised to make them eligible for US citizenship, while war criminals not only went unpunished but were recruited by western intelligence.

Michel understood that the original mission of CIC had gone awry. 'If I want to be kind, I'd say that CIC became incompetent. A mess. It did not know what it was doing. It was naïve. Period. But out of that incompetence and ignorance, out of that naïvety, came a betrayal of everything those brave young men of the Thunderbirds fought for, and some two hundred thousand Americans died for. It is a shameful legacy.'

Michel's entire family had disappeared in the course of the war, along with his world. He had adopted so many identities and lived so many lives since Hitler came to power in 1933 that it seemed as if he had passed through eternity. He could scarcely remember anything but war, and although he was still a young man with everything ahead of him, he found it difficult to imagine a world at peace. It seemed that Europe was in moral as well as physical ruin, and he felt isolated and powerless amid the wreckage.

Inspired by American friends he had made in the war, he contemplated working for the United Nations and turned away from the catastrophe surrounding him. In July 1947 he took a ship from France – together with Barry, the SS dog – and crossed the Atlantic to the New World and the future.

VIII

One weekend, after Michel had been in America for almost a year, he arranged to go to the beach with friends. It was a beautiful summer's day and the top was down on the convertible as they drove north on the Pacific Coast Highway towards Malibu. Somebody made an amusing remark and everyone laughed. Michel joined in. A sudden, awkward silence fell and an uneasy atmosphere enveloped the group. After a pause, one of the friends explained gently that no one had ever heard him laugh.

It was only then that Michel realised that at some time during the war he had lost the ability to laugh or cry. The insight shocked him. And while the gift of laughter had returned, he feared surrendering to the sadness within him. 'I realised I was filled with unhappiness and yet I was unable to cry. It was as if inside of me I had a chest filled with tears. As long as the chest remained closed I could have fun and be happy. But if it was opened, even a little, it would not be a release but disintegration. My fear was that there would be an explosion of tears. It would be a flood, and I would drown.'

The prosperity and ease of post-war life in southern California lacked reality, and Michel felt detached and remote in the comfortable world of peace. 'I identified with Gulliver, from *Gulliver's Travels*, moving alone through a strange land. But at least for Gulliver there was a visual difference when he looked about him. I was a Gulliver who looked like everybody else, but I was utterly different and removed from the people around me because of what I had been through.

'After the action of war, life was very dull. There was no real connection. As a young man I had often been in danger and always felt in charge. I was used to swimming in shark-infested waters, and I knew how to survive in that hostile environment after years in camps and in combat. It was natural to me. Suddenly, I had come from a cold, shark-infested ocean into a warm, calm lagoon and found it difficult. It was not just the adjustment from military to civilian life, which is quite an emotional upheaval, but the sense that nobody understood, or tried to understand, who I was or what I had been through. I was different and alone – Gulliver in an alien world. It took years to reintegrate.'

Michel had set sail from Le Havre in July 1947 for the USA with a wad of signed letters in his pocket from senior officers in the US Army recommending him for citizenship.[1] But although he had served and fought in the American uniform, the process was complicated because he had been unconventionally taken into the army during combat, rather than signed up on US soil. He remained stateless.

His departure from Europe had been delayed when he learned that he could not take his dog, Barry, on a military transport plane. 'They would have taken him in the hold, but I didn't want that.' He went from one shipping company to another in Paris in search of one that would agree to take the dog. Almost all of them had rules forbidding animals, but one that carried a mixture of freight and cargo agreed, subject to the captain's consent. Michel travelled to Le Havre and went to see the captain. 'I showed him Barry's glowing recommendations from the US Army and he agreed to take him as long as he remained in a certain section of the ship and did not enter the passenger cabins or the dining room. When I brought Barry on board the captain was amazed to see this giant of a dog.'

Suzanne also made the journey to Le Havre to see Michel off at the dockside, an emotional moment for both of them. The couple had met on several occasions after the war on a friendly basis. Suzanne sought rapprochement, while Michel denied the love, which remained buried. 'The truth is that I did not realise how much in love with her I was. I had a conflict within myself over how I felt, which I tried to remedy. But it was impossible.' They would remain close for the rest of their lives, in a friendship that was held in a state of love suspended, and Michel visited Suzanne whenever he travelled to France. Suzanne married the Cuban diplomat who became consul in Nice. 'But people do not remain the same and our characters went in different directions. Even if the world had collapsed, I remained positive and optimistic. Suzanne became bitter. She had everything – money, houses, diplomatic cars – but became a habitué of casinos.' On the quay in Le Havre, Suzanne gave Michel a photograph of herself. On it was written, '*Avec tout mon coeur – je reste toujours, ta Suzanne*' – With all my heart – I remain for ever, your Suzanne.

There were only a dozen or so passengers on board ship and, apart from Michel, they were all French war brides sailing to the States to join the American soldiers they had married in Europe. Despite the demanded proscription on Barry's movements, he soon took up position under the captain's table, where he was fed illicit titbits. The young brides were a happy, lively group, excited about the future, and Michel enjoyed listening to them talk about their lives. One of the women spoke of an anti-Nazi German officer she had met in Paris who had impressed her. 'I asked her to tell me about him. It was very curious. She said he was from Breslau, and called von Waldenburg, and I realised as I listened that he was the son of my aunt's closest friend, Mia.'

Later, in the United States, Michel's shipboard companion sent him Mia's address in Hamburg. He began a circumspect correspondence under an assumed name, both hoping and dreading to receive news of his aunt. 'She wrote me letters about her close friend, my aunt, and mentioned the nephew who went off to France. That was me.' But as the letters began to describe the fate of German Jews unable to escape Hitler, Michel stopped writing. 'I never revealed my true identity. I realised I did not want to know what she knew.'

Michel landed in the United States at Galveston, Texas, and was met at the dock by his friend, Colonel Wilson Gibson, the tank commander from the Thunderbirds who had given him a Silver Dollar as a token of friendship. Wilson received him like a brother, installed him in his house and introduced him to his wife and three small children, the youngest of whom had been named after Michel. He stayed for a number of weeks and Wilson persuaded him to settle in New Orleans, study law and join the legal practice he had set up. Michel was convinced by his friend's arguments and promised to return once he had made a duty visit to family living in Los Angeles. The men parted the best of friends and shook hands as potential partners.

Michel's uncle, Abraham – his mother's brother – had left Poland for New York before the First World War, and had finally settled in Los Angeles where he built up a successful wholesale cutlery and silverware business. His five children were Michel's first cousins, and he was warmly received.

An unspoken agreement came into being between uncle and nephew not to discuss the fate of the family in Europe. The subject was too painful for both of them. Abraham handed him a bundle of the last letters received from Germany and Poland. Michel took them without a word. His inability to accept the murder of his family, particularly his mother and aunt, was absolute. He knew deep within himself that they were dead, wiped from the earth, but he could not bear to face the awful truth. He was unable to say

Kaddish, the Jewish prayer of mourning that is one of the most ancient and solemn in Judaism. Traditionally, the prayer is believed to help the souls of the dead find lasting peace, and is recited over the grave of the deceased for eleven months, and on the anniversary of the death ever after. 'I could not say Kaddish. *Could not!* Knowing is one thing, accepting is another. I did not feel guilty for not saying these prayers – I would have felt guilty if I *had* said them. I would have felt a party to their deaths.

'The world's Jewish community regards the six million men, women and children who died in the Shoah as martyrs. I say No! My parents – my whole family – were not martyrs for their religion. They were slaughtered because of their race. There was no choice – that is not martyrdom.'

As Michel was preparing to return to New Orleans he received terrible news. Wilson Gibson had been taken ill with acute appendicitis and had died suddenly before he could be operated upon. It seemed unbelievable that this soldier who had landed in Africa, then battled across Sicily and up through Italy, France and Germany, could die in such a way after returning home safely to American soil. Michel's sense of himself in the New World, fragile at best during this period, was shaken.

He decided to remain in southern California and rented a house in Beverly Hills. Barry seemed to find it as difficult to adapt to peacetime life as his master, but eventually became familiar all over town. 'He learned to cross streets – I think he looked at the lights. He drove with me everywhere in the car and if he felt I had stayed too long somewhere he would put his great paw on the horn.' Man and dog had always been close, and now they became inseparable. 'He was a strong and wonderful companion to me in those years of feeling like Gulliver. I learned so much from Barry about communication with non-human animals. If I worked late in the evening he would lie down and wait for me. And he always seemed to know when I was finished and jump up in anticipation. I wondered how he did this. I thought perhaps I made some slight move or gesture that signalled my intention. I decided to test him. I made no move and did absolutely nothing except have the thought, "I'm ready to leave". And he jumped up.' There was only one thing that could make Barry revert to his previous incarnation as a dog of war, and that was the sight of someone in a uniform. He would bark and snarl in his old SS manner at the police and mailmen of Beverly Hills, who learned to give him a wide berth.

The option of working for the UN faded as it became clear that it would take years to become a US citizen. Although Michel was a legal immigrant, there seemed no shortcut, despite the fact that California Congressman Clyde Doyle and Senator Helen Gehagen Douglas introduced private bills before Congress to obtain citizenship based on his war record.

In the meantime, he concentrated increasingly on education, particularly languages. 'In a way I saw education as a continuation of the war. Democratic countries had fought not just to defeat the Nazis but to preserve free societies. I felt one of the factors that contributed to the rise of the Nazi Party was an educational system in Germany, which I had experienced as a student, that concentrated on creating a small elite to govern a vast ignorant mass. I remember professors proclaiming that graduation from high school needed to be difficult: "We want an elite – we don't want an educated proletariat!"' Michel believed the opposite to be true, and that a free society needed an effective educational system for all to produce informed and concerned individuals. He had been impressed by a statement made by Thomas Jefferson: 'If a nation expects to be ignorant and free, in a state of civilisation, it expects what never was and never will be.'

As he thought more about the necessity of an educated citizenry and the importance of learning, his thinking was given added direction by a remark made by the professor at the Sorbonne when Michel had been a student in France: 'Nobody knows anything about the learning process of the human mind.' 'I wanted to explore and probe that learning process. I needed to find out how humans learn so I could discover how to teach. And I felt that the most *alien* thing for somebody to learn was a foreign language. Not the most difficult, but the most alien – simply because you know nothing when you begin. And I took as my cornerstone the idea imparted from my maths teacher, that there was nothing so complicated that it could not be made simple. So I chose to teach foreign languages because it would allow me to probe the learning process from zero to high levels of achievement.'

The Polyglot Institute on 400 North Rodeo Drive in Beverly Hills (occupied today by Chanel) opened in September 1947. The building was a small, one-storey Californian bungalow converted into an office. A large painted sign of a parrot was placed outside. Directly across the street was Sugie's Tropics, a fashionable meeting place at the time where people enjoyed exotic and powerful cocktails such as Missionary's Downfall.

The Polyglot Institute did not prosper at first, but lurched from one financial crisis to another. Michel was joined at the institute almost immediately by Dorris Halsey, who helped translate documents, type letters, boil eggs for sandwiches, and bathe Barry. In reality, she managed and ran the school. More importantly, Dorris was a fellow alien. 'We understood each other very well. I had been stateless, like Michel, and worked with the Résistance and French intelligence and been imprisoned by the Germans. You walk around with those experiences for the rest of your life. Half of my friends who had been active in the war had been killed. So Michel was not closed down with me because I knew of what he spoke. He didn't have to explain, or dot the i's or cross the t's. We communicated in half-words. He was an alien and so was I.'

Dorris was actually a Hungarian Catholic from Budapest who had moved to Paris with her family at the age of eight. She was a fifteen-year-old schoolgirl in the south-west of France when the Germans moved into the unoccupied zone. 'They came to the school to find out if anyone spoke German, and like an idiot I put my hand up.' She was ordered to work as an interpreter at the local German command post after school. As Frenchman betrayed Frenchman, Dorris's main activity was mistranslating, losing or delaying as many of the numerous letters of denunciation as she was able. She also reported to the Résistance. The locals, however, treated her as a collaborator and refused to fill her ration allotment of eggs and butter. 'I was told by the Résistance that being thought of as a *collabo* was a good cover – but it was not easy to bear.'

The Germans eventually discovered her activities and she was sent to prison in Toulouse. 'Luckily, it was then 1944 and they were retreating all over the place so I was not sent to a camp.' St Michel's prison in Toulouse dates from 1275 and Dorris was placed in a small cell with thirty-nine other women for a total of ninety-six days. 'There was a mixture of political prisoners and prostitutes and God-knows-what, all sleeping on straw mattresses. I became the cell's champion flea and louse killer and would tell the others fairy tales from Hungary and Germany to send them to sleep at night and avoid my turn to empty the slop bucket.'

After the Liberation, Dorris returned to her village to find a photograph draped with ribbon in a local shop window identifying her as a collaborator. She moved to Paris and began to work for the Deuxième Bureau – the French intelligence service. Her mission was to deliver thousands of francs in cash to hotel porters and concierges employed as paid informers.

American troops on the Champs Elysées threw cigarettes at French girls to see if they would stoop to pick them up. Dorris ground them under her heel and was accused by the GIs of being less friendly than the German girls. But one American officer was more gracious when he asked for directions in appalling French. 'What on earth are you trying to say to me, captain?' Dorris replied in English. They went for a drink together and the American turned out to be a major in the Quartermaster Corps. 'He had access to instant coffee, cigarettes and nylons, and I was seventeen.' The couple married and Dorris moved with her husband to California, where she later met Michel. 'He was very easy to work with. He became my friend, my confidant and eventually godfather to my second marriage. Many of the friends I still have today I met through Michel. And later my second husband and I were witnesses at the ceremony for Michel's citizenship.'

One of Dorris's early tasks at the Polyglot Institute was to translate divorce papers for the actor George Marshall, whose wife was the well-known French actress Michelle Morgan. (He later married Ginger Rogers.) 'I also taught the occasional mad Hungarian if he came through the door. I became a sort of mascot and was known as Miss Polyglot.'

Another of Dorris's many roles in the office was to play romantic traffic cop in Michel's love life. 'Michel was the greatest Casanova I have ever known. Women found him a romantic *Casablanca* figure, and he had mystery and allure for people whose only hardship in the war was a shortage of gasoline coupons. There was this guilt among those who had not been in the war but remained safe and cosy in America.' The womanising had a driven quality. 'I watched all the goings-on with great amusement. Someone would be coming in as someone was going out, and I was in the front office going crazy. Everyone believed they were the one and only one, and I thought there might be a disaster sometime.'

Michel developed a reputation in Hollywood as a ladies' man. 'I love women and they know it and feel it. My relationships were very good friendships and I was open and honest and didn't make promises or cause unrealistic expectations. I always said very early on that marriage was out of the question. It's true there were a lot of ladies, and I did not tell one about the other, but everybody knew where they stood.' Dorris accused Michel of abusing his charm. He defended himself by comparing his weakness to Dorris's partiality for cake. 'You are offered a beautiful cake – chocolate, lemon, sponge or whatever – could you resist? Wouldn't you be tempted to take a slice?' From then on, when women called, Dorris would hold up a drawing of a slice of cake.

Michel disliked Dorris's first husband intensely and felt she was wasting herself on him. 'After I learned English I realised we didn't have much in common,' Dorris said, 'especially when he told me that the only thing he read was the labels on beer cans.' Michel introduced her to Reece Halsey, head of the literary department at the William Morris Agency.[2] The two hit it off, divorced their respective spouses and married. 'They had a long and good marriage. Reece Halsey quit William Morris to start his own agency and Dorris left the school to work with him.' Michel lost a colleague but gained a lifelong friend and met the extraordinary collection of writers the new agency represented, including Henry Miller and Aldous Huxley. 'I have fond memories of Henry Miller. We played a lot of ping-pong together.'[3] He met many writers at Miller's home, and quarrelled with Lawrence Durrell, irritated by his indifference and easy-going attitude towards the collaboration of Vichy.

Michel was very much on the scene, and he received endless social invitations to a wide variety of Hollywood parties and enjoyed the company of the successful and the famous. 'He learned the necessity of being a chameleon,' Dorris said. 'He could be bright and intelligent and cultured or play the simpleton. He could change.'

But even in Hollywood, the war was never very far away.

In the period directly after the war, when Michel worked for US Army Counter Intelligence in Germany, he had been largely ignorant of American politics and public opinion back in the States. He rarely read American newspapers or magazines, with the exception of the *Stars & Stripes*, although he knew that the Malmédy Massacre had outraged Americans and had resulted in a commitment to hold war crimes trials. The subsequent court case should have been a straightforward prosecution of SS criminals, but suddenly the tables were turned and the US Army would stand accused.

All seventy-three SS defendants had been found guilty in the trial. However, by the standards of American peacetime courts the army's legal procedures were open to criticism. The defendants had been tried *en masse* with only numbered white cards draped around their necks to identify them. The verdicts were hastily delivered when each of the accused received an average of only two minutes' deliberation before sentence. Punishment seemed arbitrary and illogical. Gustav Knittel, for instance, who confessed to giving the order to shoot eight unarmed American prisoners, received a life sentence while his commander, Joachim Peiper, who personally issued no such order, was given a death sentence. In Germany the verdicts were seen as victors' justice.

The lawyer assigned to defend Peiper, and several others of the accused, was Colonel Willis Everett, a Georgia attorney who was demobilised from the army directly after the trial. He returned to America feeling that justice had not been done and began to orchestrate a public attack on the army in an attempt to have the sentences overturned.

Two weeks before the trial began, Everett had objected that some of the defendants' statements had been made under duress. In addition, the prosecution admitted that in some instances interrogators had used elaborate 'mock' trials to obtain confessions. Black hoods were placed over prisoners' heads, and they were then led into a room where inquisitors sat behind a table with burning candles and a crucifix. The prisoners believed they were at an actual trial, and were told their lives were ruined and that they would never be released.

The first of thirteen investigations made by the army into the treatment of Malmédy prisoners was launched. Thirty of the SS men Everett had named as having made serious charges against the army were interviewed. Only four claimed mistreatment, ranging from blows to the head or body to being pushed down stairs. However, a review of the verdicts criticised both the conduct of the trial and questioned the admissibility of some of the sworn statements, given the nature by which they had been obtained. Temporary stays of execution were granted and the convicted men were allowed the opportunity to appeal.

Ex-SS officers used the official criticism of the army to elaborate upon the accounts of American brutality to feed a rumour mill. Wild stories went around of prisoners being starved, having their testicles crushed, their teeth knocked out, and being subjected to freezing temperatures and intense heat. Human flesh and hair was said to have been found on the walls of the men's cells together with a black hood with dry blood upon it. The rumours circulated among the American military in Germany and then spread to the States.

Everett's original intention of denigrating the procedures of the Dachau trial now expanded into a campaign to rehabilitate the convicted SS murderers as honourable soldiers. As one army review after another rejected the claims of his former clients, he petitioned the Supreme Court, continuing to cite the discredited rumours as evidence. When the petition was rejected, the lawyer met with the secretary of the army who had publicly expressed concern over the conduct of the case. Everett repeated the rumours and unsubstantiated allegations as fact. He claimed all the defendants had been tortured in their cells by Jewish refugees intent on revenge. (Correspondence written by the lawyer at this time displayed open anti-Semitism. He resented bitterly the trial judges' legal adviser, who was Jewish, and complained that three members of the investigating War Crimes Group were Jewish refugees.)

Appalled by what he took to be fact, the secretary of the army ordered a halt to all executions. The proclamation provided new ammunition for the pro-German lobby in America, and unrepentant Nazis in Germany, to attack the conduct of the entire war crimes trials. New accusations were made that confessions had been obtained from defendants by threatening to hand them over to the Russians. The secretary of the army appointed a three-man commission of American judges to investigate the way war crimes had been prosecuted, with particular emphasis on the Malmédy trial.

The judges flew to Frankfurt to spend six weeks studying the case and prepared a classified report. It found no evidence of systematic intimidation and declared the trials to have been 'essentially fair', although some of the methods used in obtaining sworn statements were again categorised as 'questionable'. The report went on to say that the evidence proved the guilt of the defendants, but suggested commuting the death sentences to atone for any injustice that might have been committed.

A separate investigation, conducted by the Administration of Justice Review Board over seven months, cross-examined all those involved in the pre-trial interrogations. It too criticised some of the methods employed but also concluded that there had been no violence. After close scrutiny of trial transcripts, the review found substantial evidence against the twelve men condemned to death.

A sensational new element was now introduced when one of the judges sent to Frankfurt on the three-man panel, LeRoy Van Roden, claimed that he had been prevented from publishing the truth. He said in a public speech that he had received statements proving that interrogators had abused, beaten and tortured the Germans to extract confessions. The effect of the judge's remarks was to destroy the credibility of the report and make it seem little more than a whitewash. The pro-German lobby in the USA attacked it, and an editorial in the *Chicago Tribune* lamented the depths to which American justice had sunk.

But Van Roden had actually received his information from Everett, and had merely repeated the lawyer's most extreme allegations. The men had been room-mates in Frankfurt after the war, and also shared prejudices. Van Roden too was an open anti-Semite and expressed the belief that Jewish refugees were using their recently acquired American nationality to pursue race vengeance. The attacks fuelled the army's critics over the handling of the Dachau cases. Most Germans now openly sympathised with the convicted Malmédy SS men, whom they saw not as criminals but as victims of the admitted malpractice and incompetence of the American Army.

The army received another blow when a German newspaper disclosed that the US military government in Germany had reduced the life sentence handed down on the notorious Ilse Koch to four years. The gruesome stories surrounding Koch, known as 'Mrs Commandant', had graphically illustrated the perverse side of concentration camp life and outraged American public opinion. Ilse Koch, who had no military rank or official position, was married to the commandant of Buchenwald, where she lived for six years. When her husband had been removed for corruption she chose to stay on. Fifty-one thousand people died at the camp through starvation, murder and torture. The stories in the American press reported that Koch had selected prisoners with interesting tattoos for extermination. The camp's pathology department skinned the corpses and then tanned the human hide to be made into gloves and lampshades. Critics of the US military now suggested that the sentence reduction was proof that Koch had not committed any crime in the first place.[4]

American politicians in those states with large German populations began to see the growing backlash to the war crimes trials as a vote-winning bandwagon. And an unknown junior senator from Wisconsin, Joseph McCarthy, hopped aboard. McCarthy desperately needed a cause to deflect attention from a court case in his home state where he was awaiting conviction by the Wisconsin State Supreme Court on charges of unethical conduct in a local trial. He now gave his support to a petition for clemency filed by the wife of Hans Schmidt, the former adjutant of the guard battalion at Buchenwald. McCarthy claimed that Schmidt had been denied a proper trial and had been tortured during interrogation to make a false confession. It was not true, but the senator demanded to know why the army had not commuted the sentence. He omitted to mention the proven fact that Schmidt had overseen executions on a daily basis for four years.

The plea was rejected, as McCarthy surely knew it would be, but the publicity encouraged a slew of petitions to the White House on behalf of hundreds of war criminals. And while the twelve remaining Malmédy death sentences were initially upheld, the publication of the previously classified judges' report added weight to the demands of Everett and allied congressmen for a reprieve. They ignored the finding that the men were guilty and chose to concentrate on criticism of the army's methods of interrogation.

Yet another inquiry into the Malmédy trial was set up, this time to be conducted by the Senate's Committee on Armed Services. An idea of the emphasis and direction this would take, along with the exaggerated and unreal atmosphere in which it would be conducted, was provided in advance by Senator McCarthy. 'It sickens me to the core of my being . . . that Americans have engaged in these brutal and unjustified acts.'

The murdered American POWs and Belgian civilians had been forgotten, and the interrogators had become the villains. Six of the twelve remaining death sentences passed on the Malmédy SS men were now commuted, while execution of the remainder was delayed until the committee reported its findings. McCarthy introduced the unique brand of low showmanship and political charlatanism to the hearings that would later turn him into a national figure. He ranted and raged about the abuse of prisoners, with particular emphasis on damage to their genitalia, but was unable to produce a scintilla of evidence to back his accusations. The witnesses he called tended towards gross exaggeration and outright lies. A German dentist claimed to have heard screams of pain coming from the jail and reported that twenty prisoners had teeth smashed by the interrogators. An independent investigator found no evidence whatsoever to support the charge.

Undeterred, McCarthy attacked foreign-born Jews, whom he claimed had maliciously abused American justice. He shouted, bullied and lied for a month, then when it became apparent that his case was about to collapse, he called a dramatic press conference and resigned. He told a room packed with reporters that the inquiry had become a whitewash to protect men who had extracted confessions under torture, 'brutalities greater than we have ever accused either the Russians or Hitler's Germany of employing'.

After McCarthy stormed off the stage, the inquiry dismissed the allegations of violence. It laid the blame for the initial acceptance of the rumours on an organised conspiracy by Nazis and their American sympathisers to discredit the trials. (McCarthy would return a year later, having discovered Communism, to reduce another Senate investigation into a circus act.)

One such German sympathiser, Senator Karl Mundt of South Dakota, wrote to a prisoner in Landsberg at the end of 1949, actually soliciting further allegations against the US Army. 'Confer with your fellow prisoners to determine if there are any notorious cases of injustice involving any of them so that you will be able to call such cases to the attention of the representatives of the Inspector-General when they arrive.'[5]

The convicted Malmédy war criminals in jail at Landsberg Fortress took heart. It was hard to believe, but powerful American politicians had willingly stepped forward to support them, American lawyers continued to petition Washington on their behalf, and a significant section of American public opinion was on their side. The men conferred daily with one another in the prison yard, met frequently with German and American lawyers, and carefully planned the most effective strategy to bring about their release.

In the winter of 1949, the *Los Angeles Evening Herald Express* ran a story outlining Michel's capture of Gustav Knittel – as one of the principal perpetrators of the Malmédy Massacre – and Emil Mahl – hangman of Dachau.[6] The story was picked up by the International News Service and reprinted in the European edition of the *Stars & Stripes*.[7] The final paragraph of the news report read: 'Next month Congress will consider giving Thomas full US citizenship because of his war services without waiting for the five-year period of residence.' The war criminals were given shrewd advice to seize upon this vulnerable area of attack. Although neither Knittel nor Mahl spoke English, and certainly did not read *Stars & Stripes*, their leader, Joachim Peiper, obtained an interpreter's diploma in English while in prison.[8] Much had been made in the various hearings of 'recently' naturalised American émigrés pursuing their interrogations in a spirit of revenge rather than justice. Here was a man who was not even American.

On the day after Christmas 1949, Mahl wrote a letter to Michel via the *Stars & Stripes* – typed in German on one side and translated into English on the other – objecting to statements he made to the paper. 'I was neither a Nazi nor at any time hangman at Dachau. I was a plain prisoner of the Third Reich and in my capacity as a concentration camp inmate it was my assignment to have corpses cremated in the camp crematorium after executions. Thus I was Kapo Crematorium. Therefore you are requested to omit in the future to mention my name in a derogativ [*sic*] manner, even if it should be your intention to do that to impress people for the purpose to get American citizenship granted to you at a premature date.'

In fact, Mahl had been sentenced to death for his activities at Dachau, although along with other war criminals his sentence had been reduced to ten years of confinement. He had sought the job at the camp crematorium and volunteered as hangman. Emboldened by support in the States, the convicted murderer now claimed that the US Army had never returned money taken from him on his arrest. He estimated the value and thoughtfully worked out the exchange rate: three hundred and five US dollars. 'You are requested to have this amount transferred to me. In case I should receive no answer from you until 1 February 1950 I shall report the case to the competent legal authorities in the U.S. to have you indicted for theft. Furthermore I shall inform members of the U.S. Congress who are competent for the grant of [sic] American citizenship to you. Sincerely, Emil Mahl.'[9]

Michel was sickened to receive the letter, but particularly outraged by a stamp in the right-hand corner of the letter: PASSED BY CENSOR. It seemed to give official sanction to a war criminal's crude attempt at blackmail. 'I made sure to bring it to the attention of the proper authorities that they might take action in the future to prevent proven war criminals from making threats with official approval.'

He prepared a statement for the press, which shared his sense of outrage and quoted his reaction. 'It is strange that Mahl should receive ten years of imprisonment, because if he is innocent, as he claims to be, then this man should be released – with all the necessary apologies. But one cannot help wondering, with amazement and some frightful doubt, what made it possible to commute a lenient life sentence given to Ilse Koch, into four years of confinement. And what caused the change of the death sentence of the Hangman of Dachau to ten years of imprisonment – the same punishment which could be given under US laws to a nineteen-year-old boy for breaking into a grocery store.'

A second, more subtle and invidious letter was written in Landsberg at approximately the same time by Gustav Knittel. It was sent not to the press – or Michel, who never learned of it – but to the US Army's Director of Intelligence at the Pentagon. Cleverly drafted, it hit on every weakness in the Dachau trials revealed in the various judicial reviews, exaggerated in the press and distorted by McCarthy. Knittel was careful not to refer to his own crimes, as he was unable to withdraw his sworn confession ordering the murder of eight American POWs. Instead, he adopted a self-righteous position in which he claimed to be intent on helping his needy wife and restoring his personal honour.[10]

The target of his attack was Michel Thomas, who had captured and interrogated him. Quoting from the article in the *Stars & Stripes* stating that Michel was not an American citizen, Knittel attempted to portray him as an émigré interrogator bent on revenge (Knittel remained unaware that Michel was a Jew). 'I should like to state that I have no interest whatsoever which persons the American Congress consider worthy to be granted American citizenship,' Knittel wrote. 'Likewise I have never borne any grudge against my apprehension by Thomas, as he was fully acting in the line of duty. However, my objection is directed against the attempt on the part of Thomas to base his "merits in the interests of the US" on untrue facts which not only touch my personal honour but which might hurt me in the future.'

Knittel had perfectly caught the mood of the times when a confessed Nazi SS murderer could appeal to the head of intelligence of the US Army to defend his personal honour against an émigré interrogator. He proceeded to launch an attack on Michel and Ted Kraus, head of CIC in Ulm at the time – who was, of course, not only American, but German-American. It repeated the rumours and lies that had been disproved in endless independent legal reviews, but were nonetheless still believed by pro-German groups in the US and a large section of the populace in Germany.

Knittel claimed that upon arrest he had been ordered to take off his blue woollen pullover, which had never been returned to him. A pair of his wife's gloves had also disappeared. He accused the men of stealing a set of china, his watch and money, and a jubilee edition of Goethe's *Faust* – the irony of which might, or might not, have escaped him. He also complained of brutal treatment at the CIC prison in Ulm after Michel and Ted Kraus had given instructions to the sergeant on duty and left. 'At first I had to stand at attention in a corner for two hours,' Knittel wrote. 'Then on order of the sergeant, a German auxiliary policeman brought in a bucket with water and a toothbrush. I was ordered by the sergeant to scrub the floor of the guard room with the toothbrush which lasted from about midnight to 0500 hours. While I was kneeling down and scrubbing the floor, I was repeatedly beaten with a dog whip by the guards under the laughter of their comrades. One evening during the second week of January my cell was locked, a guard entered, aiming a pistol at me and telling me that he would shoot in case that I should move [*sic*]. Then appeared soldiers in uniform who slapped me about thirty times in my face. When I did not react to this maltreatment, they threw all items they could get hold of outside my cell. A scar above my eye is still a visible mark of this maltreatment.'

Meanwhile, according to Knittel, his aunt, wife and child were placed in confinement two cells away from him. 'I could hear the crying of my child for reasons of not being properly fed which depended entirely upon the mood of a female warden. For eight days the little child of seven months was not allowed to be taken out in the fresh air. After my futile attempts, my wife finally succeeded that [sic] the baby was taken out for twenty minutes daily, but she and my aunt were not allowed to leave the cell for a single moment during these three weeks.'

Knittel also wrote that while unable to prove that Michel and Kraus were directly responsible for his mistreatment, he was certain they had condoned it and were the 'bad spirits' behind the action. He then addressed the manner in which he was interrogated on five occasions over three days. The interrogations opened with Michel threatening to incarcerate all of Knittel's family, including his elderly parents, unless he agreed to give up his POW status. 'Thomas declared that I would be given to the Russians in case I should be found innocent in the matter.'

It is true that immediately after Knittel's arrest he was ordered by a guard at the prison to clean his cell with a toothbrush, and the man had been severely reprimanded by Michel for his action. But there was no truth whatsoever in any of Knittel's other accusations. Neither Knittel's aunt, nor his wife – and certainly not his baby – were arrested. Frau Knittel was questioned in the comfort of her own home. The only time she entered the prison at Ulm was for the wedding condoned and organised by Michel. 'It is ironic, but I went out of my way to protect Knittel from the beginning. It was well-known that he was responsible for Malmédy and he now came under the control of American MPs. But they would not have *dared* mistreat him after I had expressed my anger over the toothbrush incident. It was the only complaint he ever made to me, and after that they knew how I would react if he was treated badly. The talk of a dog whip and the laughter during the beating is typical of the Gestapo and SS mind-set. American soldiers, of course, did not carry whips. And I rejected using psychological torture, if you can call it that. I could have destroyed him by making him suspect his wife as the person who betrayed him, but did not. I regret it – it was a golden opportunity.'

Knittel's accusations cunningly repeated almost every charge ever brought against American interrogators, short of having his testicles crushed. He claimed to have been whipped and beaten by guards, tortured psychologically through his wife and child, and physically humiliated and mistreated. The threat with the pistol, and the alleged theft of personal belongings – particularly the gloves – exactly mirrored accusations made against the SS during the Malmédy Massacre.

As a conclusion to his 'respectfully submitted' letter, Knittel hoped 'that a just solution can be found to restore my personal honour'. There is no record of any official reply, but the letter was added to the mountain of petitions and complaints the army had received. It is an indication of the anxiety of the army at the time that it was not thrown contemptuously in the bin, but preserved in the National Archives.

The stature of the incarcerated Malmédy murderers continued to grow in Germany until they were transformed from war criminals into folk heroes. The mass-circulation press continued to print stories reporting the most extreme of the discredited accounts against the American investigators. Colonel Willis Everett, the American attorney defending the war criminals, had become a white knight in the eyes of ordinary Germans, who saw him as a good man bent on justice rather than vengeance.

The authorities in America now handled the lawyer with great care and civility, and assured him in writing that eighty per cent of the sentences of war criminals under review were being recommended for remission or drastic reduction. In an extraordinary decision, the US Army said that the killings at Malmédy had been committed in a fluid combat situation when Germany was desperate. The army was arguing military necessity as a mitigating factor in a case involving the murder of its own troops.

On the surface, it seems to be a baffling position for the army to have taken, even after continued criticism. The numerous investigations found it to be essentially guilt-free and honest, yet it became strangely defensive, almost as if it had something to hide. And it did.

The army was keeping a dark secret that would have blown the Malmédy case apart, and it had nothing to do with questionable interrogation techniques or sloppy legal procedure. It was hiding a full-scale massacre of its own, perpetrated by American troops from none other than Michel's Thunderbird regiment, the 180th.

Four days after the Thunderbirds landed in Sicily in 1943, newly blooded in bitter combat, a dozen men from a company of the 180th were wounded in a firefight as they approached the airfield at Biscari. The battle raged from dawn to late afternoon, but at mid-morning two Italian soldiers emerged from a dug-out carrying a white flag. They were soon followed by a group of thirty-two more Italian troops accompanied by two Germans, all of whom were captured by a single GI, who took them to his sergeant. Word of the capture was sent to the officer in charge of the company, a young captain, who promptly gave an unequivocal order: the prisoners were to be shot. The order was carried out by a firing party of some two dozen men, a number of whom had volunteered for the task. Altogether thirty-four unarmed POWs were shot in the head or chest.

Nearby, a sergeant also belonging to a company of the 180th was given the job of escorting another group of more than forty prisoners to the rear for interrogation. The unarmed men were put into columns of two and marched several hundred yards along a road, accompanied by the sergeant and nine GIs. The prisoners were then ordered to move off the road into an olive grove. The sergeant borrowed a Thompson sub-machine gun from one of his soldiers and suggested those who did not want to witness what was about to happen should avert their eyes. He then opened fire and mowed thirty-seven prisoners down.

Both sergeant and captain subsequently faced court-martial. Although other soldiers had been actively involved, or were passively complicit in the killings, the 45th Division's inspector-general recommended in the first case that charges be brought only against the captain, as the firing squad believed it was carrying out a lawful order. Similar circumstances surrounded the sergeant, who acted alone and had also announced to his men he was following orders, although none of the accompanying troops did anything to stop him or oppose the action. Both defendants claimed at their separate court-martial that they believed they had been ordered not to take prisoners.

The captain quoted a pep talk given by General George S. Patton to the Thunderbird company commanders, while the division was still in North Africa, about to invade Sicily. 'When we land against the enemy, don't forget to hit him and hit him hard. We will bring the fight home to him. When we meet the enemy, we will kill him. We will show him no mercy. He has killed thousands of your comrades, and he must die. If you company officers in leading your men against the enemy find him shooting at you, and when you get within two hundred yards of him and he wishes to surrender, oh no! That bastard will die! You will kill him. Stick him between the third and fourth ribs. You will tell your men that. They must have the killer instinct. Tell them to stick him. He can do no good then. Stick them in the liver. We will get the name of killers, and killers are immortal. When word reaches him that he is being faced by a killer battalion, a killer outfit, he will fight less. Particularly, we must build up that name as killers and you will get that down to your troops in time for the invasion.'

As an incitement to brutality, it outstripped Adolf Hitler's speech to the SS Panzer divisions at the opening of the Battle of the Bulge. It carried the clear instruction not to take prisoners and encouraged young officers to pass the message along to green, inexperienced troops. Numerous witnesses remembered Patton's bloodthirsty remarks, and many said they took it to mean that no prisoners were to be taken.

The captain, who maintained he was following orders, was cleared of the charges against him. The sergeant offered a more muddled and unconvincing defence and was found guilty and sentenced to life imprisonment. The disparity in the verdicts was extreme and caused concern to the division's judge advocate and many senior officers, who feared political repercussions. The War Department recommended that the sergeant be granted clemency with the proviso 'that no publicity be given to this case because to do so would give aid and comfort to the enemy and would arouse a segment of our own citizens who are so distant from combat that they do not understand the savagery that is war'. The sergeant was released after serving a year of his sentence and returned to duty, reduced to the rank of private. The captain died in action in Italy later in the year.

General Patton was not called as a witness in either court-martial. By the time the verdicts were reached his explosive temperament and erratic behaviour had already created an international scandal when he slapped two shell-shocked soldiers in an Italian field hospital. This later became the declared reason for denying Patton command of US ground forces on D-Day, but as both his senior officers, General Omar Bradley and General Dwight Eisenhower, knew of Biscari it is likely that the massacre was a significant factor in that decision.

Biscari caused great concern to the US Army and the War Department, and conditions of the utmost secrecy were imposed on the court-martial proceedings. It was felt that any publicity was bound to present limitless propaganda possibilities to the enemy, trigger harsh reprisals against American troops in the field and have a detrimental effect on public opinion in the United States. The massacre was covered up so effectively that few soldiers in the division ever heard about it. 'I never heard anyone in the Thunderbirds talk of this,' Michel says. 'It was inconceivable to me when I was with them that they could act like that. It just did not happen in France or Germany. Prisoners were treated well. I am sure that very few of the men ever knew anything about it.'

But the guilty secret of Biscari haunted the army throughout the Malmédy trial and the investigations that followed. The fear was that either McCarthy, the press, or the accused SS men themselves might come to hear of it. The results would be calamitous. Biscari offers an explanation of the army's tolerant view concerning the murder of its own men at Malmédy, and the leniency later shown towards its perpetrators.[11]

The American Commander-in-Chief of European Command commuted the six remaining Malmédy death sentences on 31 January 1951. The mood at Landsberg was understandably ecstatic when the news arrived. Joachim Peiper, leader of the Malmédy prisoners, was moved to write a fulsome letter of praise to his defender. 'We have received a great victory, and next to God it is you from whom our blessings flow. In all the long and dark years you have been the beacon flame for the forlorn souls of the Malmédy Boys, the voice and the conscience of the good America, and yours is the present success against all the well-known overwhelming odds. May I, therefore, Colonel, express the everlasting gratitude of the red-jacket team (retired) as well as all of the families concerned.'[12]

For Michel, and the slaughtered Malmédy Americans long in their graves, natural justice had been grotesquely mocked. Peiper was correct in saying that the Nazi SS had won a great victory. The men who had captured, interrogated and successfully prosecuted the perpetrators of the massacre had been maligned and denigrated, while SS murderers and unrepentant Nazis had been turned into national heroes by their politically motivated American champions.

Veteran groups in America were outraged. There was also a degree of concern expressed in Congress, and the occasional critical editorial in the serious press, but the pendulum had swung in the murderers' favour. An inexorable process had begun that would eventually set all the Landsberg 'Malmédy Boys' free. Knittel was released in 1954.[13] By the summer of 1956 only three of the accused were left in jail, and they were released within the following six months. Peiper himself, the last of the Malmédy Boys, became a free man at Christmas. He was promptly hired by Porsche, the company that had made the Panzer tanks he had commanded, and duly became the first non-family member to be selected as company secretary.[14]

IX

The Polyglot Institute began to attract increasing interest. At first people walked in off the street, then, as word spread, actors and celebrities started to take the course. The press wrote articles about Michel and his method, describing him as a language wizard, and the institute became fashionable among the rich and famous.

'I considered my school as a laboratory. Early on I developed a system that promised a high level of achievement in six weeks. A very short time then.' The system would continue to evolve through ceaseless innovation and experiment over the next twenty-five years until, with the occasional refinement and polish, it became what it is today. In three days students are now guaranteed a comprehensive knowledge of a western language's grammar, together with a functional vocabulary, enabling them to write, read and converse in all tenses – without the need to memorise by rote, take notes or complete homework.

In the early days, however, not all the citizens of Beverly Hills burned with the desire to learn. One man wandered into the school, took a hundred-dollar bill from his wallet and waved it under Michel's nose. 'That's the only language I need in this world – US Green!' Michel also found it expedient to change the name of his school to the Michel Thomas Language Centre after he discovered that nobody seemed to know what 'polyglot' meant.

Some of the research conducted along the way led up the occasional blind alley. In 1958, for example, Michel was invited by Laura Huxley – the wife of Aldous Huxley – to take part in a controlled experiment with LSD at Rancho de la Puerta, in Tecate, Mexico. The drug was relatively unknown at the time and remained legal until 1968. 'I heard of this new substance imported from Switzerland and the claim that it widened reciprocity in regard to learning, so I was interested. I thought I might be able to apply it – that it might be another tool to probe the learning process of the mind. I had no idea what I was in for.'

268

The LSD was supplied direct by its creator, Dr Albert Hoffman of Sandoz, Switzerland, who had discovered it by chance in 1943 when working on a drug for migraine. Lysergic acid diethylamide was a by-product developed from a fungus that grows on rye, and the doctor accidentally ingested a dose in the laboratory. He realised he was on to something revolutionary when the short car journey home seemed to take centuries.

Michel arrived at Tecate for the two-day experiment and joined a group of a dozen volunteers, including two doctors, and Michael Murphy, founder of Esalen, the original alternative spiritual retreat in California. Most members of the group were handed a single 100 mg tab of LSD, two were given placebos, and Michel requested a double dose, as befitted a man interested in accelerated learning. Laura Huxley was one of two guides who did not take the drug, but she explained to the group what they might experience. 'It's heaven and hell and everything in between. It can bring out an angel or a devil and you do not know which one is going to pop up. You must have no preconceived opinions. You must give up control and be prepared for ego loss. It's like dying and trying not to die. Paranoia lurks, but remember the sensations are psychological not physical.'[1]

The group then swallowed the tabs of pure LSD. 'I was given a tape recorder to record my impression at all times. For a while I tried to analyse the sensations to know how the drug worked.' This approach was soon abandoned as the drug took hold. 'I tried to control it in order to experience it more fully – I thought that was what I was supposed to do. For once in my life I was not in control – which goes against my nature. I had heard about bad trips, but didn't accept I was there for a trip. I was there to experiment and research. After a few hours I was through with it, I'd had enough. I thought I would shake it off. And I couldn't! I felt controlled. I had a cold shower and started doing exercises, but it didn't work. So I gave in to it.' He moved outside into the Mexican garden. 'I was immensely impressed and overawed to step into nature and see everything differently. I saw nature through the eyes of Van Gogh.'

It had been an interesting experience, but it did not contribute anything to Michel's investigation into the learning process. 'The sensations had been emotional and spiritual, not intellectual. It was not clear to me how it could be used in a concrete way in terms of learning.' However, word spread in Hollywood that Michel's method owed its success to hallucinogens, one of the many rumours that have attached themselves to the system over the years.

Michel became involved with a beautiful actress during this time, abandoned his womanising, and sincerely believed he had met a partner for life. The couple moved in together – an almost unheard-of arrangement at the time – and began a long monogamous relationship. 'It was different to all the others and I was in love. I was thinking seriously about having a life with her. Meaning marriage.'

It came as a shock when he was challenged by the actress, who accused him of not truly loving her. Stung, he said he could not understand how she could say such a thing.

'When we make love, I feel you make love to somebody else,' she insisted. 'That I remind you of somebody you love. But it's not me.'

'That's ridiculous,' Michel protested.

Directly after the conversation he had to fly to New York on business, and thought deeply about his lover's statement during the flight. 'And I realised she was right. It was very perceptive of her. I saw that she reminded me in many ways of Suzanne and that for all these years I had still been in love with Suzanne. And all the relationships I had considered good and exciting, as close as some may have been, were marginal compared to my deep emotional involvement with Suzanne.'

The insight broke up the relationship, but also liberated Michel from the power of a past love. 'After that I felt I would finally be able to love again.'

Among the powerful and influential men Michel taught during this period was Jules Stein, founder of MCA, one of the great entertainment empires of the twentieth century. The men became friends, and Michel sometimes drove out to Palm Springs to spend the weekend. The mogul immediately understood the originality of the language system and its unlimited potential.

Julius Caesar Stein, the son of immigrant Lithuanian Jews, stumbled into the entertainment business as a medical student at Chicago University when he booked jazz bands into the gangster Al Capone's speakeasies and night-clubs. The business spread to Hollywood, where it represented movie stars and developed into the major movie studio that eventually became Universal Pictures.

Stein encouraged Michel to consider opening a network of schools nationwide and suggested a partnership. 'He was so excited that he wanted "us" to open schools across the country. He wanted ten, fifteen, twenty schools – the number increased as he spoke – to open simultaneously. It would be promoted by famous actors and be an immediate success.' Michel said he would think about it. In a town where people fought and begged to be in business with Jules Stein, this came as a surprise, almost an affront. 'I did think about it. I saw myself in the future as a financially successful owner of a chain of schools, with Jules Stein as my partner, but it would have destroyed my whole purpose. At that time I was far from completing my exploration of the learning process, defining educational goals and perfecting the system. I knew it would take many years, possibly decades.'

He went back to Stein, thanked him for his interest and explained why he could not accept. There was a moment of stunned silence. Stein seemed confounded, and said that nobody ever turned him down. Michel shrugged. Stein later wrote a letter saying he respected the decision, and enclosed share certificates for a generous allocation of his personal, preferred stock in MCA. 'In this way we will always be partners,' Stein wrote.

Whenever the men met at parties afterwards, Stein would enquire after the progress of the school. 'How are we doing?'

'Fine,' Michel answered.

'And the stock?'

'Fantastic!'[2]

But Michel certainly had ambitious plans. As he continued to probe the learning process, he began to dream of an international university. 'All great universities are national institutions. Oxford is English, Yale is American, the Sorbonne is French, and so on. I wanted to create a supra-national university with the best professors from all over the world teaching an international student body.' As he worked to turn the dream into reality, he talked to Robert Hutchins, one-time president of the University of Chicago and the Fund for the Republic, who became fascinated by the idea. Hutchins wrote in a letter to Michel: 'Long reflection on the state of the intellectual world has led me to the conclusion that the trouble with it is that there is no leadership in it. There is no concentration of intellectuals dedicated to the task of leadership anywhere in the world. There is no intellectual beacon or lighthouse to be seen. It would not take much to create one, and one should be created before it is too late. A group of ten or a dozen of the most intelligent men in the world who come together in a single place, strategically located, to work together on the identification and solution of the great problems of the second half of the twentieth century could have an overwhelming influence on the thought and the events of our time. The reason for this, of course, is that the world is waiting for the leadership that such men could supply . . . The members of the group should live together and be continuously engaged in discussion of the program.'

Hutchins said that the Fund had made a partial and inadequate attempt at such an idea, but had failed, and welcomed the renewal of such a concept under the auspices of an international university. He put forward the names of some of the Fund's own group, including Nobel prize-winning physicists Isidor Rabi, Niels Bohr and Werner Heisenberg, and the leading Catholic theologian in America, John Courtney Murray. He also mentioned the names of other international luminaries who had expressed interest in the idea, such as Paul Tillich, J. Robert Oppenheimer, Jacques Maritain, and numerous others. It was a high-powered group by any standards.[3]

It was obvious that an international university would need a great deal of money, so Michel approached Joseph Hirschorn, one of the wealthiest men in America whose fortune had been made from uranium mines in Canada. Hirschorn pronounced the project financially feasible, but suggested the greatest problem would be finding a suitable location. A supra-national university needed some kind of supra-national site, and for this Michel had a brainwave.

Grace Kelly had sought Michel's skills to teach her French after her engagement to Prince Rainier of Monaco, and teacher and pupil had become good friends during lessons conducted on the set of *High Society*, the star's last movie. Michel suggested Monaco as the ideal location for the international university, as this would also lend intellectual status to the principality, known solely as a gambling resort and tax haven. Prince Rainier expressed interest in the idea and invited Michel to join the couple for a skiing holiday at their Swiss chalet in Gstaad.

Prince Rainier listened attentively as Michel outlined his plans to build a university funded by outside investors and staffed by a collection of the world's great minds. However, Rainier pointed out a fundamental flaw: 'It's a wonderful idea, but you know Monaco. It's rather small. It is simply a question of having no land for such a large project.'

'I don't want your land,' Michel said evenly.

'What do you mean?'

'I want your territorial waters.'

Rainier was silent for a moment. 'But what on earth will you do with the Mediterranean?'

Michel explained that it was possible to reclaim land and create an island, 'but I want the island to be independent and not under the jurisdiction of Monaco. It should be a University State with the same relationship to Monaco that the Vatican has with Italy.'

Rainier listened closely. It seemed a fantastic scheme – especially at the time – but every detail had been carefully thought through. He asked to be shown detailed plans and encouraged Michel to go further.

Elated, Michel returned to the States and began pouring time and money into the project. He commissioned a prestigious firm of architects to draw up plans for the university buildings and to research the ocean bed for a suitable site.[4] Hydrographic maps were obtained from France, the ocean bed was surveyed, and an area big enough to create an island was found that would hold a full university campus, connected to Monaco itself by a bridge. The estimated cost was fifty million dollars, an astronomical sum for the day. 'It's only money,' Hirschorn said, undismayed.

A sophisticated and detailed proposal was sent to Prince Rainier. It included the hydrographic map marking the exact location for land reclamation, architectural designs for the university, a description of its academic nature, and Hirschorn's assurance of financing. 'I had to wait quite a time for an answer.'

A letter finally arrived from Prince Rainier. 'I must ask you to excuse the long delay in answering your letter, due to the fact that I have been giving the project my most earnest attention. There are several points that remain obscure . . .' Two rapier thrusts followed, effectively killing off the project. 'The site of the proposed island would interfere with the new plans for reclaiming land from the sea and for embellishing the water-front; these plans are in process of realisation.' And, 'Do you realise that, by tradition, education in the Principality is largely under the control of the Catholic Church, Monaco being a Catholic country?'[5] Unfortunately the Prince had not brought up these fundamental objections in Gstaad.

Michel was greatly disappointed. Subsequently he learned from a diary item five years later in the Louella Parsons column in the *Los Angeles Herald Examiner* in April 1963: 'The visit of Princess Grace and Prince Rainier is not entirely to be with her family and attend civic and social affairs . . . The Prince has a real estate deal up his royal sleeve, which is novel to say the least. Monaco, like many countries, is hurting for land and Rainier is sponsoring a project which calls for an artificial island adjoining his principality to be built up as a lavish resort area. Tourist trade is one of the biggest sources of income for Monaco.'[6] And it was not until Michel returned to the south of France on holiday that the extent of Rainier's 'innovative' project became clear. Suzanne told him she had something to show him, and drove him to an exhibition mounted in the Monte Carlo casino. 'And there was this maquette of a proposed new casino and hotel to be built on land reclaimed from the sea. I felt they had taken my plans for a university and built a casino instead!'

Michel left Monaco feeling depressed and disillusioned. 'It greatly embarrassed Grace. We remained friends, but did not speak of her husband.'

Michel returned to his home in Benedict Canyon one evening to find that Barry had disappeared. He began a desperate search of the immediate neighbourhood but found no evidence of him anywhere. 'The next day I put up signs all over the canyon, printed ads in the Beverly Hills paper, and tried everything. I searched and searched for a week. Each day was an eternity.'

On the seventh day he went to bed, slept fitfully and awoke early from a strange and haunting dream. 'In it, Barry came to the back porch accompanied by a man, a stranger. Barry went to his usual place where he had his food and water and the stranger stood beside him as he ate. He finished eating, looked towards me and then turned and followed the stranger out of the garden into the woods.'

Michel got up and left the house and entered the woods where Barry had disappeared in the dream. He found a steep path that led up into the hills and began to climb. 'It was not anywhere we usually went together, but I felt compelled to follow the path I saw in the dream. I walked for about fifteen minutes and found his body slumped in a small clearing. It was a lonely spot. He must have gone there to die and had a heart attack.'

The unexpected death of his wartime companion was a profound shock and a terrible loss. 'I still miss him today. After that I could not look at other dogs or touch them for a long time. To think of having another dog would have been an insult to his memory.'[7]

Yves Montand became a friend when Michel taught him English for the film *Let's Make Love*, in which he starred with Marilyn Monroe. The French film star took a large suite in the Beverly Hills Hotel with his wife, Simone Signoret. Directly opposite, across the corridor, Marilyn Monroe and playwright Arthur Miller were installed in a similarly luxurious suite. 'Simone's English was good, but not idiomatic, and the title to her had the literal and single meaning it did in French. She thought it unbelievably vulgar. She said she couldn't understand how the Americans could make a film called "Let's Have Sex".'

Michel arrived every day to teach Montand English and coach him for his part. The actor presented a challenge that almost defeated Michel, who found himself baffled by the lack of progress. He then discovered that Montand knew no French grammar and had no concept of verb tenses. Michel developed a system of hand signals to indicate past, present, future and conditional tenses, and this simple visual aid unlocked the language for his pupil. Montand was so influenced by the experience that he wrote articles, and gave interviews, describing how he had come to understand French grammar through learning English.

As Michel spent time with Montand at the suite in the Beverly Hills Hotel it became clear how close the famous couples had become. 'They practically wanted to live together.' Simone Signoret then returned to France to make a movie, and a few days later Arthur Miller flew back to New York to work on a play. 'That left Yves Montand and Marilyn Monroe alone with their front doors facing each other. And the inevitable happened.'

Montand confided to Michel about the affair in an angry outburst.

'So it happened,' Michel said philosophically. 'Why are you so angry?'

'I'm angry at Arthur.'

'At Arthur? What on earth has he done to you?'

'He has gone to New York! Why did he leave? How could he leave us alone? How could he do that to me?' Montand was on the verge of tears as he turned to Michel. '*Je ne suis qu'un homme . . . Je ne suis qu'un homme*' – I'm only a man.

Montand explained that as a kid from the slums of Marseille he had never dreamed, while running wild with his *copains*, that he might one day have an affair with somebody like Marilyn Monroe. And now he was involved with the greatest sex symbol in the world.

'How about Simone?' Michel asked pointedly. 'How do you feel about her?'

'I love Simone.'

'How do you think this will affect your marriage?'

'There is no question – I want to be with Simone.'

'I strongly recommend that you call Simone and tell her the whole story. It will make a big difference if you tell her before she finds out through some gossip column. The chances will then be strong that you will lose her.'

Montand looked depressed and sorry for himself, but he made the call. Simone Signoret flew back to Hollywood on the next plane to reclaim her husband. She remarked acidly that she did not seem to be the only person who had taken the title of the film literally. 'They all survived this brief affair. It was only a fling really. But Marilyn, so insecure and desperate to be liked, was deeply hurt by the rejection.'

Michel moved from the house in Benedict Canyon to a large apartment in the Chateau Marmont, the legendary hotel on Sunset Strip, where he lived for the next eight years. Movie star clients were fun and helped pay the bills, but Michel's focus was on setting up a model school to demonstrate revolutionary teaching techniques. He created a non-profit Foundation for Better Learning to raise funds and interest in an independent Demonstration School dedicated to advancing innovative educational approaches. 'The idea was to have children from varying social backgrounds and levels of ability, from nursery through high school. We would bring together a cross-section and provide a curriculum with outstanding teachers on the principle that no school can be better than its teachers.'

The model school was designed to be a showcase, any part of which could easily be replicated and applied. The plan was to assemble a staff of first-rate educators who used affordable programmes that any interested state school would be able to adopt. A staff of experts, each one a specialist in his own field, would assist teachers to prepare their curricula. Educational assistants and clerks would be made available to relieve teachers of routine tasks, allowing them the time and freedom to concentrate on the creative aspects of their profession. 'I saw the teacher's role as creating a relaxed atmosphere and assuring students that their questions would be respected and understood. And to encourage students to be sufficiently courageous to have opinions – to dare to be wrong.'

There was to be a Guidance Department that would work to improve greater understanding between pupils and their homes and schools. Community members from outside the school – scientists, industrialists, lawyers, artists, writers and doctors – would be invited to help on specific assignments in which they were better qualified than any available teacher. The school would also have an internship programme, similar to the one used in hospitals, where young teachers serving as apprentices would be able to watch master teachers in action. 'There would be workshops providing teachers with the opportunity to continue to develop, simplify and refine the approach to their subject. Since most teachers don't have the time or the money to keep abreast of the accelerated developments even within their own field of knowledge, the school would provide the means to bring a wide range of scholars and educational research specialists to the aid of the teaching staff.' And special attention would be paid to the design of the building for the maximum comfort of both student and teacher.

The plan was elaborated over time and attracted a great deal of attention. It was an ambitious and exciting project involving innovative and extraordinary people, but Michel now began to experience the cycle of frustration and rejection that came to dog all his attempts at educational innovation. Marvin Adelson, a professor from the University of California Los Angeles, explained: 'A lot of the opposition and distrust of the assertions that Michel makes comes out of the belief that if his method was really that good, it would have caught on before now and spread like wildfire and displaced everything else in the world. People find it hard to believe. And I found it hard to believe – at first.'

But Adelson soon became a convert to Michel's revolutionary educational ideas, and an avid proselytiser. An original thinker and brilliant scientist himself, the professor laid claim to an eccentric academic background spanning a number of disparate disciplines. After leaving the army he took a degree in electrical engineering and then made a dramatic switch to study for a PhD in psychology. 'Had the war not started I would probably have been a doctor.' He became associated with various non-profit think-tanks involved in national policy studies, and worked on a project connected with the space programme. He then managed the command, control and information systems at Hughes Aircraft for five years. He moved on to become the principal scientist at the System Development Corporation, a think-tank that was a spin-off of the Rand Corporation, and then abruptly changed career yet again when he was appointed professor of architecture at UCLA, a post he held for twenty-three years.

Among Adelson's particular interests were the educational needs of the future and the potential of accelerated learning. 'If you do it right you might not be able to teach everybody everything, but you can teach a lot of people a lot of things. I was initially sceptical of Michel's claims, but I listened to his tapes. They were simply better than anything else I'd ever run across in my life. Since then I have never encountered a person who has heard them and not been impressed.'

But he was mystified by the mumbo-jumbo and rationalisation that many people seemed to need to accept the success of the method. 'People attached all sorts of attributes to Michel, and one was that he hypnotised students. Why that should work, or what was wrong with hypnosis if it did work, there was no way to understand.

It was clear to me that Michel had thought through his system from the learner's perspective, which is what is missing from so many other approaches, including the academic approach.'

Enthused, Adelson began to talk about the method within the academic world and made an astonishing discovery: not only were there people in the language-teaching community who were not prepared to try the method, there were also a large number who did not want anybody else to try. 'It was a shock. I was very dismayed.' Adelson did not have to go far to discover the reason. 'Vested interests. If you make it possible to learn a language in a weekend, a week, or even a year, you're going to thrust into obsolescence a whole institutionalised structure. And that puts people's livelihoods and professional status at risk. I was amazed, over and over again, by the essential conservatism of the system of thinkers who are supposed to be leading-edge. Michel drives these people crazy. They don't like the idea that the teacher takes responsibility for the student's progress; they don't like the concept of no written work, not allowing students to do homework or take notes – it all violates the conventional idea that students screw up because they are not doing enough work. Teachers don't like to admit that it might be their fault, that they are simply teaching badly.'

Adelson, who was with Systems Development Corporation at the time, worked with Michel for more than a year to develop a detailed prospectus for the Demonstration School. The proposal had already been fully approved by the Ford Foundation, after eighteen months of consultations, and only needed a signature. 'Unfortunately there was a potential struggle going on at Systems at the time with regard to education,' Adelson explained. 'The proposal fell into the hands of a person who mirrored the attitudes of the university faculty, which was murder for the programme and the result was that nothing happened.'[8]

'I was completely disillusioned and emotionally drained by the experience,' Michel says. 'After so much work and coming so close to realising the dream, this wiped me out. I gave up!'

Rejection by the educational establishment began to become something of a routine, and followed a pattern. An enthusiastic university chancellor, ambassador or lawyer would take the course and excitedly recommend it to an academic body or government department. Reasons would then always be found by elements within the particular organisation concerned not to adopt it.

At the University of Pittsburgh, for example, the chancellor, Wesley Posvar, invited Michel to give a ten-day demonstration programme in French and Spanish to a group of forty faculty, staff and students. 'Most took up the language at the beginning level, and achieved a satisfying degree of conversational, reading and writing proficiency in that period of time,' Posvar wrote in a letter to the futurist Herman Kahn, at the Hudson Institute. 'Some had previously studied the language but felt they really did not know it, and they were brought to what they described as a state of fluency. Whatever claims or comparisons might be made, of this I am sure: eighty or ninety hours spent in this method is more effective than two or three semesters in college training, which is several times as time-consuming and not nearly as exciting.'[9]

The chancellor expected sceptics, but was unprepared for everyone on the staff of the various language departments to refuse to attend the demonstration. A professor in the linguistics department dismissed the system without further investigation because he said that he only accepted a method as viable when it was theory-based and empirically proven. The head of the French department also stayed away, declaring that she was always suspicious of methods that claimed quick results.

People even found reasons to reject the method after its results had been clearly demonstrated to them. Charles Morin, an attorney in Washington DC – from the large and powerful law firm Dickstein, Shapiro, Morin – introduced Michel to a number of political clients, including John Connolly, when he was governor of Texas, and Lyndon Johnson, when he was vice president. (Michel taught LBJ's daughter, Lynda Bird, French. At dinner with the Johnsons one evening, Michel was surprised to see that everyone's massive steak was exactly the same odd shape. They had all been trimmed to resemble the outline of the state of Texas.) Morin took two days of French with Michel and was so impressed by the results he talked about it all over Washington. The CIA heard about the method and sent a French woman to test the attorney. 'I was certainly not fluent, but felt I could communicate,' Morin said. 'I asked the woman, in French, if she could speak more slowly. She said she was from Paris and Parisians always spoke fast. We talked for about an hour.' The woman returned to the CIA and wrote a report on the encounter in which she declared that Morin had to be making false claims as it was impossible to learn to speak grammatically correct French in such a short time.[10]

The proof of the system, for anyone who cared to investigate, lay with the students. Sometimes, these came from the most unpromising backgrounds and circumstances, such as a class of fifteen-year-old black ghetto youths in a Los Angeles inner-city school still reeling from the aftermath of the Watts riot. Academic activity had been brought to a grinding halt after a series of student sit-ins developed into violent demonstrations culminating in a full-scale riot which almost completely destroyed the school. Teachers walked out, claiming unreasonable working conditions. The principal had a breakdown and had to be replaced. The new principal appealed for outside help. In the circumstances it seemed an almost quixotic gesture on the part of Michel to volunteer to enter the war zone to teach for a week. 'One of the criticisms of the militant community then was that what was taught to black youth was irrelevant. So I thought the most irrelevant thing I could do was to drive down to South Central and teach French.'

The principal was pessimistic about the entire enterprise. The government had given the school an emergency grant of thirty thousand dollars – a large sum at the time – to clean up the debris from the riot, but not a cent extra for education. Discipline in the school had declined to the point where teachers were forbidden to close classroom doors, as this provoked troublemakers to break them down. Authority was flouted to the point that couples fornicated in the corridors. Most students had no interest whatsoever in learning anything. Some were violent. Michel was warned that he might be exposed to verbal or even physical abuse.

'Just give me a class and I'll handle the rest,' Michel said.

'No, no, no – it's not so simple,' the principal said over the phone. 'You have to come down here first and assess the situation. It's wild!'

'I don't need to come down. Just arrange a class and I'll be there at eight o'clock Monday morning.'

The class to be taught was described as 'consisting of twenty-four recalcitrant eighth-graders, markedly below-average students, severely deficient in reading skills or other basic skills for that matter, but judged to be of average intelligence'. The principal remarked ironically in a letter to a colleague that he was interested 'in determining whether Mr Thomas could take an irrelevant subject, French, and make it relevant'.[11]

Michel arrived at the school to find police with attack dogs patrolling the grounds. Many of the buildings looked as if they had been bombed, the flagpole had been bent to the ground and the Stars and Stripes removed and burned. No undamaged classroom was available, so a storage room was found. The students proved as difficult, academically dull and potentially dangerous as promised. Michel was confronted by the simmering mix of dumb insolence and hostility presented to every teacher who attempted to broach the shield of defiant ignorance. Michel responded philosophically: 'I have always learned the most from teaching students who are very difficult.'

From the first moment he wrong-footed his surly crew, who were unprepared for a tutor whose unspoken maxim was, *The student is never wrong.* 'Teaching is my responsibility, not yours,' he told the class, assuming a quiet, unhurried manner. 'Don't worry about remembering. That's my responsibility too. I don't want you to take notes. There will be no homework. No tests. The work involved here is mine, not yours.' He asked the class whether anyone knew where French was spoken. There was no reply. When pressed, one student suggested London. Why? Because London was in Paris. Michel made no comment, but quietly began to explain, without sarcasm or censure, that French was spoken in France, and also in a number of African countries. As he elaborated on the importance of the language in Africa, he began to teach, but in such a casual, offhand way that no one felt obliged to object. 'Much of English is French badly pronounced,' he said, illustrating the point with the French pronunciation of a number of words used in everyday conversation: experience, realisation, gratitude. 'In fact, you know a good deal of French already, much more than you realise.'

As he talked, he attempted to estimate the size of the problem facing him. Not only were the students below average, they were completely uninterested in learning at best, and disruptive and potentially violent at worst. Mentally, he divided the class into three groups. The first was made up of those who were shy and tried to hide behind others. The second, and largest, group comprised the passive and indifferent, some of whom had trouble sitting still: they rocked, drummed on desks with their fingers, tapped their feet, moved about, or even slept. Finally, there was a troublesome minority who were defiant or actively belligerent. Even to ask one of these students his name was to provoke an abusive answer. Michel decided to concentrate on the first group – whom he designated the Shy Group – while hoping to bring in members of the second group – the Indifferent Group – over time. He ignored the belligerent faction.

The first objective was to give as many students as possible an early sense of achievement within the first half hour. Using one of his many heuristic techniques – described as 'mental hooks' – he demonstrated to the class that they already possessed a French vocabulary of as many as three thousand words or more. And that these were not 'baby' words, but complex adult words, so they did not have to begin learning as children. He pointed out that most English words ending in -tion, -able, -ence and -ism were the same in French (condition, capable, experience, realism). And that many English words ending in 'y' had an 'e' in French: fraternity, paternity, liberty and so on.

No one was ever questioned directly or allowed to raise his hand. Students were never called on by name but were encouraged through eye contact. If anyone apologised for making a mistake, Michel asked, 'Why are you apologising? Why are you concerned? Eliminating mistakes is my problem. Why are you worrying? You are not supposed to know the language yet.' His gentle, continued insistence that he alone was responsible for each student's progress, and his acceptance of blame for all mistakes, led to an immediate reduction in anxiety and tension. He had removed what he describes as 'the terrible burden of expectation'.

Once members of the Indifferent Group saw the Shy Group respond, they began to take an interest. Those who were usually ignored by their peers, and rarely dared speak up in English, were beginning to form sentences in French. Even the most timid students lost their self-consciousness, while the indifferent were pulled in one by one. No one was ever urged to try harder or respond faster, but was advised to slow down at the first sign of tension or nerves. And while individual students progressed at different rates, the learning process moved very rapidly. Unannounced, informal exercises that seemed effortless were in reality carefully planned, and while the pace seemed relaxed and unhurried, the speed at which learning occurred was dramatic.

Within two hours Michel was helping any student who bothered to listen through such complex sentences as, 'If I had known you were coming to town this evening, I would have made reservations for us at a restaurant, and would have tried to get tickets for the theatre.' Or, 'I am very glad you are going to come and have dinner with us at the house tonight because I would like to speak to you and I would like to know when you are going to be here because I am going to cook.' By the end of the first day he had the class pretty well in hand, and the interest of the first two groups had been greatly enlarged. He continued to ignore the belligerent group.

Before dismissing the class he felt secure enough to take a strong hand. Speaking in a friendly (in order to show that his purpose was not to punish) but firm manner, he said: 'I came here to teach. To show you that you can learn. That you can learn anything. If you want me to come back tomorrow I want to know I can teach without disturbances. There are some here because they want to learn. I also notice that some of you are not interested in learning. I feel it is unfair that those who want to learn should be disturbed and interfered with by those who do not. So I am going to separate the class and only teach those who want to learn. Will those who do not want to learn French please raise their hands.' Not one hand went up.

The next day started very differently. Everyone was involved, and even the belligerent group was quiet. Minor disturbances were punished by sending the offending student out of the room for ten minutes. The classroom had to be evacuated during the lunch hour, something many of the students feared because the playground had become an unpleasant and dangerous place. Michel told them he would be pleased to let them stay in the room if they could be trusted. Some of the larger, 'belligerent' students immediately volunteered to police the others. 'No. There are to be no bosses. If you want to stay in the room each of you has to accept responsibility for his own behaviour.' The students insisted they could control and protect the room.

After lunch, Michel was still in conversation with colleagues when the bell went. One or two of the regular teachers were sceptical when they heard of the progress achieved by a class generally acknowledged to be made up of hostile, dead-end losers. As the discussion continued there was a knock on the faculty door and one of the students stuck his head in. 'Please, Mr Thomas, the class is waiting.'

One of the most obvious student deficiencies was a general inability to listen, either to Michel or each other. He introduced a game in which he would try to 'catch' someone not listening. The students began to take satisfaction in not getting caught, and after a day the game became redundant. At the end of the third day an extraordinary thing happened: the students pleaded with Michel, and the school administration, to have the class continued for an extra week. This was arranged.

On the fourth day, Michel was reasonably satisfied with the performance of the class but still suffered occasional interruptions when talking broke out. By merely pausing for a couple of moments, these incidents stopped. Although remarkable progress had been made, he decided the intellectual habits of the class could benefit from further tightening. Choosing a minor lapse in attention on the part of several students, he staged a walk-out towards the end of the day.

'I told them I was quitting. I repeated that I was there to teach and could only do that to people who wanted to learn. "I will not teach with disturbances. So fine, I'm leaving."' Although there was an immediate chorus of protests, he left the room and made his way to the common room. 'The purpose of the walk-out was not to establish a reputation as a strict disciplinarian, but to further train the students as persons willing to control their own impulses out of concern for fellow students and in the interests of their own learning.'

He waited five minutes, but the expected delegation failed to materialise. He feared he had misjudged his timing, and at the end of ten minutes was very tense, alarmed that he had made a serious mistake. He began to think of a way to correct this when five students appeared to say that the class had discussed the matter and had voted unanimously to request his return. As he re-entered the classroom he was touched to find that during his absence the students had swept and tidied the room, and found a chair and desk which they placed at the front for him.

'There is one more thing,' Michel said. 'No bubble gum. I don't want to see it or hear it!'

This was almost immediately ignored, but two large youths from the formerly belligerent group jumped up of their own accord and confiscated gum from the others.

During the lessons Michel had been shocked to learn that none of the students had seen the sea, even though they had lived in Los Angeles, on the Pacific Ocean, all their lives. At the weekend he organised a convoy of minibuses and offered to take anyone who was interested to the beach. The entire class went along. It was an easy, pleasant time, and the group had fun. A genuine affection and friendship had sprung up between Michel and his unpromising class.[12]

Back at school during the second week Michel began to talk about the importance of education not only in getting a job and being successful in the world, but as an end in itself. Learning, he told his students, should be fun. For the first time in their lives they listened and tended to agree. By the end of the week each had drawn up a list of subjects of special interest. Michel organised for various students to take music and drawing lessons, and so on. To the stupefaction of the other teachers, this group of sub-standard, recalcitrant non-readers requested to stay on twice a week after regular school for the remainder of the term, purely for the privilege of meeting and talking with Michel.

Both the principal and the professor monitoring the experiment were profoundly impressed by the results. Black youths who spoke English in the jargon of the ghetto were now speaking grammatically correct, properly accented French. Where truancy had been the norm, attendance for Michel's lessons had been one hundred per cent. Noisy, disruptive behaviour and occasional violence had been replaced by self-imposed discipline that never broke down. Most startling of all was the increase in the attention span of the class, especially in view of the long sessions. Michel had the complete attention of the group all day, while the only control method he ever used was the threat of suspension from the class for ten minutes. Unruly youths written off as academic duds had been transformed into students with a passion to learn. The professor who monitored the class under Michel wrote: 'He uses no aversive controls, never scolds, never raises his voice, never acts as if he were disappointed in a student's performance, never frowns . . . The reports I've had from other students convince me that the excitement and satisfaction which I experienced were in no way unusual, but something experienced by virtually all of Mr Thomas's students, whether poorly educated youngsters from the black ghetto or presumably better educated persons with graduate degrees.'[13]

Language block is not confined to the poorly educated but is found in every class of society at every level of intelligence. The French film director François Truffaut considered himself an extreme case and despaired of learning English. His inability to communicate led him to take an interest in stories of children who had been brought up wild and were unable to speak any language, and resulted in the film L'Enfant Sauvage (The Wild Child). An added interest in educational experiments with autistic or delinquent children made it almost inevitable that he would eventually find his way to Michel.[14]

'Block', Michel believes, is a result of bad teaching in childhood. 'We handicap and hobble and put a heavy lid on the immense innate learning potential of the human mind that is in everyone. Education has become a conspiracy between parents and governments to control children. Every child is institutionalised at the age of five or six and sentenced to at least ten years' hard time until so-called graduation. Children serve time by law, and I call it a conspiracy because parents consent to it and the government enforces it. So children become prison inmates – except unlike prison inmates they do not have a voice with which to protest, or advocates to protect their rights. Children don't have anybody. They have to serve their time unconditionally. After such an experience many naturally feel they have had enough of education and learning. They have no wish to continue. School's over and done with – learning's finished. From childhood on we are conditioned to associate learning with tension, effort, concentration, study. In essence, learning equals pain. The educational experience has been a painful one, and has capped the immense learning potential of each child. This is a tragedy.'

Conventional teaching, Michel argues, closes rather than opens the mind and cripples even the best students, blocking the subconscious because of the tension it creates. 'Why not make use of the full potential of the human mind, by combining the conscious and subconscious? And you can only tap into that if someone is in a relaxed and pleasant frame of mind. It is important to eliminate anxiety and tension. Then and only then is a person completely receptive to learning. People do not want to expose themselves to more pain, or face what they think are their own inadequacies. Yet these are the very people who become most excited when they see that they can absorb and progress quickly and easily.'

Michel's approach overcomes the most stubborn cases, and he insists there is no such thing as someone being unable to learn. He emphatically rejects the idea that a person has to have a gift, or 'ear', to be able to learn a language. 'Have you ever met anyone, however stupid, who cannot speak their own language? Everyone is gifted. Anyone who can speak his native tongue has already proved his gift for language and can learn another.'

In a letter to a friend about his experience with Michel, Truffaut wrote, 'He has never criticised me. His manner is a little like that of a psychoanalyst and he has the patience of an angel . . . Anyway, he told me that he would make it his job to teach me and that I wouldn't leave here without being able to write, read, speak and even understand.'[15] Michel was as good as his word, and after sixty hours of lessons Truffaut was able to read his first book in English (Selznick's *Memo*[16]), watch and understand the Nixon Watergate hearings on TV, and write the following inscription on a photograph for his teacher: 'At first I learn from you the word "impeachment" and four weeks later I was able to have a meeting in English at Warner Bros headquarters. Thanks, Michel, warmest regards.'[17] Truffaut presented him with a beautiful set of Proust – in French.

A further success with both teachers and children in a Los Angeles primary school was also ignored by the educational establishment. In the early 1970s Michel was approached by Andrea Kasza, principal of Norwood Elementary School in the heart of South Central Los Angeles. The principal had a serious and fundamental problem with her five hundred pupils. The school had originally been split between sixty per cent black and forty per cent Hispanic students, but was moving rapidly towards a Spanish-speaking majority. None of the new arrivals spoke English, and there was not a single Hispanic teacher on the staff. 'There were only two who knew any Spanish at all – one of whom was Jewish, and the other Japanese.' There were no government programmes at the time to help, and while Kasza attempted to hire Spanish-speaking teachers, she sought desperately for something to fill the gap. 'I wanted the staff to learn enough Spanish quickly to be able to communicate with the students. I had heard about Michel's Foundation and contacted him. We set up a class for twenty teachers who had no Spanish at all, and they took one of his crash courses.' It was an unqualified success. 'The teachers were very happy with the programme and many of them went on to become fluent in the language.'

During the course, Michel decided he also wanted to work with the young children, which he had not done before, to help them speak English. 'I didn't have the money to hire him for a year, and he did it pro bono,' Kasza said. 'It would never have happened otherwise.' Michel was given *carte blanche* for a year to teach not just languages but every subject. 'I had thirty kids in the class and divided them into two groups. One used a teacher and one used tapes, and I rotated them. It worked like a charm.' A six-week block was set aside when the primary school children who spoke only sub-standard *barrio* Spanish were taught nothing but English as a foreign language. 'A child in America must speak English or become a permanent second-class citizen. So they learned English and also had their level of Spanish raised. They learned how to speak and write in both languages in these six weeks.' The second six-week block course was in mathematics, again using a rotating combination of teachers and tapes.

Kasza watched Michel at work and devised a curriculum over time to enable ordinary schools to adopt the method without disruption. The programme started with kindergarten and spread to involve all grades and the entire staff. The Spanish community approved because the programme maintained the use of both languages. The school became recognised as having the best transition programme in the country, and people came from all over the world to study it. 'We developed an outstanding programme,' Kasza said. 'The teachers loved it, the children loved it, the parents loved it and we had great press.'

287

The courses were given the official endorsement of the California Teachers' Association and the National Education Association. Michel was greatly excited and waited for the various state and federal educational bodies to express interest. 'I waited for the phone to ring. I expected the Education Department to hammer on my door. Instead, there was silence. Nothing.'

'I don't know why people don't support things,' Kasza said. 'It's so difficult to create change. Certainly don't look for it in the language departments of the universities. They're the most resistant to change of any educational group I know. They ignore the practitioners. A new approach means asking a whole department to change its attitude, and that's the problem. In the academic world people get comfortable with what they're doing. What would happen to all those Spanish professors with tenure? They'd have to change their ways. If the man who invented the paperclip needed the approval of a university department we would never have had the paperclip. They would say people had never used paperclips before, so who needs them?'

One of the young teachers at Norwood Elementary School, Alice Burns, approached Michel one day with two tickets for a concert. 'I had been on the course and after just one day I was in awe,' Alice said. 'I had just never seen anybody synthesise the things that we learned as theoretically sound. I had been sent on a university course at USC and there was no comparison. The course I took there was the same sort of fragmented language instruction that we're all familiar with.'

The couple began to go out regularly together. One evening, after dinner, Michel suggested that they drive to the airport and get on the first plane to wherever it happened to be going.

'That would be great,' Alice said calmly. 'Let's do it.'

Michel looked closely at his date. 'I realised that it would be wonderful to travel with this woman. To me, to travel with somebody is even more of a test than living with them. And I decided this was somebody I could travel with – possibly settle down with. So we looked at each other, bypassed the airport and drove to a hotel in Newport Beach and spent the weekend together. It was the beginning of a very special relationship. It started me thinking in a different way. Over the years I always had a strong desire for a family and children, especially during the war when I thought I might be killed. I had the need for someone to survive me. But I had hidden the desire, and convinced everyone in Hollywood I was not the marrying kind, not a family man. Alice brought this out of me as my feelings for her deepened.'

They were married within a year.[18]

Alice was born and brought up a Catholic, but had converted to Judaism in her teens. Her father, a history professor in Oklahoma, was part Osage Indian. 'I was a spiritually orientated person, but I was constantly in conflict with Catholicism. I seemed always to be breaking some rule and nobody gave me an explanation why. I never had that conflict with Judaism.'[19]

The couple wanted children quickly, and a son was born in the first year of their marriage. He was named Gurion, the Hebrew word for lion. When Michel saw the baby, tears of emotion welled in his eyes – the first he had shed since long before the war.[20]

After the birth of a second child – a daughter, Micheline – the couple decided to move to the east coast where they set up house in Larchmont, New York, half an hour's drive from Manhattan, where Michel opened a school. 'I brought the children up with a reverence for life – for people, for animals and even plants. When the kids picked wild flowers and threw them down, I tried to make them feel responsible by putting the flowers in water and taking care of them.' Micheline took the lesson to heart and grew attached to a cockroach. She travelled into Manhattan on the train with her unlikely pet in a jam jar and showed it to fellow travellers for them to admire.

Michel often worked late in his study on the ground floor of the house. One night, as he sat at his desk, six-year-old Guri came down the stairs from his bedroom. The child entered the study and immediately made for a half-open drawer where he spotted an SS dagger from Michel's wartime collection. 'I brought up both of my children not to have military toys – no guns, no shooting – and here he had stumbled on all this Nazi stuff. It was a contradiction. I felt caught.'

To the small boy, the dagger seemed like a sword, and he was thrilled by it. 'Why do you have this sword?' he asked. 'How did you get it?' Michel felt uncomfortable, and was wondering how to respond to the six-year-old when Guri answered his own question. 'You took it from a bad guy.' Michel nodded as the child came up with another question. 'Who are the bad guys, Daddy?' Again the child answered his own question with information picked up at Bible study. 'It must be the Assyrians.'

Michel thought, 'Oh my God, I don't want this. The Assyrians will become the Syrians, and then it will be the Arabs. I don't want him to go down this road.' It was a critical moment. He could either burden his son with a legacy of hate – albeit the legitimate hatred of Nazi evil – or introduce him to a more complicated world of personal responsibility. 'One is not born with hatred, one learns hatred. Children are injected with it and then they grow up with it. As adults they have to find reasons to justify their hatred, and they find these reasons. Hatred is dangerous because it can last for ever, be handed down from one generation to the next. There are antidotes to most poisons, but none for the poison of hatred. Especially if it is inculcated in children.'

He told Guri that he had taken the sword from a Nazi bad guy.

A few days later Guri had a new question. 'If God created all life, did he create bad guys and Nazis?'

Michel told his son to fetch his latest favourite toy, a space figure with a revolving head that revealed different expressions ranging from benign to downright evil. Michel rotated the head, moving from one expression to another, and asked Guri to tell him whether the face was a bad guy or a good guy. The child became engrossed in the game, emphatically differentiating between the two.

'We are all created by God but we are not puppets of God,' Michel explained. 'We are not being played or manipulated by God. Good or bad is within all of us and it is what we do with our lives, and with ourselves, that brings it out. Those who do not suppress the bad side of themselves, but allow it to dominate, will be bad guys. There are people in whom sometimes the bad will triumph and sometimes the good, and nobody can trust them because they can't trust themselves. They are people with many faces. It is important to know what we have in us, to work towards one strong, good face.'

Later, he explained to his son that nations too had many faces, and what they made of their history shaped their nature. 'I taught my children not to follow the crowd, and elevated a couple of lines from the Bible to the level of commandments: Thou shalt not follow the multitude to do evil, and Thou shalt not stand idly by. I'm not a religious man. But let me say that my life has led me to believe in God. A more precise explanation would be that I believe in the divine spirit of God, a universal God. I am happily Jewish because it is a religion without dogma – there is nothing that cannot be questioned. I accept the differences between human beings. I see a brotherhood of mankind regardless of colour, creed or race, and believe in what is God-given in all of us. But what Eichmann, Himmler and Hitler were capable of doing is something we all carry. We have the same seeds in us, the same potential for evil in certain conditions and in certain circumstances. It is up to us what we become.'

The encounter between Michel Thomas and Klaus Barbie at St Joseph's prison in Lyon more than forty years after they had last met was a calm and dignified affair without emotion or histrionics. In a gloomy room set aside for judicial investigations, Michel sat at a table flanked by a judge and a lawyer. Across from him, beside an interpreter and a court reporter, but so close the men could almost touch, was wartime Gestapo chief Klaus Barbie, the Butcher of Lyon.[21]

The meeting was part of the preliminary hearings in the course of collecting evidence for the trial against Barbie. Michel had already given testimony in Paris to the police, in the presence of prosecuting attorney Serge Klarsfeld, and now he had been called as a witness to establish the identity of the man who had interrogated him forty years earlier. Barbie argued in German that when he was in 'police' training a professor of criminology had stated that it was impossible to recognise anyone after such a long time. Especially if that person, on his own admission, had only been in the other's presence for two hours. 'I did not expect ever to agree with the defendant, but in this case I do,' Michel said. 'If I had passed the man sitting there in the street I would not have recognised him. But facing him and staring at him here close-up, I know. His voice, his demeanour. It is clear. That is Klaus Barbie.'

Michel drew attention to a distinguishing mark he had noticed all those years earlier: a right ear lobe lower than the left. 'And that effeminate gesture, the flicking of his hand with his little finger bent inwards. The mocking, sarcastic smile. And nobody could forget those eyes, those rat's eyes with no mercy in them.'[22]

After the war, Klaus Barbie had disappeared for thirty-three years. Although wanted by the Americans, British and French, he managed to keep one step ahead of them all through a mixture of his own low cunning and the gross incompetence of his pursuers.

Ever since he left Lyon, he had been on the move. As a member of the Gestapo he came under the automatic-arrest category, so he took an assumed name one month after Germany's surrender, and worked on farms to survive. He was soon back in touch with clandestine Nazi and SS organisations, however, and learned to make a living forging identity papers. In the winter of 1945, he was arrested by the Americans at Darmstadt, for reasons that remain unknown. He received a fourteen-day prison sentence but his true identity was not discovered and he was released.

He became a common criminal, posing as a policeman on one occasion to rob a baroness of her jewellery in Kassel, and moved from one town to another, selling forged identity papers and black-market goods. As his circle of underground SS contacts grew, one proved to be a double agent working for the British. Barbie was subsequently arrested and told, 'Well, my friend, we are not the Americans. You are not going to run away from us!' A bold statement that was to prove entirely incorrect. The British moved him to a safe house in Hamburg and locked him in a room, but Barbie found a crowbar, levered the padlock from the door and fled. He would later claim that the British had roughed him up. 'I lost all interest in the British and all faith in their promises.' He acquired new forged ID papers and returned to Marburg and a life of petty crime.

The Americans and the British had launched a crackdown at this time on Nazi resistance groups. Operation Selection Board targeted numerous suspects, and in February 1947 agents simultaneously raided dozens of addresses all over Germany. Barbie was thought to head an underground Nazi group, made up of seventy members, that was involved in smuggling fugitives out of the country. He later claimed to have escaped through a bathroom window as CIC agents burst through his front door.

Soon after this narrow escape he decided that his only long-term chance of remaining at liberty was to switch sides and work for Allied intelligence. He sought out Kurt Merk, a former wartime colleague and Abwehr (German military intelligence) officer who had been recruited by CIC to run a spy network. The men met in the small town of Memmingen, just a short drive south of Ulm, and Merk agreed to introduce his former colleague to his American masters.

Barbie's name was immediately recognised by CIC as one of the principal Selection Board targets still at large, but the regional commander saw him as a valuable informant and neglected to inform HQ. And so it came about that one section of CIC secretly protected the Gestapo officer, while another searched for him. The American agent who recruited Barbie found him to be 'an honest man, both intellectually and personally, absolutely without nerves or fear . . . a Nazi idealist'.[23]

'The new CIC officers were totally and completely incompetent, with no idea of how to run an intelligence operation,' Michel explains. 'They looked for help from "professionals" – Nazis who had worked in intelligence. Most of these men just sold them newspaper reports they had read in the Czech press, or the like. They got zilch from Barbie.'

Barbie's past was no secret to his masters. He had been on the CROWCASS directives since 1945, accused of the murder and torture of civilians, and CIC had further identified him as head of the Gestapo in Lyon. A brief profile on him was also among the multitude written by Michel while in Munich. Barbie did not deny his position – which, after all, was his sole claim to expertise in intelligence work – but insisted he had not been involved in torture and murder. However, Merk later reported to CIC that Barbie had tortured Résistance members and had boasted of hanging them from their thumbs until they were dead. 'If the French ever found out how many mass graves Barbie was responsible for, even Eisenhower would not be able to protect him,' he said.[24]

A report was now sent to HQ and an internal squabble broke out within CIC between Barbie's protectors and those who arrested him. After being a paid informant for nine months, he was finally arrested and taken to Oberürsel for investigation. Barbie was scared and angry when he was locked up, alarmed that he might be handed over to the French and shot. In a hollow attempt at defiance, he told his captors, 'You are not going to get anything out of me!' It took only a week of solitary confinement for him to change his mind. He began to write lengthy, heavily edited accounts of his activities in Lyon and admitted being a member of the SD, but claimed he was attached to foreign espionage rather than the Gestapo. A CIC officer reported, 'It is not believed that he had wilfully withheld information.'

It became clear to Barbie that the Americans were only interested in his post-war activities, and his captors seemed satisfied with his account. They prepared to release him to return to work with CIC in Memmingen. The French, however, took a different view when their investigations revealed that US intelligence knew of Barbie's whereabouts. As early as 1948 there were newspaper reports in France, and then official notes between the countries, demanding his extradition from Germany. CIC was faced with a situation that was diplomatically embarrassing and potentially explosive.

French intelligence demanded the right to interrogate Barbie. After first feigning ignorance of his whereabouts, two CIC officers took him to a rendezvous with French agents. He denied that he was Klaus Barbie, and the Americans warned the French not to ask unauthorised questions, breaking off the interview after only ten minutes. A second meeting was demanded, during which the French agents formed the clear opinion that Barbie had been given immunity by the Americans. No questions regarding his whereabouts or activities were allowed, although he did admit his identity.

'He is very important to the United States,' the CIC officer accompanying Barbie said. 'He does dangerous things.'

A third unproductive meeting convinced the French that Barbie had been offered full American cover. CIC's reaction to a statement by the French government charging him with 'murder and massacre, systematic terrorism and execution of hostages' was to hide him from French war crimes investigators. They decided to keep Barbie under wraps, claiming that the French security services were 'thoroughly penetrated by Communist elements' who wanted to 'kidnap Barbie, reveal his CIC activities, and thus embarrass the United States'.[25]

Barbie was moved to Augsburg, where he worked with spy networks designed to penetrate the French intelligence service, and employed agents to infiltrate right-wing Ukrainian émigré organisations inside Germany. He also used German agents to penetrate the local KPD (German Communist Party) and was paid a bonus of one hundred Deutsch Marks when he obtained a list of the Augsburg membership. However, his overall contribution to American intelligence was insignificant in comparison to his crimes.[26]

Continued pressure from the French government persuaded CIC HQ that Barbie should be quietly dropped as an informant without being told of his altered status. He continued to be paid for writing worthless reports while CIC made plans to spirit him out of Germany along a ratline – espionage jargon for a clandestine route used to smuggle out agents. They chose the Monastery Line, run by a certain Monsignor Kruoslav Dragonovic, a high-ranking prelate in the Croatian Catholic Church. Dragonovic, known inside CIC as the 'Good Father', was himself a war criminal. He had been a 'relocation' official with the Croatian Fascist Ustachi in Yugoslavia, a regime responsible for the murder of at least four hundred thousand Serbs and Jews. The priest fled to the Vatican in 1944 and created an escape route out of Croatia for members of Ustase.

Monsignor Dragonovic knew his business as the man in charge of the single largest and most important ratline, and the CIC used his services extensively over a number of years. In particular, CIC in Vienna used the Monastery Line to 'establish a means of disposition of visitors' – meaning prisoners – whose continued residence in Austria constituted a security threat as well as a source of public embarrassment to the commanding general. A deal had been struck with the monsignor, who agreed to provide false IDs, visas, safe houses and transportation to South America for a thousand dollars a head. In exchange, CIC helped certain fugitive Ustachi selected by Dragonovic to leave the US zone, even though many of them appeared on Allied lists of war crime suspects.

Barbie was duly given his new ID – Klaus Altmann – and Dragonovic was paid his usual fee to arrange papers and passage to South America. When Barbie went to say farewell to his mother, CIC agents took elaborate security measures in case she was being watched by French agents in search of her son. Then, together with his wife, son and daughter, Barbie was driven by CIC agents from Augsburg to Salzburg and escorted by train to Genoa, where the party was met by the Good Father. The family was issued with substitute passports from the International Committee of the Red Cross and given immigration visas to Bolivia. Then, on 23 March 1951, Barbie and family sailed on an Italian liner to Buenos Aires, Argentina. CIC HQ congratulated themselves on a job well done. Those involved were commended for the 'extremely efficient manner in which the final disposal of an extremely sensitive individual was handled. This case is considered closed.'[27]

Klaus Barbie took up residence in Bolivia, where at first he was reduced to begging from fellow Germans and took on the appearance of a tramp. Later, he obtained a job managing a remote sawmill in a tropical mahogany forest where he attempted to indoctrinate bemused local Indian workers with 'good Nationalist Socialist ideas'. Barbie had been working on the estate for a month when he found out the German owner, who had emigrated to Bolivia before the war, was a Jew. Untroubled by his previous convictions, he remained in the man's employ for a further three years.

Barbie was sentenced to death *in absentia* by French courts in 1952, and again in 1954, for the murder of members of the Résistance. He was granted Bolivian nationality in 1957 and made himself useful to subsequent right-wing military regimes. He became financially solvent after founding his own sawmill and began to boast of his more acceptable wartime experiences to fellow members of the town's racially exclusive German club. His open enthusiasm for Nazism was not even dulled when Mossad commandos from Israel kidnapped Adolf Eichmann in Argentina. And when the West German ambassador visited the German club in La Paz, Barbie responded to a toast by shouting, 'Heil Hitler!'[28]

The Vietnam War temporarily turned Barbie into a rich man when there was a large demand for chinin, the bark used to make quinine. In 1965 US Army intelligence remembered their embarrassing asset and moved to reactivate Barbie as an agent. The plan was scotched by the CIA after enquiries made by Senator Jacob Javits regarding America's employment of war criminals as intelligence agents. But although the CIA, US Army and State Department all knew that Klaus Altmann was Klaus Barbie, neither body felt obliged to inform the French or German governments, both of which had outstanding legal files on him.

No one informed US Immigration either, and in 1970 Barbie visited America on two occasions. As a partner in the state-owned Transmaritima shipping line, he had developed close connections with the Bolivian military and was suspected of transporting large quantities of arms. He was granted a diplomatic passport by Bolivia and used it to visit Germany. Barbie's particular expertise was called upon when Hugo Banzer, a notoriously oppressive military dictator even by South American standards, took over the government in 1971. Barbie was given power to create internment camps for the regime's political enemies where torture and execution were common. He also served in the Bolivian secret police and was involved in drug smuggling.[29]

The public prosecutor in Munich recommended dropping the Barbie case in 1971 on the legal grounds that a German court could not prosecute cases involving Nazi crimes against France. News of this reached Serge and Beate Klarsfeld in Paris, a couple who had dedicated their lives to hunting down Nazi war criminals.

Serge Klarsfeld had lived as a child with his family in Nice during the war, where five thousand French Jews and as many as twenty thousand Jewish refugees had taken refuge under the tolerant jurisdiction of the Italians. The Klarsfelds themselves were refugees from Romania. The fall of Mussolini and the armistice meant the withdrawal of the Italians from occupied France, as the army demobilised and fled across the border. The Nazis entered Nice and began a ruthless manhunt during which they searched hotels and Jewish homes, and stopped trains and cars leaving the city.[30] On the night of 30 September 1943, the Gestapo raided the home of the Klarsfelds. The father had built a false space in the rear of a cupboard to hide the family in just such an event, and they squeezed into the airless refuge the moment they heard the Gestapo pound on the apartment door. To refuse to answer meant that the Germans would break the door down. The father let them in and explained that his wife and children were away in the country. The Gestapo searched the apartment and actually opened the door to the cupboard, but suspected nothing. The last that Serge Klarsfeld saw of his father was a hand appearing in the cupboard to take the front door keys from his wife. Their hands touched in the dark. The father was careful to lock the front door after him so that nothing would seem out of order. The Gestapo sent him to his death in Auschwitz.

Beate, a German Protestant, felt a profound need to expiate the crimes of her country, one of which was the murder of the father of the man she loved. She was enraged that known Nazis were allowed to remain free 'because of the apathy of governments'.[31] Her father had served in the Wehrmacht and she felt that her parents' generation appeared indifferent to the crimes of the Nazis and had learned nothing from the great disaster that had overcome them.

Serge and Beate Klarsfeld launched a relentless publicity campaign against Klaus Barbie that gathered increasing momentum over time. Beate organised a successful demonstration outside the court house in Munich to get the case reopened. The couple researched the assumed name that Barbie lived under and obtained photos of him. Two taken in 1943, and another in La Paz in 1968, were given to anthropometric experts – scientists who determine similarities in people by minute analysis of facial features. Once it had been established that Klaus Altmann was definitely Barbie, the next step was to persuade the French government to demand extradition. The Klarsfelds released the photos to the press to put pressure on the bureaucracy in France to make a move. As a result, journalists in South America swarmed around Barbie, who protested, 'I am not Klaus Barbie but Klaus Altmann, a former lieutenant in the Wehrmacht. I've never heard of Klaus Barbie and I've never changed my identity.'

Beate Klarsfeld travelled to La Paz to publicise the case, which became an international issue. Barbie was paid two thousand dollars to appear on French television, where he changed his previous story and admitted to being a member of the Waffen-SS who had served in Holland, Russia and France. He said he had been in Lyon, but not as Klaus Barbie. He claimed not to be able to speak French, but then said fluently in the language, 'I am not a murderer, I am not a torturer.'

A change of government in Bolivia removed Barbie's protection, and France finally demanded his extradition. This was problematical as there was no formal extradition agreement between the countries, besides which Barbie was not French. But Beate travelled once more to La Paz to keep the issue alive, accompanied by a woman who had lost a husband and three children as a result of Barbie. The women chained themselves to a bench outside his office.

The Bolivians arrested Barbie on charges that he had defaulted on a contract with the state-owned mining corporation, owing ten thousand dollars. He was hustled on to a Bolivian military jet and flown to French Guiana, and transferred at dawn under tight security to a French military transport plane. He was flown directly to Lyon and taken to Monluc, the prison where he had incarcerated and tortured so many of his victims. He remained unrepentant. 'I did my duty. I have forgotten. If they have not forgotten, that is their business.'[32]

While Barbie sat in jail awaiting trial in Lyon, an extraordinary report of his dealings with US intelligence was delivered to the US attorney general. It was the result of a highly unusual six-month investigation triggered by Barbie's abrupt expulsion from Bolivia. 'As the investigation of Klaus Barbie has shown, officers of the US government were directly responsible for protecting a person wanted by the government of France on criminal charges and in arranging his escape from the law. As a direct result of that action, Klaus Barbie did not stand trial in 1950; he spent thirty-three years as a free man and a fugitive from justice.' The US issued an unprecedented formal diplomatic apology to France.

The original death sentences passed upon Barbie in the 1950s were no longer valid under French law because of the statute of limitation. He was now charged with eight new counts of crimes against humanity. These included the liquidation of Jews arrested at the UGIF in Lyon on the day Michel had been present; the deportation of six hundred and fifty men, women and children on the last French transport to Auschwitz; the torture and execution of scores of Lyon's Jews; and the deportation of fifty-two Jewish children from an orphanage in the village of Izieu.

Of all Barbie's monstrous crimes, the murder of the orphans was the most heartless and pointless, carried out only weeks before the end of the war. Izieu, a tiny, remote village of grey stone houses and thirty inhabitants, had scarcely been affected by the war. A Jewish couple who had fled the anti-Semitism of Poland in 1939 had rented an old manor house there at the end of 1942 and converted it into an orphanage. The village initially came under the jurisdiction of the Italian zone and the orphanage was left alone throughout 1943. Most of the children had spent time in French prison camps from which their parents had been deported to their deaths. A young teacher, who came fifteen kilometres each day from the nearest town, noticed how old the children were for their years. 'They were children who had already lived . . . they never talked about themselves, their families or their lives. They never said anything. They were very secretive. They were used to being distrustful. They explained nothing, they said nothing.'[33]

The orphans had suffered horribly, but found refuge in the shabby, rambling manor house that became their new home. In summer, they swam in the rivers and walked in the mountains, and in winter enjoyed snowball fights and tobogganing. They drew pictures for their murdered parents and wrote letters to them. The children retreated into a quiet rural life despite wartime scarcity and hardship.

The Italians left in September 1943, and when the Germans took over there was concern. A Jewish doctor from a neighbouring village was deported, but the orphanage remained untouched. Life continued its tranquil and uneventful course, although the adults lived in a state of permanent anxiety. Madame Sabin Slatin, co-founder of the orphanage with her husband Miron, left for a few days to search for safer premises, and while she was away a dozen German soldiers arrived from Lyon. They drove up in two trucks, followed by Gestapo officers and Milice in an open convertible, and pulled into the courtyard of the manor house. The children were dragged from a breakfast of hot chocolate and bread.

A local farmhand witnessed what happened next: 'The Germans were loading the children into the trucks brutally, as if they were sacks of potatoes. Most of them were frightened and crying. The little ones who didn't know what was going to happen were frightened by all the violence. But the older ones knew well where they were going. I knew it was finished for them.' The children called out to the farmer, and he walked towards them, but a soldier blocked his way and slammed him in the ribs with the stock of a rifle. One of the older boys tried to jump from the back of a truck but was grabbed, beaten and kicked. 'A German came up to me,' the farmer said. 'I'm sure it was Barbie. It's simply a face one does not forget. For a moment he looked at me, spoke to another German, then said, "Get out!" I left, walking backwards.'[34]

The children and the adult staff from the orphanage were driven to Montluc prison. That night a telex was sent to SD HQ in Paris: 'This morning, the Jewish children's home Colonie d'Enfants in Izieu (Ain) was closed. Forty-one children in all, aged three to thirteen, were pulled from the nest. In addition, the arrest took place of all the Jewish personnel, that is to say ten persons, including five women. We were not able to find any money or other valuables.' The telex was signed 'Klaus Barbie'.[35]

The following day the children were put on a passenger train to Drancy. They were under guard and the older boys were manacled. Miron Slatin and two of the most senior boys were shot at the French fortress Revel. Less than a week later thirty-four of the forty-four children were deported to Auschwitz, along with three hundred other children, on a train carrying a total of fifteen hundred Jews. The journey took two days, and when they arrived they were lined up hand-in-hand on the ramp of the concentration camp in rows of five. The children were all gassed later the same day.

It took four years of legal wrangling after Michel's first confrontation with Barbie before the actual trial finally got under way. It was not until 11 May 1987 that the defendant stepped into the Lyon courtroom to face his accusers. Michel approached his own day in court with feelings both of foreboding and high expectation. He dreaded the emotion and memories that Barbie would inevitably stir, but nurtured the simple hope that the trial would force France to face a dark side of its recent history. Even though Vichy was not in the dock, Michel believed that the shameful story of collaboration and betrayal could not fail to be exposed.

The actual experience in court, and the trial itself, were to prove a bitter disappointment. Michel arrived to find an empty chair instead of the defendant. 'It was a terrible anti-climax for me. I had prepared myself both intellectually and emotionally for the confrontation with Barbie. But the whole trial was conducted with Barbie absent, which was his right under French law. He remained in his comfortable double cell.'

At first, the absence of the man himself confused and threw Michel. Then, as its significance sank in, he became enraged. 'Where is the defendant?' he cried out angrily. 'I expected to confront him! But what I see is an empty chair behind bullet-proof glass. Empty! While the defendant Barbie is comfortable in his two-room apartment next door. To me this is unacceptable!'

Michel then gave a detailed account of the visit in February 1943 to the UGIF offices in Lyon and his subsequent encounter with Barbie. The single exchange Michel had with Barbie's defence lawyer, Jacques Vergès, was when the attorney asked for the names of people arrested in the office. Michel explained that the only people he recognised were café acquaintances, and even if he had once known their names he could not remember them after almost fifty years.

'I believed Michel's evidence absolutely,' Serge Klarsfeld, who was one of the prosecuting attorneys, said. 'I knew it was true, and the police knew it was true, because when at the very beginning Michel came to us in Paris he gave us accurate details about the raid on UGIF. He could not have known them unless he was there on that day. But I feared a catastrophe when he gave his testimony in court before a jury, and there was a catastrophe. The jury wanted to see a meek, modest man with sad stories about treatment by Barbie – they wanted a victim. They did not want somebody who was aggressive and defiant and who challenged the procedure of the court. It was not a truth some of them were prepared to believe. There were some witnesses for the prosecution who were lying. But they were old, or crying, or seemed broken, so they were believed. It is a great lesson about the truth people are prepared to believe.'

In addition to his angry demand to have Barbie brought before him in court, Michel had also given his evidence in an anecdotal manner that included an account of his premonition on the stairs of the building, and hearing voices warning him of the presence of the Gestapo. 'I was naïve. I expected to be asked to show documents proving I had been with the Résistance, which I had with me, to establish my credibility. I expected to show the report, signed and stamped by Dax of the Résistance in 1944, of my arrest by the Gestapo in Lyon the previous year, and my subsequent escape. But I was asked no questions by the prosecution and was not given an opportunity to present the documents to the jury.'

Alarmed that some members of the jury did not seem to accept Michel's account, the chief prosecutor, Pierre Truche, asked for the testimony to be recused. The prosecutor later received Michel in Paris and explained the reasons for his action. He said that as he had listened to the evidence he was reminded of the line by the seventeenth-century French poet Nicolas Boileau: '*Le vrai peut quelquefois n'être pas vrai semblable*' – The truth is sometimes unlikely. He explained that he was unable to base the prosecution on testimony that was unlikely, even if true. To convict Barbie, irrefutable documentary evidence was needed, linking him to the crimes.

The experience left Michel deeply wounded and caused him as much pain as anything in his life. A subsequent careless mis-translation of the English subtitles for the documentary on Barbie, *Hotel Terminus*, was yet another blow when it gave the impression that Truche had found the testimony 'inconsistent', a word he had never used. He had actually said Michel's story did not gel for the jury. After the post-war attacks from Mahl and Knittel, the Barbie trial almost provided the hundredth blow of the whip, and Michel staggered beneath it. 'Not to be believed after what I had been through! To have my integrity questioned! I felt my whole life was dismissed. It was deeply disturbing to me. I was wounded not by my enemies but by those for whom I stood up. It was immensely painful – not for days or weeks, but for ever. I wish I had never gone to the Barbie trial. A hundred times!'

The trial of Klaus Barbie was stood on its head by the defence in the same manner as the appeals of Emil Mahl and Gustav Knittel. Once again the victims of war crimes would be cast as the perpetrators, and it would not be the accused Nazi murderer who would be on trial but France herself. And not the collaborationist Vichy government, but the colonial French administration that had ruled Algeria, Indochina and its African colonies. The truth was given a rough ride as forces of the extreme right and the extreme left united to defend the indefensible.

A wealthy Swiss banker, François Genoud, who was a declared Nazi both during and after the Second World War, had stepped forward to bankroll Barbie's defence. Genoud had appealed to the extreme-left lawyer Jacques Vergès for help, and the attorney flew to Geneva to confer with the Nazi paymaster. This unlikely couple had more in common than at first appeared in that they shared a deep and fundamental antipathy towards Israel. Genoud funded Arab liberation movements of the extreme left, while Vergès had defended Arab terrorism. The lawyer had flown to Lyon to meet his new Nazi client and was appointed as the mastermind for the defence. From now on Barbie would merely be a pawn in an elaborate political agenda.

On the surface, Jacques Vergès appeared quintessentially, almost affectedly, like a member of the French establishment. He dressed in the immaculate, formal style of a lawyer, worked at a Louis XV desk in his office, and boasted old Flemish tapestries on the wall. But his entire life and political philosophy had been shaped by the conviction that the culture in which he was immersed secretly dismissed him as a colonial half-caste. Vergès was half Vietnamese, and therein lay the root of his intellectual and political rage against France. He was born a twin in Thailand in 1925 – then known as the Kingdom of Siam – where his father, a doctor and diplomat, had married a Vietnamese woman. She died when the twins were only three years old. The children seem to have been brought up by their father in a poisonous atmosphere of resentment and hate. As a young man Vergès saw the world through a distorting prism of racism, while his twin brother received a life sentence when he murdered the man competing with his father for a minor political position.

As a student in Paris, Vergès became a Communist and president of the Association of Colonial Students at the Sorbonne. One of the more active members was the young Cambodian Pol Pot, who became a lifelong friend. (Pol Pot went on to become leader of the Khmer Rouge and the architect of the mass murder of more than a million of his fellow countrymen.) The French Communist Party sent Vergès to Prague for four years in 1950, where he met Josef Stalin. He left the party when it failed to take a radical position against France over Algeria, insisting that French crimes in Algeria were as bad as Nazi crimes in the Second World War.

Vergès became well-known for defending Arab terrorists, and his court tactics were so aggressive that he was jailed for two months and temporarily lost his licence to practise law. In 1962 he moved to Algeria, converted to Islam and married an Algerian woman whom he had defended against charges of placing bombs in cafés.[36] (The conversion had a practical side as the lawyer was already married with children in France.) He spent his honeymoon in China, where he met Chairman Mao and became an avid Maoist, and when he returned to Paris he edited the Maoist review *Révolution*. (It was Vergès who sent Régis Debray to Bolivia to hunt for Ché Guevara.)

He now adopted a new enemy: Israel. Fundamentally opposed to the existence of the Jewish state, he defended Palestinian terrorists charged with hijacking an El Al plane. He argued that the act was political, not criminal, and that Israel was to blame for the passengers' deaths. This outrageous claim attracted international notoriety, but did nothing to help his clients, who were found guilty. Most of Vergès's clients were found guilty, despite all the rhetoric and political posturing. The press began to call him Maître Guillotine.

In 1970, Vergès disappeared. Left-wing conspiracy buffs believed him to have been murdered by Mossad, while his enemies secretly hoped it might be so. He did not reappear until 1978, when rumours from the right suggested he had spent the time with his friend Pol Pot in Cambodia and with Palestinian guerrillas in the Lebanon. 'I am a discreet man,' Vergès said when questioned about the eight-year gap in his life. 'I stepped through the looking-glass where I served an apprenticeship. I have come back battle-hardened – note that word, it's the right one – and optimistic.'[37]

Once again he picked up radical cases, defending neo-Nazi bombers and Armenian terrorists, and used the courts as a platform from which to attack his political enemies. He continued to lose many cases, and some clients went to jail for long periods. The high-profile Barbie trial provided a magnificent stage, complete with an international audience, for him to vent his rage both against the French establishment and Israel.

Essentially, Vergès argued that if France could try a man for crimes committed forty years earlier, while operating under orders from a foreign government, then France herself was equally guilty of crimes against humanity in Indochina, Algeria and Africa. The lawyers he assembled for the defence team were all from Third World countries: 'In this trial made in the name of humanity it is important that the defence is made of the colours of the human rainbow: black, white, brown and yellow.' There was not an Aryan among them, but the Nazi Barbie raised no objections.

The irony of this fanatical representative of racial purity being thus defended was not allowed to go unremarked. The French-Jewish intellectual Alain Finkielkraut – who would later describe Barbie in print as 'this paltry underling, this monstrous subaltern, this poor man's Eichmann'[38] – stood on the steps of the court and declared, 'We should be indignant over the situation in which a black man, an Arab, a Bolivian and Vergès – a man who claims his Asian ancestry – rise to the defence of a Nazi, and furthermore defend him in the name of their race, in the name of their non-European identity. Imagine you're in 1945, at the end of the war, and someone says, "You'll see, in twenty or thirty years when they accuse and condemn a Nazi torturer, it'll be the subhumans (that's what the Nazis called them) who will defend him." Everyone would have laughed.'[39]

Vergès continued to argue throughout the trial that Barbie's crimes were no different to those committed by the French state sitting in judgement, and that the defendant was a small criminal in comparison to French colonialism. The French were no better than the Nazis, and neither were the Jews, as Israel's actions clearly demonstrated. When Barbie claimed in a brief statement in German that he was only a cog in the machine following orders and should not be punished for doing his job, he was silenced by his lawyer. It was not the defence that Vergès had planned and could only serve to remind jurors exactly what Barbie's job had been and the monstrous nature of the Nazi machine for which he had worked. And when the defendant declared that he remained an honest Nazi, and had been doing a soldier's job in time of occupation, Vergès handed him a note. Barbie read it and took the advice to claim the right not to be present at his own trial. Vergès then had the stage to himself.

As the fifty-eight witnesses were interviewed over three weeks – each one numerically representing fifty victims – the intellectual and political arguments faded in the face of grim facts. One woman, who had been thirteen years old when Barbie tortured her, said she had never recovered from the experience. Another, who had been tortured nineteen times, described how her back was torn apart by a spiked ball on a rod, and was unable to say any more: 'I excuse myself from recalling the rest.' The evidence against Barbie piled up, the most damning of which was proof of his involvement in the murder of the forty-four orphans of Izieu.

Vergès dismissed the order for the deportation of the children presented as evidence by Klarsfeld as part of a Zionist plot to justify Israel's existence and its oppression of the Palestinians by morally blackmailing the world with the sufferings of the Jewish people during the Holocaust. He described Klarsfeld as a 'Zionist hitman' and said the order was a forgery. Experts proved beyond doubt that it was not. Vergès switched arguments. The Nazis were not to blame for the deportation and gassing of the children, but the Jews themselves. He held the UGIF in Lyon responsible for keeping files on the orphans and placing them in an unsafe region, and for collaborating with Vichy and the Nazis.

The plea made on Barbie's behalf by his Arab lawyer consisted of a long rant against Zionists and Israel for crimes committed against Arabs. He again claimed that Israel was responsible for the deaths of thousands of Palestinian refugees, and that 'the Israelis were just as guilty as the Nazis'. The attorney did not actually mention Barbie once, merely attacked Israel, until the judge finally silenced him for digression.

After six hours of deliberation the jurors found Klaus Barbie guilty of crimes against humanity. He was sentenced to life imprisonment. Vergès predictably proclaimed the trial a farce. Barbie made a final statement, speaking in French for the first time: 'I did not commit the raid on Izieu. I fought the Résistance and that was the war, and today the war is over. Thank you.'[40]

But perhaps the most eloquent argument against Barbie was made by Sabin Slatin, the woman who had founded the orphanage at Izieu, and the sole surviving adult. 'Barbie said that he made war on *résistants* and *maquisards*, but the forty-four children of Izieu were neither *résistants* nor *maquisards*. They were innocents. Neither pardon nor forget.'

*

Michel returned to America from the Barbie trial deeply wounded by his own experience and disappointed by the outcome in general. Barbie had been found guilty but the reality of wartime France had been further obscured in the process. Michel was bruised and angry, and felt that a great opportunity to expose the truth had been missed.

In the circumstances, he had to dig deep to find the emotional resources and stamina needed to resume the battle with the educational establishment. Fortunately, in this he had stalwart allies. Undeterred by previous rejections of Michel's revolutionary method, Marvin Adelson approached Herbert Morris, the Dean of Humanities at UCLA, in the early 1990s and asked him if he was interested in improving the quality of foreign-language instruction in the university. 'I sort of smiled at him,' Morris remembered. 'Given the fact that we were teaching eighty-six languages at UCLA at that time with what you might imagine to be a rather substantial investment of resources. Of course I was interested.'

Adelson told the dean – another gifted polymath with degrees in philosophy, law and literature – that he knew someone who could teach students of any ability a foreign language in days. Morris nodded politely, and while he knew the professor of architecture to be a brilliant and original man, he dismissed the conversation as fanciful. However, he agreed to meet and listened with fascination over a three-hour lunch as Michel spoke of his teaching method and his life.

As the men left the faculty dining room, Morris said, 'Michel, either more miracles are associated with your life than anyone I could possibly imagine or you're the biggest charlatan who ever walked the face of the earth.'

'Give me a weekend and I'll give you a language,' Michel replied calmly.

Despite an impossibly busy schedule, Morris agreed. He drove to Michel's hotel for three twelve-hour sessions, and on the third day woke up with a bad case of vertigo caused by an ear infection. 'The room was swimming around me but I told my wife I couldn't stay in bed – I had to get to Michel's hotel. Even getting in the damn car was a high-risk activity, but I was so highly motivated, convinced that I was on my way to acquiring a facility in Spanish. I don't know where my mind was during that day but I sat down and had another twelve intensive hours without a break for lunch. It was extraordinary. I had acquired a competence in Spanish after three days! A remarkable achievement. People ask me how it came about and I don't know how to answer them. It's a mystery to me. Michel has a charismatic quality, an intonation of voice, accompanied by extraordinary patience and self-assurance. I think he has managed to survive and achieve what he has done by having a degree of self-confidence that matches that of anyone I've ever known.'

Herb Morris talked the course up to the various heads of the language departments in an attempt to gain their interest. Nine months after taking the three-day course, without any continuation or revision, he was asked by the head of the Spanish department to take the university's placement exam, a test given to students to establish their level of competency in a language. 'I missed, by one question, passing the test that would have placed me as having a year of Spanish at college level. After nine months! Had I taken the test immediately after I would have been in the ninety percentile. I know that for certain because I began to audit classes in Spanish at UCLA. I would sit in on these classes and raise my hand, and was more advanced in my understanding of the language than native speakers taking Spanish Twenty-Five.'

A meeting was arranged between Michel and the heads of the language departments. 'It was a catastrophe!' Herb Morris remembered. 'A disaster! A fiasco! The paradox of someone with Michel's degree of self-confidence is that it can be perceived as arrogance and become self-defeating. A salesman would have gone into the meeting and humbly suggested he had something that might just complement their efforts in some modest way. I've had a lot of experience in academic politics and anyone who has any feeling for that world knows that what you have to do before you even dream of getting them to listen to you, or move in the direction of modifying what they're doing, is butter them up. It's just a given. Faculty are hypersensitive about their position, what people think about them, and how much they are respected. There are few groups more conservative than academics. They are distrustful of someone suggesting that there is a completely different way to do things, and that it is much better than what they are doing. They are simply not prepared to acknowledge someone else has got the answer and they don't.'[41]

Michel challenged the language heads' methods, calling them obsolete and ineffective. And he made it clear that he was not prepared to allow his method to be diluted, but wanted it adopted in its entirety. The French department wanted Michel to submit the course for them to study before they gave permission for a demonstration class. 'You can observe the demonstration,' Michel told them, 'and you're welcome to participate and evaluate the results. What more can you want?' The various heads of the language departments seemed to Michel to feel threatened and went on the defensive. From then on, academic politics appeared to take over. The head of the French department wrote a dense, jargon-laden memo rejecting the method – of which the department had no experience – on the grounds that it would cause 'a potentially serious disturbance'.

However, the continued support of dean, chancellor and vice chancellor – all of whom were Michel's enthusiastic ex-students – resulted in a small experimental programme being organised under the auspices of the UCLA's Summer Sessions. Fliers went out to the students asking them to test the possibility of learning a year's French in ten days. 'Guaranteed success! The University cannot guarantee that any student will learn what is taught in any class, of course – we provide the instruction, but the student must do the learning. Michel Thomas is so confident of his program, however, that he is willing to make a guarantee: if you fail to pass the proficiency exam after this course, he will provide additional tutoring at no cost until you pass the exam.'[42] UCLA even pointed out that the cost of the course was considerably less than its own twelve-unit summer intensive course. The appeal hoped to find twenty students willing to volunteer for the experiment. Two hundred and fifty signed up.

Ten days before the first students were supposed to begin, it was abruptly cancelled. 'The reason for this action is that the support of the UCLA's French Department was withdrawn, and University policy requires that all summer classes be approved by the academic department responsible for the area covered,' the director of the Summer Sessions wrote in dismay. 'There was considerable interest in this program among our students.'[43]

Clearly, if a ten-day course was on offer that was both cheaper than the university's own intensive course and also succeeded in meeting a standard usually acquired after a year, the department would look ridiculous. 'So the experiment never went through. And yet only I could have lost! If I failed I would have been wiped out, my reputation would have been in tatters. And they could have gone on teaching in the same old way getting the same level of results. And if the experiment succeeded all they had to do was think about it.'

*

Today, the educational establishment remains as impregnable as ever, but individuals, corporations, diplomats and film stars still beat a path to Michel's door.[44] (The French, to their credit, have recognised Michel's talents, and the Société d'Encouragement Au Progrès, which comes under the guidance of the Académie Française, have awarded him their gold medal.)[45] The waiting list for personal tuition grows ever longer. Among the stars Michel has taught are Warren Beatty, Candice Bergen, Tony Curtis, Bob Dylan, Princess Grace of Monaco, Melanie Griffith, Yves Montand, Diana Ross, Peter Sellers, Barbra Streisand, Raquel Welch, Natalie Wood . . . the list goes on and on and includes ambassadors, politicians, cardinals and industrialists. Woody Allen described learning with Michel as 'effortless . . . a psychological breakthrough, some sort of miracle'. The most recent star to be taught by Michel is Emma Thompson, who learned Spanish. 'You follow these threads he creates with you as he slowly weaves it into your brain. He knits the structure of the language into your head. It's magical.'[46]

And yet, despite all the plaudits heaped upon both man and method by those who have spent a small fortune to take the course, there are still those who remain convinced he must be a fraud. Perhaps it is all the talk of magic and miracles that puts people on their guard. When producer Nigel Levy approached the Science Department at the BBC to make the first film of the method, he experienced the disbelief and suspicion that has dogged Michel all his life. 'They rejected it out of hand. On the grounds that they did not believe it was possible. They were quite dismissive.' Eventually, a commissioning editor in the Education Department of the BBC agreed the method sounded fascinating, and it was arranged that Nigel Levy should take a language course and then be tested by independent adjudicators. 'I didn't speak a word of Spanish, so I chose that. I learned more in four days than I would have in years at any school or institute. Because the way he teaches is just so fundamental.' Michel's parting words were, 'It's important not to open any grammar textbooks – it will only confuse you. It's very important to leave it alone. Do not try to remember.' Nigel Levy found the advice impossible to take. 'It was all I could think about. I desperately wanted the technique to work for the sake of the film I wanted to make. I tried to revise my grammar and got thoroughly confused.'

A week later he prepared to take the various tests the BBC had organised. He was examined by the Cervantes Institute, which was given no indication of his level of knowledge of Spanish. He felt that by attempting to revise the grammar he had muddied the pool and feared he had made a thorough mess of the exam, but his Spanish was judged to be commensurate with a student who had spent a year at college and done homework. A second test was held later at the BBC with the commissioning editor and a teacher from a college of higher education. 'This time I was relaxed. And I sat and chatted to the teacher for half an hour or so and could express myself easily. He couldn't believe it when I told him how long I had been learning Spanish. He assumed I was intermediate level, which meant two years. It had been four days!' The BBC went ahead and commissioned the programme.

Michel was challenged in the documentary, the first time he had allowed even a part of his method to be filmed, to demonstrate his technique by teaching half a dozen students French in a single week of term. At first sight the volunteer guinea pigs from Islington Sixth Form Centre in north London – described as 'academically very average' – did not instil confidence. All had failed whatever language GCSEs they had previously taken and were studying for vocational qualifications because they did not like exams. One had been written off as a hopeless case with regard to learning any language, told to give up trying and advised to take up woodwork. It almost seemed that the language master had been set up. Unfazed, Michel guaranteed without reservation to have them all speaking French in five days.

The standard, institutional classroom was changed into a cosy den. Desks and blackboards were replaced with armchairs, carpets and potted plants. Bright lights were dimmed and curtains drawn. After three days of lessons the pupils appeared as transformed as their surroundings. Animated and full of excitement, they interrupted one another to enthuse over the joys of long hours in the classroom. They spoke of Michel as a magician, insisting he could anticipate questions, banish inhibitions, create confidence – even read minds. Their imaginations had been captured and, perhaps for the first time, they found themselves in the grip of intellectual excitement. They had discovered they were not language duds after all. The surprise and thrill of this unexpected revelation made once dead eyes shine. And, sure enough, after five days they were able to speak French to one another in long, complicated sentences.

The head of French at the school, Margaret Thompson, was shown at the beginning of the documentary to be thoroughly sceptical. 'I think there are different aptitudes for language. I think it requires things like attention to detail and hard graft that kids find boring and don't want to be bothered with.' At the end of the week, after witnessing the progress of the class, she was converted. 'Impressive,' she conceded graciously. 'Very impressive. As the students say, they have done in a week what normally takes five years. I think the real lesson is that the sheer interest in learning is enough for the students. Knowledge keeps them interested. He's really on to something here, something very important.'[47]

Michel has spent the whole of his life since the war teaching languages, and more than ten thousand students have passed through his schools. But he regrets that his influence has been minimal, a pebble cast in an ocean. 'I feel that I have not made a dent in improving the educational system. All we are doing at best is re-arranging the deckchairs on the sinking *Titanic*. It leaves me greatly frustrated that I have never managed to get the model school going as an educational showcase, and failed to set up the international university – although I'm not giving up. I have done and tried everything – and I mean everything – but have been defeated by an educational establishment that believes it is enlightened but is really autocratic and dictatorial.

'My idea in essence has been to create excitement. To succeed with youngsters where others failed. With those who are wild, even with delinquents locked up for major crimes. I attempted to expose them to the experience of learning, which becomes the excitement of learning, which becomes the excitement of living. All you have to do is turn the key to unlock what is already there in every individual.

'The desire to learn never really dies. It cannot be killed, it just becomes dormant. At all ages and in all conditions of life it can be awakened and can flourish. Every human being – I should say every living being – has a natural, inherent drive to learn. And this desire doesn't have to be created or force-fed. It craves satisfaction.'

Michel Thomas never really wanted to teach languages, or anything else – it just turned out that way. Teaching became a way of carrying on the various battles he has waged throughout his life. 'I fought, and continue to fight, an entrenched educational system to try to make it more open. I wanted to show what could be achieved with learning by removing the heavy lid and opening the mind. I wanted to demonstrate that anybody can learn. I didn't devise my system to teach languages quickly. I did it to change the world.'

X

At a time when Michel Thomas should have been celebrating the unprecedented success of his recorded language courses in Great Britain, and in the United States, a shadow was cast across his life. A long, mocking article appeared in the *Los Angeles Times* inviting readers to entertain the idea that he was perhaps a fantasist and a fraud. The piece succeeded in raising questions without answering them, but readers were left in little doubt that the paper believed Michel to be less than a war hero, and possibly something of a con man.

The original request for an interview seemed straightforward. The hardback edition of this biography — first published in the United States under the title *Test of Courage* in 1999 — had been favourably reviewed by the paper and briefly appeared on its best-seller list.[1] Michel was well-known in the city where he had spent thirty years and was happy to grant an interview.

Reporter Roy Rivenburg, accompanied by a photographer, arrived at Michel's hotel and asked to see 'the packet of letters'. At first, Michel did not understand until the reporter explained that he wanted to read the letters mentioned at the beginning of the book. These are the ones described as having such explosive emotional content — the despair of parents trapped in Germany facing deportation and death — that Michel himself had never been able to read them. He ignored the crude demand but did produce documents and photos and submitted to a four-hour interview.

The reporter reached me later in London by phone and it was clear that he was someone on the warpath. The relentless, negative nature of the questioning felt like a police interrogation. I warned Michel that I feared a hatchet job. 'I welcome scepticism,' Michel said. 'It is to be expected. I am going to talk to him again and answer all his questions.'

I was aware that despite all my efforts to provide convincing documentation, there were undoubtedly readers who might remain sceptical of such an extraordinary life. Perhaps the reporter, I reasoned, was merely exploring similar reservations. In that case, an honest investigation would do Michel a service. All we had to do, despite the reporter's clumsy manner, was answer questions and keep providing proof of the book's veracity.

Michel submitted to a second long interview, flying in from San Francisco especially for the encounter. The reporter now demanded details that would confound anyone's recall after sixty years. Michel was asked for a description of the foyer of the Monte Carlo casino in 1941 and the position of the slot machines; he was asked to describe the terrain surrounding Dachau, the position of rivers and bridges, and the layout of the camp; he was expected to remember the number of storeys in the building that housed the Jewish refugee association in Lyon during the war, whether it had an elevator, and if the office doors carried identifying plaques; he was asked the colour of various Nazi Party membership cards discovered in Munich.

Michel attempted to answer all the questions courteously, but finally he lost his temper. 'I seem to remember no sign on the door of the office of the refugee committee — but if there was one you will say I am lying? And I am supposed to remember the colour of cardboard cards after sixty years?'

I wrote to the editor of the Southern California Living section, Bret Israel, to ask about the editorial motivation of spending weeks investigating a proven Holocaust survivor, member of the French Resistance, war veteran and Nazi hunter. 'I am aware that there are frauds in the world feeding off the Holocaust, and that it is certainly the job of a newspaper to report on and expose such men. By anyone's estimation — even your reporter's — Michel Thomas is a million miles away from this category. Your reporter says that he seeks to make Michel prove the events of his life. And that he will write a fair and balanced story, and is open to hearing "evidence" on behalf of Michel. Has the *LA Times* put him on trial?'[2]

From the beginning, the thrust of all the questioning seemed aimed at discrediting Michel. The reporter insisted that his methods were standard procedure for the *Times* — methods like running checks on Michel for court judgements against him, and demanding documentary proof for every aspect of his life. There was even a request for a copy of Michel's birth certificate. 'I don't have one,' Michel said. 'Does this mean that to this man I don't exist?'

The investigation was certainly following different rules to those in force when the *Times* conducts advance negotiations with public relations companies to obtain access to a movie star. Feature editors regularly make deals with powerful publicists prior to interviews with celebrities and agree to questions in advance, even allowing them to choose favoured reporters and photographers. The bigger the star, the more concessions made by the paper. Clearly, Michel was to be held to a more demanding journalistic standard.

Later research disclosed that Rivenburg was an accredited member of the faculty of the World Journalism Institute, a division of God's World Publications, a Christian fundamentalist publisher located in Asheville, North Carolina, heart of the Bible Belt. The Institute, founded in 1998, is committed to providing a 'focused, rigorous and highly theological journalism academy' that trains Christian journalists from a 'biblical worldview' to infiltrate the mainstream media.

However, I continued to answer Rivenburg's deluge of questions by email and to supply copies of documents. I provided the names of people to interview who would confirm aspects of Michel's life — Serge Klarsfeld, a French lawyer and acknowledged expert on the experience of French Jews during World War II; Pierre Truche, a senior French judge who had prosecuted Klaus Barbie; Dr Ted Kraus, Michel's commanding officer in the Counter Intelligence Corps; and Professor Herbert Morris, of the School of Law at the University of California, Los Angeles, who had firsthand knowledge of his language skills. I provided copies of Counter Intelligence Corps (CIC) identity documents, Army documents and much more.

Ted Kraus, one of Michel's post-war CIC commanders, was duly interviewed by phone. 'During my phone conversation I disclosed several key events beyond dispute. Thomas's persistence and vigilance resulted in our capture of SS Major Knittel, a priority war criminal. . . . We visited the Grenoble area on leave where he introduced me to a number of his former *maquisards* who were delighted to be reunited with him.' Kraus also told the reporter that he had spoken to Michel in 1945 about his Dachau experiences and had seen the photographs — and had even asked for a set to be printed from his negatives. He said that shortly before he was transferred to another CIC unit, in Schwabisch Hall, he had secretly tape-recorded several meetings at a Nazi-decorated locale in which Michel, posing as SS Dr Frundsberg, interviewed and infiltrated a post-war SS terrorist organisation, and learned later that leaders of this group were arrested and tried before a US military court. Kraus was disconcerted, however, by the uniformly negative tone of the questioning. 'I sensed where he was headed.' Not a word of the interview would appear in the subsequent article.[3]

Professor Morris, of UCLA, was also interviewed by phone. 'It became clear to me, based upon the reporter's questions and statements, that the forthcoming article would be sceptical in character and that it would in all likelihood call into question the truthfulness of a number of Michel Thomas's claims about his World War II experiences. Because I had become concerned about the negative tone adopted during the interview I expressed strong reservations about the motives of the *Times* in what appeared to me an attempt at an exposé. Specifically, I told Mr Rivenburg that I believed it was undisputed that Thomas had lost his parents in the Holocaust, that he had been in the French underground and interned in concentration camps, that he had served with US forces in Germany. Mr Thomas had lived an extraordinary life, simply granting these undisputed facts. Given this, I did not understand why he and the *Los Angeles Times* would want their readers to question Mr Thomas's truthfulness and character.' Professor Morris also confirmed — 'without qualification' — the effectiveness of Michel's language courses from personal experience in taking Spanish and French. He concluded the conversation by saying that what the *Times* and the reporter were about to do was 'tragic'.[4]

I continued email contact with the reporter, growing increasingly exasperated by the petty, nagging quality of the questions, but answered them at length and faxed documents. These included the top copy of the bill introduced to Congress by Californian Senator Helen Gahagan Douglas supporting citizenship by Special Act of Congress based on Michel's war record.[5] Among others was a translation of a meeting with the French prosecutor, Pierre Truche, in Paris after the Barbie trial, two ordres de mission, one from Sécurité Militaire Française (French CIC), and another from the Alpine Division. I also sent various CIC documents — authority to operate civilian vehicles, orders and letters of commendation from Michel's commanding officers.[6]

Nothing seemed to satisfy. As soon as one avenue of enquiry had been exhausted, another one was taken up. The reporter became fixated on the technical status of Michel's military service, dismissing all documentation shown to him as insufficient evidence of service with the US Army or CIC. The book explains that because Michel was a stateless Jew and not an American national, his position with both the Army and the CIC was highly unusual, and possibly unique. I wrote a final email in exasperation. 'I do not understand why you are so focused on the "technical" nature of Michel Thomas's service in the US Army. Surely, the point is that he VOLUNTEERED and

FOUGHT with the US Army for NINE MONTHS, during a period of intense combat in France and Germany. He then spent a further TWO YEARS AND THREE MONTHS with CIC, during which time he did much useful work, including the capture of the US Army's most wanted war criminal.

'The CIC card reproduced in the book is an official document issued by CIC *identifying* Michel Thomas in order that he may go about his work. He did, of course, wear the uniform of a US Army CIC special agent at all times. You may insist that a private from the typing pool in some Kansas Army base, who never saw combat or even went overseas, is somehow a more "fully fledged" soldier than somebody serving with GIs in battle. Few American veterans would agree with you.' I suggested that if he wished to avoid confusion he could safely state that Michel fought with the US Army and served with the CIC.[7]

Finally, there was silence. I genuinely believed that the reporter had been convinced and had decided to call it a day. But the paper had invested too much time for no article to appear, and reputations apart from Michel's were now on the line. A feature duly appeared. Headlined 'Larger Than Life,' it dominated the front page of Sunday's Southern California Living section and covered an entire inside page. From the opening paragraph onward, the thrust of the entire 4,000 words was to sow doubt with the reader in regard to Michel's credibility. '"Everything is fully documented," Thomas says, "Don't take my word for it. Ask me how I can prove it." Easier said than done. Many of his claims are impossible to prove — or disprove.'[8]

Abundant documentary proof had been provided, of course, to support *all* of the major events of Michel's life. The article ignored anything concrete and consisted of a farrago of innuendo written in an unappealing tone. The reporter employed the technique of interviewing and emailing various experts who had never heard of Michel and knew nothing of his life, and inviting their scepticism by suggesting the *Times* had serious reason to doubt certain incidents. An example of the method used with almost everybody interviewed is the published response of an army archivist when told that Michel claimed to be at the liberation of Dachau: 'Who wasn't?' says Army archivist Mary Haynes, noting the proliferation of Dachau liberator claims in recent years. No mention was made to the archivist — or to the reader — of twenty-eight photographs taken at Dachau, the negatives of which remained in Michel's possession, or the signed reports from crematorium workers, or the subsequent arrest of Emil

Mahl, Hangman of Dachau. This was all fully documented from verifiable, independent sources but ignored.

Further doubts were sown about events that appeared to an outsider to have been well researched by the reporter. Had Michel been captured and released by Klaus Barbie on a raid on the Jewish refugee centre in Lyon in 1943? Was Michel really a CIC agent, or merely employed as a civilian interpreter who had exaggerated his importance? Had he discovered the Nazi Party Master File at the end of the war? Was his language teaching method effective, or merely an over-hyped, over-priced rehash of old techniques? His personal honesty was also undermined by suggesting that he could never have won money by playing *boule* in the Monte Carlo casino because the machine mentioned never existed.

The paper provided no hard evidence in answer to its own questions, but, using carefully crafted weasel words, succeeded in a devastating job of character assassination. The feature did irreparable harm to Michel in Los Angeles, a town where he had spent a third of his life and enjoyed a considerable reputation. Worse, it damaged his good name among those whose opinion he valued most — combat veterans from the Second World War, fellow Holocaust survivors, and the Jewish community in general. An invitation to speak at the Museum of Jewish Heritage, in Battery Park City, New York, was withdrawn. Other institutions seemed to turn their backs, while old friends subtly changed their attitude towards him. The Wiesenthal Center, in Los Angeles, which previously had always been friendly, now turned icy. Numerous calls to various people at the Center made on Michel's behalf by myself and researchers were not returned. A librarian at the Center, who had read the article, indicated she believed Michel to be a fraud.

One statement attributed to Michel understandably offended everyone: 'Other Holocaust victims could have escaped death too, if only they hadn't given up.' This is a grotesque misinterpretation of a view, described in detail in this book, in which Michel maintains that the stifling of hope of those interned in concentration camps was an indication of the 'total collapse of human morality' and 'an unpardonable sin'. To write that he believed camp inmates who succumbed to despair were somehow responsible for their fate, and to apportion blame to the victims rather than their murderers is the opposite of what he believed. It is also a remark, of course, guaranteed to alienate and enrage any Jewish reader. And the article's casual statement, 'His own family, he believes, died at Auschwitz,' betrayed the emotional indifference of the reporter. 'I do not *believe* they *died* there,' Michel responded, 'I *know* they were *slaughtered* in Auschwitz.'

A number of letters hostile to the article were printed in the paper a week after its publication, albeit tucked away between advertisements in the Southern California Living section, rather than published in Letters to the Editor. Ted Kraus, Michel's wartime CIC commander, wrote questioning why all of the vital information he had provided had been ignored. 'Yes, Mr Rivenburg, some people just happen to be more unique than others and "larger than life." You could have better served your newspaper and readers by probing the more challenging question of why this is so.'[9]

Rift Fournier wrote: 'Have you no sense of decency, sir? That story must rank among the major newspaper cheap shots of the new millennium. . . . The article proved nothing except that with lawyers on hand the writer was able to question the heroism and extraordinary accomplishments of a unique man. . . . Is Thomas guilty of living with an enormous amount of bravado? Of course he is, but that doesn't mean he's a fraud.' One letter described the article as a 'mean-spirited, tabloid-toned diatribe.' Another declared that the 'tedious, toothless attack was a disgrace.'

One letter from CIC historian Conrad McCormick seemed to support the article. Except, McCormick did not write the letter. It was cobbled together from emails, without his knowledge, edited by Rivenburg, and printed without McCormick's permission — despite a strict policy at the Times requiring a check on the authenticity of all letters considered for publication.[10] In a sworn statement McCormick declared, 'I did not write any letter to the editor of the *Los Angeles Times*. I recognise some of the contents of the letter published with my name as text from email correspondence that I exchanged with Mr Rivenburg in the course of our contact regarding his inquiries for the article. However, whatever words of mine appeared in the alleged Letter to the Editor were not written to Mr Rivenburg or the *Los Angeles Times* with the intent that they would be published.'[11] The paper has refused to comment or answer questions regarding this.

I sought the right of reply from the *Times* to the questions raised but was refused. A lawyer representing the paper was dismissive of a formal request submitted by Michel's lawyer for either a correction or an apology, claiming that the article was merely a book review, written within the accepted journalistic practices of a reviewer, and that Michel either could not or would not provide verification for his version of events.[12] The article, of course, was not a book review.

Indeed, the hardback edition of the biography had been positively reviewed by the paper — 'A story that highlights the power of the human mind and will' — four months before the publication of the article.[13] And the *Times* had since been bombarded with documentation to verify Michel's version of events.

There seemed no alternative for Michel but litigation, although most of his friends — myself included — strongly advised against such a course. 'You expect me to sit here and do nothing?' Michel said. 'To wait and hope they apologise one day? This is the worst time in my life — which is quite a statement. This is an attack on who I am — a denial of my life and my psychological self. What else do I have but my reputation? When I was in physical danger I always found ways to defend myself, but here I am defenceless. I *must* go to court to put my case before a judge and jury. I have no choice.'

Such a course of action would involve Michel in an unequal struggle against a powerful newspaper with unlimited resources intent on placing every legal obstacle in his path. In addition, the paper's entire staff would be obliged to close ranks against him — even journalists who had expressed their distaste regarding the article. And there would be those who would unjustly attempt to characterise the litigation as an attack on the First Amendment and free speech. 'This is everything to me,' Michel said. 'It is a battle for everything I have stood for. It is a fight for my good name. For my whole life.'

Michel was now obliged to commit most of his financial resources and summon the mettle of earlier days in a contest that would pit David against Goliath. The battle would be long, uncertain, expensive and emotionally draining. 'I found the article deeply humiliating and damaging to my reputation,' he wrote. 'To me the overall impression given was that I am a charlatan, a liar and a fraud and that I have exaggerated or fabricated the story of my life.'[14] From the outset, he declared that whatever damages he might win would be donated to a charitable educational trust.[15]

The Supreme Court has held that public figures — as Michel was defined — must prove that a newspaper published with 'constitutional malice,' a standard that requires proof of either intentional defamation or a 'reckless disregard for the truth.' Although a mass of documentation had been unearthed for the book that might reasonably be expected to satisfy most readers, a court case demanded that evidence meet a legal standard of proof.

Expert witnesses from the fields of journalism and linguistics, of a sufficiently high calibre to be officially accepted by federal courts in

California, were asked to evaluate the extent of defamation contained in the article. The verdict of Robin Lakoff, professor of linguistics at the University of California, Berkeley, for the past thirty years, was straightforward. In a sworn declaration, she wrote that she found the article one-sided, biased, and highly defamatory.[16] Sherrie Mazingo, professor of journalism at the University of Minnesota, was equally harsh in her judgement, citing inaccuracy, factual errors, undocumented facts, bias, lack of balance, and the critical exclusion of vital information. 'The reporter Rivenburg chose to disregard documentation that could have verified information that he presented in his story as lacking credibility. But what is perhaps most grievously unethical about the article "Larger Than Life" is the overwhelming presence of editorialising, bias, superfluous information and cheap shots. . . . the reporter woefully fails to meet the ethical standards of fairness and balance.'[17]

The legal team of the *Times* wisely chose not to defend the veracity of the article, but to concentrate on the paper's constitutional right to publish it. The lawyers adopted a strategy intended to stop the case from getting to court for a hearing before a jury, employing a legal mechanism to have the case dismissed. Fully aware of the dangers of a jury trial, the *Times*'s lawyers invoked the so-called Anti-SLAPP Statute. This had been introduced by the California legislature with the intention of helping to protect tenants' associations, environmental groups, and individual activists confronting large corporate developers with deep pockets. These corporations often used litigation to stifle protest by bringing libel actions against people who made statements in public meetings. The statute, therefore, aimed to provide a means to expose and dismiss early on, worthless actions filed for the purpose of chilling 'the valid exercise of the constitutional rights of freedom of speech.' But the statute's original purpose had now been stood on its head as a media conglomerate with unlimited resources employed it in an attempt to stifle the lone voice of an individual. The bully was crying victim.

The burden of proof was now shifted to Michel to establish 'reasonable probability' that he would prevail in the claim, or he would not even be allowed a hearing. Although a wealth of sworn declarations from people of impeccable academic qualifications had been presented to the court, and this expert opinion was supported by a mass of new evidence, the court found against him. In essence, the judgement stated that the article was defamatory but constitutionally protected, as it merely stated opinion and could not be proved to be malicious.

'Implications that Thomas lied about his past would be defamatory. . . . A reasonable reader or juror might conclude, after reading the article and considering the various points of view presented, that Thomas had in fact lied about his past. But no reasonable juror could find that Defendants intended to convey that impression.'[18] This makes no sense and seems contrary to simple logic. By the exclusion of documents, and the omission of facts, the whole thrust of the article was that Michel was lying. Otherwise, there was no peg for the article to hang upon.

The ruling seemed to have nothing to do with freedom of speech but supported the overweening and uncontested power of the press. The might and money of the *Times* — owned by the enormously rich *Chicago Tribune* group — had been wielded against a man attempting to salvage his good name. No right of reply had been offered in a town where there was effectively only one newspaper. The former Presiding Judge of the Alameda County Superior Court, Michael Ballachy, who later studied the evidence that would have been presented in a trial, stated that based on his experience as a trial judge, 'I suspect that if the case had been presented to a jury they would have found for the plaintiff and would have gone very high on punitive damages.' One law professor, who felt Michel had been dealt with unfairly, nevertheless suggested that he needed to see himself as a lamb sacrificed on the altar of free speech. 'I've never been a lamb,' Michel replied, 'and I don't intend to be one now.'[19]

Under the provisions of California's anti-SLAPP statute, the dismissal of the case automatically entitled the *Times* to be awarded attorneys' fees. The Los Angeles media law firm Davis, Wright, Tremaine, which represented the *Times* in the case, promptly submitted a bill for $120,000. The Court later ruled that the amount was 'clearly excessive' and that the lawyers for the paper had 'engaged in rampant multiple billing, billing up to four separate items for a single meeting or review of a single draft or document. Padding in the form of inefficient or duplicate efforts is not subject to compensation.' Defence counsel was 'ORDERED to submit new documentation of hours, limited to time spent and costs incurred on the special motion to strike alone, with all duplicate billing eliminated.' This highly unusual ruling was a humiliation for the lawyers representing the *Times*, who had been publicly reprimanded for padding their legal costs and attempting to cheat Michel out of money.[20] It was a sadly fitting conclusion to a shabby business.

Denied his day in court, Michel slipped into a deep and uncharacteristic depression. 'This man has stolen my life,' he said of the reporter. 'I now feel that even my friends greet me with doubt in their eyes. Most hurtful is that the Jewish community thinks I'm a liar.' I truly feared that his despair was such that it might kill him.

There was, however, to be a silver lining to this thunderous dark cloud. A knight in shining armour appeared from San Francisco in the north, mounted on in-line skates rather than a charger and armed not with a lance but a laptop. Alex Kline is one of the most experienced private investigators in the country, and he had been brought in by the lawyers to head the research team.

Kline's background was impressive. He had majored in human biology at Stanford before working at a major San Francisco law firm, and then he had gone on to law school. He later took an internship at San Francisco's Center for Investigative Reporting. Research was both his passion and his genius, and for the previous twenty years he had been employed by the most demanding attorneys in California, researching cases for litigation. He had worked as an employee for two of the country's largest corporate investigative firms, Kroll Associates and the Investigative Group International, before setting up his own business. He had earned the reputation through the years for being painstaking, meticulous, honest — and relentless.

There was only one problem. Kline was initially sceptical of Michel Thomas's extraordinary life story. 'I had never heard of Michel Thomas and my first exposure to him was from reading the article,' Kline said. 'Investigators take professional pride in a stubborn sense of scepticism, and my first reaction was that the reporter had done a skilful job dissecting the dubious claims of a man whose past was simply too extraordinary to be believed. There was precious little hard evidence mentioned in the article to bolster the claims of such an extraordinary life, and plenty of indication of the kind of bombast of a con man who had worked the gullible celebrity circuit successfully for decades, with hard-to-verify claims of wartime derring-do, and a too-good-to-be-true method of language teaching. The reporter's snide attitude about his subject was off-putting, but his research appeared detailed and thorough. Roy Rivenburg had succeeded in implanting in me a great scepticism about Michel Thomas.'

Kline reasoned, moreover, that a competent investigative reporter with the resources of the *Times*, especially someone allowed months to prepare a major article, could quickly run down the details of the story. 'It should have been easy to expose a fraud definitively. If the details did not fit together, if the documents and the witnesses did not exist, it would be very hard to maintain the face.'

Kline met with Thomas and talked to him at length, and studied the documents in his possession. 'He was inviting me to dig as deeply as I wanted, and he shied away from nothing when I asked him for details. This was precisely the opposite of what I would expect from a con man, whose greatest expertise is at changing the subject and dodging the explanation of details. It cost Michel many thousands of dollars to research these questions over the following year. Again, this was hardly the action of a con man intent on concealing his fraudulent past.

'Had we advanced to trial, a jury would have seen the same extensive parade of powerful evidence Mr Rivenburg saw prior to publication but ignored,' Kline said. 'But my objective was to go further and produce such overwhelming evidence that no juror could doubt the truth of Michel's World War II experience. I therefore set about bolstering the already abundant evidence of the biography with even more detailed evidence — more documents, more witnesses, more corroboration.'

In the years to come, both in preparation for a court case and long after a hearing had been denied, Kline spent thousands of hours — most of them unpaid — researching the facts questioned by the *Times* profile. Documents were sent to photo and handwriting experts for verification. Steven Jones, an 'archives rat' at the National Archives in College Park, Maryland, spent months hunting for fresh supporting evidence. Wartime colleagues were tracked down, and the curators of relevant museums were asked for expert opinion. People interviewed for the article were contacted, re-questioned, shown documents, and asked to share email correspondence exchanged with the reporter. As each question raised by the *Times* was researched, an abundance of new evidence, confirmed by the most exacting experts in the field, supported Michel's original account without exception.

'As I spent months methodically researching dozens of aspects of Michel's story,' Kline said, 'I found a wealth of evidence in every instance to support his "claims" for his wartime experiences.' Over time Kline became, and remains, a passionate defender of Michel's reputation. 'Everything has checked out one hundred per cent!'

Perhaps the most damaging attack on Michel's credibility was the suggestion that he had not been at the liberation of Dachau. The first troops into the camp on the day of liberation were led by twenty-seven-year-old Lieutenant-Colonel Felix Sparks, of the 3rd Battalion, 157th Regiment of the Thunderbirds. Colonel Sparks had been quoted in the article saying that he did not recall anyone named Thomas. Interviewed by Kline after publication of the article, Sparks said he had been told by Rivenburg that Michel Thomas claimed to have accompanied him and his troops into Dachau on the day of liberation, and only later learned that he had never said any such thing. Sparks said he could hardly be expected to remember the names of the hundreds of US military personnel who had been at the camp on the day of liberation, and added that he would not have recognised a CIC agent if he saw one. 'I never knew what those guys did — I don't even know if I was aware of their existence during the war!'[21]

Michel had told me that he arrived in Dachau in a jeep on the heels of the troops who forced the main gate. In my research I inaccurately identified these troops as Sparks's men, unaware that his unit had entered the camp earlier by a side gate. Michel had no way of knowing — and little interest in — the identity of the GIs in front of him. There were, of course, thousands of troops from two separate divisions present at the liberation of the camp, which was vast and spread over many acres, and the men were operating in an atmosphere of chaos, murder and high emotion. I emailed the reporter prior to publication to explain my mistake — and emphasise this was not a false claim by Michel. This was later twisted around to mean: 'Even his biographer admits Michel's Dachau claims are false.'

Ian Sayer, author of a history of the CIC, was quoted in the *Times* article as saying that although the records do not specify when the first CIC agents arrived at the camp, the first unit was not the 45th Detachment. But Michel specifically told Rivenburg — and I confirmed in emails — that he went to Dachau on his own initiative, for which he had both the motivation and the authority.[22] The records show that Michel's unit was at Schrobenhausen, less than twenty miles from Dachau, on the morning of liberation. No power on earth would have kept him away.

No mention was made of author Sayer's earlier statements when first contacted by Rivenburg outlining Michel's claims and asking if the stories checked out. Sayer had initially replied that Michel sounded plausible, and later wrote with the 'good news' that he had found a reference to Special Agent Thomas from 45th CIC. He then faxed a photocopy from a page of the unpublished, thirty-volume history of CIC: 'Agents Thomas and White, on their way to pick up an automatic arrestee, were informed at Hersbruck that the town for which they were heading was in Germans hands.'[23] This referred to an incident just before the liberation of Dachau and the battle for Nuremberg, when Michel found himself in a city still held by the enemy. Confronted by Americans in a jeep, the Germans promptly surrendered. Although aware of the event, I had not included it in the book because I had been unable to find verification. But not a word of Sayer's documentary support of Michel's claims appeared in the article.

Lieutenant Colonel Hugh Foster, who has spent years researching the liberation of Dachau, was quoted in the *Times* as saying that Michel's account differs from other eyewitness accounts and National Archive records. But the reporter never told Foster of the supporting documentation and photos, and repeated that Michel claimed to have gone to Dachau by tank and entered the camp with Sparks's 157th infantry.[24] When subsequently shown Michel's documentation by Kline, Foster wrote a letter stating that the evidence he had seen demonstrated to him that Michel was at the camp on or very shortly after the day of liberation — the best evidence being the arrest of Emil Mahl, Hangman of Dachau, two days after the liberation,[25] 'because the only information about who Mahl was had to come from the concentration camp.'[26] Handwriting expert Dr Timothy Armistead declared that the handwriting on Emil Mahl's original statement in Michel's possession was consistent with that on the prisoner's later statement presented as evidence by the prosecution at Dachau in November 1945.[27] A log of Mahl's correspondence while in prison at Landsberg also proves he wrote to Michel via the *Stars & Stripes* newspaper.

The article had completely ignored the photos and documents in Michel's possession linking him to the liberation. Peter Mustardo, a photo expert recommended by the New York Museum of Photography, examined Michel's Dachau negatives and photos. His expert opinion was that they were consistent with negatives and photos from the period of 1945.[28] Large prints were blown up from the negatives and sent to Barbara Distel, head of the Dachau Concentration Camp Memorial Museum. She and her staff examined the photos and formed the opinion that they could only have been taken on the day of liberation — or at most a day or so later. The museum's staff of photo archivists had never seen twenty of the twenty-eight photos and, therefore, concluded that Michel must have taken them as he had the negatives. When later informed that Michel also had negatives for at least three of the eight photos in the Dachau Museum archives, Curator Distel said that he must have taken those as well because they had never been able to discover the name of the original photographer and possessed no negatives.[29]

Michel had also shown the *Times* originals of the ten typed reports of the interrogation of four crematorium workers at Dachau. One is signed Eugen Seybold, who was photographed by Michel along with another crematorium worker dragging corpses and pushing them into a crematorium oven. Curator Distel confirmed that Seybold was one of the crematorium workers at the time of the liberation of Dachau.

The question of Michel's service in the CIC should have been settled definitively by the ID documents shown to the *Times* and the statements made by Ted Kraus. 'But thanks to a list Steve Jones found at the National Archives of former members of his CIC unit, I was able to locate a handful of surviving wartime comrades who had not seen Michel in nearly sixty years,' Alex Kline said. 'They all remembered him clearly, were outraged by the *Times*' treatment of him, and unhesitatingly went to bat for him every way they could.'

However, one CIC document from the archives, signed by Michel, does say 'Civilian Employee' — a term he always found insulting, and one dismissed as meaningless by American colleagues who served with him. Walter Wimer, a CIC agent who worked with Michel, made a sworn statement describing his role with the Corps, and the reality in the field: 'Michel Thomas worked in the capacity of a CIC Agent, and the uniform he is pictured in, with the US insignia on each side of the collar and on the cap, was worn by fully-fledged Agents, not civilian employees. We did have French officers who worked with our unit, from the Deuxième Bureau, but they wore French uniforms. Mr Thomas was sent out on missions, by our commanding officers, in the same capacity and with the same duties and powers as the other Agents of our unit.'[30]

The widow of Frederick White, another CIC Agent who served with Michel, provided a photograph of the men together in the uniforms of US CIC agents. (Agent White had been given a set of Michel's Dachau photographs. On the back of one, a picture of the corpse of a young man lying facedown, he had written: 'Looks as though the kid cried himself to death.')[31]

Any questions that a sceptic might harbour concerning Michel's service with the Thunderbirds were decisively answered when he was invited to a reunion of the 45th Division in Oklahoma City in 2002, where he was reunited with former comrades-in-arms. Henry Teichmann, whom he had not seen for fifty-eight years, greeted him warmly. As a young captain in the Thunderbirds at the time, it was Teichmann who had signed Michel's orders in 1944 releasing him from combat intelligence with the 180th Regiment and transferring him to the 45th Division. Another Thunderbird veteran and comrade-in-arms, Bedford Groves, who had served in combat with Michel in both the 180th regiment and later in the CIC, remembered how Michel undertook the workload of three agents.[32] Informed at the reunion of Michel's treatment by the *Times*, more than 130 Thunderbird veterans sent handwritten cards and letters to the paper deploring the article. No acknowledgement or reply was ever received, and nothing was published.

The article had also attempted to demonstrate that Michel did not discover the Nazi Party membership file. It quoted an account by Stefan Heym, a writer who worked as a journalist for the US Army before becoming a committed communist and settling in East Germany. Heym's account did not concentrate on the discovery of the file in May, about which he only knew what he was told by the manager of the paper mill where the documents had been taken to be pulped, but on the announcement of the discovery at a press conference the following October. He wrote a lengthy, fictional account of the discovery in the form of a satire of the Americans; his nonfictional account is highly unreliable. Kline tracked down Heym, who wrote to him only weeks before his death to say that despite the suggestion in the article that Rivenburg had made contact, he had no recollection of it.[33]

George Leaman, who wrote an official history of the Nazi files for the Berlin Document Centre, was asked by the *Times* to compare Stefan Heym's account and Michel's. Leaman declared that the former was more 'on the mark.'[34] But when contacted by Kline after publication of the article, Leaman admitted that he had not read Heym's account for at least eight years. Kline showed him a document he had just located at the Archives that corroborated Michel's account of the files having been initially discovered in early May 1945 by CIC agents. Other documents in the archives established that the agent, or agents, were from the 45th Division CIC — which consisted of fewer than twenty men, of whom Michel was one of only six who spoke German. A report written on May 20 records CIC having 'been advised' of 68,000 kilos of documents at the mill, going there, posting guards, and informing the authorities.[35]

Rivenburg chose to ignore an account published in his own newspaper, which quoted the manager of the mill remarking on the arrival of 'an American GI' in early May 1945.[36] Also ignored were the documents taken from the mill that Michel kept in his possession. These include an original letter written by Himmler to a Dr Ludwig Dittmar; a court case filed by Goering against Julius Streicher concerning the employment of a Jew on the anti-Semitic *Der Sturmer* and mentioning Streicher's sexual abuse of young boys; a lithograph of the hanging of Court Jew Suss in Stuttgart in 1737; an album of watercolours given by Himmler to Hitler's adjutant, Julius Schaub, commemorating the SS campaign in Greece; and a Nazi propaganda recording.

The undisputed authority on the Berlin Document Centre is Robert Wolfe, senior archivist for thirty-five years at the National Archives for captured German and European war crimes records and post-war occupation records. He unreservedly accepts Michel's account after a detailed examination of all the relevant documents. A Purple Heart veteran and combat infantry officer in the war as well as press censor and military government official during the post-war occupation, he also understands the reality behind the paper.

Wolfe was the consultant to the State Department for the Berlin Document Centre for more than three decades and has written official reports on the history of the records. Among these is a scholarly paper describing their discovery and capture at the paper mill at Freimann, the Munich suburb. 'Michel Thomas's most important contribution to history and justice is unquestionably his discovery, identification, and preservation of the Nazi Party and related records awaiting pulping at the Josef Wirth Papier-Papper-Wellpappenfabrik (paper-cardboard-corrugated paper mill). These records were the most important documentation of the war. If they had been pulped in that paper mill, we would not have been able to prove, in spite of the deniers, that the Holocaust or other victimisations occurred. Whatever success the victors had in the punishment of war criminals and the denazification of Germany was based in considerable part on the possession and access to these personnel records of the Nazi Party and its subordinate formations and organisations, discovered, identified and reported by CIC Agent Thomas. If any one of us could make such a contribution in our lifetime it would be enough.'[37]

The section in the article questioning Michel in regard to Klaus Barbie relied on the account of the debacle over the trial described in this book, but was heavily and unfairly edited. Again, no mention was made of a Résistance document, written in 1944 and verified by the French government, of Michel's arrest and escape from the Gestapo in 1943 at the time of Barbie's raid on the Jewish refugee association in Lyon. Rivenburg claimed to have spoken to Serge Klarsfeld, but the lawyer later denied he had ever been contacted. The article also quoted the French newspaper *Le Monde* as saying at the time of the trial that Michel had 'a taste for make-believe.' This was a mistranslation of 'À une manière de s'exprimer, à un goût trop prononcé de paraitre, de multiplier les détails.' An accurate translation of this would be: 'A way of expressing himself, a taste for showing off, and for overindulgence in detail.'[38]

The article even challenged Michel's account of playing a *boule* slot machine in the foyer of the Monte Carlo casino in 1941. 'Casino officials, after consulting their archives and various experts, say the type of slot machine Thomas describes "to our knowledge was never in Monte Carlo".' Contrary to the reported opinion of these unnamed 'archivists and experts', the Historical Department of the Société des Bains de Mer — the company that owns and runs the Monte Carlo casino — later provided Michel with a copy of the annual agreement between the casino and the maker of a *boule* slot machine from the beginning of September 1940 to the end of August 1941 — the exact period that he describes playing such a machine.[39]

In regard to Michel's language courses, the paper implied that they were no better than other intensive courses, could not be replicated, and essentially consisted of nothing more than a traditional technique re-packaged. 'Although vague on details, Thomas says his approach is to create excitement in students. . . . He doesn't want to reveal his methods for fear his ideas will be stolen or distorted.' Far from being vague on details or refusing to reveal the method, the language tapes at the time of the article's publication were available in French, German, Spanish, and Italian and widely sold in both the United States and Great Britain. In Britain, where Michel became a minor celebrity through his courses, they occupied fourteen of the top fifteen best-selling language audio titles at the time of the article's publication. To date his courses have sold an extraordinary one and a half million units worldwide.[40]

In the fall of 2007, Michel's British publisher — where the retail value of sales had topped $60 million — produced courses in Russian, Mandarin, and Arabic using teachers well versed and passionate about the Michel Thomas method. 'A vindication at last of Michel's belief that the power of his teaching lay in his methodology,' Katie Roden, a director of Hodder Education, wrote, 'rather than in, as some sceptics claimed, a hypnotic quality in his personal presence.'[41]

An analysis of all the language teaching courses on the market made by journalist Marcus Dunk in 2006 led him to write an article about the Thomas method in the *Daily Express*: 'They are the best language CDs of all time and continue to outsell and out-perform their rivals.'[42]

Jackie Kearns, the headmistress of a British school experimenting with Michel's method, was quoted in the article as saying it was merely an old technique brilliantly repackaged. She denies saying any such thing and insists she was misquoted and misunderstood. Michel had taught a number of thirteen- and fourteen-year-olds French for four days at her school, and their grades rose instantly. Her real assessment of Michel's technique — 'Outstanding!' — was buried at the very end of the article.

A great many people came to Michel Thomas's support after publication. By early 2004, nearly 400 people signed a letter of protest to John Puerner, publisher of the *Times*, and to John Carroll, at that time the paper's editor, asking that the paper consider the evidence it had been shown and publish an article setting the record straight. The signatories included scores of prominent people from the worlds of business, law, diplomacy, academia and the arts. Among them were Flint Whitlock, author of *Rock of Anzio*, the definitive history of the 45th Infantry Division campaign in Europe in World War II; Mortimer Zuckerman, owner of *U.S. News and World Report*; and Walter Curley, former US ambassador. Michel's celebrity students who have sent letters of protest include Carl Reiner, Emma Thompson, Raquel Welch and Warren Beatty. Actor Kevin Kline quoted William Shakespeare in his support: '"He who steals my purse steals trash, but he who filches from me my good name robs me of that which not enriches him, and makes me poor indeed." That this man at age eighty-eight refuses to let his word, his honour, and his name be publicly filched, I find inspiring. It smacks of the same courage he demonstrated fighting the Nazis.'[43]

New York Times columnist Anthony Lewis wrote, 'The case of Michel Thomas is indeed troubling.'[44] Alan Dershowitz, the acclaimed celebrity lawyer and Harvard law professor, described the battle with the *Times* as 'an incredible and horrible story.'[45] A group of supporters calling themselves The Friends of Michel Thomas produced a web site — michelthomas.org — reproducing all of the documentary evidence supporting his life story. But not a word about the controversy — neither the lawsuit, nor its aftermath, nor the hundreds of letters to the editor, nor the impressive roster of distinguished supporters — ever appeared in the *Times*.

Finally, out of a sense of profound disillusionment and disgust, Alex Kline confronted *Times* editor John Carroll. The editor was addressing a group of students on the campus of the University of California, Berkeley, with a talk, sponsored by the School of Journalism, aptly entitled 'Selling Out the First Amendment'. The editor spent an hour outlining his newspaper's commitment to high-minded journalistic ideals, such as the persistent pursuit of the truth — and developed an odd concept of his own that he described as the paper's duty to 'sovereign readers'.

But before the innocuous evening wound up, Kline rose in the audience during the question-and-answer period. He asked why the editor of the *Times*, or anyone else on the paper, had not responded to the nearly 400 letters from sovereign readers, respectfully requesting that the paper carefully reconsider the story of Michel Thomas. Visibly rattled, and so angry he almost came out of his chair, Carroll was contemptuous in his reply: 'I hate to get into this one, but I figure we're going to since we're in Berkeley.'

The editor told the students that his paper had run a story about a man who had written his autobiography. 'And if you read the autobiography you'd be amazed you'd never heard of this man because he pretty much single-handedly won World War II for us. It was a preposterous book, and our review of it was an investigative review. It debunked many of the claims in this book, and had some fun doing it, had a few laughs at the author's expense. . . . We were sued by this author . . . and the case was so weak that the poor author who sued us not only had to pay his own legal fees, he was ordered by the court to pay ours, which was a nice outcome for us.'[46]

Like the original article — even down to the snide tone — Carroll's account of the aftermath was wrong in almost every detail. The book is not an autobiography, of course, and Michel Thomas is not the author; the article is not a book review and does not pretend to be; I did not sue the paper and advised against such course. And while Michel did indeed have to pay the paper's expenses, this was only because California's anti-SLAPP statute automatically awards attorneys' fees to plaintiffs in defamation cases that do not advance to trial. Carroll did not mention that the court ordered the lawyers to cut their fees nearly in half because of double-billing and padding. The reader must decide which is the most preposterous, this book or the statement that the *Times* 'had some fun and a few laughs' at the expense of a Second World War veteran and survivor of a French concentration camp already in his late eighties at the time.

Carroll stated that he was 'very proud of that story — we haven't

retracted a word of it, and we don't intend to, because it was true.'
He refused to be drawn into a debate, and the moderator quickly
moved on to safer ground, but not before Carroll demanded to know
'where the money comes from for lawyers to pursue a case for years
that they've already lost?' In the few seconds in which he was
allowed to respond, Kline declared that all of the facts of Michel's life
challenged by the *Times* had been shown to be demonstrably true
and thoroughly documented, and that a number of supporters
believed so strongly that what the newspaper did was wrong they
were willing to work for free.

'In the face of such intransigence, and a wilful refusal to
acknowledge such thoroughly documented facts, I was at a loss how
to respond to such an angry and defiant public assertion,' Kline said.
'Carroll was terribly misinformed about the case, and had not read
any of the materials we had worked so hard to put before him, the
publisher, and others at the paper.'

After I received a transcript of Carroll's remarks at Berkeley, I
wrote to the editor at his Pasadena home and sent a copy of a revised
edition of my biography, which included much of the new evidence.
I asked the editor to extend me the professional courtesy of
reviewing the material concerning the legal battle with his paper. 'I
believe you will find the book and the nature of the case very
different from the version reported to you. I am appealing to you, as
a newspaper editor of known integrity, to review this new
information.' I suggested that a reporter might write an article
answering the previous questions raised by the paper, and this need
be neither an apology nor a retraction, but simply a follow-up. 'To
leave a shadow over the reputation of a brave man, a lifelong warrior
against hate who is now ninety years old, seems to me unbearably
sad.' I received no reply.[47]

The brute realities of big media were best explained to me by Bret
Israel, the editor who had originally commissioned the article. In a
telephone interview in February 2007, he told me he had not read
Test of Courage but felt that Michel's claims in regard to his language
courses were 'interesting'. He assigned the story, which he then
edited and ran past the paper's lawyers. He seemed blithely
unconcerned of the anguish the piece had caused its subject, and he
had shown scant interest in the subsequent legal battle.

Israel said that he had reviewed none of the new material
concerning Michel, had not read the chapter in the new edition of
the book concerning the court case, had spoken to the *Times* lawyers

only once during litigation, and had never had a conversation with the editor on the subject. There is no reason to disbelieve him, although the indifference displayed regarding the casual destruction of a man's reputation is chilling. The pressure of working on an important daily paper, he seemed to suggest, left little time for reflection. The dogs bark and the caravan moves on. 'I grant you that in a perfect world there would be follow-up on every story, but that just isn't possible.'[48]

Israel said he was unaware when he assigned the story to Rivenburg of the reporter's affiliation with the World Journalism Institute. He seemed shaken when I quoted from a link posted on the reporter's own web site: 'The brave Rivenburg had the guts to call Thomas out. This is one Jew who managed to get away from the Nazis and feed the fire of another of the great hoaxes of the 20th century. (Did you know that the gas chambers at Dachau were never used, except perhaps for de-lousing of prisoners to prevent the spread of typhus?)'[49]

The *Times* claims in its own published code of ethics: 'Our duty is to the truth. We pledge to seek and report the truth with honesty, accuracy, fairness and courage. . . . We will deal with people fairly and compassionately. In every case, we should strive to achieve balance and fairness in all reporting and news decisions. Fairness should be used in sourcing, writing, editing, photo play, layout and headline writing. Getting all sides of the story is the minimum requirement.'

This code has been trampled in regard to Michel Thomas, and a great newspaper has demeaned itself and perpetrated a great wrong. To ignore the evidence supporting Michel's life is to express contempt for those who suffered through a terrible time in history, and shows an utter lack of respect for those who risked their lives to fight the evil that caused it. If the well-documented story of Michel Thomas is not to be believed, then whose is? What combat veteran or Holocaust survivor can meet a greater standard of proof? What evidence will ever be sufficient for the sceptics?[50]

The arrogance and indifference of the *Times* and its editors to the serious business of character assassination — especially that of someone with the background of Michel Thomas — shocked Kline. He had backed up the events chronicled in this biography — already well-documented — with a wealth of new evidence designed to persuade any reasonable person who reviewed it. Until the confrontation with the editor, he had always held out hope that one day the paper would correct the record, but he now accepted that would never happen.

Long after most of Michel's supporters had reluctantly resigned themselves to defeat and accepted the gross injustice meted out to him, Kline battled on alone. His commitment began to seem hopeless — and many people advised him to drop his quixotic campaign — but he never gave up.

Denied any response to letters imploring the *Times* to look at the evidence amassed over many months of serious research, he began to work tirelessly to organise the vast amount of assembled documentation and witness testimony to lobby the US Army to review Michel's wartime record, with a view to awarding the Silver Star for which Michel had originally been written up while in combat with the Thunderbirds in France. Given the nature of Michel's service with the US Army — and that he was not an American national at the time and did not have an official army ID number — this was the most demanding undertaking of all. For two years Kline doggedly worked on the task, putting forward Michel's case.

After fruitless petitions to Congressman Tom Lantos, the sole Holocaust survivor in the US Congress, to Los Angeles Congresswoman Jane Harman, and to New York's newly elected Senator Hillary Clinton, the formal petition to the Army to award the Silver Star was finally submitted by Michel's Democratic member of Congress for New York, Carolyn Maloney, and Republican Senator John McCain. Nearly a year passed until finally, against all the odds, Michel received word in February 2004 that sixty years after his action in wartime France he was to be awarded the medal for his bravery.

The US Army overlooked the eccentricity of Michel's service and concentrated on his courage. The award of America's third highest medal for valour reads: 'The President of the United States of America, authorized by Act of Congress, has awarded the Silver Star to Michel Kroskof-Thomas for gallantry in action against the enemy in France from August to September 1944, while a Lieutenant in the French forces of the Interior (Maquis Commando Group) attached to the 1st Battalion, 180th Infantry Regiment, 45th Infantry Division. During this time in adverse weather conditions and against intense enemy resistance, Lieutenant Thomas successfully led reconnaissance patrols into enemy territory to gain vital information necessary for the continued advance of allied forces. Often he led as many as three patrols in one day and on several occasions volunteered to go on these patrols alone with utter disregard for his personal safety. Lieutenant Thomas was instrumental in capturing many enemy prisoners whom he personally interrogated and obtained much vital information. His fluent knowledge of various languages was beneficial in interrogating enemy prisoners and captured slave laborers and French civilians. The gallantry displayed by Lieutenant Thomas was in keeping with the highest traditions of the military service and reflects great credit on himself, the 180th Infantry Regiment, and the French Forces of the Interior.'[51]

In May 2004, on the eve of the dedication of the new World War II Memorial, old soldiers gathered at the site to witness the award ceremony. The medal was presented by Senators Bob Dole and John Warner, both decorated World War II veterans. Dole had spearheaded the creation of the memorial and took time from his packed schedule during the week of its dedication to honour Michel. French ambassador Jean-David Levitte was also present, as were Michel's children. An honour guard of Rangers stood at attention and presented arms. Emotion was high, as wartime colleagues looked on proudly. Among old comrades-in-arms were Ted Kraus, his CIC commander, and Bedford Groves, who had served with Michel in both the Thunderbirds and the CIC. Groves had insisted on making a painful and difficult journey in a wheelchair to attend the ceremony.

'The horrible conflict we call World War II took the lives of at least sixty million people,' Michel said in a moving speech of acceptance. 'An inconceivably large number for any of us to comprehend, and an inconceivable large sacrifice in humanity's slow groping towards the ideals of peace and freedom. The rubble was cleared long ago, the bones of the millions lie at rest, and a handful of us who survived are gathered here today. Veterans all carry the scars of that terrible war. We carry them in our minds and in our bodies. But we also carry the spirit of that time, and this is our gift to bear from the ashes of that awful inferno.

'We fought to destroy an enemy who sought world domination while carrying out the genocidal extermination of millions of innocents — including my entire family. It is our duty to carry on the struggle, by insuring that those who would distort, devalue, or deny our sacrifices be held accountable to the truth.

'It is with pride that I stand here today with fellow comrades in that worthy battle to defend both freedom and the sanctity of human life. I can think of no greater honour than to have my contribution to our common struggle recognized by you here today. I am deeply moved and humbled by this gesture from each of you, and immensely honoured to receive this recognition from the United States of America.'

The Silver Star ceremony received international press coverage. Michel was interviewed by the French and Spanish national television networks, and he was featured in a five-minute Memorial Day segment on CNN by Wolf Blitzer. The US Army's news service published a feature story entitled 'Sixty Years After Nomination, Veteran Gets Silver Star at WWII Memorial': 'In 2001 a newspaper questioned some of Thomas's claims, and a movement to authenticate his Silver Star picked up momentum. Key members of Congress got involved; the Pentagon reviewed his case; and soldiers who hadn't seen him in sixty years came forward to attest to his bravery.'

Two days after the Silver Star award, the Holocaust Memorial Museum honoured Michel at a large public event, Salute to Liberators, for his role in the liberation of Dachau. Introduced by the director of the museum before a large crowd, Michel was given a standing ovation.

It had been a week in which justice had finally been done and was seen to be done. Today, Michel's reputation is proven and secure.

Michel Thomas died in January 2005. There is no doubt that without the commitment, research skills, and relentless battle for justice waged on his behalf by Alex Kline, he would have gone to his grave a broken and unhappy man. 'I put my heart and soul into this case for years and it began to seem like something of a hopeless cause,' Kline said. 'But in the end it was worth it to see him honoured by the Holocaust Museum and awarded the Silver Star — his ultimate vindication.'

The obituaries of Michel in Great Britain were respectful. I wrote one for *The Guardian* and was interviewed sympathetically in the United States by National Public Radio. In fairness, the *Los Angeles Times* went out of its way to be even-handed, and the obituary writer gave the impression of a man walking on eggshells. Despite the award of the Silver Star and the recognition of the Holocaust Museum, the *Washington Post* relied almost exclusively on the earlier *Times* article for its obituary, and portrayed Michel as a bit of a rogue and an adventurer, a characterisation no one who knew the man would recognise. The *New York Times* published nothing.

For Michel Thomas, the war never ended. The experiences and memories from those years dominated the remainder of his life, as they have dominated this book. Wherever and whenever he traveled, he carried a suitcase stuffed with photos, letters and documents from the past, and he never went anywhere for more than a few days without this small holdall of history. Once, when he thought he had lost everything, he experienced uncharacteristic emotions of panic and despair.

The suitcase contained the haphazard archive of a long and eventful life and provided both anchor and backdrop in the various rented apartments, houses and hotel rooms he temporarily inhabited around the world. After a few days in any location its contents slowly spread, covering tables and shelves, until Michel was surrounded by his past. He rooted endlessly through the familiar disorder of his papers, often pausing over a faded document or creased photograph as if in a trance. Each item was a reminder of some significant event or person, brought to life by the emotional memory he had developed as a child.

An old love letter from Suzanne, sent from Lyon reminiscing about their days together in Paris, jostled with faded newspaper cuttings and pictures of his children. Horrific private pictures of corpses at Dachau lay beside a glossy magazine containing an article on the language course. Pictures of past loves were mixed in with ID cards from the Résistance, old CIC reports and correspondence. Photographs of Michel's mother and aunt were scattered over the handwritten pencil confession of Dachau hangman Emil Mahl. To me, the assortment was always a jarring combination of great love and absolute evil.

For Michel, the war continued and the enemy remained the same. The adversary was never really the Vichy government, or SS storm troopers, or even the Nazi war criminals that he captured after the war. The true enemy, and the one that generated instant, boiling rage, was the nameless, faceless bureaucrat who condemned Michel's family to death for lack of a quota number. Forever with us, in peace as in war, he lives on as the symbolic leader of those who do not care.

Michel continued to battle the cohorts of this great grey mass. It included the officials who side-stepped his numerous attempts to bring the dark secrets of the Vichy years into the open, and ambitious political opportunists on the extreme left and right who have manipulated the experiences of the victims of the Nazis to their own post-war political ends. It also numbered unimaginative educators who resist new methods of learning and are prepared to sacrifice a child's future to protect their own interests.

As a boy Michel instinctively admired and emulated courage. Later, when life became hard and almost unbearable, he came to value it as the first of all virtues without which no other could exist. In the war he conspired to surround himself with men of courage, from his French comrades in the Résistance to the American GIs of the Thunderbirds. In the soft times of peace and prosperity, when quiet and undramatic acts of real courage are often overlooked, he clung to it more than ever as the moral quality that stands between humanity and ruin.

But some human pain penetrates so deeply into the soul that courage is not enough. Even at his death, at the age of ninety, the precious family letters in the battered cardboard folder remained unread.

In Les Milles, when Michel thought he was about to be discovered by guards and transported to his death, he cried out to his universal God to be spared and he made a covenant. He never disclosed the terms of the agreement to another living soul, but his life suggests it must have included the promise to keep alive the memory of those slaughtered, and to struggle to prevent such a thing happening again.

Michel's much-vaunted charisma was really no more than the energy of his belief in himself and those like him. He believed in the inestimable power of the individual. 'I believe in the power of one. Never to give in. And that a person should never feel or say that he or she is powerless as an individual.' His energy remained boundless to the end as he left his base in New York to travel around the world, teaching for weeks at a time in London, Los Angeles or Monte Carlo. He seemed to be forever on the move. On the weekend prior to his death, he visited Charleston, South Carolina, for a Renaissance Weekend attended by political and cultural movers and shakers, flew on to Los Angeles for the ninetieth birthday party of the ex-mayor of Beverly Hills, and returned to New York to confront a punishing workload. After twenty years of serious heart trouble and ignored ill health — 'I have to keep going, there's too much to do' — he was felled by a fatal heart attack.

As a tidal wave of fresh hatred engulfs the world, Michel Thomas's example of a single man's struggle not to be overwhelmed by a previous deluge of evil offers hope. The story of his life records something more than survival, courage and heroics — it provides a portrait of a great warrior against hate.

ACKNOWLEDGMENTS

The first person I have to thank is the six-year-old child who made a vow not to forget the significant events of his life. This book would not have been possible without the originality and sensitivity of that small boy who was Michel Thomas. I also need to thank the adult he became, who early in our relationship told me, 'You can ask me any question about any area of my life and I will try to answer it honestly.' This has often been difficult and painful, but Michel always proved as good as his word.

I would also like to thank my lifelong friend Charles Fawcett for first bringing the life of Michel to my attention and for introducing us. Charles is one of the few men who Michel rates as a genuine unsung hero of the Second World War. As a young American art student living in Paris when the Germans occupied the city – before the United States entered the conflict – Charles married a total of six Jewish women he had never met to save them from deportation and death. He later worked with Varian Fry in Marseille in a dangerous enterprise smuggling literary and artistic figures wanted by the authorities over the Pyrénées. (Michel was unaware – because Charles had never mentioned it over the decades – that he went on to fly with the Royal Air Force and fight with the French Foreign Legion.)

Many of the French documents from the camps and courts, including much of the documentary evidence of the deportations in general, have been made available as a result of the life's work of the Parisian lawyer, Maître Serge Klarsfeld. His archive of the papers of foreign and French Jews deported to their deaths during the war, including many thousands of identifying photographs of the individuals themselves, guarantees that no one died unremembered. It is a magnificent undertaking.

For many years after the war, Michel's was a lone voice in his insistence that the Vichy government of France was not directed by Germany, but was an independent and enthusiastic proponent of home-grown fascist, anti-Semitic policies. It was not until 1977, with the publication of *Vichy France* by Robert Paxton – which met with a firestorm of hostile criticism in France – that this view began to receive scholarly support.

Similarly, Michel was first ignored and later contradicted, in his charge that the US Army Counter Intelligence Corps knew the true nature of Klaus Barbie's Gestapo past when they first employed him. And also that he was merely one of a number of known Nazis recruited by American intelligence. Even when the United States Department of Justice published its official report on the intelligence community's connection with Barbie, the government insisted it was an isolated case. Further research, most notably by Tom Bower in a series of books linking Nazis to the post-war scientific, banking and intelligence worlds, has proved that Michel's view was not only correct but understated.

And perhaps one day, some government, university or school might even be prepared to investigate Michel's method of teaching languages. It is a tragedy that this is not being done. At first the attitude of obstruction and rejection displayed by the educational establishment was a mystery to me, and I am grateful to Marvin Adelson and Herbert Morris, of UCLA, for an insight into world of academic *Realpolitik*.

There is, however, one gap in Michel's remarkable memory. Recall has been less than perfect in the case of the names of certain people and places from long ago. While every effort has been made to give the correct ones, these have not always been possible to verify. And some names in the book have reluctantly been changed by the author at Michel's insistence.

I am particularly grateful to Ted Kraus, Michel's Counter Intelligence colleague in Ulm, after the war. Ted gave me his time to explain a complicated world and reproduced numerous photographs for me. Thanks are also due to Nigel Levy, the producer of the BBC documentary on Michel's language teaching technique, for his generosity in sharing contacts and personal experiences.

I owe thanks to many people who have helped me in all sorts of areas during the writing of this book: Don Bachardy, Daniel Balado, Margaret Barrett, Sara Bodle, Livia Bracamonte, Taina Dundas, Jenny de Gex, Harold Goodman, Carroll Gray, Dorris Halsey, Donald Hawkins, Linda Howard, Sally Hughes, Laura Huxley, Hans Joohs, Behram Kapadia, Angelina Kasza, Alex Kline, Leo Marks, Charles Morin, Catherine Munson, Joseph November, Danny Parker, Walter Platz, Mike Reynolds, Patrick Robertson, Leslie Robinson, Andy Savoie, Emma Thompson, James Weingartner, and Darrel Whitcomb.

ACKNOWLEDGMENTS

I owe a particular debt of gratitude to my agent and friend Mark Lucas, who contributed time and effort far above the call of duty.

Alex Kline has generously shared the fruits of his extensive research conducted over more than two years.

And as always, I am indebted beyond words for the love and support of my trusted critic and confidante, Mary Agnes Donoghue.

PICTURE CREDITS

1. Michel's ID photo in Le Vernet. (Michel Thomas Collection)
2. Michel's mother, Freida. (Michel Thomas Collection)
3. Michel in Breslau, Germany. (Michel Thomas Collection)
4. Michel in Vienna as a student. (Michel Thomas Collection)
5. A French gendarme surveys prisoners in a French concentration camp. (Courtesy of the Contemporary Jewish Document Centre, Paris)
6. Prisoners arrive at a French concentration camp. (Courtesy of the Contemporary Jewish Document Centre, Paris)
7. The Vercors in the Alps. (Courtesy of the trustees of the Imperial War Museum, London)
8. Résistance fighters in the mountainous terrain around Grenoble. (Imperial War Museum/Comité de la 2ème Guerre Mondiale)
9. Mademoiselle Thérèse Mathieiu. (Michel Thomas Collection)
10. Young members of the Maquis are given a demonstration in the use of arms. (Courtesy of Halton Getty)
11. Michel in the commando outfit of the Grésivaudan Maquis. (Michel Thomas Collection)
12. Official French government recognition of military and Résistance service. (Michel Thomas Collection)
13. Citizens of Grenoble welcome liberating US troops. (Imperial War Museum)
14. *Collabos Horizontales*. (Imperial War Museum)
15. An old lady regards the ruins of her home. (US Army Military History Institute)
16. Giant Tiger tank used by the SS Panzer divisions. (Imperial War Museum)
17. Troops from Kampfgruppe Peiper in a *Schwimmwagen* (amphibious Volkswagen). (Imperial War Museum)
18. The killing field of the Malmédy Massacre. (US National Archives/Keystone)
19. Gustav Knittel. (Michel Thomas Collection)
20. Thunderbirds line up SS officers at Dachau. (US Army Military History Institute)

21. The centre of Ulm after the war. (Courtesy of Ted Kraus)
22. Michel at work in his office at Ulm as a special agent of the US Army Counter Intelligence. (Michel Thomas Collection)
23. The notorious Nazi and RSHA officer, Dr Frundsberg – aka Michel Thomas. (Michel Thomas Collection)
24. CIC ID document. (Michel Thomas Collection)
25. Michel skiing in the mountains. (Michel Thomas Collection)
26. Michel at the CIC Villa Kauderer in Ulm. (Ted Kraus Collection)
27. The children of Izieu. (Courtesy of Serge Klarsfeld)
28. Michel and Ted Kraus, head of Counter Intelligence in Ulm, in the mountains. (Ted Kraus Collection)
29. Michel collaborating with the enemy. (Ted Kraus Collection)
30. Klaus Barbie, the Butcher of Lyon, manacled and surrounded by police, as he is taken to the Lyon courthouse for trial. (Popperfoto)
31. Michel standing in front of the photos of many of the celebrities he has taught languages in his office in New York. (Michel Thomas Collection)
32. Michel with students from the City and Islington Sixth Form Centre, North London. (Courtesy of the British Broadcasting Corporation)
33. Michel after receiving the Silver Star. (US Army photo by Spc. Lorie Jewell)

BIBLIOGRAPHY

Ambrose, Stephen E. *Citizen Soldiers: The US Army from the Normandy Beaches to the Bulge to the Surrender of Germany, June 7, 1944 – May 7, 1945*. New York, Simon & Schuster, 1997.

Anthology. *Reporting World War II: American Journalism 1938–1944*. Two vols. New York, Library of America, 1995.

Amouroux, Henri. *La Grande Histoire des Français sous L'Occupation*. Ten vols. Paris, Robert Laffont, 1976–93.

Aron, Robert. *The Vichy Regime, 1940–44*. Boston, Beacon, 1969.

— *France Reborn: The History of the Liberation*. New York, Scribners, 1964.

Asprey, Robert B. *War in the Shadows: The Guerrilla in History*. Volume I. New York, Doubleday, 1975.

Baecque, Antoine, & Toubiana, Serge. *Truffaut*. New York, Knopf, 1999.

Bishop, Leo V., Fisher, George A., & Glasgow, Frank J. *The Fighting Forty-Fifth: The Combat Report of an Infantry Division*. Baton Rouge, Louisiana, Army & Navy Publishing Company, 1946.

Boileau-Despreaux, Nicolas. *The Art of Poetry*. 1674.

Bower, Tom. *Klaus Barbie: Butcher of Lyon*. London, Michael Joseph, 1983.

— *The Paperclip Conspiracy: The Hunt for Nazi Scientists*. London, Michael Joseph, 1987.

— *Blind Eye to Murder*. London, Little, Brown and Company, 1995.

Bradley, Omar N., & Blair, Clay. *A General's Life*. New York, Simon & Schuster, 1983.

Bruckman, F. *180th Infantry, A Regiment of the 45th Infantry Division*. Munich, 1945.

Bruckberger, Raymond Leopold. *One Sky to Share: French and American Journals*. New York, P.J. Kenedy & Sons, 1952.

Bullock, Alan. *Hitler, A Study in Tyranny*. Revised edition. New York, Harper & Row, 1962.

Burrin, Philippe. *Living with Defeat: France under the German Occupation 1940–1944*. London, Hodder Headline, 1996.

Camus, Albert. *Notebooks (1935–1942)*. New York, Alfred A. Knopf, 1963

— *Notebooks (1942–1951)*. New York, Alfred A. Knopf, 1965.

344

Cesarani, David. *Arthur Koestler: The Homeless Mind*. London, William Heinemann, 1998.

Chambard, Claude. *The Maquis: A History of the French Resistance Movement*. Tr. Elaine P. Halperin. Indianapolis/ New York, Bobbs Merrill, 1976.

Cole, Hugh M. *The Ardennes: Battle of the Bulge*. Washington DC, US Government Printing Office, 1965.

Cookridge, E. H. *Gehlen*. New York, Random House, 1971.

D'Este, Carlo. *Bitter Victory: The Battle for Sicily, 1943*. New York, Dutton, 1988.

Dippel, John V.H. *Bound Upon a Wheel of Fire: Why So Many German Jews Made the Tragic Decision to Remain in Nazi Germany*. New York, Basic Books, 1996.

Dupuy, R. Ernest, & Dupuy, Trevor N. *The Encyclopedia of Military History*. New York, Harper & Row, 1970.

Eisenberg, Azriel. *Witness to the Holocaust*. New York, Pilgrim Press, 1981.

Ehrlich, Blake. *The French Resistance*. London, Chapman & Hall, 1966.

Fest, Joachim. *Hitler*. London, Weidenfeld, 1974.

Finkielkraut, Alain. *Remembering In Vain: The Klaus Barbie Trial and Crimes Against Humanity*. Tr. Rozanne Lapidus & Sima Godfrey. New York, Columbia University Press, 1992.

Foot, M.R.D. *S.O.E. in France: An Account of the Work of the British Special Operations Executive in France 1940–1944*. London, HMSO, 1968.

— *Resistance*. London, Eyre Methuen, 1976.

Franks, Kenny. *Citizen Soldiers: Oklahoma National Guard*. University of Oklahoma, 1984.

Frenay, Henri. *The Night Will End: Memoirs of a Revolutionary*. New York, McGraw Hill, 1976.

Friedlander, Saul. *Nazi Germany and the Jews: The Years of Persecution, 1933–1939*. Volume I. New York, Harper Collins, 1997.

Fry, Varian. *Surrender on Demand*. New York, Random House, 1945.

Fuller, Major-General J.F.C. *The Second World War*. London, Eyre & Spottiswoode, 1948.

Gay, Peter. *My German Question: Growing Up in Nazi Berlin*. New Haven & London, Yale University Press, 1998.

De Gaulle, Charles. *War Memoirs*. Vols 1–6. London, Collins, 1955.

Gedye, G.E.R. *Betrayed in Central Europe*. New York, Harper, 1939.

Gehlen, Reinhard. *The Service: The Memoirs of General Reinhard Gehlen*. New York, World Publishing, 1972.

Gilbert, Martin. *The First World War*. New York, Henry Holt, 1994.

— *The Holocaust: The Jewish Tragedy*. London, Collins, 1986.

Halls, W.D. *The Youth of Vichy France*. London, Clarendon Press, 1981.

Hastings, Max. *Das Reich: The March of the 2nd Panzer Division Through France*. New York, Holt, Rinehart & Winston, 1981.

Hilliard, Robert L. *Surviving the Americans – The Continued Struggle of the Jews After Liberation*. New York, Seven Stories Press, 1977.

Hitler, Adolf. *Mein Kampf*. New York, Reynal & Hitchcock, 1939.

Hohne, Heinz, & Zolling, Herman. *The General Was A Spy*. New York, Coward, McCann, 1971.

Horne, Alistair. *To Lose a Battle: France 1940*. London, Macmillan, 1969.

Hunt, Linda. *Secret Agenda: The United States Government, Nazi Scientists, and Project Paperclip 1945–1990*. New York, St Martin's Press, 1991.

Huxley, Laura. *This Timeless Moment*. New York, Farrar, Straus, Giroux, 1968.

— *Between Heaven and Earth*. New York, Farrar, Straus, Giroux, 1975.

Irving, David. *Hitler's War*. New York, Viking, 1977.

Jenks, William A. *Vienna and the Young Hitler*. New York, Columbia University Press, 1960.

Johnson, Paul. *A History of the Jews*. New York, Harper & Row, 1987.

Kaplan, Marion A. *Between Dignity and Despair: Jewish Life in Nazi Germany*. Oxford & New York, Oxford University Press, 1998.

Jones, Ernest. *The Life and Times of Sigmund Freud*. London, The Hogarth Press, 1956.

Kahn, Herman. *On Thermonuclear War*. Princeton, Princeton University Press, 1960.

— *The Year 2000: A Framework for Speculation on the Next Thirty-Three Years*. New York, Macmillan, 1967.

— *Things To Come: Thinking About the Seventies and Eighties*. New York, Macmillan, 1972.

— *The Future of the Corporation*. New York, Mason & Lipscomb, 1974.

— *The Next 200 Years: A Scenario for America and the World*. New York, Morrow, 1976.

— *The Coming Boom: Economic, Political and Social*. New York, Simon & Schuster, 1982.

— *Thinking About the Unthinkable in the 1980s*. New York, Simon & Schuster, 1984.

Kedward, H.R. *In Search of the Maquis: Rural Resistance in Southern France, 1942–1944*. Oxford, Clarendon Press, 1993.

— *Resistance in Vichy France: A Study of Ideas and Motivations in the Southern Zone, 1940–1942*. Oxford, Oxford University Press, 1978.

— *Occupied France: Collaboration and Resistance 1940– 1944*. Oxford, Basil Blackwell, 1985.

Keegan, John. *The Second World War*. London, Century Hutchinson, 1989.

— *Six Armies in Normandy*. New York, The Viking Press, 1982.

Kershaw, Ian. *Hitler: 1889–1936: Hubris*. London, Allen Lane, The Penguin Press, 1998.

Klarsfeld, Serge. *The Children of Izieu: A Human Tragedy*. New York, Abrams, 1984.

Klein, Theo. *Oublier Vichy*. Paris, Criterion, 1992.

Koestler, Arthur. *Scum of the Earth*. London, Jonathan Cape, 1941.

Knight, F. *The French Resistance 1940–44*. London, Lawrence & Wishart, 1975.

Laqueur, Walter, & Breitman, Richard. *Breaking the Silence*. New York, Simon & Schuster, 1986.

Langer, William L. *Our Vichy Gamble*. New York, Knopf, 1947.

Lasby, Clarence G. *Project Paperclip: German Scientists and the Cold War*. New York, Atheneum, 1971.

Le Chene, Evelyn. *Mauthausen – The History of a Death Camp*. London, Methuen, 1971.

Linklater, Magnus, Hilton, Isabel, & Ascherson, Neal. *The Nazi Legacy*. New York, Holt, Rinehart & Winston, 1984.

Lytton, Neville. *Life in Unoccupied France*. London, Macmillan, 1942.

MacDonald, Charles. *The Battle of the Bulge*. London, Weidenfeld & Nicolson, 1984.

Marks, Leo. *Between Silk and Cyanide: The Story of S.O.E.'s Code War*. London, Harper Collins, 1998.

Marrus, Michael R. *The Politics of Assimilation: The French Jewish Community at the Time of the Dreyfus Affair*. Oxford, Oxford University Press, 1971.

— & Paxton, Robert O. *Vichy France and the Jews*. New York, Basic Books, 1981.

Michel, H. *The Shadow War: European Resistance 1939–1945*. New York, Harper & Row, 1972.

Morgan, Ted. *An Uncertain Hour: The French, the Germans, the Jews, the Barbie Trial and the City of Lyon, 1940–1945*. New York, Arbor House–William Morrow, 1990.

Mosley, Leonard. *Dulles: A Biography of Eleanor, Allen and John Foster Dulles and their Family Network*. New York, The Dial Press, 1978.

Novick, Peter. *The Resistance Versus Vichy: The Purge of Collaborators in Liberated France*. Columbia University Press, New York, 1968.

Ousby, Ian. *Occupation: The Ordeal of France 1940–1944*. London, John Murray, 1997.

Paris, Erna. *Unhealed Wounds: France and the Klaus Barbie Affair*. New York, Grove Press, 1985.

Paxton, Robert O. *Vichy France: Old Guard and New Order, 1940–1944*. London, Barrie & Jenkins, 1972.

— *Parades and Politics at Vichy*. Princeton, Princeton University Press, 1966.

347

Pearson, Michael. *Tears of Glory: The Heroes of Vercors, 1944*. New York, Doubleday, 1979.

Porch, Douglas. *The French Secret Services*. New York, Farrar, Straus, Giroux, 1995.

— *Report of the Subcommittee on Armed Services, United States Senate, Malmédy Massacre Investigation. 81st Congress, 1st Session*. Washington DC, US Government Printing Office, 1949.

Ranelagh, John. *The Agency: The Rise and Decline of the CIA*. New York, Simon & Schuster, 1986.

Regler, Gustav. *The Owl of Minerva*. New York, Farrar, Straus & Cudahy, 1959.

Reynolds, Michael. *The Devil's Adjutant: Jochen Peiper, Panzer Leader*. Revised & updated. New York, Sarpedon, 1997.

Rousso, Henry. *The Vichy Syndrome: History and Memory in France since 1944*. Tr. Arthur Goldhammer. Cambridge, Massachusetts, 1991.

Ryan, Allan. *Klaus Barbie and the United States Government*. Washington DC, US Government Printing Office, 1983.

— *Quiet Neighbors*. New York, Harcourt Brace Jovanovich, 1984.

Ryan, Donna F. *The Holocaust & The Jews of Marseille*. Chicago, University of Illinois Press, 1996.

Sartre, Jean-Paul. *Paris under the Occupation*. Included in *French Writing on English Soil: A Choice of French Writing Printed in London Between November 1940 and June 1944*. Ed. & Tr. J.G. Weightman. London, Sylvan Press, 1945.

Shalit, Levit. *Beyond Dachau: Memories, Reflections*. Johannesburg, Kayor, 1980.

Shirer, William L. *The Rise and Fall of the Third Reich: A History of Nazi Germany*. London, Secker & Warburg, 1959.

— *The Collapse of the Third Republic*. New York, Stein & Day, 1969.

Simpson, Christopher. *Blowback*. New York, Weidenfeld & Nicholson, 1988.

Singer, Israel Joshua. *The Brothers Ashkenazi*. New York, Knopf, 1936.

Smith, Michael. *Foley: The Spy Who Saved 10,000 Jews*. London, Hodder & Stoughton, 1999.

Smith, R. Harris. *OSS: The Secret History of America's First Central Intelligence Agency*. Berkeley, University of California Press, 1972.

Stein, Gertrude. *Wars I Have Seen*. New York, Random House, 1945.

Tanant, Pierre. *Vercors, Haut-lieu de France*. Paris, Arthaud, 1951.

Taylor, A.J.P. *The Origins of the Second World War*. New York, Atheneum, 1962.

Toland, John. *Battle: The Story of the Bulge*. New York, Random House, 1959.

— *Adolf Hitler*. New York, Harper & Bros, 1976.

Truffaut, François. *Correspondence: 1945–1984*. New York, Farrar, Straus, Giroux, 1990.

Van de Velde, T.H. *Ideal Marriage: Its Physiology and Technique*. New York, Random House, 1926.

Wall, Patrick. *Pain: The Science of Suffering*. London, Weidenfeld & Nicolson, 1999.

Warner, Geoffrey. *Pierre Laval and the Eclipse of France*. New York, Macmillan, 1968.

Wasserstein, Bernard. *Britain and the Jews of Europe 1939–1945*. London, Leicester University Press, 1979.

Webster, Paul. *Pétain's Crime: The Full Story of French Collaboration in the Holocaust*. Chicago, Ivan R. Dee, 1991.

Weingartner, James J. *Crossroads of Death: The Story of the Malmédy Massacre and Trial*. Berkeley, University of California Press, 1979.

— *Hitler's Guard: The Story of the Leibstandarte SS Adolf Hitler, 1933–1945*. Nashville, Battery Classics, 1992.

Weisberg, Richard H. *Vichy Law and the Holocaust in France*. New York, New York University Press, 1996.

Whitcomb, Philip W. *France During the German Occupation, 1940–1944*. Vol. 2. Stanford, Stanford University Press, 1957.

Whiting, Charles. *Massacre at Malmédy*. London, Leo Cooper, 1971.

Whitlock, Flynt. *The Rock of Anzio: From Sicily to Dachau: A History of the 45th Infantry Division*. Boulder, Colorado, Westview Press, 1998.

Wyman, David S. *Paper Walls: America and the Refugee Crisis 1938–41*. New York, Pantheon, 1985.

Zuccotti, Susan. *The Holocaust, the French, and the Jews*. New York, Basic Books, 1993.

— *The Italians and the Holocaust*. New York, Basic Books, 1987.

END NOTES

I

1. *Expulsion of German Jews to Poland:* See Marrus & Paxton, *Vichy France and the Jews*, p 25.
2. *Uncle's letter:* The letter was written in Sosnowice, Poland, on 4 December 1939, and hand-delivered to New York by Edgar Schlesinger, a friend of the family, on 18 February 1940.
3. *Quota numbers:* In contrast, Frank Foley, passport control officer at the British Embassy in Berlin, provided forged passports to numerous Jews, and broke the rules of his own government by providing visas for Palestine. Foley was actually head of MI6 in the German capital and at great personal risk went into concentration camps to save Jews. He is credited with saving many thousands of lives. See Smith, *Foley, passim.*
4. *American haven:* Germany and Italy did not declare war on the United States until 11 December 1941, in support of Japan. America had declared war on Japan on 8 December 1941, the day after the attack on Pearl Harbor.
5. *Unfilled quotas:* The quota for refugees to the United States from Austria and Germany for 1938, the year the visa was applied for, remained unfilled. Wyman, *Paper Walls*, p 221.

II

1. *Birth date:* Michel does not believe in chronological age. 'People pigeonhole you the moment they know your age. So I do not tell them. Let people work it out. My birth date is a footnote to my life.' He was born on 3 February 1914.
2. *Russian Poland:* The Poles in Prussian Poland were subjected to a similar, if less severe, form of Germanisation. Poles in Austrian Poland were treated more liberally. After the revolution in 1917, Russia recognised Poland's right to self-determination; the defeat of the Central Powers in 1918 led to the recreation of Poland as an independent republic.
3. *German army in Lodz:* Gilbert, *First World War*, pp 103, 106–7, 347.
4. *Casualties during Lodz campaign:* Dupuy & Dupuy, *Encyclopaedia of*

Military History, p 944.

5. *Lodz in First World War:* See Singer, *The Brothers Ashkenazi, passim.*

6. *Childhood memory system:* Michel is well aware of the pitfalls of recovered memory. Memories can merge and blur, or be superimposed with information gleaned at a later date. But he feels confident that, because he consciously thought about preserving memory at such an early age, he is able to differentiate between the real and the received.

7. *Freida's collapse:* Michel remained dry-eyed throughout the many interviews and conversations about his life which explored almost unbearably painful areas, but as he described this incident he almost broke down.

8. *Breslau between the wars:* Lacqueur & Breitman, *Breaking the Silence*, pp 28–30, 36. Due to the fortunes of war and the ironies of history, Breslau is now a Polish city. Although German since the Middle Ages, it reverted to Poland after its capture by Soviet troops in May 1945. It was the one major city in the country not to surrender before VE Day. The German population was subsequently deported and largely replaced by Polish settlers. The town was renamed Wroclaw.

9. Legends of the Gods: This was one of the books Adolf Hitler had in his room as an impoverished student in Vienna. Kershaw, *Hitler: 1889–1936: Hubris*, p 41.

10. *Wagner's influence on Hitler:* see Fest, *Hitler*, p 56.

11. *Hohenzollern:* The great Prussian family of leaders dating back to the eleventh or twelfth century. They created strong, disciplined armies dedicated to military excellence, and eventually united and ruled Germany. Their reign came to an end with the defeat of Germany in 1918 when William II was forced to abdicate.

12. Ideal Marriage: Dr Velde seems to have been a champion of little women. 'Women of short stature and small bones can often meet all requirements in the flexibility and capacity of their *vaginae*. And in their sexual vigour and efficiency are also conspicuous, not only in coitus, but in their buoyant reaction to the mental and physical stress and strain of menstruation, pregnancy and parturition, their fine flow of milk, and easy conception. In short, little women approximate most often to the typical womanly ideal.' In support of this view the doctor quotes 'the saying among the English common people: "Little women – big breeders"' Van de Velde, *Ideal Marriage*, p 206 and *passim.* (The doctor went on to write post-honeymoon marriage manuals such as *Sexual Tensions in Marriage* and *Fertility and Sterility in Marriage.)*

13. *Nazis come to power:* Bullock, *Hitler*, pp 253–7. Keegan; *Second World War*, p 27.

14. *Jewish life in pre-war Germany:* 'Quoting Goethe at every meal', see

351

Kaplan, *Between Dignity and Despair*, pp 3–93 *passim*.

15. *Saarland:* Under the Treaty of Versailles, in 1919, coal mines in the rich Saar valley were handed over to France for a period of fifteen years in compensation for the destruction of French mines during the war. The treaty also provided for a plebiscite to decide its future. In 1935 more than ninety per cent of the electorate voted for reunification with Germany.

16. *Karl Hamburg:* A lifelong friend, the men lost touch until after the war when Michel found a book on philosophy written by Hamburg in a Beverly Hills bookshop. He wrote to the publisher for his friend's address. Dr Charles Hamburg taught at Columbia University, New York, before becoming the Dean of Philosophy at Tulane University, New Orleans.

17. *'Praised be that which toughens':* See Irving, *Hitler's War*, p 377.

18. *Michael Nelken:* Michel Thomas was later to use the name Kent as a middle name in memory of his friend.

19. *Dachau:* 'Empty huts in a gravel pit', the camp was run by the local SS, already known as one of the most savage and brutal platoons in Bavaria. The camp was immediately enlarged to hold five thousand prisoners. It was further expanded throughout the war to become a notorious death camp. Gilbert, *The Holocaust*, pp 32–3.

20. *Wilhelm Furtwangler:* The conductor remained in Germany through most of the Second World War and although an avowed anti-Nazi, his position and prestige were such that he avoided direct persecution. He was exonerated of charges of collaboration after the war and enjoyed a highly successful international career.

21. *Just a matter of time:* For the grim fate of the Jews of Lodz during the war see Gilbert, *The Holocaust, passim*.

22. *Jews of Lodz:* See Singer, *The Brothers Ashkenazi, passim*.

23. *Oscar (Usher) Kohn:* Only Uncle Usher survived. Despite the dismissal of his great-nephew's predictions, Oscar Kohn did leave Poland a year later, and went to live in Cuernavaca, Mexico. When the Germans invaded Poland, less than two years after the conversation with Michel, the occupying Nazi governor, Hans Frank, appropriated the Kohns' luxurious house. The Russians also took a large slice of Poland for themselves. After the Nazi–Soviet non-aggression pact dissolved on Hitler's invasion of Poland the country was reduced to a battleground. And after the Germans lost the war the Soviets dominated Poland, until the collapse of Communism. Michel had been prophetic.

The men met up in Mexico after the war and Uncle Usher vividly recalled their conversation in Lodz. He admitted to being so removed from reality that when he finally fled, he was shocked and offended to be jostled in the chaos. But he kept his wry sense of humour. The only hurt he suffered, he said, was to his dignity: 'I lost my high silk top hat.'

The novel, *The Brothers Ashkenazi*, written in 1936 by Israel Joshua Singer – brother of Nobel prizewinner Isaac Bashevis Singer – about the rise of a great industrial family in pre-war Lodz, is in many ways a fictional biography of the Kohns. The story charts the rise and fall of two brothers in the textile manufacturing business. One is generous and outgoing, the other hard and miserly. Asked which one best represents Uncle Usher, Michel replied: 'Both!'

III

1. *Suzanne Adler:* Suzanne de Lhosa, née Adler, died in Nice, France, in 1992.

2. *Nuremberg Laws:* In September 1935, Adolf Hitler introduced the Nuremberg Laws. These deprived German Jews of fundamental civil rights, reducing their status to that of foreigners within their own country. They were forbidden to marry non-Jewish Germans, and not allowed to employ German females in their homes under forty-five years old. They were also forbidden to fly the German national flag bearing the swastika. Friedländer, *Nazi Germany and the Jews*, p 142.

3. *Alfred Adler:* By the time Michel was studying in Vienna Adler had already moved on from the city – to the United States in 1935. He had been one of the founders of psychoanalysis, together with Carl Jung, as a student of Sigmund Freud. Freud later denounced both men as psychoanalytical heretics. He died in Aberdeen, Scotland, in 1937.

4. *Hitler on Anschluss:* Hitler, *Mein Kampf*, p 3.

5. *Hitler's youth in Vienna:* See Jenks, *Vienna and the Young Hitler, passim.*

6. *Cardinal Innitzer:* Shirer, *Rise and Fall of the Third Reich*, p 350.

7. *Freud leaves Vienna:* The colleague was Ernest Jones, who became Freud's biographer. Jones, *Life and Times of Sigmund Freud*, Vol. III, p 235.

8. *Excesses in Vienna:* Other eyewitnesses to events following the *Anschluss* were William L. Shirer, legendary foreign correspondent of the *Chicago Tribune*, and G.E.R. Gedye of *The Times*. 'The behaviour of the Vienna Nazis was worse than anything I had seen in Germany. There was an orgy of sadism' (Shirer, *Rise and Fall of the Third Reich*, p 351); 'The streets of Vienna were an inferno. As I walked through or drove past the mobs . . . one of the many sentimental phrases applied by the Viennese halted my brain – *Das gold'ne Wiener Harz*. There was little trace of golden hearts written on these hate-filled, triumph-drunken faces, and the memory of it makes one's stomach queasy'. (Gedye, *Betrayal in Central Europe*, p 284.)

9. *Polish passports rescinded:* The first law modifying citizenship was passed by the Polish parliament on 31 March 1938, followed by a decree cancelling the passports of foreign residents in October of the same year. Friedländer, *Nazi Germany and the Jews*, p 267.

10. *Evian Conference:* See Friedländer, *Nazi Germany and the Jews*, pp 248–9.

11. *Dianne Dudel:* Michel's cousin married Ileahu Ben Elissar, who became Israeli ambassador to the United States, and at the time of writing is the ambassador to France.

12. *Ernst Ehrenfeld:* After completing his prison sentence, Ehrenfeld served in the French Foreign Legion throughout the war. He survived to marry a French woman, and settled in France.

13. *English general rages:* Major-General J.F.C. Fuller, in Fuller, *The Second World War*, p 55.

14. *Maginot Line:* Horne, *To Lose a Battle*, pp 25–32; Kemp, *The Maginot Line, passim.*

15. *Jean-Paul Sartre quotation:* From his memoir, *Paris Under the Occupation;* quoted by Ousby, *Occupation*, p 22.

16. *General de Gaulle:* See De Gaulle, *Memoirs*, pp 30–1.

17. *Italians held off:* Horne, *To Lose a Battle*, pp 564–5.

18. *Hitler at Compiègne:* William Shirer wrote notes in his diary after watching Hitler through binoculars. Shirer, *The Rise and Fall of the Third Reich*, pp 742–3.

19. *Defeat of France and armistice:* The fullest accounts are carried in Shirer, *Fall of the Third Republic*, and Horne, *To Lose a Battle*.

20. *Albert Camus quotation:* Camus, *Notebooks 1935–1942*, p 146.

21. *Resisters of the First Hour:* See Paxton, *Vichy France*, p 39.

22. *Vichy's anti-Semitic laws:* See Marrus & Paxton, *Vichy France and the Jews*, pp xi-xvi, 3–20.

23. *Influence peddling:* Court document No. 69, Correctional Judgement 600, Nice Tribunal, 9 January 1941.

24. *Acquittal:* Court document No. 175, Case 17, registered in Nice, 17 January 1941.

25. *Residence denied: Refus de Séjour*, issued by authorities in Nice on 14 February 1941.

IV

1. *Internment order:* Proposition Internment, Nice: Code # 131W21898: Transport 17 Juifs au Camp Le Vernet, 26 April 1941. Document provided from the archive of Serge Klarsfeld.

2. *Gardes Mobiles:* A section of the police 'notoriously' reactionary and brutal, according to the writer Arthur Koestler, 'both in human material

and tradition', in *Scum of the Earth*, p 116.

3. *Refugee goes mad:* Marrus & Paxton, *Vichy France and the Jews*, p 66.

4. *Concentration camps:* The term *camp du concentration* was the official term, first used by Interior Minister Albert Sarraut in 1939. Marrus & Paxton, *Vichy France and the Jews*, p 165.

5. *French Dachau:* This was the headline of the first article to appear in the international press in the *New Republic* on 11 November 1940. Other reports decrying conditions in the Vichy camps soon followed in the *New York Times*, the British papers *The Daily Telegraph* and *The Sunday Times*, and the Swiss paper *Journal de Genève*.

6. *Le Vernet:* The description of Le Vernet appears in the memoirs of the novelist Gustav Regler, *Owl of Minerva*, pp 333–4, 352–3. In 1941 Arthur Koestler published an account of his time in the camp after escaping to England. Undesirable foreign refugees are the 'scum' referred to in his title. Koestler's description of the camp tallies closely with that of Michel Thomas. The account here is an amalgamation of Thomas's memory and Koestler's written record, made only months after his internment. See *Scum of the Earth*, pp 101–65, *passim*.

7. *Thirty-one camps:* The totals were reported by the Kundt Commission, a Gestapo tool authorised under the Franco-German armistice to visit French camps and extract any prisoner the Germans wanted under a system known as 'Surrender on Demand'. Marrus & Paxton, *Vichy France and the Jews*, pp 165–6; Fry, *Surrender on Demand*, *passim*.

8. *Honour of France:* André Jean-Fauré, Vichy inspector-general of the camps, prepared reports for the Chief of State, Marshal Pétain himself, although it is doubtful that he ever saw them. A member of the marshal's staff scribbled in pencil across a report on Gurs, 'Not to be acknowledged'. Marrus & Paxton, *Vichy France and the Jews*, pp 172–3.

9. *Unit C:* The huts of Unit C were finally rebuilt in October 1942 but there were no Jewish inmates to benefit from the improved conditions. They had all been deported 'to the East'. Marrus & Paxton, *Vichy France and the Jews*, p 175.

10. *Dysentery of the soul:* Regler, *Owl of Minerva*, p 336.

11. *Walking skeletons:* Michel Thomas has photographs in his possession taken of inmates for a later report on the camp. Their shrunken, emaciated forms are identical to the survivors of the Nazi death camps.

12. *Man of bad reputation:* The report stated: '*Mauvaise réputation, moralité douteuse. A fait l'objet d'une information pour trafic d'influence. N'a pas obtemperé au refus de séjour. Decision Ministerielle d'internment, 7 Mai, 1941.*' Report provided from the archive of Serge Klarsfeld.

13. *Bureaucratic obstruction:* See Marrus & Paxton, *Vichy France and the Jews*, pp 162–3; Fry, *Surrender on Demand*, p 157.

14. *Arrival in Les Milles:* Michel Thomas's arrival in Les Milles was registered with the authorities on 22 December 1941. He was given the number 2539.

15. *Les Milles:* For a history of the camp, see Ryan, *The Holocaust and the Jews of Marseille*, pp 95–6.

16. *Saint Louis:* Great Britain, Belgium and France finally agreed to grant asylum to the passengers, taking a third each. Only the refugees admitted to Britain survived.

17. *Powerful deterrent:* Ryan, *The Holocaust and the Jews of Marseille*, p 104.

18. *Never saw the sun:* Many years after working in the mine Michel Thomas discovered that the respiratory problems he had been suffering were as a result of black lung. X-rays showed that his left lung manifested 'increased interstitial fibrosis . . . a complication of exposure to coal dust'. Report by Gerald Salen MD, New York, 1993.

19. *Round-up of French Jews:* The BBC had announced the deportation plans to the Résistance on 24 July 1942. Ryan, *The Holocaust and the Jews of Marseille*, p 120.

20. *Drancy:* All but twelve of the seventy-nine deportation trains left from Drancy, as did over sixty-seven thousand of the seventy-five thousand Jews. Marrus & Paxton, *Vichy France and the Jews*, p 252.

21. *Extra beer and cigarette rations:* Porch, *The French Secret Services*, p 209.

22. *Vichy ambassador married to a Jewess:* The wife of Fernand de Brinon, Vichy's representative in Paris, was exempted from having to wear the Star of David, but virtually condemned to house arrest. The Germans insisted that the exemption was only good for her residence in the family property in the Basses-Pyrénées near Biarritz and suggested she live continuously on the estate. Her brother was later arrested, despite being in possession of an official paper stating he did not belong to the Jewish race. Marrus & Paxton, *Vichy France and the Jews*, p 237.

23. *Jews constitute a national danger: Le Matin*, 16 December 1941.

24. *Violation of armistice:* The Prime Minister was quoted in the article 'Laval Losing Confidence', *Manchester Guardian*, 30 September 1942.

25. *Without brutality:* Ryan, *The Holocaust and the Jews of Marseille*, p 121.

26. *Security strengthened:* Ibid. p 120.

27. *Police chief's statement:* Ibid. p 122.

28. *Turkish citizens protected:* Michel's friend Nic Levy, interned with him both at Le Vernet and Les Milles, was one such Turkish Non-Deportable. He witnessed deportation after deportation at Les Milles but was never touched. After the war he opened an elegant men's shop – Dorian Guy – opposite the Georges Cinq Hotel, and another – Soirées Elysées – in the Champs Elysées. The experience of Vichy convinced him to reverse his name to Yvel.

29. *Number of children deported:* These figures have been painstakingly compiled by Serge Klarsfeld from camp records in France and Germany. The figures for 1942 are: one thousand and thirty-two under six; two thousand, five hundred and fifty-seven between six and twelve; two thousand, four hundred and sixty-four between thirteen and seventeen. Klarsfeld, *Le Memorial de la deportation des Juifs de France*, unpaginated.

30. *Quota requirement:* By the end of 1942 a total of forty-two thousand, five hundred Jews were sent from France to Auschwitz, a figure the Germans found disappointing. For a detailed analysis of this period, see Marrus & Paxton, *Vichy France and the Jews*, pp 217–69 *passim*.

31. *Willpower:* One of the legacies of the camps, Michel Thomas jokes, is an ability to go for superhumanly long periods without feeling hunger or the need to urinate. Nigel Levy, the producer of the BBC documentary on Michel, remembers: 'I went in at nine in the morning and left at eight at night. In all that time he did not move from the armchair, ate a single packet of crisps and, as far as I remember, never used the bathroom.'

32. *Escape attempt:* Many years after the war Michel Thomas met one of the children who had been taken from Les Milles on the bus that he had tried to board. The man had survived the war, and remembered the adult prisoner who had tried to escape by riding with them. The guards quickly found the escapee and arrested him.

33. *Children separated:* Donald Lowrie, who was active in relief work for the World Alliance of the YMCA, wrote a memorandum in August 1942 based on eyewitness accounts of this incident. Ryan, *The Holocaust and the Jews of Marseille*, pp 122, 254.

34. *Sam Fischer:* Not the real name, which Michel was unable to remember.

35. *Bummed a cigarette:* The cigarette was given to Michel by Nic Levy, the Turkish Non-Deportable (see note 28).

V

1. *'What silence!':* The observer is quoted in Bower, *Barbie*, pp 29–30.

2. *Lyon's history of rebellion:* See Morgan, *An Uncertain Hour*, pp 18–19.

3. *Communist resistance:* The secret agenda of the FTP was revealed in archives released by Moscow in the first half of the 1990s. Porch, *The French Secret Services*, p 214.

4. *Lyon and the Résistance:* See Aron, *France Reborn*, p 346; Porch, *The French Secret Services*, pp 175–264 passim.

5. *The Maquis:* The term that came to describe the whole underground movement in France. The word is Corsican and describes the rough gorse into which the bandits of the island disappear.

6. *Abbé Alexandre Glasberg (1902–82):* Kedward, *Resistance in Vichy France*, pp 175–6; Marrus & Paxton, *Vichy France and the Jews*, p 207;

Morgan, *An Uncertain Hour*, p 170; Zuccotti, *The Holocaust, the French and the Jews*, pp 73–4, 131.

7. *Hitler's communication with Pétain:* Irving, *Hitler's War*, pp 444–8.

8. *Italian zone:* See Zuccotti, *Italy and the Holocaust*, pp 75, 82–3.

9. *Lyon and UGIF:* Morgan, *An Uncertain Hour*, pp 199–216.

10. *Disappointing results:* The report is quoted in Morgan, *An Uncertain Hour*, p 207.

11. *Michel at UGIF office:* One published account of Barbie's life identifies Michel at the UGIF office as 'Michel Kroskof, a Polish artist'; see Bower, *Barbie*, p 58.

12. *'Without them':* The quotes by Barbie are from Bower, *Barbie*, pp 41, 51.

13. *Darnand's quotes:* Morgan, *An Uncertain Hour*, p 105.

14. *Background to Milice:* Kedward, *Occupied France*, pp 66–7; Marrus & Paxton, *Vichy France and the Jews*, p 335; Ousby, *Occupation*, p 267–75.

15. *Arrested by Milice:* Michel's arrest was in Grenoble on 30 March 1943. Report on the service and activities of Mr Michel Kroskof-Thomas in the Résistance and Maquis, French Forces of the Interior, Isère, Section IV: signed by Captain Dax, St Ismier, 4 December 1944. Copy read and certified by Secretary General of the Departmental Committee of National Liberation of Grenoble, 22 August 1957 (signature illegible).

16. *Michel's betrayal:* Today, Michel Thomas says of this incident: 'I always wondered what I would do if I saw the young man who betrayed me again – and I did, on a street in Paris at the end of the war just before I went to the United States. Instinctively, I stepped forward and embraced him. And we had a very pleasant lunch together. I was happy to see him, and happy for him to see me alive so he wouldn't have guilt. It was done and finished.'

17. *Control of pain:* This is not as unusual or extraordinary as it sounds. Professor Patrick Wall, a practising London physiologist, has spent a lifetime studying pain. His research has led him to believe that whether a sensation is interpreted as painful depends on what else the brain is attending to at the same time. Soldiers in the heat of battle often do not know they have been wounded; athletes continue to play after sustaining severe injuries. The brain prioritises. See Wall, *Pain, passim.*

18. *René Gosse:* For the role of academics in the Résistance, see Kedward, *Resistance in Vichy France*, pp 74–5. Gosse and his son were later murdered and their bodies were found in a ditch outside Grenoble. His colleagues deduced that both men had been tortured, and that the son had been killed in front of the father.

19. *Sammy Lattès:* After the war Lattès, a professor of Italian literature, became a national inspector of education.

20. *Résistance positions:* All these roles are recorded in the FFI (Forces

Françaises de l'Intérieur) report.

21. *Dax:* The *nom de guerre* of Jean Berfini, a well-known Résistance figure based in Montbonnot.

22. *BBC coded message:* Kedward, *In Search of the Maquis*, p 174.

23. *Capture of head of Secret Army:* General Delestraint survived torture and two years' incarceration in a German concentration camp. He was murdered by the Nazis as Allied troops advanced in 1945.

24. *André Valat:* After the war he became president of the veterans of the Grenoble and Grésivaudan Résistance until his death in 1996. There is a memorial to the memory of Georges Chappuy and Jean Nogues on the site of the encounter with the Germans outside Biviers. It reads: 'French Résistance, Biviers Group. Here fell our comrades shot by the Germans on 17 June 1944 during a dangerous mission.' The men were awarded the Croix de Guerre.

25. *Henri:* The *nom de guerre* of Henri Segal, a French Jew – 'one of the heroes', according to Michel.

26. *Attack on Fort Murier:* Aimé Recquet wrote his own account of this incident – see Nal & Recquet, *Autres Recits* (published with *La Bataille de Grenoble*), pp 274–81.

27. *Thérèse Mathieu:* Michel did not see Thérèse Mathieu again in the war, but kept in touch and met her years later. After the war she was sent by the Ministry of Education to French Africa to set up a system of education. At the age of seventy she complained that there were certain Alpine peaks she was no longer able to climb. She died in 1955 in a car accident in her beloved mountains.

28. *Battle of Vercors:* The best and fullest account is chronicled in Michael Pearson's book, *Tears of Glory* (*passim*), in which the author interviewed survivors and gained access to classified documents. See also Aron, *France Reborn*, pp 182–95; Chambard, *The Maquis*, pp 173–94; Ehrlich, *The French Resistance*, pp 168–88; Foot, *SOE in France*, pp 357–8, 391–9; Kedward, *In Search of the Maquis*, pp 174–81; Morgan, *An Uncertain Hour*, pp 292–300.

VI

1. *Germans turned:* Foot, *Résistance*, p 252.

2. *Liberation of Grenoble:* See Aron, *France Reborn*, pp 344–6; Chambard, *The Maquis*, p 193; Foot, *SOE in France*, pp 412–13; Recquet, *Bataille de Grenoble*, pp 296–9; Pearson, *Tears of Glory*, pp 301–12.

3. *Résistance report on Michel Thomas:* Report on Service and Activities of Michel Kroskof Thomas, FFI, Isère, Section IV, 4 December 1944: 'After escaping from the deportation camp he joined the Résistance in Lyon in September 1942. He acted as liaison officer, charged with

hiding *refractaires* (Frenchmen resisting being drafted into forced labour in Germany), furnishing them with false identity papers, recruiting them into the Corrèze and Isère Maquis, or helping them escape to Spain. Arrested at the end of January 1943 by the Gestapo in Lyon, he managed to escape and went to Grenoble where he continued his activities. After being informed on, he was arrested on 30 March by the Grenoble Milice (French Gestapo) and was tortured for six hours. With outside help he escaped, and for the fifth time, changed his identity. Moving to Biviers (Isère) he was in charge of *refractaires*, of supplying food to the Maquis, and serving with SRD (Resistance Intelligence Services). Organising a group, he affiliated it with the AS (Secret Army). He and his group built a refuge in the mountains for the Maquis. In September 1943 he was named Section Chief in the Secret Army. In June he and his group repeatedly destroyed telephone lines. He was among the first to join the Maquis de St Marie-du-Mont. He and his group took part in attacks on German convoys. During one mission (a commando raid to resupply the Maquis) he and his group were attacked by the Germans who killed two of his men and seriously wounded a third. Surrounded and under fire from two groups of Germans, tracked for almost an hour, he managed to escape thanks to an adroit manoeuvre. (The three men in his cell were later cited and decorated with the Croix de Guerre.) He returned to the Maquis de St Marie-du-Mont which on the next day came under heavy attack by German troops. He was the part of my Commando Group from the time of its inception, at the same time serving as liaison officer (to the Grésivaudan and Chartreuse resistance areas.) He accomplished his missions despite German roadblocks, and in combat zones. He participated in the destruction of bridges between Grenoble and Chambéry, and with his group interdicted the reconstruction of them in wood, sawing and otherwise destroying all material brought in for the purpose. He took part in the daylight raid on Fort du Murier and on Fort Barraux. After the liberation of Grenoble he joined the Special Police Groups, serving with the 2ème Bureau (Intelligence). He was in charge of investigations and arrests. On 29 August 1944 he was detached to the American Seventh Army (Intelligence) and left for the front. Thus MICHEL has served the cause of Liberation with honour and bravery.' The report is signed by Captain Dax, Territorial Commandant, Sector 6. It was later read and certified as genuine by the Secretary General of the Departmental Committee of National Liberation.

4. *Horizontal collaborators:* Bruckberger, *One Sky to Share*, pp 23–4.
5. *Coiffure of 1944:* Stein, *Wars I Have Seen*, pp 121, 243.
6. *Thunderbirds' history:* For a complete history of the division, from its

entanglement with Pancho Villa through the Korean War, see Franks, *Citizen Soldiers, passim*; Whitlock, *Rock of Anzio, passim*.

7. *Praise from Patton:* Quoted in Whitlock, *Rock of Anzio*, p 53.

8. *Italian campaign:* see Keegan, *Second World War*, pp 287–301.

9. *Thunderbirds:* Background on the 45th Division, together with a combat chronology, is provided in *45th Division News*, Thunderbirds Special Edition, Second Anniversary edition, Vol. V, No. 38, 10 July 1945.

10. *Liberation of Lyon:* The Milice witness was Max Pyot; the priest tortured by the Gestapo was Abbé Boussier; the Bron airport supervisor was Joseph Bouellat; the Résistance leader who sent the signed letter to the Gestapo was Yves Farge. See Aron, *France Reborn*, pp 345–6, Bower, *Barbie*, pp 104–7; Morgan, *Uncertain Hour*, pp 308–9, 314–16.

11. *Liberation of Culoz:* Stein, *Wars I Have Seen*, pp 215–16, 244–5.

12. *Thunderbirds' prisoners:* By the end of the war the Thunderbirds would have a tally of one hundred and three thousand, three hundred and sixty-seven POWs to their credit. It is impossible to calculate how many enemy were killed or wounded. *45th Division News*, 10 July 1945.

13. *Cracow ghetto:* The chemist who witnessed the events in Harmony Square, Cracow, Poland, in the first week in June 1942 was Tadeusz Pankiewicz, who wrote a detailed account. Unknown to him the deportees were sent to Belzec and gassed. Eisenberg, *Witness to the Holocaust*, pp 194–203.

14. *Silver Star:* The recommendation was written – and appallingly spelt, in what seems to be the house style of American military reports – by Martin F. Schroeder, executive officer, 1st Battalion, 180th infantry, 45th Division, Seventh Army (undated). The medal was never awarded, possibly because Michel was a foreign national. 'I never looked into it or followed it up. I believed in Mathieu's credo that we were not in it for decorations. I still do.'

The recommendation reads: 'From the time of the liberation of Grenoble, France, in August 1944 through the battle of the Vosges mountains in Alsace in November of the same year, Michel Kroskof-Thomas, a Lt of the French Forces of the Interior (Maquis Commando Group), was attached to the S-2 section of 1st Bn, 180th Infantry. During this time in adverse weather conditions and against intense enemy resistance, he successfully led reconnaissance patrols into enemy territory to gain vital information necessary for the continued advances of our forces. Often he led as many as three patrols in one day, and on several occasions he volunteered to go on these patrols alone with utter disregard for his personal safety. He was instrumental in capturing many enemy prisoners whom he personally interrogated and obtained much vital information. His fluent knowledge of various languages was beneficial in interrogating German prisoners and captured slave laborers, and French civilians.

In September 1944, in the vicinity of Aubry, France, one of the companies of the Bn was holding a bridgehead across a river, and was in an exposed position which was continuously threatened by counter-attack. Michel Kroskof-Thomas personally established contact with an agent of the FFI in a strongly held enemy town and obtained vital know-ledge and exact information as to movements, positions, enemy strength, installations, armor, and minefields. Later, he supervised the main-tenance of contact with agents in other enemy-held towns in the vicinity, and thus he daily received information concerning enemy movements, reinforcements and proposed activities of the enemy on a larger scale. On one occasion when two patrols had been captured while attempting to obtain further information concerning enemy positions he volunteered to go alone into the positions. On this patrol he personally observed all the enemy minefields in the vicinity, and succeeded in reaching a single house where he captured an enemy soldier and obtained additional information as to positions and activity. When other enemy soldiers approached the house, he succeeded in withdrawing with the prisoner and returned to friendly positions and with information concerning artillery targets in the vicinity. A few minutes after he left the house, it was set afire by the enemy. By knowing the location of strategic positions and installations, and giving personally observed results of our shelling, he was able to effectively direct fire on these enemy positions causing them to withdraw from their prepared positions. This greatly relieved the strain on the forces holding the bridgehead.'

15. *Temporary release from Thunderbirds:* 'To Whom It May Concern: This is to certify that Michel Kroskof-Thomas, of Grenoble, France, has been attached to our Intelligence Unit S-2 since 27 August 1944, in the capacity of interrogator and scout. His services proved invaluable to this organization. He disregarded personal safety to carry out hazardous patrol missions and as a result was able to submit important information on enemy installations and strength. His ability to speak French, German and Polish has aided this organization in the interrogation of French civilians and German PWs. Reluctantly, we are forced to release Michel Kroskof-Thomas, in accordance with AG 230, Headquarters, VI Corps, dated 6 October 1944. He leaves with our sincere thanks and highest recommendation.' Henry F. Teichann Jr, 1st Lt, Infantry, Headquarters, 1st Battalion, 180th Infantry, APO 45, Postmaster, N.Y. New York, 19 October 1944.

16. *Take no prisoners:* The quoted written order was given to the US 38th Infantry Regiment. Whiting, *Massacre at Malmédy*, p 62.

17. *Battle of the Bulge:* A library of books has been written on the Ardennes campaign. The fullest account is Cole's *The Ardennes: Battle of the Bulge*; the best is MacDonald's *The Battle of the Bulge*; the most readable is Toland's *Battle: The Story of the Bulge.*

18. *Transfer to CIC:* The date of the transfer, 28 March 1945, is quoted in a recommendation written by Michel's senior officer, Captain Rupert W. Guenthner, 20 July 1945.

19. COWARDS AND TRAITORS: Quoted in Bishop, *Fighting 45th*, p 161.

20. *Battle for Aschaffenburg:* Reports on the battle appeared in *Time* magazine and the Associated Press, 2 April 1945.

21. *Landseer:* The breed is considered to be the black and white variant of the Newfoundland. It is named after the artist Sir Edwin Landseer (1802–73) who featured it in many of his paintings. By 1920 the breed was virtually extinct; German breeders recreated it by crossing the St Bernard with the Great Pyrénéan Mountain dog.

22. *A fabric of moans:* The words are those of Staff Sergeant Donald Schulz. Bower, *Paperclip Conspiracy*, p 104.

23. *Unrecognisable as humans:* Report by the US Signal Corps, quoted in Gilbert, *Holocaust*, p 796.

24. *Murrow in Buchenwald:* CBS radio broadcast, 15 April 1945. Text reproduced in *Reporting WWII*, Vol. II, pp 681–5.

25. *Liberation of Dachau:* Associated Press and various other correspondents mistakenly reported that the 42nd Division helped capture the camp, but in fact it did not arrive until after it had been liberated solely by the 3rd Battalion, 157th Infantry of the Thunderbirds. *The Seventh Army Daily News Summary*, 1 May 1945.

26. *Combat rage:* The GIs' rage is described by Whitlock, *Rock of Anzio*, p 360.

27. *SS men killed:* A 'secret' report on the killings was prepared by the Seventh Army's assistant inspector-general, Lt Col Joseph Whitaker. It recommended that four members of the 45th Division be charged with murder and tried by court-martial. One of the officers to be charged later reported that General Patton destroyed the report in his presence. No disciplinary action was taken. Whitlock, *Rock of Anzio*, pp 388–9.

28. *Female journalist:* Martha Gellhorn, then married to Ernest Hemingway, visited Dachau after the troops liberated it. 'Actually she came in days later and struck people as self-important and pretentious,' Michel says. Gellhorn, 'Dachau', *Collier's*, 23 June 1945.

29. *Infernal fire:* The journalist was Sam Goldsmith, a Lithuanian Jew who had sought asylum in Britain before the war. His report appeared in *Haboker, Tel Aviv*, 1945. Quoted in Gilbert, *The Holocaust*, p 799.

30. *Emil Mahl:* Mahl was actually captured and interrogated in Munich,

where he had fled at the approach of Allied troops.

31. *Confession:* Michel has kept the document of yellowing paper, 'a souvenir of one of the gruesome testimonies of our time'. It is signed twice by Mahl on the final page.

32. *Work detail in Dachau crematorium:* The detail was made up of: Eugen Seybold, from Munich; August Ziegler, from Mannheim; Franz Geiger, from Augsburg; and Johann Gopaz, from Hariborg (Yugoslavia). All the men were interviewed at length by Michel and volunteered to give testimony in writing.

33. *Dachau doctors:* Gellhorn, 'Dachau', Collier's, 23 June 1945.

34. *Fritz Spanheimer:* After the war Spanheimer remained in Munich and became a prominent attorney.

35. *Nazi Party membership profiles:* The mill owner, Hans Huber, later claimed to a reporter from the *Los Angeles Times* that he was against Nazism and had 'preserved the files and kept them hidden' until their discovery by 'an American GI'. 'Berlin Document Center Aids Nazi Hunters', *Los Angeles Times*, 11 March 1979.

36. *Freight cars of documents:* Robert Wolfe, *A Short History of the Berlin Document Centre*, 1994, p xii.

37. *Post-war reorganisation of American forces:* Franks, *Citizen Soldiers*, p 139.

38. *Child in Buchenwald:* The American officer was Rabbi Herschel Schechter. The child, Israel Lau, was kept alive by the cunning and love of his nineteen-year-old brother, Naftali. After the war Israel Lau became Chief Rabbi of Netanya, in Israel. His brother became consul-general in New York. Bonnie Boxer, *The High Holidays: Israel El Al*, p 11. The incident is also quoted in Gilbert, *The Holocaust*, p 792.

VII

1. *Dr Frundsberg:* Ted Kraus, Michel's senior officer in CIC at this time, was party to the SS sting operation. 'Michel posed as an important SS figure, and had an elaborate place set up which was very impressive, and he was able to put it all over. He had a theatrical touch.' It was Kraus who organised and ran the tape recordings of the meetings. 'I doubt very much if the transcripts still exist.' Ted Kraus, interview with the author, New Haven, Connecticut, 30 October 1997.

2. *'Systematic . . . imbecility':* The quotation comes from a British Foreign Office official, Con O'Neil. Bower, *Blind Eye to Murder*, pp 142, 166; *'politically . . . indifferent':* The quotation comes from Saul Padover, an American member of the SHAEF Psychological Warfare Division who arrived in Aachen two months after the war to find committed Nazis back in power.

3. *Failure of de-Nazification:* For a scathing and convincing account of the

Allies' failure at de-Nazification, see Bower, *Blind Eye to Murder, passim.*

4. *Gestapo official:* Six months later, after Michel had moved to Ulm, the man was arrested and interned. He wrote to Michel asking for help. 'I went to Munich with Ted Kraus and got him officially released.'

5. *Vatican seal:* Many years after the ODESSA raid in Munich, Michel's ex-student, John Cardinal O'Connor from New York, borrowed the seal to show it to Pope John Paul.

6. *Werewolves:* The single effective act carried out by the Werewolves seems to have been the assassination of Franz Oppenhoff, an ardent Nazi who was made mayor of Aachen just after the end of the war. The Werewolves considered him a collaborator. Bower, *Blind Eye to Murder,* p 142.

7. *Churchill quotation:* Winston Churchill, 28 October 1948.

8. *D-Day list:* see Bower, *Blind Eye to Murder,* p 85.

9. *Martin Bormann:* Ruthless and hard-working, Bormann rose from obscurity to a position of great power within the Nazi Party. Condemned to death *in absentia* at Nuremberg, he disappeared and was never found. His whereabouts and eventual fate have been the subject of endless speculation.

10. *Georg Lermer:* Although the Department of the Army released a sanitised version of CIC records on Georg Lermer and Rainbow to Michel Thomas, it stated in a letter: 'This information is exempt from the public disclosure provisions of the Freedom of Information Act.' US Army Intelligence and Security, Arlington, Virginia, 22 August 1986.

11. *Soviet contracts:* Bower, *Paperclip Conspiracy,* p 228.

12. *General W. Dornberger:* Far from being held responsible for the exploitation of slave labour, Dornberger was granted top secret security clearances, citizenship and national honours in the United States. He joined Bell Aircraft in 1950 and became senior vice-president of Bell Aerosystems Division of the multinational Textron Corporation. He died in 1980.

13. *Pajamas and Apple Pie:* See Simpson, *Blowback,* p 73.

14. *Project Paperclip:* For a full account of the political machinations surrounding Paperclip, see Bower, *Paperclip Conspiracy*; Hunt, *Secret Agenda*; Lasby, *Project Paperclip,* Simpson, *Blowback.*

15. *Villa Kauderer:* Ted Kraus returned to the villa in Ulm in 1987 and found it transformed into a YMCA hostel, although it remained virtually untouched inside. On a walk through the city with Hans Joohs he turned a corner and bumped into ex-agent Hans Meyer. Ted Kraus, interview with the author, 8 April 1999.

16. *Leo Marks:* A lifelong friend of Michel, Marks was head of the code department of Britain's Special Operations Executive that worked with

the Résistance in the Second World War. He devised a code system for agents dropped behind enemy lines into occupied Europe based on his poems that were printed on silk handkerchiefs, underwear or coat linings. The most famous, written for the female agent Violette Szabo, begins: 'The life that I have Is all that I have And the life that I have is yours . . .' The poem was used in the film about Szabo, *Carve Her Name With Pride*. Leo Marks's memoirs are both revealing and entertaining: Marks, *Between Silk and Cyanide*.

17. *Hans Joohs:* Michel became convinced of Joohs's integrity and saw him as a victim of the war. Sponsored by Swifty Gearheart, Joohs won a scholarship to Syracuse University, New York, in 1949. He visited Michel on the West Coast the following year. 'He still had his dog, Barry, who recognised me.' The men remained friends until Joohs's death in 1999. Joohs, interview with the author, 6 June 1998.

18. *Ulm refugees:* Screening teams at camps at Hersfeld, Hof, Ulm and Giessen processed three hundred thousand refugees during this period.

19. *Ebensee revolt:* The incident is recorded by Evelyn Le Chene, historian of Mauthausen and surrounding camps. When American troops liberated Mauthausen itself they found one hundred and ten thousand survivors – twenty-eight thousand of whom were Jews – and ten thousand bodies in a vast communal grave. Quoted in Gilbert, *The Holocaust*, pp 808–9.

20. *Malmédy Massacre:* Although a misnomer, the term Malmédy Massacre is used here to describe the killing of all unarmed American POWs during the Battle of the Bulge – not just the Baugnetz crossroads, where the greatest number were murdered. Ironically, no POWs were actually killed in the town of Malmédy, but half a dozen US troops and one hundred and seventy-eight Belgian civilians lost their lives through pilot error in three US bombing raids on the town, the last of which was on Christmas Day 1944.

21. *Original Malmédy inquiry:* See Bower, *Blind Eye to Murder*, pp 133–6.

22. *Lowing of cattle:* The description comes from a survivor of the massacre, James P. Mattera – see 'Murder at Malmédy', (with C.M. Stephan Jr), *Army* magazine, December 1981.

23. *Malmédy Massacre:* The account here is a composite taken from the following sources: Toland, *Battle*, pp 55–8; McDonald, *Battle of the Bulge*, pp 213–23, 437–8; Cole, *The Ardennes*, pp 261–4; Weingartner, *Crossroads of Death, passim*; Whiting, *Massacre at Malmédy, passim*; Reynolds, *The Devil's Adjutant, passim*.

24. *Shed murders:* See Weingartner, *Crossroads of Death*, p 113.

25. *POWs to be shot:* Attributed by Knittel to SS Stabaf Weiser, adjutant to Dietrich. From pre-trial statement of Knittel, National Archives,

declassified on 16 September 1997.

26. *Gustav Knittel in Stavelot:* The account of the killing of the American POWs is taken from two pre-trial, sworn statements made voluntarily by Knittel himself. The commander of the anti-tank guns was SS Obersturmführer Wagner; the wounded soldier was SS Obersturm-führer Leidreiter. Knittel claimed not to know the names of the two soldiers who carried out the executions as they were from another unit. See Knittel sworn statements, National Archives, Record Group 338, Entry 147.

27. *Anna Konrad:* Not her real name.

28. *Ted Kraus:* Quotation and information provided by Ted Kraus, interview with the author, 30 October 1997.

29. *Blaicher Haag 19:* The address of the house and the names of the aunt and uncle are taken from a letter written by Gustav Knittel to the Director of Army Intelligence, Washington DC, from Landsberg Prison, 5 January 1950.

30. *Gustav Knittel's background:* See Weingartner, *Crossroads of Death*, p 26.

31. *Nazis recruited by* CIC: See Simpson, *Blowback*, pp xiv, 6.

32. *Gehlen's reputation:* Heinz Hohne, a senior editor of Germany's *Der Spiegel* magazine, wrote a critical book on the spymaster charging that he was much less efficient and effective than credited. Nevertheless, it is estimated that seventy per cent of all the US government's intelligence on the Soviet Union in the early years of the Cold War was supplied by the Gehlen Organisation. See Hohne & Zolling, *The General Was a Spy.* Gehlen responded to the criticism with a self-serving autobiography, *The Service: The Memoirs of Reinhard Gehlen.*

33. *'Secrets of the Kremlin':* Gehlen is quoted by Mosley, *Dulles*, pp 115–16, 125, 234.

34. *OSS Communists:* See Ranelagh, *The Agency*, p 92.

35. *Gehlen Organisation:* For comprehensive accounts of this remarkable organisation and the man who ran it, see Hohne & Zolling, *The General Was a Spy* and *Cookridge, Spy of the Century.* For the relationship with US intelligence, see Simpson, *Blowback* pp 40–51.

36. *Dr Franz Six:* On his retirement he went to work for Porsche. In 1961 he gave evidence as a defence witness in Adolf Eichmann's trial in Israel for crimes against humanity, despite the fact that his former boss then worked for rival Daimler-Benz.

37. *Intelligence files empty:* The dire and dangerous situation is described by Harry Rositzke, the CIA's chief of espionage against the Soviet Union at the time. He worked closely with the Gehlen Organisation to fill the empty files. See Rositzke, *CIA's Secret Operations*, p 20.

38. *CIA copies reports:* See Cookridge, *Spy of the Century*, p 201.
39. *'Anatomy of a Soviet Spy':* The original typewritten manuscript in German remains in Michel's possession.
40. *Hans Meyer:* Not his real name. Although contacted by the author through an intermediary on several occasions, Hans Meyer declined to be interviewed.
41. *Rudolf Schelkmann:* One of the original typed reports for CIC on Schelkmann is in Michel Thomas's possession. It dates the first contact as 1 November 1946 and the meeting in the hunting lodge as 26 November 1946.

VIII

1. *Recommendations:* Among the many recommendations was one from his commander in the Thunderbird combat CIC: 'The ability displayed by Kroskof-Thomas in interrogations of suspects is graded Superior. His attention to duty was at the cost of his own health – interrogating certain individuals unceasingly from twenty-four to forty-eight hours. Investigations by Kroskof-Thomas based on said interrogations drew excellent results. The devotion of Kroskof-Thomas to the assigned mission of this unit *far* exceeded the demands placed on other personnel. By superior performance in service to the United States Army it is believed that Kroskof-Thomas be favorably considered in his application for United States citizenship.' Rupert W. Guenthner, Captain, Inf. 0-1302642, 20 July 1945.

Excerpts from another recommendation read: 'I am particularly aware of the very high calibre of the work you performed in Munich, where I worked with you most closely. The fact that we occasionally disagreed on investigative methods pursued doesn't in the least detract from my appreciation of your work. You have turned in an excellent performance. You have exhibited intelligence, initiative, superior devotion to duty, and an admirable comprehension of counter-intelligence techniques and work . . . I understand you have made an application for an immigration visa to the United States. I trust that this will be possible for you, and would be proud to know that a man of your principles and experience would be interested in eventually becoming a citizen of the United States.' Ernest T. Gearheart Jr, Special Agent in Charge, Ulm Team 970/35, 307 CIC Corps Detachment, HQ Seventh Army, APO 758.

And another from his CIC commander in Ulm: 'Due to a lack of experienced personnel and an overabundance of work, it was necessary to depend extensively on the qualities of Mr Thomas. He assumed these new responsibilities conscientiously, often exhibiting extraordinary initiative in investigations of CI interest. Particular commendation is given to him for his thorough work in the establishment of a well-organised informant network and in the pursuit of subversive groups detrimental to the interest of the American occupation policy . . . As a result of his long contact with Mr Thomas, the undersigned has only the highest praise for him both for his work and his person. At all times he kept the interests and aims of the United States paramount.' Theodore C. Kraus, Special Agent, CIC, 2 October 1946.

2. *Reece Halsey Agency:* The agency is still in business on Sunset Boulevard, opposite Le Dôme restaurant, and continues to represent the estates of Huxley and Miller. Dorris attends the office every day and can be found at lunchtime at her reserved table in Le Dôme. Interview with the author, 3 March 1999, Le Dôme, Los Angeles.

3. *Henry Miller:* Later, in 1978, Miller put pressure on his powerful literary friends to lobby the Swedish Academy on his behalf suggesting he be given the Nobel Prize. It was an outrageous suggestion and certainly had no effect on the deliberations of that august body, which gave the prize to Isaac Bashevis Singer. The new Nobel laureate penned a generous note declaring that he felt Miller should have won. Miller replied that he wasn't interested in the literary glory, only the money. Singer sent him a cheque for $5,000, whether as a generous hand-out or a calculated insult is unsure. Miller cashed it. 'That story, from lobbying the Nobel Committee to cashing Singer's cheque, described Henry's personality exactly,' Michel says.

4. *Ilse Koch:* In an effort to save face, the US Army handed Ilse Koch over to the Germans for trial. She died in a mental asylum. Bower, *Blind Eye to Murder*, p 285.

5. *Senator's letter:* Bower, *Blind Eye to Murder*, p 291.

6. LA Herald Express *report:* The headline of the story ran: THRILLING TRAP OF NAZI WHO ORDERED DOOM OF YANKS. *Los Angeles Evening Herald Express*, 23 November 1949.

7. *Stars & Stripes report:* The headline of the story ran: EX-AGENT TELLS HOW HE CAUGHT MALMEDY CHIEF. *Stars & Stripes*, 17 December 1949.

8. *Peiper's diploma:* See Reynolds, *Devil's Adjutant*, p 259.

9. *Mahl's letter:* The letter, which is in the possession of Michel Thomas, was sent from Landsberg Fortress on 26 December 1949.

10. *Knittel's letter:* The letter was sent from War Criminals prison No. 1, Landsberg/Lech, 5 January 1950. National Archives, Record Group 338, Entry 147, Box 57.

11. *Biscari massacre:* The massacre has received scant attention over the years. Even in the detailed, and excellent, history of the 45th Division – *Rock of Anzio* – it receives only two paragraphs, and is described as 'two

unfortunate incidents that reflected negatively on the Thunderbirds'. Whitlock, *Rock of Anzio*, p 50. For a full account of the trial, see Weingartner, 'Massacre at Biscari: Patton and an American War Crime', *The Historian*, November 1989.

12. *Red-jacket team:* Condemned men at Landsberg were obliged to wear regulation red jackets.

13. *Knittel's release:* According to Hans Joohs, Knittel returned to Ulm and worked for a company that manufactured trucks. He died in 1976.

14. *Peiper's release:* Peiper died in a fire-bomb attack on his home in Traves, in the Hautes Saône, in 1976. For an account of his life and his murder, see Reynolds, *The Devil's Adjutant*, pp 259–69.

IX

1. *Tecate experiment:* Laura Huxley, interview with the author, 5 May 1999.

2. *MCA stock:* MCA went through corporate reorganisation on 1 September 1959 when all of its subsidiaries were merged into MCA Inc. The original Nine Old Men, who owned twelve hundred shares in the old corporations, now owned 170,400 each. The new stock's par value was seventeen cents. When the company was formally listed for the first time on the New York Stock Exchange three months later it began trading at $17.50 a share. Within a year the stock hit $38 a share. When Jules Stein died in 1981 he left in excess of two hundred million dollars – from an original investment of five thousand dollars. McDougal, *The Last Mogul*, pp 254, 423.

3. *Hutchins's letter:* The letter was sent from the Fund for the Republic, New York, to Michel on 4 February 1959. Isidor Rabi was an Austrian-born US physicist who developed a highly accurate technique for measuring the nuclear magnetic movements of atoms; Niels Bohr was a Danish physicist whose work formed the basis for modern atomic theory; Werner Heisenberg was a German physicist who was one of the principal architects of quantum mechanics; Paul Tillich was an American Lutheran minister, theologian and academic whose work related Christianity to contemporary life; J. Robert Oppenheimer was the American physicist in charge of the US atomic bomb programme, who later opposed the development of the hydrogen bomb; and Jacques Maritain was a French Roman Catholic theologian interested in applying the methods of St Thomas Aquinas to contemporary social problems.

4. *Architectural plans:* The firm of architects was Victor Gruen Associates, a company based in Los Angeles with offices all over America.

5. *Prince Rainier's reply:* The letter, from the Palais de Monaco, is dated 6 February 1959.

6. *Rainier's real estate deal:* See Parsons, *Los Angeles Herald Examiner*, 26 April 1963.

7. *Barry's death:* Michel was reluctant to have the story of Barry's death included in the book. 'It seems so unbelievable. I don't expect people to believe it, but that is what happened.'

8. *Marvin Adelson:* Interview with the author, 19 March 1999.

9. *Pittsburgh University:* Letter from chancellor, Wesley Posvar, to Herman Kahn of the Hudson Institute, January 1981.

10. *CIA rejects method:* Charles Morin, interview with the author, 20 May 1999.

11. *Letter from principal:* Dr Andrew Anderson, principal of the George Washington Carver Junior High School, to Edward Mead of the Ford Foundation, 16 May 1969.

12. *School experiment:* The week of French instruction at the George Washington Carver Junior High School was used as a case study in a paper by Dr Garth Sorenson, chairman of Educational Counselling at the Graduate School of Education at the University of California Los Angeles. Sorenson, previously a self-confessed defeatist in learning French before contact with Michel, wrote a paper on schools of thought on the improvement of public education. See, 'On the Use of the Case Study in Developing Better Instructional Procedures'.

13. *Professor's report:* The report was written by J. Michael Fay, instructional co-ordinator at the George Washington Carver Junior High School, April 1969.

14. *L'Enfant Sauvage:* For Truffaut's interest in educational experiments in teaching difficult children, and the evolution of the film, see Baecque & Toubiana, *Truffaut,* pp 260–5.

15. *Truffaut letter:* Letter to Helen Scott, 9 July 1973. See Truffaut, *Correspondence 1945–1984,* pp 395–6.

16. *Selznick's* Memo: Selznick, *Memo from David O. Selznick,* Viking, 1972.

17. *Signed Truffaut photo:* The photo hangs in the offices of Michel Thomas Language Systems in Beverly Hills, California.

18. *Marriage:* Rabbi Dr Charles Steckel was the rabbi at the ceremony. He had been a friend of the family in Breslau and had stimulated Michel's interest in archaeology as a teenager. The rabbi had left Germany for Zagreb, in Yugoslavia, and escaped to Istanbul during the war. He moved to Budapest in 1942 posing as a German Lutheran priest and worked with Raoul Wallenberg, the Swedish diplomat who saved the lives of many Jews by issuing travel documents. Steckel moved to America after the war and settled in Pasadena, California. Michel found him through a chance item published in the newspaper. 'It was meaningful to me to be married by him. There was a connection to the

family and the old world in Breslau.'

19. *Alice Burns:* Interview with the author, Los Angeles, 8 May 1999.

20. *Birth of children:* Gurion was born on 28 November 1978; a daughter, Micheline Freidessa – a name created by combining the first names of Michel's mother and aunt – was born on 16 February 1980.

21. *Barbie hearing:* Michel Thomas gave preliminary evidence to the *juge d'instruction* in Lyon in April 1984.

22. *Confrontation with Barbie:* 'Barbie Confronted', *Le Matin*, 21 December 1983; Michel's quotation on Barbie from the *New York Times*, 24 May 1987.

23. *Barbie recruitment:* US Nazi hunter Allan Ryan prepared a two-hundred-page study on Barbie for the Justice Department. Its findings were first made public in a press conference at the US Department of Justice, Washington DC, on 16 August 1983. Ryan, *Klaus Barbie and the United States Government*.

24. *Barbie's past:* Agent's monthly report, 15 September 1948. Quoted in Simpson, *Blowback*, p 189.

25. *CIC rationalisation:* Ryan, *Klaus Barbie*, p 69n.

26. *Barbie's CIC activities:* Top-secret report by Lt Col Ellington Golden, commanding officer of HQ 970th CIC Detachment, 11 December 1947. Quoted in Simpson, *Blowback*, p 185.

27. *'Case closed':* The report is quoted in Ryan, *Quiet Neighbors*, p 307.

28. *Barbie in South America:* See Ryan, *Quiet Neighbors*, pp 275–9; Bower, *Klaus Barbie*, pp 205–24.

29. *Bolivia's internment camps:* See 'Nazi Impénitent, Agent Américain, Homme D'Affaires Bolivien', Jean-Marc Théolleyre, *Le Monde*, 16 May 1987.

30. *Manhunt in Nice:* See Zuccotti, *The Italians and the Holocaust*, p 89.

31. *Beate Klarsfeld:* Her words are quoted by Paris, *Unhealed Wounds*, p 188.

32. *'I did my duty':* The quotation appeared in the *New York Times*, 14 February 1983.

33. *'They said nothing':* See Linklater et al, *Nazi Legacy*, p 113.

34. *Eyewitness account of raid:* The farmhand was Julien Favet, then aged twenty-four.

35. *Barbie telex:* The telex survived, and was marked Lyon, 8.10 p.m., 6 April 1944.

36. *Vergès's wife:* The lawyer's bigamous marriage was to Djamala Bouhirid, an Algerian Communist sentenced to death for terror bombings. She was spared execution and eventually released after a campaign by André Froissard – who happened to be one of the *résistants* tortured by Barbie in 1943.

37. *Jacques Vergès:* For a detailed account of Vergès's life and an analysis of his politics, see Paris, *Unhealed Wounds, passim.*

38. *'Paltry underling'*: See Finkielkraut, *Remembering In Vain,* p 3.

39. *'Everyone would have laughed'*: Finkielkraut appeared in the documentary on Barbie by Marcel Ophuls, interviewed on the court house steps in Lyon while awaiting the verdict on 14 July 1987. Ophuls, *Hotel Terminus.*

40. *Barbie's fate:* Klaus Barbie died of leukaemia in September 1991.

41. *Herbert Morris:* Interview with the author, Los Angeles, 23 February 1999.

42. *UCLA summer course:* The flier for the summer experiment, which was part of UCLA's extension programme, went out in April 1990, and the courses were scheduled for 20 August through September.

43. *Experiment cancelled:* Letter to Michel from Gary Penders, director of the Summer Sessions, UCLA, 10 August 1990.

44. *Impregnable educational establishment:* The British remain similarly impermeable. A letter from an enthusiastic publisher extolling the virtues of Michel's system sent to David Blunkett, Secretary of Education, received a stock reply from a civil servant. 'Whilst the Department sets the framework for teaching in school through the National Curriculum, it is for schools and teachers to determine how to deliver it . . . We will keep your letter on our files.' Janet Haworth, Curriculum & Assessment Division, Department of Education and Employment, 18 March 1998.

45. *Gold medal:* The medal was presented to Michel on behalf of the society by M. Raoul Aglion, Ministre Plénipotentiaire, on 16 January 1982.

46. *Emma Thompson:* Interview with the author, London, 23 November 1998.

47. *BBC documentary: The Language Master,* first shown on BBC2 on 23 March 1997.

X

1. Michel Thomas's biography, *Test of Courage,* was published in the United States by The Free Press, 1999.

2. Email from author to Bret Israel, editor of Southern California Living, *Los Angeles Times,* 26 March 2001.

3. Sworn Declaration from Theodore C. Kraus, Ph.D., Cheshire, Connecticut, 14 December 2001.

4. Sworn Declaration from Herbert Morris, Emeritus Professor of Law and Philosophy, Former Dean of the Division of Humanities, and Interim Provost of the College of Letters and Science at UCLA, Los Angeles,

California, 16 November 2001.

5. Bill introduced to Congress by Senator Helen Gahagan Douglas, HR 5255, 80th Congress, 2nd Session, 1948.

6. Email from author to Roy Rivenburg, 28 March 2001.

7. Email from author to Roy Rivenburg, 4 April 2001.

8. 'Larger Than Life' by Roy Rivenburg, *Los Angeles Times*, 15 April 2001. Copyright prevents the reproduction of the article in full.

9. 'Response to Story on Michel Thomas': six letters were published in the Southern California Living section of the *Los Angeles Times*, 7 May 2001. They were all heavily edited by the editors of that section, rather than the editor in charge of Letters to the Editor.

10. Roy Rivenburg admitted editing the letter in a posting on the michelthomas.org bulletin board, February 18, 2006.

11. Sworn Declaration from Conrad R. McCormick, Sierra Vista, Arizona, 8 January 2002.

12. Letter from Karlene Goller, attorney for the *Los Angeles Times*, to Michel Thomas's attorney, Anthony Glassman, 3 May 2001.

13. Book review, *Los Angeles Times*, 18 December 2000.

14. Sworn Declaration from Michel Thomas, New York, 10 January 2002.

15. The lawsuit between Michel Thomas, plaintiff, and the *Los Angeles Times* Communications LLC, Roy Rivenburg, and Tribune Company, defendants, was filed 9 October 2001.

16. Sworn Declaration from Professor Robin T. Lakoff, Berkeley, California, 16 December 2001.

17. Sworn Declaration from Professor Sherrie Mazingo, Roseville, Minnesota, 9 January 2002.

18. Tentative Ruling by Judge Audrey B. Collins, granting Special Motion to Strike the Complaint pursuant to California Code of Civil Procedure, 4 February 2002.

19. A 'mock' trial of the case was staged in April 2003, sponsored by the University of California Schools of Law and Journalism. The idea was not to reach a verdict but to examine the evidence.

20. Defendants' Motion for Attorneys' Fees, *Michel Thomas* v *Los Angeles Times Communications, LLC, et al.*, US District Court, Central District of California, 2 April 2002.

21. Phone interview with Alex Kline, March 2002.

22. 'CIC personnel will be permitted to operate with minimal restrictions of movement, CIC personnel will not be delayed in the execution of their assigned duties by the observance of standard military customs or prohibitions, nor by the military police or other military agencies. CIC badges and credentials will be honoured at all times.' CIC order from General Dwight Eisenhower, Supreme Commander, Allied Forces,

issued from HQ, US Army, signed by Lt Col Richard P. Fisk, Assistant Adjutant General, and by Capt Rupert W. Guenthner, Commander 45th CIC Detachment, HQ, US Army, 2 December 1944.

23. Email from Ian Sayer to Roy Rivenburg, 7 April 2001. The reference to Thomas appears on page 2862, Volume XX, of the unpublished *History of the Counter Intelligence Corps*. The thirty-volume history was compiled between 1950 and 1959 at the Army Intelligence School in Fort Holabird, Maryland.

24. From the outset Foster had 'cautioned' Rivenburg of the official definition of 'liberator.' 'The Army gives divisions "liberation credit" if ANY element of that division passed through OR NEAR a concentration camp within forty-eight hours of its occupation by US Forces.' Email to Roy Rivenburg from Hugh F. Foster III, 1 March 2001.

25. Emil Mahl was arrested on 1 May 1945 in Irschenhausen, near Munich. Letter from Mahl, Landsberg Prison, to the Modification Board, Heidelberg, 30 December 1951.

26. Letter from Lt Col Hugh Foster III stating his conviction of Thomas's presence at Dachau on day of liberation, May 2002.

27. Handwriting expert Dr Timothy Armistead gave his opinion in March 2002.

28. Expert opinion on Dachau photos given by Peter Mustardo, March 2002.

29. Letter from Barbara Distel, Curator of the Dachau Memorial Museum, 18 April 2002.

30. Sworn Declaration from Walter Wimer — CIC Agent from 1944 through 1945 — 8 January 2002.

31. Sworn Declaration from Doris White — widow of CIC Special Agent Frederick White — Worcester, Massachusetts, March 2002.

32. Videotaped Thunderbird Reunion, Oklahoma City, Oklahoma, August 2002.

33. Letter from Stefan Heym to Alex Kline, November 2001.

34. Stefan Heym wrote two accounts of the announcement of the discovery of documents from the Nazi Party master file. One is fictional and is contained in his book of short stories, *Die Kannibalen und andere Erzälungen*, Paul List Verlag, Leipzig, 1953. The unpublished nonfiction manuscript is lodged with the author's papers at Cambridge University. Heym gave credit to Hans Huber, the manager of the mill, for the discovery. Huber, of course, had received the documents directly from the SS.

35. Discovery of Party Documents in the Josef Wirth paper mill in Freimannn, by 45th CIC Detachment, 20 May 1945. The report is headed Weekly Counterintelligence Report #16, and the discovery

comes under the sub-heading Special Cases of CIC Interest. It was an interesting week — other cases include documents from Germany's top commando Otto Skorzeny reporting on the attack on Hitler's life, the freeing of Mussolini, and the diary written by Mussolini while imprisoned. Seventh Army, Western Military District, Annex No 2, Part 4 of 8, CIC Reports/Reporting Section G-2, period 20 May–20 June 1945. Now lodged in the National Archives.

36. The quote from Hans Huber about the discovery of the documents by 'an American GI' appeared in an article headed 'Berlin Document Centre Aids Nazi Hunters,' *Los Angeles Times*, 11 March 1979.

37. Open letter from Robert Wolfe, To Whom It May Concern, 13 June 2002.

38. Mistranslation of phrase from article on Klaus Barbie trial, *Le Monde*, 23 May 1987.

39. Letter from the Historical Department, Société des Bains de Mer, Monaco, 5 July 2001. The agreement between the casino's director general of the time and Monsieur M. Dufour, engineer, is dated 7 April 1941.

40. See Top 15 Language Audio Tapes, *The Bookseller*, September 2001. More recent figures provided by US publisher McGraw-Hill in March 2007.

41. Katie Roden, Director, Consumer Education, Hodder Education, in letter to the author, 22 March 2007.

42. 'Why the Michel Thomas Method Is the Best,' *The Daily Express*, 3 July 2006.

43. The quote is from *Othello*, Act III, Scene 1.

44. Letter to the author, 18 June 2002.

45. Email to Alex Kline, 28 October 2006.

46. "Selling Out the First Amendment: The Collision of News, Entertainment, and Politics," Wheeler Auditorium, University of California, Berkeley, 14 February 2004.

47. Letter to John Carroll, 12 April 2004.

48. Bret Israel was the only member of the *Times* who agreed to speak with me: 'I can hardly refuse.' The interview was conducted by phone on 19 February 2007. Roy Rivenburg repeatedly refused to submit to a phone interview. Carroll has also avoided answering questions.

49. Roy Rivenburg's web site Off Kilter gives a link to Les Jones. The posting here was placed by one Jeff Jones, 22 March 2005. At the time of writing — April 2007 — the link remained.

50. Documents and details of the preparation for the disallowed defamation trial can be found at michelthomas.org.

51. The award certificate of the Silver Star is dated 11 February 2004.

INDEX

Note: Most entries refer directly or indirectly to Michel Thomas, except where otherwise indicated. Subentries are in alphabetical order, except where *chronological* order is more significant.